Who Was Cousin Alice?

Also by John Matthias

Poetry
Bucyrus (1970)
Turns (1975)
Crossing (1979)
Bathory & Lermontov (1980)
Northern Summer (1984)
A Gathering of Ways (1991)
Swimming at Midnight (1995)
Beltane at Aphelion (1995)
Pages: New Poems & Cuttings (2000)
Working Progress, Working Title (2002)
Swell & Variations on the Song of Songs (2003)
New Selected Poems (2004)
Kedging (2007)
Trigons (2010)

Translations
Contemporary Swedish Poetry (1980)
    (with Göran Printz-Påhlson)
Jan Östergren: Rainmaker (1983)
    (with Göran Printz-Påhlson)
The Battle of Kosovo (1987)
    (with Vladeta Vučković)
Three-Toed Gull: Selected Poems of Jesper Svenbro (2003)
    (With Lars-Håkan Svensson)

Editions
23 Modern British Poets (1971)
Introducing David Jones (1980)
David Jones: Man and Poet (1989)
Selected Works of David Jones (1992)
Notre Dame Review: The First Ten Years (2009)
    (with William O'Rourke)

Criticism
Reading Old Friends (1992)

Who Was Cousin Alice?
and Other Questions

Memoirs, Essays, Poems

John Matthias

Shearsman Books
Exeter

Published in the United Kingdom in 2011 by
Shearsman Books Ltd
58 Velwell Road
Exeter EX4 4LD

www.shearsman.com

ISBN 978-1-84861-168-9
First Edition

Cover:
Photograph of Alice Green Hoffman embossed on multiple gift
jewelry boxes presented to family members. An original print is in the
Hoffman archive, East Carolina University Manuscript Room,
Joyner Library, Greenville, NC.

Contents

Poem: Family Apocrypha:
    A Slashed Painting by John Singer Sargent   9
Foreword   11

I

1. Who Was Cousin Alice?   13
    Poem: Ohio Forbears   34
    Poem: After Years Away   38
2. Kedging in 'Kedging in Time'   41
    Poem: Geneva Pension   55
    Poem: Some Letters   57

II

1. Poetry and Insomnia   59
2. Poetry and Murder   76
3. Prince Marko   101
4. Grand Old Dirty Old Men   122

III

1. Mendelson's Early Auden   155
2. The Haunting of Benjamin Britten   167
3. From Mauberley to Middagh Street:
    Ways of Meeting the British   185
4. The Poetry of Roy Fisher   194
    Poem: Left Hands and Wittgensteins   218
    Poem: Longs and Shorts   219
5. British Poetry at Y2K   220

IV

Modernisms: Five Poems
    Modernato Pizzicato   271
    Their Flims   273
    The Baronesses   275
    Ashville Out   277
    Xoanon: Gunnar Ekelöf   280

V

1. Pleasures and Situations:
    The Prose of Robert Hass and Robert Pinsky   282
2. Two Kinds of Autobiography   306
3. John Berryman I–III   327
4. The English Poetry of Göran Printz-Påhlson   346
    Poem: Interlinear Dialogue   357

Notes to the Essays   359

For Laura, Elliot, Ian, and Leila

And for my ten cousins whom Alice has always perplexed and intrigued

And for my wife Diana's nieces and nephew who grew up at
100 Bayswater Rd. and thought of her as a sister

And in memory of Wayland

Family Aprocrypha:
A Slashed Painting by John Singer Sargent

The large Sargent painting, subsequently slashed,
Of my distant cousin Hoffman, Alice Green,
Was photographed in Paris by Michelle's Studio
In 1909. Alice had complained of standing still

For hours at what Sargent called a "sitting," and
That she was forced to bring, day after day,
The fresh roses herself. But *he* was who he was.
This would be a "Sargent," after all, and grand

As it could be, grand as his pictures of the other
Ladies in her circle captured by the genius
Of his hand. *Dab dab dab* she heard, and *Stand still*
Will you please Miss Green, and *Mind the rose.*

She minded roses, was in fact allergic, just like
Monsieur Proust, and she had to dab dab dab
At her running nose with a little handkerchief she
Brought from her hotel. Three of them, in fact.

He asked her to open up the book he had brought her,
Place it on the table with the roses, read a poem.
Oh it was John Keats! *Now look up!* he said,
And gaze at the lawn through the magic casement

At a thing fled forever from its image in the poem.
It's lost, he said, *but you—I'll save you for the ages*
If you just stand still another hour, another month.
Tell me once again who this Hoffman is.

She wondered if she really knew. She would marry him
Of course, but she doubted that she loved him.
What did it matter, he was wealthier than she. He was
A (white) descendent of George Washington, and

He was paying for this portrait as a wedding gift.
Hoffman, that is, and not the father of her country—
If indeed it *was* her country any more, if indeed
He were the father of it. Hoffman had her reading

Aaron Burr and other members of the Founding Fops,
As he liked to say, telling her she'd make a better
Picture even than the *Portrait of Madame Pierre Gautreau.*
I am a Washington, he said, *but only on the side.*

She didn't know the oldest of old tales—*A man of means,*
My dear, and mean enough to many when he'd
Met them with the line he'd taken from the artist's
Great new friend: You are a woman out of Henry James!

That had taken them exactly to this point and not beyond.
She stood. The artist dab dab dabbed. As yet she didn't know
That Hoffman was an outrageous rake who stalked
The beautiful and famous through salons and country houses

And the continental spas. Standing tall and straight as
Archer's arrow held in Eros' hand, she didn't know
He'd tell her *all* when every honest hour ticked beyond
The help of any art. Would he rip the white bodice

From her even whiter breasts while she, before she
Slashed the canvas worth a Whistler or Dégas,
Looked into his smirking face and said *My raffish*
Mr. Crass: I leave an image only of an image.

Take it for a song—a kind of testament, a trespass.

Foreword

I have always enjoyed books that combine a poet's prose with his or her poetry, but there are not very many of these. I'm thinking both of books that combine ambitious statements of poetics with a poetic text, like David Jones' *The Anathemata*, as well as less formal volumes, miscellanies of prose and verse like Stanley Kunitz's *Next-to-Last Things,* some of Robert Duncan's books, or, on a very ambitious scale, Pasternak's *Dr. Zhivago.* Memoir, criticism, fiction—it doesn't matter, but I like to see some poetry with the prose of a poet-critic or a poet-who-also-writes-prose. When I published my first volume of essays, *Reading Old Friends,* I included a section called 'Three Poems on Poetics.' I'm doing something similar here. There is of course more prose than poetry in the book, but I hope the reader will pay attention to the poems, since they are entangled for me in the stories being told, and the literary-critical observations being made.

Who Was Cousin Alice? begins with stories. I have written a certain amount of what might be called autobiographical criticism in the past, but have only recently attempted the autobiographical (and biographical) narrative that is true memoir. My first shot at this was the commentary on *Kedging in Time,* some reflections on my wife's British family requested by the editors of *Chicago Review* to clarify the long poem by that title which had been published earlier in the magazine. Having written that, I thought I might explore in a similar way some memories of my own American family in what became *Who Was Cousin Alice?* The poems that frame these pieces, and those that appear within them, were sometimes written before the prose, and sometimes after. They tell some of the same—or closely related—stories, but in another way. 'Poetry and Insomnia,' 'Poetry and Murder,' and 'Prince Marko' are also narrative memoirs, but poems appear internally in these three pieces in order to expand implications or refocus perspectives.

The more strictly literary-critical pieces begin with a long essay about the erotic writing of the old or ageing, 'Grand Old Dirty Old Men,' and continue with essays on the early work of W.H. Auden, a biography of Benjamin Britten, and Paul Muldoon's '7 Middagh Street.' The Auden, Britten, and Muldoon essays are a kind of three-part reflection on immigration, homecomings, and trans-Atlantic issues in the arts. They also include the first of several re-printings from *Reading Old Friends.* Though the original Auden essay appeared in that book, it really requires the Britten and Muldoon essays to complete it. I have written italicized headnotes for revised, re-printed, and re-contextualized essays from *Old*

Friends (as well as for some of the others). Four of these pieces appear at the end of the book: on Robert Hass and Robert Pinsky, Michael Anania and Jiri Wyatt, John Berryman and Göran Printz-Påhlson. The Berryman essay is much expanded from the *Old Friends* version, and the others take on new meanings by the new organization of their parts. The Hass, Anania, and Wyatt pieces also comment obliquely on my own recent practice of autobiographical narrative.

'The Poetry of Roy Fisher' and 'British Poetry at Y2K' are the most academic selections of the work collected here. The first was commissioned for *Contemporary British Poetry: Essays in Theory and Criticism*, edited by James Acheson and Romana Huk. The second was published on *Electronic Book Review*. If the British Poetry essay had footnotes, they would far exceed in length those to the Fisher essay. I have not added footnotes to essays that did not initially contain them in journal publication. This is not really an academic book, so I hope my inconsistency on this matter of notes will be forgiven.

I have not re-printed any of the essays originally published in *Reading Old Friends* that make clear my long interest in modernism. In their absence is the section called: 'Modernisms: Five Poems.' That is the only uninterrupted block of verse. The poems to Roy Fisher and Göran Printz-Påhlson are intimately related to these.

I am deeply grateful to publishers and the editors of journals and books that originally printed some of the work appearing here. Acknowledgment is made to *Boulevard, Chicago Review, Parnassus, Cambridge Literary Review, The Common, Electronic Book Review, Fifth Wednesday, Harvard Review, The Southern Review, PN Review, Tärningskastet,* Salt Publishing, SUNY Press, Swallow Press and Shearsman Books. I am even more grateful to friends and colleagues who have read and commented on various parts of the book. In no particular order, twenty who helped a lot: James Walton, William O'Rourke, Stephen Fredman, Gerald Bruns, Vincent Sherry, Michael Anania, Joe Francis Doerr, Robert Archambeau, Richard Berengarten, Romana Huk, Herbert Leibowitz, Lars-Håkan Svensson, Maggie Nerio, John Peck, Peter Robinson, John Wilkinson, Alex Davis, Keith Tuma, Heather Treseler, Igor Webb, and of course my wife, Diana Matthias. Most of all, my thanks to Tony Frazer, who has shown amazing patience with me as we have put this thing together for Shearsman.

John Matthias
January 2011

Who Was Cousin Alice?

I've been trying for some time to remember all the rooms in my grandfather's house. The downstairs is not difficult. There was a large living room full of heavy furniture; a "music room" that contained two pianos, one in tune and one not, and lots of Victorian bric-a-brac; a dining room that could seat maybe twenty people; a long passageway full of cabinets and shelves that led to the kitchen; and, behind the kitchen, a pantry. The house was very dark, even when the sun was shining. Made of large, split stones mortared together in an irregular pattern, its appearance of solidity belied its actual fragility. Even when I was young a large stone from high on the tall chimney might come tumbling down having loosened itself from the mortar. Uncle Edward, suffering from the after-effects of the Spanish Influenza, which he had been among the first to contract after the First World War, sat immobile in his corner of the living room—frozen like a statue most of the time, one of those unfortunates whose survival of the flu itself brought on the Parkinsonian condition made famous by Oliver Sacks in *Awakenings*. Uncle Edward was the specter of my childhood.

Upstairs, there were many bedrooms, all named for someone. There was "Grandfather's Room," directly at the top of the stairs, "Grandmother's Room," down the hall to the left, and "Uncle Edward's Room" to the right. At this point I become confused. Somewhere beyond Edward's room, down the right side of the hall, was "Mary Derbyshire's Room"—Mary was my grandfather's widowed sister—and beyond that, back where the house became darker and darker, way back where the hallway turned behind the attic stairs, was "Cousin Alice's Room." But who was Cousin Alice? My cousins were Jim, Robert, Richard, Marilyn, Nancy, Judy, and Joan. Cousin Alice's room, though always empty, was kept tidy and clean, as if Cousin Alice were expected back at any moment. Now and then I'd ask about her. "Who is Cousin Alice?" "Oh," someone would say, "Aunt Alice was named for Cousin Alice." That confused me a lot—how could an aunt be named for a cousin, who was obviously much younger? Or sometimes people would say: "She's very rich, you know. She went to Paris. She went to China. She was a friend of Eleanor Roosevelt." One day I asked Fanny, the cook who seemed actually to live in the kitchen (which, of course, was called "Fanny's Room") about Cousin Alice. "You know," she said, "your Cousin Alice actually owns Bogue Banks." Immediately I thought of a whole lot of banks along a street called Bogue where possibly family members had their accounts. "Does she have a lot of money, Fanny?" "Piles of it! Johnny, she's got money to burn. But you know, the Bankers nearly burned her out one year. Your father had to go and fix things up." This of course made no sense at all. "*Burned* her out?" I asked. "*Burned* her out," said Fanny, "*Burned* her out. Then they all went back and fished. That was all they really ever wanted."

I'm looking at a rather elaborately produced 'Christmas Greeting' from "The Matthias Household, 2135 Iuka Avenue, Columbus, Ohio." Fifteen pages in length and bound with a gold ribbon between black, imitation-leather boards, its glossy pages are still in very good condition. There's no date, but it must have been sent out in the late 1920s. It contains two photographs of the house on Iuka, a summer scene and a winter scene, along with a photograph of an earlier house in Van Wert, Ohio, under which a picture of youthful Grandfather M. appears in his Spanish–American War uniform and another of a youthful Mary Crouch in a dress suit with a kind of bow tie. Then comes Mary Crouch Matthias's poem, 'Goodbye, Old Home.' The poem was a farewell to the home in Van Wert, in fact, written when they moved to Columbus when my grandfather began the first of many terms on the Ohio Supreme Court. Then there is a photograph of the children: Edward, John, Mary, and the twins, Florence and Alice. Pictured sitting in a rocking chair before the fire is Mary Green Crouch, my great grandmother, known to everyone as "Grandma Crouch." Then another poem, 'Club Life,' by Mary Crouch Matthias. Then the 'Class Poem' of the Ohio Northern University class of 1894. That must have been the class that at least one of my grandparents belonged to, for they met at Ohio Northern. Finally, in this Parnassus of a Christmas card, is '1917' by John M. Matthias, my father. Presumably written when he was an undergraduate at The Ohio State University, it's a World War I poem that is clearly a protest poem. Written in regular tetrameters, it imagines a young officer moving red and black buttons around on a battle map. I have to admit that it's not half bad:

> The young lad laughs, the thoughtless jest:
> He moves the buttons one inch west.
> Ten thousand boys in France's mud,

Some twist in pain, some soaked in blood.
They pray for death—for death is best,
With Flanders Field—just one inch west.
Ten thousand crosses "row on row
In Flanders Field where poppies grow."
The young lad laughs—the cost?—who'd guessed
To move the buttons—one inch west.

The 'Christmas Greeting' does not include a word about the family's hopeless war veteran, Edward, nor anything about Cousin Alice. Where was she at the end of the 1920s? Edward was where he always was, a frozen statue in his corner.

Fanny would tell me other things about Cousin Alice from time to time. "You know", she'd say, "she was really a Green. As far as anyone knows, she was married to that Paris Hoffman man for about two days. But she kept his name." The Greens were on my grandmother's side of the family, and I knew nothing about them at all. As far as I knew, I'd never met a Green, and I didn't know that Grandma Crouch had once been married to one. Fanny said she had never seen a Green in the house, except for Cousin Alice. My grandmother, crippled with rheumatoid arthritis and already beginning to live exclusively in the past, would sometimes confuse Cousin Alice with my Aunt Alice, her daughter. Then I too would get confused again. "Did Aunt Alice marry Paris Hoffman?" I'd ask. "No", she said, "Alice married Bob Jacoby. There was no Paris Hoffman. Your Aunt Alice *lived* in Paris after she went to China and before she bought Bogue Banks. Johnny, she spoke six languages. She sued your father for fraud, but she was so fond of her niece, Eleanor Roosevelt." I knew Eleanor Roosevelt was the widow of our last president before Truman. We had studied the presidents in school. But how could someone so old be Aunt Alice's niece? Or was she Cousin Alice's niece?

She was Cousin Alice's niece. A Green family genealogy following the descendants of Thomas Green, Sr., born in Leicester, England, in 1606, marches steadily to Albert William Green, b. February 12, 1830 in North Bloomfield, Ohio, and his daughters Alice, Grace, and Mary. Alice married J. Ellis Hoffman. Grace married Henry Alexander and their daughter, Eleanor, married Theodore Roosevelt, Jr. Mary's first husband was Martin V.B. Lewis, who died in the Civil War, and her second husband was Arthur Van Wye Crouch. My grandmother was the third of their eight children. But nobody in the family ever gave me such a simple timeline as that, so I continued to thrash about in my confusion. I was especially upset that my father, a municipal court judge, had been dragged into court for fraud. He himself sometimes talked about hearing fraud cases in his own courtroom, and I knew people who had committed this act, whatever it was, got sent to jail.

What one heard repeated most often about Cousin Alice among family members was that "she would rather go to court than to the theater." And go to court she did—in Paris, New York, North Carolina, and elsewhere. Many of the papers in the Alice Green Hoffman collection at East Carolina University's Joyner Library deal with her endless legal battles. But I am getting way ahead of myself and my story.

At some point early on in my life I began to read poetry. In fact, I date my reading of poetry from about the same moment that I learned to read. I would browse around in my grandfather's large library and pull out volumes of Longfellow, Whittier, Oliver Wendell Holmes, and Kipling. My grandfather was a super-patriot and an orator. He liked poetry to have the same kind of ring to it as a good jingoistic harangue.

When it became possible to make scratchy 78 rpm records at small local studios, he recorded himself reading a thing called 'A Toast to the Flag' and distributed copies to all members of the family. There was talk at the time that my grandmother should make a companion recording of 'Goodbye, Old Home.' Grandfather would sometimes read poems aloud to his grandchildren, thumpers like 'The Charge of the Light Brigade.' He had a fine, resonant baritone voice. We all loved these poems and, as the 'Christmas Greeting' makes clear, everyone was expected to versify. My cousin Joan wrote the family's most proficient occasional verse, most famously her poem for our grandparents' golden wedding anniversary, which was meant to be sung to the tune of 'Daisy, Daisy, give me your answer true.' Around this time, someone put in my hands an eight-line poem that a classmate at Mrs. Porter's School for Girls in Farmington, Connecticut, had written for Cousin Alice. It was not quite my sort of thing, but I saved it anyway.

A queenly air,
A stately grace,
Diana' s form,
And Juno's face,
A heart that's true,
And has no malice,
The whole divine,
And your hair, Alice.

By the time I was in junior high school, my grandfather's library had yielded up Walt Whitman and Edgar Allan Poe, though I was given to understand that there was something not quite right about both of them. At least Poe rhymed. But Whitman was an entirely new world after all that Longfellow and Whittier. To my surprise, we even started reading him in school. I had already developed what has become a life-long habit of turning to the end of any book before starting off at the beginning, and I did that with *Leaves of Grass*: "Good-by my Fancy! / Farewell dear mate, dear love! / I'm going away, I know not where, / Or to what fortune, or whether I may ever see you again." The poem made me cry, though I wasn't sure what "my Fancy" meant—or, for that matter, "dear mate." Probably Whitman's wife. My grandfather believed in memorizing poems and had pressed on me just what you would expect—'Oh Captain, My Captain.' One day I was called in from a school recess to find my mother waiting for me in the principal's office. My grandfather had fallen to his death from the attic window just above Cousin Alice's room. He was the Grand Old Man in Ohio legal circles and the Republican Party, so it made headlines in the evening papers. The story was that he had lost his balance while trying to show exterminators where squirrels were getting into the house. My father always thought it was suicide.

In the general re-orderings of life following the death of a patriarch, a lot of things change places, go missing, or get passed down a generation or two. Somehow I ended up with a box of materials pertaining to Cousin Alice. I was more keen on getting hold of the Civil War books, the Spanish-American War dress sword, and one of the uniforms that had epaulettes attached, but it is true that I had always "expressed interest" in Cousin Alice, so I took what I'd been given, put it in a cardboard box on a closet shelf, and forgot about it.

Lots of names from the past came up at my grandfather's funeral, but Cousin Alice's wasn't one of them. The Captain had fallen, and the ambiguities surrounding his death were serious and troubling. For years I heard nothing more about the fancies and fortunes of the lady on Bogue Banks, or Diana's form and Juno's grace.

By the time I was in high school, I had acquired the family vice of committing verses myself. My ambitions, however, exceeded the patriotic ode or homestead elegy. I had read *Song of Myself* and was full of my "simple separate person . . . from top to toe." One thing that I especially liked about Whitman was that *he did go on*, unlike Emily Dickinson, who stopped abruptly before I could get the gist of anything she said. Whitman seemed to say everything three or four times, so you couldn't miss the point. But my reading of the American classics coincided with the emergence in the 1950s of Whitman's nephews, the Beats; and poets like Allen Ginsberg praised not only the Good Gray Poet, but also modernists like Pound and Williams. I remember very clearly standing in Long's Bookstore across from Ohio State and pulling both Pound's *Selected Poems*, concluding with excerpts from *The Cantos*, and what was then the latest installment of Williams' *Paterson*, off the shelf. As usual, I turned to the conclusions first:

> but if Senator Edwards cd/ speak
> and have his tropes stay in the memory 40 years, 60 years?
> in short / the descent has not been of advantage either
>   to the Senate or to "society"
>   or to the people
>   The States have passed thru a
>   dam'd supercilious era.
> Down, Derry-down /
>   Oh let an old man rest.

I loved the way that moved. Also, it seemed to be a protest poem of some kind, though not quite as protesting as Ginsberg's 'America.' But I had no idea what Senator Edwards' "tropes" were, and to this day I still misread it as "troops," like I did then. Did Pound's Senator have his own militia? The *Paterson* installment ended this way:

This is the blast
the eternal close
the spiral
the final somersault
   the end.

I was hooked. I bought both books and told my English teacher the next day that I was going to write a book-length modernist poem. Instead of laughing at me, he smiled gently and said something wise (which has now become commonplace advice in poetry workshops): just don't write it about yourself. Almost at once I decided to write it about Cousin Alice.

When I pulled down the box from a high shelf in my bedroom, I found it didn't contain half of what I thought I remembered. There were a few legal documents, a yellowing newspaper article cut out in such a way that I could only read 'Tuesday, April' and 'The Twin-City Dial' at the top. I think the twin cities were Morehead City and Beaufort, North Carolina. I'm still not sure of the date and year. There was also a photograph of a house with my very young-looking parents standing on the front porch. And there was the Green family genealogy that I've already mentioned.

The newspaper article, by James McEwen, told me about the history of Bogue Banks, "a thirty-mile-long sand spit, running east and west and separated from the mainland—or 'country' as the bankers call it—by Bogue Sound. For generations Salter Path remained, for all practical purposes, isolated from the rest of the world . . . so isolated that their very speech retains the flavor of Elizabethan pronunciation. Not even the oldest resident knows how long the settlers have been there." They all seemed to be fishermen and had intermarried for so long that they were all related to each other. Most of them were called Willis or Guthrie. More than that, the economy of the Salter Pathers was communal. "All of the 350 people in the settlement take part in the fishing, and all the families get equal shares of the profits, no matter how much effort has been put into the work." The article goes on to explain that the life of this community had been disrupted twice— recently during World War II when a Marine post was stationed there with rocket emplacements and a free gunnery range, and before that

---

when Alice Green Hoffman acquired 1,500 acres of Bogue Banks from "a wealthy man from Maine who was there very seldom and had little to do with the locals." McEwen refers to Hoffman as follows:

> [A] wealthy cosmopolite. She lived much of the time in Paris, and she bought the Bogue Banks property at the time of World War I, when things were perhaps uncomfortable in France. Why she chose Bogue Banks is a mystery to most people as it was hardly a place for a woman accustomed to international society. However, buy it she did and made a showplace out of it, although she managed to keep it well hidden. She planted rose gardens and cultivated lawns and imported furniture from all over. She frequently had guests from New York or even Paris. She determined to do something for the Salter Pathers, but she wanted to do it in an orderly manner, and she expected it to be appreciated. There were plans for clothing for the children and other things in that vein. But the Salter Pathers were not to be regimented. They resented her attentions, especially when they were accompanied by restrictions. There was considerable excitement out on the island when on one occasion the islanders marched around the Hoffman house shooting off guns and in general acting like a tribe of Indians. She was besieged for a couple of days. When she did get out, she took the matter to court.

The legal documents in the box pertained to a history of conflict between the Salter Pathers and Cousin Alice. But they were long, complicated, ultimately discontinuous, and didn't at first seem to offer me anything very "poetic." It appeared that my father at first represented Cousin Alice in court, but was very soon defending himself against her. What I finally liked best in the legal documents was the rhythm of a passage in one that seemed to be the final settlement in the quarrel between Alice and the Salter Pathers that stepped off the boundary lines demarcating what would henceforth be, as it were, the "reservation" of the Salter Pathers.

> save and except the area described
> as follows:

beginning at the southwest
corner of the Atlantic Beach
on the Atlantic Ocean (the
southwest corner of the property
known as the Hoffman Property)
thence running westwardly with
the Atlantic Ocean waters to
a point on the ocean two miles
from the beginning thence northwardly
and parallel with the west line of
the Atlantic Beach to the waters
of Bogue Sound to the
northwest corner of the Atlantic
beach thence with that line
which is the east line of the
Hoffman property to the beginning

As for the narrative, I couldn't figure out how to tell the story because I didn't have all of its parts. But consistent with my enthusiasm for endings, I did manage to write what I thought might be the final lines:

dunes drift
sand covers
the crops
    And you have been here?
    Three hundred years.
    And your people?
    Fish in the sea.

Not knowing what to do next, I put the lines, along with the legal documents, the newspaper article, and the Green family genealogy back in the box and stopped worrying about how I might write a long modernist poem. But I didn't stop thinking about Cousin Alice. Now and again I'd turn to James McEwan's article and ask family members for some amplification.

§

Alice had been a daughter of extreme privilege. Albert Green was a successful businessman who moved his enterprise from Columbus, Ohio to New York City. Although Alice lived for a few years with her Ohio grandparents for the sake of her health and a good outdoor life, she returned to New York after her mother died, following the birth of a third daughter. This was the "Gilded Age," and young Alice glowed in it, first at Miss Porter's School for Girls, where she had as expensive an education as money could buy, and then among the whist-playing and horseback-riding set. Scarcely out of her teens, she inherited one fortune upon her maternal grandmother's death and then another when her father died. Fluent by now in French, German, and Swedish, she headed for Europe, where she first lived in St. Moritz and studied music. She became an accomplished pianist and singer.

In London, she was presented to Queen Victoria; in Stockholm, she danced with Prince Eugen; in Germany, she traveled with a scion of the Van Munchausen clan; in France, she acquired a stable of horses and raced them at Chantilly and Longchamps. Then she suddenly and inexplicably married J. Ellis Hoffman, a man McEwan calls "an international playboy who traced his descent to the Washington family." It was 1909 and she was just over twenty.

When I asked my father about Hoffman, he told me that the marriage really didn't survive the wedding night. The day before the wedding, Hoffman evidently confessed something of his rake's progress through the capitals and spas of Europe. He expected his new wife, sophisticated and wise in the ways of the world, to accept this the same way his two previous wives had accepted it at first—not only in the past, but also for the future. But Alice, along with her education, had acquired an early feminist intolerance of boorish husbands, and she decided to bolt. Surprisingly, she went through with the wedding first. It had been planned as an extravaganza, as one can imagine, and it was simply too late to call it off. One wonders how she kept up the act on her wedding day. As for the wedding night, no one in my family thought the marriage was ever consummated. Marriage was a mistake that Cousin Alice would never make again.

And yet why did she ever agree to marry Hoffman? My father said, "Well she was only twenty." But she had already turned down other suitors, including an extremely dashing cavalryman who had been wearing, rather surprisingly, a Civil War uniform at some kind of New York horse show or hunt before Alice left for Europe. In an unpublished and unfinished autobiography now in her archive at East Carolina University, Alice writes that "next to the inestimable treasure of real love which exists, though so difficult to achieve, I have always considered my personal liberty as my most precious possession." She must have thought briefly that Hoffman represented "the inestimable treasure of real love," only suddenly to realize that her "most precious possession," her "personal liberty," would be threatened by the marriage.

There appear to be no further romances in Cousin Alice's story, and J. Ellis Hoffman disappears for good well before the official 1911 divorce. One can begin to imagine a number of Henry James plots for this unlikely episode and its hypothetical aftermath. What was said to her family, the wedding guests, all those well-connected friends? Having lived in Paris from 1900 to 1910, Alice returned to New York with whatever explanations she wanted to give and began acquiring real estate. These investments included property on 54th Street intended as a gift for her niece Eleanor and her family, an island off Connecticut, and, in 1917, Bogue Banks. She had been taken to Bogue Banks for a visit and evidently found it promising, though, after establishing Grove Farms, she only stayed there briefly until she actually moved to the property permanently in 1934. While she went on traveling between New York and Paris, her land was in the hands of managers and available to guests. One of them found it much as my parents did when they arrived in 1939 to deal with Cousin Alice's legal difficulties. Alice quotes this quatrain from a guest book in her autobiography:

> Abounding in beauties of nature
> This island's inhabited too,
> Wild boar, cattle-ticks, red-bugs & serpents,
> Thrive, as not many living things do!

By citing materials in the archive, I again anticipate things. Neither I nor anyone in the family knew that there was an archive, nor that anyone beyond the family might have any interest in Cousin Alice.

We speculated about her values. Was she a proto-feminist, a rich old maid, an early conservationist, a crazy lady obsessed with law-suits? By now it was around 1960 and I was again thinking about that modernist poem. I was also thinking about how problematic my relationship with my family and its traditions had become. I couldn't join in celebrating the legacies of the Grand Old Man and his jingo certainties. I declared myself a Democrat, then a Socialist. I read C. Wright Mills' *The Power Elite* and Ferlinghetti's *A Coney Island of the Mind*. I liked progressive jazz. I also began wondering if Cousin Alice couldn't be recruited as an ally before-the-fact, someone in but not of the family, a subversive influence, a ghostly partner in rebellion, Simone de Beauvoir to my Jean-Paul Sartre. By this date I had tried out my early run of lines on John Berryman at a University of Utah summer "Writers' Conference," which I attended straight out of high school. He pretty much said, "Why don't you write something else?" But he was interested in Cousin Alice and Bogue Banks. What did my parents do down there? Berryman wanted to know. (He also said it all sounded more like Faulkner than something Williams or Pound would be interested in.) I told him that for my mother and father it must have almost been a honeymoon trip, as they had been married only shortly before they headed south. Alice had asked my grandmother to urge my grandfather to intervene in her legal difficulties, not understanding that a Supreme Court justice couldn't represent her in a law suit. My grandmother sent her son instead.

This was well after the attack on Alice's house by the Salter Pathers that kept her locked inside for about two days and nights. Once their advocate in her eccentric way, she now mocked them to my father and parodied their Cockney-like accent: "Hoigh toid's the time for feeshing," she said. My father would walk around the island getting the lay of the land, but my mother was terrified of the poisonous coral snakes and stayed in the house where Alice would play the harpsichord through the afternoons with all the heavy curtains drawn, burning several candelabra full of tall candles in the 95-degree heat. Berryman said she didn't sound much like the Joan of Arc I was seeking for my poem.

He wondered what it had been like there in the war. I told him that my father had said the German U-boats hunted merchant ships in the waters beyond Bogue Sound and that Alice could hear exploding shells and anti-submarine mines going off. Bodies even washed up on the beach. Because of her fondness for France and the French, Alice had been in favor of the U.S. entering World War II well before Pearl Harbor. Various projects around her property were intended to further the war effort.

Berryman and I sat cross-legged in his room at a University of Utah dormitory. At that time he had only recently begun to write and publish the *Dream Songs*, but he could easily improvise a self-parody after a couple of drinks.

> Henry's Cousin Alice settled on Bogue Banks.
> Her fame not yet achieved, she was obscure
> Like him. The Sherman tanks
> Dug up the sand in moonlight, General Patton's Yanks
> Down south to guard contentious ranks
> From U-boats and that Lady. Told she must abjure

But there my notes break off. I don't know what he went on to say that Alice must abjure. "What was the settlement?" he asked. "It was complicated", I explained, "since the Salter Pathers didn't legally own their land and didn't pay taxes. But basically, the court said they could stay where they were if they kept away from Cousin Alice's property." In trying to protect both the property in the short run and Alice's long term intentions of passing on the land to the descendents of Eleanor Roosevelt, my father established a trust with himself as trustee. That was his big mistake.

§

Time passed. I studied fiction with Peter Taylor at Ohio State and thought about turning Alice's story into a novel. Taylor knew the terrain quite well and was enthusiastic about the project in his quiet, southern way. He urged me to get as much information as I could from my parents while they could still remember it all. Taylor was an acquaintance of Berryman's and probably Robert Lowell's best friend. He also advised me to look at the combination of memoir and poetry in what was then Lowell's most recent book, *Life Studies*.

I tried Cousin Alice in fiction, but it didn't work. During three years at Stanford, I studied with Yvor Winters, who had little interest in Cousin Alice and was against long modernist poems. When I went to London on a Fulbright grant, it was in time for a late resurgence of British Modernism, especially with the later work of David Jones and the publication, in 1967, of Basil Bunting's *Briggflatts*. "Brag, sweet tenor bull, / descant on Rawthey's madrigal," the poem began. My London roommate, who listened patiently to Cousin Alice stories, used to sing out in parody of my intentions:

> Howl, baritone hound,
> disgorge on Hoffman's property

During these years I did obtain a few more details from my parents. It seemed that Alice was first drawn to Bogue Banks when in 1915 she answered an advertisement regarding a house for sale three miles from Beaufort, North Carolina with "fourteen bedrooms, three baths, steam heat, electricity, 40 acres of fig orchard, 120 acres of pines, perfect climate, no malaria, no snow." The owner expected to sell it as a hunt club or sanatorium. In fact, Alice didn't buy that house, but during her visit to Beaufort she was taken to Bogue Banks and fell in love with the island. Instead of acquiring the hunt-club sanatorium, she bought three hundred acres of Bogue Banks, along with a cottage which she began to expand. By the time my parents arrived two decades later, Alice had obtained two other large tracts of land and expanded the house into an elaborate structure of eighteen rooms. Her gardener and mason had begun to construct formal terraced gardens on the French model. These were mostly overgrown by 1939, though my mother remembered some beautiful roses still poking up through the weeds. Six years later, military hardware was left rusting in the underbrush from the 101st Infantry and the 244th Artillery, many of whose soldiers were entertained by Alice in the house and who had left behind various kinds of gifts, including the inevitable verse, this time presented by a young Marine:

> At the edge of the forest, by the bank of the Sound
> Alone and secluded, there may be found,
> Aloof, yet inviting, enchanting Bogue Banks
> Apart and protected from humanity's pranks.

The pranks organized by the Salter Pathers, however, had demonstrated that Cousin Alice was not as secluded and protected as she may have thought. With a little urging, I got my parents to elaborate on the famous "attack." They said it was really a kind of comical harassment—the banging of pots and pans, pigs and cattle released into Alice's garden, that kind of thing. The Salter Pathers helped themselves to her fruits and vegetables, threw gravel at her windows in the night, and someone shot a crow out of the sky in such a way that it fell right at Alice's feet while she was walking near her house. The various lawsuits were too many and too complicated for my parents to remember accurately.

Alice had sued to get the Salter Pathers off her property. The Salter Pathers had counter-sued to preserve their fishing and grazing traditions. When Alice established a dairy farm on her property, the Salter Pathers complained that her cattle were dying of TB and infecting their own livestock. But Alice was still often in New York and Paris and therefore had to fight her legal battles at long distance and by proxy.

"When," I asked, "did Alice stay in 'her' room in Columbus?" My parents weren't quite sure. "When she went to and fro she'd stop off at the old house on Iuka," they thought. She came to Columbus "now and then." I asked if she had had much interaction with other family members in town. "Not much," they said. "She kept to herself and mainly stayed in her room." They thought they remembered Alice and my grandmother having long conversations. They thought she might have spent some time with her namesake, my aunt. It was doubtful, they said, that anyone in the family knew Alice better than they did themselves, and they felt they knew her hardly at all. After my father was sued for fraud and had to get his friend, Paul McNamara, to represent him against Alice herself, they wanted nothing more to do with her anyway. As for what I wanted to have to do with her, my position had changed. She clearly couldn't serve as my Joan of Arc or even my Simone de Beauvoir. My sympathy was now entirely with the Salter Pathers. It was now the mid-1960s. Weren't the Salter Pathers a good prototype for a Sixties commune? Whatever deceptive glamour and nonconformity Alice might have represented in her Paris heyday, it now seemed that she wanted to be the queen of her small realm. Or an imperialist invader like her in-law forebear, Teddy Roosevelt. So off with her head. When I went back to my long modernist poem—at last having taken Charles Olson as a model because he dealt so well with coastal geography and history in his own long modernist poem—I really stuck it to her as I exaggerated the violence of the "attack" on the

Hoffman establishment by the Bogue Banks squatters. (*Revolutionaries,* I said to myself, fiery with the energy of a Mayakovsky.)

> Fires there, and
> each man with
> torch. Crazy through
> the houses
> scattered round
> the backbone of
> the bank. Crazy up the island nob
> and down the
> Salter Path through
> underbrush and
> over dunes and
> under over-
> hanging limbs
>> Did they murder the cooks? Hack
>> The Butler up? Did they
>> Drink the blood of
>> The maids?

> Solid world / measure incomplete

> ends and beginnings
> cannot be regarded
> as fixed

When I was back in Columbus during the Christmas holidays in 1967, I came in late one night to find my father in tears. The end of my grandparents' old stone house on Iuka had been fixed. With the death of my grandmother, my cousin Nancy and her large family had moved in for a few years, but now the heavy stones were loosening from the mortar so quickly that the structure was clearly unsafe. The property had been sold and the wrecking ball was due to arrive the next day.

In the morning my father and I watched as the old house was destroyed. It came down very quickly. At a certain point, when about half of it had fallen to the ground, rooms and hallways could be seen as if one were looking into the open back half of an enormous doll's house. "There's Dad's room", my father said. "There's Edward's." The cleanup before the wreckers arrived had evidently been incomplete as various objects flew out into the sky with each swing of the ball: a baby cradle, a small desk, a bookcase. Once more they swung the ball and my father said—"And there's Cousin Alice's room." Another swing and out flew an object I couldn't identify. It hovered in the air for a moment and seemed as if it actually might glide away rather than fall. When it crashed into the limbs of a tree it made a strange sound, like breaking music. "What was that?" I asked. My father smiled wanly and said: "That was Cousin Alice's cello."

§

When I returned from England in 1968, I had enough poems for a book. At the very end of what would eventually be published as *Bucyrus* came the Bogue Banks poem, preserved as a series of fractured narrative fragments combined with two other poems, one on medieval witchcraft and the other a quasi-Jungian take on alchemy—two counter-cultural enthusiasms of the decade—as 'Poem in Three Parts.' By itself, the Bogue Banks part of the triptych turned out to be only about ten pages long, and not the *Paterson* or *Maximus* I had hoped to produce. It's just as well! And that would have been the end of the story of Alice Hoffman had I not received a telephone call one morning almost thirty years later from someone identifying herself as Kathleen Guthrie from Bogue Banks, North Carolina.

Mrs. Guthrie's voice sounded a little hesitant as she asked if I could possibly be the son of John Marshall Matthias who had been one of the lawyers representing Alice Hoffman against her own Salter Path community in the 1930s and 40s. And was I also a poet? She had been working on a master's thesis at East Carolina University about Mrs. Hoffman and needed to ask me some questions. I was, of course, surprised and delighted. It turned out that she had just spoken with Paul McNamara, my father's old friend and his own lawyer when he was charged with fraud. It had taken McNamara a minute or two before he began to get the picture, but when it all came into focus he said—"Good Lord, are you one of *Them*?" Indeed she was. She told me that her husband was a descendant of David John Willis, who figures in the poem. And she explained that up until her own children's generation, all the men and women in the community fished for a living, although now, because of the area's development as a tourist center, fishing resources had been depleted. For years her husband had fought just to keep beach fishing in the fall from being prohibited. She had already made contact with my aunts, the twins Alice Jacoby and Florence Merkel, and Paul McNamara had promised to take a list of questions to my mother, whose worsening dementia would probably not allow her to remember much from so long ago. My father had by then been dead for a decade and more. So I told her what I knew, which was much less than what I have written above, as I have been drawing without acknowledgment both on her eventual thesis and on the East Carolina archive, which she was the first to tell me about. She mainly wanted to know about J. Ellis Hoffman and the Paris years.

I could tell her only what my parents had told me. As for the legal entanglements, she had worked those out with an exacting patience. One appendix in the thesis lists fifteen different lawyers and, among many others, the following cases from the North Carolina Superior Court of Beaufort, North Carolina:

> Alice Hoffman v. J.C. Lewis, et al.
> Alice Hoffman v. David John Willis
> Alice Hoffman v. Henry Willis and David John Willis
> Alice Hoffman v. John A. Royall
> Alice Hoffman v. J.M. Willis, S.A. Duplanty, and C.S. Wallace
> Alice Hoffman v. E. Abott
> Alice Hoffman v. John Marshall Matthias and Roosevelt children
> Alice Hoffman v. Lewellyn Phillips
> Alice Hoffman, Bogue Banks, Inc. v. Lewellyn Phillips, John
> Marshall Matthias, the Alden Corporation, and R.N. Lorrimer.

And so on. It is almost a poem. So is this.

> Mrs. Hoffman shall receive from the fishing two shares.
> No green wood shall be cut or burned in the Community.
> No one shall trespass on her property from the line to the East
>   of Salter Path to her eastern property.
> No cattle, hogs, horses, sheep, goats or any other livestock shall
>   be allowed within these lines.

No one shall interfere in any way with her property or the
   people in her employ.
In case any of the members of the Community are unwilling to
   be guided by the above requests it is understood that they
   will leave the village of Salter Path before the 1st September
If at any time it should be found that any one has broken this
   agreement he would expect to be dispossessed without
   further notice.

Mrs. Guthrie agreed with me that these austere documents had a kind
of weight that was certainly missing from the unintentionally comic
"verse" also quoted in her thesis, some of which I have reproduced
above. But she had enjoyed the fragments she had read in *Bucyrus* and
wanted to print them as an appendix. Though the poem, such as it was,
had finally found its right reader, what a pity it is that I hadn't received
such a phone call thirty years before.

Mrs. Guthrie was perplexed about something else. Did Cousin
Alice ever reside at my grandfather's Columbus, Ohio house on Iuka?
I assured her that she had and that family members had always spoken
of "Cousin Alice's Room" in the house. But she told me that in her
phone conversation with Alice Jacoby she had been told of only a single
meeting between the two Alices, in a Washington, D.C. hotel where
my Aunt Alice was condescended to and felt herself a kind of intruder
in the suite where Cousin Alice was attended by several servants and
received her as if she were a peasant petitioning a queen. According to
my aunt, it was not a happy visit. But what about "Cousin Alice's Room"
in Columbus, my father's tears, the sailing cello? Mrs. Guthrie said she
had the feeling that Alice Hoffman had never stayed in Columbus. I
said I'd check with the cousins of my own generation and get back to
her.

For a long time I had been pretty much out of touch with the
Merkels, Jacobys, Borders, and Carlsons, the families of cousins Jim,
Marilyn, Robert, Richard, Judy, and Joan. For thirty years I had been
more or less adopted by my wife's British family which I found so
fascinating that I forgot everything that might be interesting about
my own. Though I was the only family member still called by the old
paternal surname, I was on the whole disaffected from what remained
of the Matthias clan. Marilyn had told me at some point that she and

I, in her opinion, were "out of the loop" in our different ways. And it's interesting that she too had developed a particular interest in Cousin Alice over the years. But now Marilyn told me that it was true Cousin Alice never stayed in Columbus and that "Cousin Alice's Room" was a kind of joke. She explained: "It's what our grandparents and Fanny called the one room in the house that nobody slept in, the one behind the attic stairs. Since all the other rooms had names," she said, "they gave that one a name as well—the name of the person who never visited but sometimes wrote letters containing strange tales or requests for legal advice." Marilyn had actually visited the archive at East Carolina and had read the unfinished autobiography. She still admired Alice, she said, because she was "an outsider in all respects, and she knew her own mind." I asked her about the cello that had flown out of "Cousin Alice's Room" during the demolition of the house. She told me it was Edward's cello, an instrument he had taken up before going off to the First World War which of course he couldn't play once his illness crippled him. The family put it out of the way in "Cousin Alice's Room" where, of course, it eventually became "Cousin Alice's Cello." I asked Marilyn why she thought I hadn't realized these things. She said that maybe I was a little dense. But she thought we were drawn to Alice's story for the same reason. It represented something well beyond the world view of Ohio Republicanism, the Broad Street Presbyterian Church, the United Spanish-American War Veterans, family chauvinism, the sentimentality of 'Goodbye Old Home' and the jingoism of 'A Toast to the Flag.' And yet Alice was still family, a romantic and female version of the proverbial bachelor uncle who has strange habits and a complicated past. Marilyn thought Cousin Alice might yet be "taken up" by the North Carolina Historical Society, especially if Kathleen Guthrie's thesis were published as a book. And what a good movie she thought it would make: *The Queen of Bogue Banks*, maybe starring Meryl Streep.

§

I suppose it was good to get the business about the room clarified, but I was nonetheless disappointed to abandon the imagined lonely afternoons when Cousin Alice sat there behind the attic stairs playing her cello until Fanny brought her dinner up on a tray and I followed behind hoping to hear about Paris and China and her island off the coast of North Carolina. I had spent more time thinking about Cousin Alice than I cared to admit, but she had given me in return materials and mysteries for the first real poem I had tried to write, tried and tried to write for twenty years. And then, distant relation that she was, she gave me an excuse to get back in touch with my own kin, even when I thought they hadn't been quite "my own free kind" (upon the crags in the cool light), as Mr. Pound must have said somewhere at about the time Cousin Alice married her own Europeanized American. I suddenly realized that I had missed all these blood relatives of mine and that I enjoyed their company.

Alice Hoffman died on Bogue Banks in 1953. Kathleen Guthrie's thesis tells us that "the Roosevelt heirs conveyed title of a portion of the island land to the State of North Carolina. The remainder of the property, except for another gift to the state on June 3, 1980, was developed into business and residential areas, including houses and condominiums." But the Guthrie family and the Salter Path remain.

Mrs. Guthrie concludes her study by referring to a 1923 judgment that established legal heirs of thirty-five men who were living in the village at that time. In a 1979 civil suit, "each head of household in Salter Path was required to trace his or her ancestry to at least one of the original thirty-five men named in the 1923 judgment." All but three families could do this and so stayed on. The presiding judge, assessing them only a few years' back taxes, obtained deeds for their properties from the Roosevelt heirs. He also, says Mrs. Guthrie, "[testified] to the character of the Salter Path villagers and the unity among them."

Ohio Forebears

Albert C.

He'd vaccinate at gunpoint if he had to
when there was an epidemic. Out he'd go
in what his son still called a "buggy"
in the 1940s. Friendly with the gun strapped

on his hip, he'd had it since a rebel
shot him through the elbow in the Civil War.
Eventually, he lost the arm, but not
before he used both hands delivering

uncounted babies in Gilboa and McComb.
Born on the battle's anniversary, his son
was given "Shiloh" as a middle name.
With 10,000 dead on either side, who would

light the candles on his cake? Beauregard retreated.
Pittsburgh Landing held. But the dark
in the covenant was truly arked.
Albert kept his arm in a bottle of formaldehyde

underneath a cupboard by the coal chute.
Now and then he'd go and have
a look at it. The gun was given in his will
to Edward Shiloh and the arm

was buried with him when he died.

Edward Shiloh

The gun was quite antique in '98, but
he took it with him anyway. No Rough Rider,
he nonetheless claimed Teddy R as his
own man and spoke with jingo confidence.

Although he never got to Cuba, Supreme Court
pages said they'd seen him in his uniform
that hangs in tatters in my closet by
the judge's robe that he and then my father wore.

He was distinguished for the wisdom and the style
of his opinions which are studied even now
in schools of law. He'd pace the upstairs study floor
incanting: *Goddamn the goddamn damn.*

My father said to him one night: *I wish you'd taught
me how to curse.* His bookshelves bulged
not only with The Law, but poetry:
With Kipling & with Whitman & with Tennyson . . .

At ten I sat there on his floor with Gunga Din.
I loved each button on his uniform, his
epaulettes, the dull dress sword. But most of all
the pistol brought from Shiloh with a shattered arm.

A large bronze bust they made of him
and put it in the State House where for fifty years
he was Ohio's Justice Holmes. The plaster cast,
intact for many months, shattered into pieces

in the hallway where it stood beside our phone.
A call from someone with bad news—
all about the trouble I'd got into at my school—
and suddenly the patriarch was dust.

The papers said he'd slipped and fallen
from a window where he tried to show exterminators
where the squirrels got into the house. But I knew
this synchronicity was all my fault. Although the bronze

statue stood upon its pedestal, I knew
that phone call somehow broke the plaster cast and

pitched him out the window, too. I believed in the uncanny:
Pittsburgh Landing calling yet to Shiloh & to Beauregard,

the finger on a severed arm pointing straight at me.

John Marshall

It's hard to be a judge and named for Marshall
but at least he wasn't monikered
for some battle in the Spanish War. The family
used to sing the bully anthems and they all

remembered the Maine. He missed the war his
own generation fought because rheumatic fever
licked his heart with flame and made him, unlike
Albert C and Edward S, unfit to serve.

His ill health followed him in ways I never knew
until he died. What he wanted was to serve.
The state. His family. Something, anyway.
When Edward Shiloh fell out of that window

and I thought my truancies from school had been
the cause, he won the unexpired term
and wore his father's robe as if it were a uniform.
And that was what destroyed him.

He was a shy and rather simple man and what
he could do well he did before
he had to live up to his name. His level
was Municipal, and traffic court his calling.

Although they made no bust of him, they cast
his name in bronze and screwed it
to his office door. It might as well have said:
Give up hope all Ye who enter here.

He entered every day. A hundred yards away
his father's statue stood.
He stuck it out for something like a dozen years
and then resigned, humiliated by his frailty.

John Edward

Ohio forebears on a shelf imported from
all over: Pooh and Rupert,
Paddington and Roosevelt, Delmore Schwartz.
And books to tell their tales.

Even Pooh's is sad, abandoned in the end
by the boy he loved and served.
To all of them I'm Albert's severed arm,
I'm Edward Shiloh's plaster cast,

John Marshall's dickey heart, the clumsy foot
of Paddington at tea time—
a badly broken covenant with
hearth & home, and exiled in a place

I thought I chose that isn't Rome or Tomis
either one but closes borders on your
marches where the cars are stalled and all
the horses sleeping in their harnesses

& Sherman's not recruiting any more, Ohio.

After Years Away

I. My Bed, My Father's Bell

First my bed, then his, now mine again—
just for a week.

He died in it, my father, where for years
I'd lie beside my pretty love,

alive and indiscreet.
He moved in here so she, my mother,

might sleep undisturbed while he gazed darkly
all night long into the dark.

In need, he'd ring a small brass bell
molded in the shape

of a hoop-skirted lady
sweeping with a broom and looking grim.

I see it now,
lying sideways on a row of books.

He'd ring it and she'd come to him.

II. My Father's Bell, My Grandfather's Books

The books are remnants of a city gardener's
life; the works of Emerson,

a Tennyson collected, *Paradise Lost*.
He's written in his Milton

1650
1608

   42 years. And on the title page:
Begun in January, 1893, and never finished.

In another hand: *Happy New Year to you, 1892.*
He's figured that J.M. was 42 and 1650

when he wrote his answer to Salmasius
and lost his sight.

Defensio pro Populo Anglicano.
At the Presbyterian funeral a cousin

asked: *are you religious?* And I said
In callow family disaffection:

Gnostic. Bogomil. Albigensian for heaven's sake.
On the *Ex Libris* plate:

Poetry. This book will not be loaned.
And underneath: *couldn't dig this month.*

Ground as old as hell.
I replace the book. I pick up the bell.

III. My Mother's Broom, My Father's Bell

My mother stashed those books in here
for me to find. My father

would have seen them, reaching for his bell,
but they were not for him.

She left them here, her father's only legacy,
as she began to sweep.

She swept the hearth, the porch and drive,
She even swept the street.

(She swept my father once entirely
off his feet.)

While he lay dying & while I sat reading books,
she swept his mortal breath away,

I think.
When she heard the ringing here . . .

And then swept circles round & round the bier
as I said *Gnostic, Bogomil.*

Although the ground was cold as hell
they dug the grave & dug it deep.

Sweet sleep. Sweep sweep.
There's no one here to listen or to care,

and so I ring the bell—
creating great commotion *there.*

Kedging in 'Kedging in Time'

After the first version of the poem now called 'Kedging in Time' was published in *Chicago Review* using only its first line as a title—'Thirty-Nine Among the Sands, His Steps'— I was asked by the editors of that journal to give an account of its occasion and composition. Although it was impossible to pass up such an offer, I was aware that there are always dangers that come with any experiment in self-reading.[1] One doesn't want inadvertently to shut down any passages—a resonant word in the watery context of this poem—while opening up a lock here and there by way of some auto- and bibliographical heaving and hoing at cranks, gates, gears, and other kinds of machinery. Most of the ships in this tale are too heavy to portage; and a clogged sluice may now and then require a better trained nautical sleuth than the maker of the poem and author of these notes. Still, the essay was generally enjoyed and a number of readers suggested that I reprint it in the book, *Kedging* (Salt Publishing, 2007) where it can in fact be found in a slightly different form.

To begin with, the title of the piece changed after its appearance in *Chicago Review*. The first line is now just a first line, though still splicing the titles of two popular fictions of the early Twentieth Century, Erskine Childers' *The Riddle of the Sands* (1903) and John Buchan's *The Thirty-Nine Steps* (1915). The title is now as given above, while the version in the book, re-formatted to encourage a slow reading, follows the title with a modified quote from the OED and a dedication:

> [Kedge, v. *intr*. A. To warp a ship, or move it from one position to another by winding in a hawser attached to a small anchor dropped at some distance; also *trans*. To warp. B. Of a ship: To move by means of kedging.] Poets, too, may cast an anchor well before them, pulling forward when attached to something solid, only then to cast their anchor once again.

For some families involved:

Drury-Lowe, Adams, Bonham-Carter, Hilton-Young, Young

And for friends

The addition of a dedication serves, I hope, to suggest at once that the poem is not entirely impersonal in the mix of literary and historical materials encountered by the reader following the first fourteen lines. In fact, by the end of the piece, it should become clear that an elegy for Pamela Adams, along with her forbears and some in her extended family, has emerged out of the various dissolves, re-windings and general historical parataxis of the text. Although fictional characters, historical figures, and family members keep an extended and perhaps an initially perplexing company in the piece, Pamela is at the center and draws the others together as daughter and wife of sailors, reader of Childers, Buchan, Anthony Hope and Rider Haggard, writer of memoirs, step-mother, mother, mother-in-law, cousin and friend of those many members of "families involved." Although it's going to sound like name-dropping, a bit of family history may help to open up the poem.[2]

At some point in the fall of 1966 I found myself at a party in London talking to the most beautiful woman in England. Reader, I married her. But not for a year or so. I was inconveniently married to someone else at the moment and, of course, I had to meet Ms. Diana Adams' family. That very night I made a start at what was a very long process. At the end of the party Ms. Adams suggested dropping back to "my sister's place," what I assumed would be a student flat. Her sister's name, "Liz Young," sounded reassuring enough, but my London roommate (my American wife was at Stanford), drove the four of us—the fourth was a friend who had met Liz's husband, Wayland, at I.U. in Bloomington, and *that* sounded downright Hoosier—straight up Bayswater Rd. to a private house amid hotels and high rises more or less across from the Round Pond in Hyde Park. I still thought the "student flat" might be at the back or maybe in the attic, but became a little alarmed when I saw a blue plaque near the door saying that James Barrie had written *Peter Pan* inside. Liz and Wayland lived, along with their five children, in the whole house, not just in part of it. After I got to know Wayland I sometimes thought he, with all his polymath's enthusiasms, might *be* Peter Pan.

It was quite late and all children save the eldest—that was Easter, eighteen—were in bed. After a while Wayland, and a little later Liz, came down from wherever they had been upstairs. The backdrop to a sherry and a couple of hours conversation was a large library, art on the walls by some artists I recognized—Duncan Grant in his Matisse phase, for example—and both a piano and harpsichord. As Wayland talked a little shop, it turned out that he was a member of the Wilson government and had another name—Lord Kennet. (His paper trail is hard to follow as he's published books under the names Wayland Hilton-Young, Wayland Young, and Wayland Kennet. The changes of name suggest an intellectual restlessness that has been part of his character.) Liz, as it turned out, was Diana's half sister, daughter not of Pamela, but of Bryan Adams' first wife, Audrey, who had drowned in a swimming accident. Liz was a poet, a published authority on arms control, and co-author, with Wayland, of books ranging in subject from old London churches to Northern Lazio in Italy. On the literary side of things, they were friends of people like Wole Soyinka and William Golding; on the political side, they entertained ministers, ambassadors, and a range of high-flying academics including a man I met later that year called Henry Kissinger. Liz and Wayland were about forty. Diana was twenty-one. I was twenty-four and felt like an American pilgrim out of Henry James.

Diana had been living at Liz and Wayland's house while attending Russian classes at what was then called Holborn College. And she had lived there before, when she was doing A-levels at Queens. It must have been a heady environment for a teenage girl. Her own home was in the tiny village of Hacheston, in Suffolk, where her father had retired after serving in two World Wars. He was over eighty. Pamela was twenty years younger. They had met at the League of Nations before the Second War. Captain Adams had been pleased when his first daughter married the son of an old shipmate, Edward Hilton Young. They had served together on *Vindictive*, about which Hilton Young wrote in his book *By Land and Sea*. (It is my main source for the attack at Zeebrugge.) The Captain had been pleased enough with Wayland's early books, but didn't like his famous contribution to the zeitgeist of the Sixties, *Eros Denied*. "All about sex," he sniffed when I mentioned it some years later. (It was research at the Kinsey Institute that had led Wayland briefly to Bloomington.)

Though Edward Hilton Young had proposed to Virginia Woolf in a punt on the Cam, he eventually married the widow of Captain

Scott of the Antarctic. So Lady Scott was Wayland's mother. She was a sculptor and a friend of T.E. Lawrence, who sat to her for a bust. I eventually imagined both a polar waste and a desert at opposite ends of the house: one the province of Scott, the other of Lawrence. Wayland would sometimes dress up in Lawrence's Arab robes (somehow in his possession) and dash about the house with his dagger. His daughter, Louisa, writes her grandmother's life in *A Great Task of Happiness*. Another daughter, Emily, is a sculptor, like Lady Scott—and perhaps the finest living stone carver in the tradition of Gaudier-Brzeska, Eric Gill, and Mestrovic.[3]

The Scott, Young and Adams families are all from Naval backgrounds. Louisa writes in her biography that the Youngs "came from a line of runaway cabin boys and pirates which developed into Admirals." I have in my library the midshipman's log book composed by Sidney Drury-Lowe, Pamela Adams' father, from the time he was thirteen. No runaway or pirate, he came from a branch of the family which one associates with the poetry of John Donne. He, too, "developed into" an Admiral. Bryan Adams, born in Australia, also went to sea at an early age. Along with Hilton Young, he served under Sir Roger Keyes at certain points in the First World War. Thoby Young, Diana's ten-year-old nephew when I met him, eventually married Roger Keyes' granddaughter.

"And Pamela was nine." The passage that introduces Pamela to the poem finds her "near Rosyth in the little coastal / village, Aberdour." Here she waits for her father's occasional visits, reading Hope, Buchan and Childers, playing games, looking out to sea where the naval war is in progress. Part II of the poem concludes looking forward to her 94th year and her memories of the Kiel Regatta, the war-time patrols of destroyers and dreadnoughts, and eventually the surrender and scuttling of the German fleet. At the end of her life, she thought she was the last to have seen *Der Tag*, The Surrender. Her father had seen to it that she and a few other children of officers were taken out in a launch as the German ships steamed past. She tells the story in one of her unpublished memoirs, *The Iron Pier*, which is a source for this part of the poem. Out at sea her future husband was also aboard his ship. She wouldn't marry him for twenty years, but there he was. Like Pamela herself, and like her father, he had a copy of Childers' *Riddle of the Sands.* Churchill had sent copies to all ships at sea after Childers' participation in The Cuxhaven Raid in December 1914—a raid that depended on the observations of shores, islands, canals, sandbanks, tides and military strategies of a fictional character living in a novel.

"On Vindictive . . . nothing flying in the sky except the gulls." At the end of Part III, the poem returns to Pamela by way of Bryan Adams' and Hilton Young's participation in the attack on the guns at Zeebrugge. The strategic importance of the raid would take too long to explain here, but it's worth saying that it was a nearly suicidal assignment for those, led by Captain Adams, who dashed from their ship in a land attack against the lighthouse on the mole. (Maps of the coastline from Dunkirk north to Borkum and Cuxhaven can be found in Robert Massie's history, *Castles of Steel.*) Adams survived intact while Hilton Young, still on *Vindictive*, lost an arm to enemy fire. The narrative passage describing the attack merges in the text with Pamela's half-dreaming memories on the early morning of Remembrance Day, 1966. This was my first visit to Hacheston, and there I am, "the young American / walking with the family to the little Norman church."

By the time I wrote this passage, Pamela was dead. Or, perhaps, I was writing it as she died. It is rather uncanny. Diana had flown to England in February of 2005 and had been there for a month or so, nursing her mother. The poem turned biographical and elegiac during that period. The remembered events included the Remembrance Day celebration, a first meeting between "the young American" and Pamela and Bryan Adams, pleasure sailing on the Alde, a dinner, and some awkward literary conversation in which the American tries to talk about Virginia Woolf—he was reading *Jacob's Room* coming up on the train— when the Captain said (the poem only has him "looking rather bored"): "Perhaps we've had enough of *her*," maybe referring to his future son-in-law's blather, or maybe to his own memories of his shipmate's infatuation with Virginia Woolf herself. The bookshelves there in Hacheston held some serious literature—complete sets of Hardy, Austen, Scott—but it's the talismanic Kipling, Buchan, and Hope toward whose books, unfortunately, the American has his back. As for Childers, he finally read *The Riddle of the Sands* when it was urged on him by, of all people, Geoffrey Hill.

The poem ends—aside from the echoing questions meant for "Mr.

Memory"—where it began, with sailing on the Alde. I had placed "Wayland, Nigel, and Ian" in the yacht at the Kiel Regatta—an actual yachtsman, a Bonham-Carter cousin, and my newborn grandson— while, of course, the little sailing boat in the Suffolk river contains the Captain, his wife, his daughter, and the troublesome American. Diana "sailed the Alde" quite early in life and her head was full of sometimes frightening fantasies—"children's strategies on tidal rivers / where the toy wooden soldiers rose / in marshmist reeds and tipped their Bismarck helmets / to the girls, *Achtung!*" The rest of the opening passage, however, introduces an altogether different strand of the poem: "Cousin Erskine had preceded /by some leagues

> And even Uncle Win. Sons of Lord Anchises,
> Prophesying war, sang of arms and men who had come back again
> *By whom the bundled fasces were restored . . .*

Biographically speaking, there is no Uncle Win or Cousin Erskine in the Adams, Young, or Drury-Lowe clans. The references are to Childers and Churchill, who "had preceded" the principal family members of the poem into historical waters—and in the wake of Aeneas and Lucius Junius Brutus. Early on, Childers—an enthusiastic combatant in the Boer War—was as bullish an Imperialist as Churchill himself, and the "bundled fasces" resonate equally of Imperial Britain, Augustan Rome, Bismarck's Germany, and the Italy of Mussolini.

To compound the fiction braided at the outset around biography, Childers, as far as I know, never sailed from the Alde in Suffolk on any of his pre-World War I explorations of the Frisian islands, the coasts of Holland and Germany, and the Baltic that provided material for *The Riddle of the Sands* and, eventually, his official paper for the Admiralty, *The Seizure of Borkum and Juist*. He sailed out the mouth of the Thames. However, his journey on *Vixen*, and the journey of his characters Davies and Carruthers on *Dulcibella*, enter the poem at once as fiction and fact. Sailing *Vixen*, Childers carried with him and read Book Six of *The Aeneid* and Anthony Hope's *Rupert of Hentzau*, sequel to *The Prisoner of Zenda*. Pamela would also be reading Hope—as would Churchill.

The mapping of Davies and Carruthers, their discovery of German military secrets, and the epilogue by "the editor" dealing with the deciphered memorandum Carruthers pulls from a stove at Norderney, became a matter of great interest at the War Office after *The Riddle of the Sands* was published in 1903. Fictional characters began at that point their instruction of statesmen, Admirals, and Generals who continued listening up to and beyond the Cuxhaven Raid of December 1914. From the first page of the poem, fictional characters move in the same world as men and women like Bryan and Pamela Adams, Hilton Young, Sidney Drury-Lowe, John Buchan, Kaiser Wilhelm, Tsar Nicholas and Childers himself.

The next several pages of text, following the introduction of motifs in the initial fifteen lines, braid together Childers' articulated fear that Germany could easily launch an invasion of Britain from the Frisian islands with Churchill's reading of *The Prisoner of Zenda* and his composition of *Savrola*, the Ruritanian romance he wrote in 1897 and published first in *MacMillan's Magazine* and then, in 1900, as a novel with Hodder and Stoughton's "Sevenpenny Library." Unlike *The Riddle of the Sands*, *Savrola* would be of no importance at all if it weren't by Churchill. Written in the wake of *Zenda's* extreme popularity, and between Malakand and the River War when its author was twenty-four, *Savrola* is dedicated to "The Officers of the IVth (Queen's Own) Hussars in whose company the author served for four happy years." In the poem, the adventures of the republican Savrola as he battles in fictional "Laurania" with dictator Morala on the right and radical Kreutz on the left, merge with an account of the actual attack at Kilid Bahr in the Bosphorus.[4] While Laurania's fleet is recalled from Port Said to quell Savrola's rebellion—*Fortune*, *Petrarch* and *Sorato* exchanging fire with shore batteries as they attempt to gain access to Laurania's major harbor—*Agamemnon*, *Inflexible* and *Irresistible* encountered in fact a similar situation steaming up the strait to the Hellespont in the Dardanelles campaign that sent the novelist who had become First Lord of the Admiralty plummeting into temporary obscurity. Edmund Wilson said that in some ways Churchill's career gave him the impression of a person living perpetually in a boy's adventure story; the same might be said of Childers. In the case of both, their fictions prefigure events in the First War and after. And Churchill knew his Childers well. Carruthers' fear of a German attack from the Frisians became Childers' memorandum recommending a British attack from

Borkum and Juist, supported by the Russians in the Baltic. Churchill chose the Dardanelles and disaster. Who knows what might have happened at Borkum and Juist?

As Morala and Churchill "dream of power" and Churchill pauses in his 1897 composition, the poem's clock is re-set for 1915 and Gallipoli. If only the fictional Carruthers saw the dangers of a German invasion of the eastern coast of Britain from the Frisians (British barges now diverted from the Baltic to the Dardanelles), it was Richard Hannay, John Buchan's hero in *The Thirty-Nine Steps* (1915), *Greenmantle* (1916), and two subsequent novels, who knows that Kaiser Wilhelm "gave it out he was a secret / Muslim and proclaimed a Jihad in Islamic lands / against the Brits." From this point to the end of Part I, Buchan and his fictions become a new strand in the braiding, anticipating a transition from the British failure against the Turks and Germans at Gallipoli to the success of Brits and Russians—aided by T.E. Lawrence, who may be the model for Sandy Arbuthnot in *Greenmantle*—at Erzerum. As he wrote his novels, Buchan, who worked (sometimes with Lawrence) in intelligence and decoding, also wrote the ongoing chronicle (verging on propaganda) that became *The Nelson History of the War*. The strange story about the Kaiser's feigned conversion to Islam is evidently true, as it is told in the history as well as the fiction.

The poem continues with the first references to Childers' adventure running guns to Ireland on the *Asgard*—guns which, though intended for the Dublin Volunteers, were eventually taken by the Irish Republican Brotherhood and used in the Easter Rebellion. While Childers was at sea, Austria sent its ultimatum to Serbia. The war began, and Childers returned to England to fly as navigator in a Short 136 from which he pointed out details from the maps made in his head sailing *Vixen* back in 1897. Because of that, "1903's fiction [does indeed, drawing on *Vixen's* log] prefigure 1915's fact." Childers spent the rest of his life trying to reconcile his commitment to the cause of Ireland with his loyalty to the Empire. In the end, of course, that couldn't be done.[5]

How do these and other texts function in the poem? As secure holds for the kedge-anchor of my reefed verbal craft. When I first read *The Riddle of the Sands*, I had to look up "kedge" and "kedging" in the OED. In seconds I had on my screen just the kind of list I like—*kechel, Kechua, keckle, kecksy, keddah, kedje, kedge-anchor, kedger, kedging, kedjeway*—and immediately wrote a short poem bouncing phrases off these K's. ("K,K,K, Katie" sang the Tommies and the sailors shipped to foreign ports.)[6] The phrases include some that find their way into the present, longer poem when its poetics, as it were, is made plain:

> . . . what's the future of the future tense?
> What's propitious in the past? Passing through the present
> Kedging's all you're good for
> With a foot of water under you, the tide gone out, the fog so
>   thick
> You can't see lights at Norderney but enter history in spite
> Of that by sounding in its shallows with an oar.

In the end, I thought an epigraph could make this even plainer.

The "young American" of Part III bores the Captain by going on at dinner about Virginia Woolf. I've mentioned that he was "in fact" reading *Jacob's Room*. (By 1922, when Woolf's novel was published in the same year as *The Waste Land*, modernism had begun making fiction like Buchan's look even more unsophisticated and jingoistic than it is.) [7] In *Jacob's Room*, Jacob and his friend Timothy Durrant sail from Falmouth to St. Ives Bay before the war, following the same route around Land's End that Childers took in *Asgard* in July 1914. *Asgard*, indeed, sailed with its load of guns right through massive exercises of the British fleet which occurred at the same time, George V observing from a dreadnought. Jacob, like the characters in *Greenmantle*, travels eventually to Turkey before he is ground up in the gears of war and becomes a casualty in a world that came into being, while, as Woolf has it, "A voice kept remarking that Prime Ministers and Viceroys spoke in the Reichstag; entered Lahore; said that the Emperor traveled; in Milan they rioted; said there were rumours in Vienna; said that the Ambassador at Constantinople had audience with the Sultan; the fleet was at Gibraltar."

The fleet would be at Scapa Flow. The conclusion of Part II quotes a passage from Childers' *Vixen* log and finds Wilhelm sailing in the Baltic just before the outbreak of war. He had always envied the Royal Navy and participated enthusiastically with those other heirs of Queen Victoria, cousins Nicholas II and George V, in the parties and regattas held at Osborne House on the Isle of Wight. Admiral Jellicoe brought

150 British ships down into the North Sea to support the Cuxhaven Raid. Zeppelins and submarines ventured out, but not the great ships of Wilhelm's *Hochseeflotte*, which were hiding in the estuaries and rivers known so well to Childers. The raid achieved little and, subsequent to that, the Germans would not be drawn. There would be no early Trafalgar. There would be no Trafalgar at all, even at Jutland.

I need only identify two or three more texts—though one is a film—into which the kedge-anchor digs in order to haul this contraption forward (winds and retreating tide also sometimes pushing it back). The film is Alfred Hitchcock's version of Buchan's *The Thirty-Nine Steps*. While Part II of the poem begins with a quote from Childers' paper on Borkum and Juist and an evocation of the response in East Anglian coastal towns to seeing aircraft and ships of war, a central figure called "Mr. Memory" is soon introduced. There is no such character in Buchan's novel. He is added by Hitchcock to the 1935 film along with a love-interest for Hannay. (The latter's name is Pamela, but because of the more important Pamela in the poem, references to this character use the name of the actress who played her, Madeleine Carroll.) While ships in the North Sea, Hannay in *The Thirty-Nine Steps*, Buchan in Room 40 (working on codes, like his hero), and the secret agents of Black Stone all try either to establish or penetrate an "atmosphere," the aim of Buchan's villains to acquire intelligence about the disposition of the British fleet becomes—once "Buchan's Hannay" morphs into "Hannay's Buchan" in the film—a search for secret plans to build a silent aircraft engine. Mr. Memory, whose music hall act involves his ability to recall an infinite number of unrelated facts when questioned by members of the audience, substitutes for Hannay's code-breaking in the novel. At the end of the film, Mr. Memory begins to reveal the secret formulas in a Palladium performance and is immediately shot. Hannay has shouted out, "What are the 39 Steps?" Mr. Memory, evidently programmed in some way to carry all the information in his head and deliver it to the villains, says "The 39 Steps is an organization of spies collecting information on behalf . . ." Which is as far as he gets. But the 39 Steps in the novel is a set of stairs down to the sea where full tide occurs at 10:17. At that time, Hannay finds the villains at Trafalgar Lodge—with its 39 steps—where, in the poem as well as the novel, he accosts them. He has decoded his information and followed his clues to this place and time, which is not performance time at the Palladium. "The day [when] the book which [Hannay] inhabits enters time"— publication day in 1915—happens to be a day when the evacuation was under way at Gallipoli. Mr. Memory is not asked in the poem about that, or indeed about what he happens to be doing in a poem in the first place. But he becomes the most important single figure other than Pamela. The questions that are put to him derive either directly from Hitchcock or from kedging activities already introduced. By the end of the poem he has run out of answers and, like Erskine Childers, has been shot.

Which does not mean that the reader will be unable to answer questions for him. *Did Erskine Childers eat Carruthers' / heart?* Yes. *Who returned to Ireland in a German submarine when / Asgard's captain still served Empire and Ascendancy in Short 136 / In skies above the Heligoland Bight?* That was Roger Casement. *Who was hanged and who was shot / and why?* Childers was shot, Roger Casement was hanged. For carrying an illegal weapon. For treason against the crown. *Did Churchill cheer and did Cuchulain weep?* Yes. *Who steps thirty-nine among the sands or riddles there / who also may have sailed the Alde?* Erskine Childers, Edward Hilton-Young, Bryan Adams, Diana Adams, a visiting American who'd just read *Jacob's Room*, and Pamela both old and young.

> On 29 July the fleet leaves
> Portland in the dark to pass the straits of Dover, eighteen miles
> Of warships steaming toward the foggy empty waters
> In the north . . .
> and Pamela was nine.

We have now again reached the family memoir section of the poem, the long run of lines about Pamela and her father ending with their playing the parts of characters from *The Prisoner of Zenda*. Mr. Memory falters while Mrs. Adams, 94, remembers; the child Pamela reads her romance to the exhausted Captain Drury-Lowe.

> She lived near Rosyth in the little coastal
> village, Aberdour. Her father was a captain & she sometimes
> saw his ship out on patrol. She wished she were a boy
> and could go to sea herself and didn't like it when

her mother & the other naval wives would say
But you can marry a sailor! Precocious reader, she'd go down
to the rocks emerging at low tide with Buchan or Childers,
Rider Haggard or Hope. She'd be the hero on the run,
she'd be the spy, she'd be the swashbuckling master
of a masked identity. Then she'd make a large uncovered stone
her ship, fire a broadside at the Germans who were hunting
through the fogs to find her father and, although
she didn't know it, her future husband too. Her own child
would also be a captain's daughter and the strategist of
tidal rivers to the south where toy wooden soldiers rose in marsmist
reeds and tipped their Bismarck helmets to the girls, *Achtung!*
Achtung! her father joked, running towards her laughing down
the iron pier where landing craft left officers and men
who now and then were granted leave. He'd walk with her along
the narrow path between the bay and village, rightful
king of Ruritania, prisoner freed from Zenda and engaged
to Princess Flavia; and she'd be Rudolph Rassendyll
dueling for his borrowed crown & honor with Black Michael's
black usurping henchmen on the castle bridge.
Then her father's utter great fatigue would overwhelm him
and he'd lie down in the sun,
shade his aching eyes with his daughter's open book . . .
If you asked Mr. Memory about these two, he'd be
confused. Father, daughter? Captain, mate?
Two red-headed Rudolphs? Richard Hannay and his scout Pienaar
cloaked entirely in an atmosphere & sharing stories with
the very man who stalked them? Mr. Memory at the Palladium
might falter, but not Mrs. Adams, 94, perhaps the last alive to have
seen the things she's seen, telling ancients at the ancient public school
converted to a home: *And I was Pamela, a child, and yet I*
saw it all. Every ship on the horizon steaming in formation
while the two of us would sing dispatch or distich there
beneath the sign of all these sails: darting in and out & crossing tacks
at fifteen knots, the yachtsmen heading for the Kiel Regatta,
Wayland, Nigel, Ian: Monarch firing from the
forward turret out of fog by whom the bundled fasces or
the kingdom come. She kissed her father's eyes
And read him stories from her book.

At the beginning of section III, "Cousin Nicky"—Tsar Nicholas II—also reads to comfort the frightened and exhausted. Amazingly, he actually read Buchan's *Greenmantle* to his imprisoned family before their execution, finding information in it Buchan got about the strategies leading to the Russian cavalry attack at Erzerum from some visiting Russian journalists, including Vladimir Nabokov's father, whom he had shown around Scapa Flow in February 1916.[8] Buchan wrote to his mother in October 1917: "I saw a letter from the Grand Duchess Olga saying that she and her sisters and Papa had been greatly cheered and comforted in their exile by *Greenmantle*. It is an odd fate for me to cheer the prison of the Tsar." The narrative of *Greenmantle* is twined around Pamela's story and that of Buchan's work on codes in Room 40, details of which fascinating operations derive from a masterful source, David Hahn's remarkable *The Codebreakers: The Story of Secret Writing*, which I've used off and on ever since I wrote *Pages* in 1995. Surprisingly, Buchan gave the characteristic stare of Admiral Hall, head of decrypting in Room 40 and known as "Blinker" because of a twitch that accompanied the stare, to one of the villains in *The Thirty-Nine Steps*.

For the rest, the poem kedges on by way of its fictions and facts—many of the latter opened up by another masterpiece, Robert K. Massie's *Castles of Steel*—toward Zeebrugge and *Vindictive*—and Hilton Young's account of Bryan Adams' landing party. When this attack occurred, Pamela was still in Aberdour, still only nine, though she would marry Bryan Adams in the end. On Remembrance Day 1966, she must have been younger than I am now. Strange to think I'm sixty four. I wonder what she made of me. I'm sure Captain Adams knew I'd come to take his daughter away. What a loss, for me, that I was really still too young to speak to him sympathetically about his participation in two World Wars and a long life at sea. He could have told me, a sedentary grad student, much that I had to learn from books for thirty years. He was by then quite deaf. Almost the first thing he said to me was that he wished the Brits were fighting with us there in Vietnam. For a 1960s peace activist, such as I then was, that made things quite awkward. At lunch that day in 1966 there was a British Foreign Service type whose father had been a Commander and who had an upper lip so stiff that you could pluck it. "I do like Richard Palmer," said the Captain as my rival left the table under which Diana had been kicking me. Soon enough I did in fact take the Captain's daughter away to America and, shortly after that, he died. Pamela lived on for years, and for years we spent our summers at her house there in Suffolk. My favorite response to this poem came from one of its first readers: "I like Pamela," he said.[9] He is not alone. She had a kind of goodness that everyone who met her felt; a Christian would say she was touched by Grace, but that would have embarrassed her terribly. Her house was a kind of Howards End, and she was a kind of Mrs. Wilcox. Any lonely waif might be invited there, and many were. She outlived everyone in her generation; she even outlives Mr. Memory in the poem

Liz and Wayland are now in their eighties and I've literally lost count of the numbers of grandchildren and great-grandchildren there are. Their magical house on Bayswater Rd., Peter Pan at the door and Lady Scott's studio at the back, still holds its magnificent past, though one wonders when the future will arrive with a wrecking ball and hotel. In the sixties, an Indian journalist called Abu Abraham lived in the studio. He once told me about his elementary education in New Delhi and a British history teacher who lectured them on what he claimed was the most powerful influence in the modern world since the 18th century. It was something that Abu wasn't quite able to get, and he wrote down "British Seepa" in his notes. British sea power.

Because of certain medical problems and an accompanying claustrophobia, I never go to England any more. For many years I was adopted by a family and conscripted (willingly enough) by a history not my own. I owe them a lot. I owe them at the very least a poem.

Geneva Pension

Once a year my wife's mother, Mrs. Adams, 93,
receives in her mail at Farnam, Surrey,
a letter from Geneva asking, in effect,
are you still alive? It comes along with her

League of Nations pension, still paid
to her as the widow of a naval attaché.
She laughs and says: *I guess we are not many.*
Out of curiosity, she once wrote back

and asked: *How many are we, in fact?*
A polite letter came a few weeks later
in which an official—one wonders just what kind—
had written at the end, *In fact, six.*

By the time it reached the secretary to be typed
evidently things had changed: she or he had lined out "six"
and just above it written "five."
But indeed Captain Adams was a League of Nations

officer in residence. There they were, a veteran
of the World War and his so much younger wife.
Their high hopes faded like a sunset
on the lake. Or like the hopes of a tall hieratic

figure they would see standing with a walking stick
beside the lake and evidently talking to
himself: O.V. de L. Milosz, metaphysician, French poet,
citizen of Lithuania. "Will the hour be new

in some archaic future?", Milosz asked before
the war. *Nouvelle, mais si peu neuve . . .*
By 1922 he heard an insect's cry within him,
underneath the ashes of his heart . . .

Thinking in French or Polish or maybe even German,
he stood there by the lake and, in a highly formal way,
inclined his head politely to the English Captain
and his wife as they passed him on their promenade.

There in Surrey, early June, Mrs. Adams looks a little
quizzically at the check, then at the picture of
her husband leaning on the window sill in
morning sun. Elsewhere, four other widows of the League

receive Geneva pensions and may also greet the day.

Some Letters

In the end it was his daughter who would write
the book about his mother, but Wayland
fended off biographers for years after academics
on the trail of Robert Falcon Scott

trashed her on their way to the pole. It was 1980
and I lived that year at Clare Hall in Cambridge
with my wife, half-sister of Liz, wife of Wayland Young,
Lord Kennet. Wayland had been Hilton-Young at first,

like his father, Lady Scott's second husband, but he
scrapped the Hilton part when he joined the Labour Party
(at the same time, about, that Wedgwood-Benn had
smashed the Wedgwood saying, You can call me Tony).

Anyway, Wayland phoned one day and asked if I
would go identify myself at the U.L. archive and bring him
something to The Lacket, a small cottage in Wiltshire where
Lytton Strachey had written *Eminent Victorians*, I think,

sometime after Wayland's father, the first Lord Kennet,
had proposed to, and been refused by, Virginia Woolf.
He wanted the letters, deposited by him on extended loan,
that T.E. Lawrence wrote to Lady Scott after she became

a Hilton-Young and T.E.L. became a Ross, and then a Shaw.
Or was it Shaw, and afterwards Ross? I showed them my ID,
an Indiana driver's license, and they gave me a large envelope
with all the letters. I said, Can I just walk out with these?

The librarian said I could, being "Lord Kennet's representative."
So I took them to the station and caught a train for
Wiltshire, reading in astonishment Lawrence's account to
Wayland's mother, then a sculptress keen to do his bust,

about his changes in identity and habits. At one stop I got out,
Xeroxed all the letters, and caught another train.
Lawrence of Arabia! Or Shaw. Or Ross. He wrote to
Wayland's mother: "T.E. Lawrence is no more."

Wayland's mother, too, had changed from the days
when Scott would dine with her at luncheon parties that
included Barrie, Beerbohm, Isadora Duncan, Gertrude Stein.
(Peter Scott, Wayland's half-brother, had been named

for Peter Pan, a work written not in Wiltshire at The Lacket
but at Wayland's London house on Bayswater Rd.
You may have seen the blue historic plaque affixed above the door.)
When I got to The Lacket, Wayland told me that another biographer

had been in touch and that he'd grown wary, thought he'd
better see what T.E.L. had written before granting access
to the file. I gave him the originals and sat there having tea
and thinking about Lawrence, Scott, Strachey, Barrie, Beerbohm

and Virginia Woolf. After a while, Wayland leaned over
and passed me something—my driver's license, it appeared, had
been slipped by the archivist in among the letters.
Our eyes met for a moment, and I suddenly remembered all

those photocopies I had made coming down. Better burn those.
But I smiled and took the Indiana License, another cup of tea,
a scone with marmalade, and said: Lawrence of Arabia! Good Lord!
And Wayland said: Yes. A very strange little man.

Poetry and Insomnia

But I sleep well
J.V. Cunningham

Funes could not sleep
Jorge Luis Borges

Television advertisements for over the counter sleeping aids are everywhere at the moment, especially perhaps on the network news where other weaknesses of aging baby boomers are addressed: impotence, piles, incontinence, osteoporosis. Ah, for a good night's sleep. Just one pill and awaken refreshed. With the peacefully sleeping spouse beside the agonizing insomniac, it's even implied in these ads that a good night's sleep might also cure some of the other ills.

My own bouts with insomnia began in graduate school. The crisis was reached when I had to take a final exam in a *Beowulf* class and finally realized that I had never managed to learn Anglo-Saxon. The only solution was to memorize the trot, at least those passages that seemed most important to our professor. Three days before the exam, I began spending nights in a gloomy office for teaching assistants trying to do just that. I didn't dare go home, or I knew I'd fall into bed out of exhaustion. This was all more important than it should have been because the Stanford English department had accepted more graduate students than they could really afford and our grades were going to determine whether we were given a stipend for the following year. If you got a B- you would probably be sent home. In three nights I managed to memorize most of the epic, went to the exam, and recognized enough of the Anglo-Saxon in passages chosen for translation that I was able to vomit the memorized trot into my bluebook. I walked out of a two hour exam in about twenty minutes knowing I'd done well while everyone else in the room assumed I had just given up. Then came my punishment. We'll call it the late night *Beowulf* movie.

Even now I hardly dare to open the text of that poem. One year a while back, a well-meaning student of my own gave me Seamus Heaney's translation in thanks for a letter of recommendation. She stood there smiling and I thought I'd better open it up and take an appreciative look. The book was bilingual, and it all came swimming back:

Hwæt we Gar-Dena in gear-dagum

"So!" writes Heaney in his translation, "the Spear-Danes in days gone by," etc. etc. "So," he says in his Introduction, clears the table for an Irishman (and maybe an Anglo-Saxon too). For me it brought those sick days back to the pit of my gut.

After the exam, I had ridden my Rabbit motor scooter back to my Mountain View digs and fallen into bed. But no sleep came. Okay, I thought, my body's not used to sleeping in the afternoon. I fussed about the apartment until a little after dark, then back to bed. All I could do was recite the poem to myself, while before my eyes danced the memorized trot. How do actors avoid this happening, I wonder. And musicians. Doesn't Pollini whistle the 'Appassionata' concerto to himself all night long? Evidently not, or he wouldn't be able to play it the next day. Perhaps it's all muscle memory and he doesn't have to think about it. In the morning, I went to the student health service and told my story. The doctor found it funny and told me it would pass. Just go back and go to bed. I did, and re-played the *Beowulf* movie. By that time I had been awake for five nights. When I saw the health service doctor again, I was quite desperate, and managed to coax a small green pill out of him. It did no good at all. The next day he gave me a bigger pill; the day after that two of the bigger pills. By that time I was stumbling around campus like a drunk, slurring my words, utterly stupid in my under-water world. Though I realized it was not really safe for me to ride the motor scooter in that condition, I had no alternative. It was by then the week-end and the doctor told me that if there were no improvement they would give me an injection on Monday. Most of my support during this siege came from my then girl-friend who was sympathetic but no more able to find a practical solution than I was. And what finally cured me of the poem nearly killed both of us.

We had stayed in my apartment until about midnight when I told her we'd better ride back to her Stanford dorm (which still had an official witching hour for undergraduate women) so she wouldn't get in trouble with the authorities and I could come home and take my pills. On El Camino Real, halfway between Mountain View and Stanford, a car pulled out of a parking lot directly in our path and we slammed into it at about thirty miles-an-hour. I woke up in the hospital with a lot of cuts and abrasions, but alive. She has a five inch scar on her thigh to remember me by. But *Beowulf* was gone. When they discharged me from the hospital, I took a taxi home and slept like a baby.

There is a moment in Benjamin Britten's orchestral song cycle, *Nocturne*, that will strike terror into the heart of any insomniac. Most of the settings of poems in this great composition are about sleep and dreams—Shelley's 'On a poet's lips I slept' from *Prometheus Unbound*, Tennyson's 'The Kraken,' Keats's 'Sleep and Poetry,' Shakespeare's Sonnet 43—but the setting of twenty lines from Book X of Wordsworth's *Prelude*, 'Residence in France and the French Revolution,' has to do with sleeplessness, and the young Wordsworth had more to worry about than his Anglo-Saxon exam. With pounding timpani obbligato, Britten's tenor sings:

> But that night
> When on my bed I lay, I was most mov'd
> And felt most deeply in what world I was;
> With unextinguish'd taper I kept watch,
> Reading at intervals; the fear gone by
> Press'd on me almost like a fear to come;
> I thought of those September Massacres,
> Divided from me by a little month,
> And felt and touch'd them, a substantial dread;
> The rest was conjured up from tragic fictions,
> And mournful Calendars of true history,
> Remembrances and dim admonishments.
> 'The horse is taught his manage, and the wind
> Of heaven wheels round and treads in his own steps,
> Year follows year, the tide returns again,
> Day follows day, all things have second birth;
> The earthquake is not satisfied at once'
> And in such a way I wrought upon myself,
> Until I seem'd to hear a voice that cried,
> To the whole City, 'Sleep no more.'

Britten's orchestra builds to those last two lines with a furious forward motion and triple forte timpani until the tenor, audibly anguished and nearly hysterical with dread, all but shouts out: "Sleep no more." Peter Pears' voice was known, at its upper range, nearly to crack, and there were critics who never tired of commenting on this. In his version of these lines, the effect is exactly right. He was no Pavarotti, and the tone and confident high notes of Pavarotti's voice would be almost comical here. Pears' and Britten's Wordsworth sounds as if he hasn't slept for weeks. The Wilfred Owen setting that follows this one in *Nocturne* finds only a single woman asleep and dreaming of Keatsian "golden gardens and sweet glooms" while ghosts of men from the trenches of World War I lurk in her walls, her rooms, her tapestries; their torn red mouths make her roses bloom. The woman is "not afraid of their footfall," but one might suppose that Wordsworth's tenor hears nothing else but their steps, sleeps no more, staggers from the French Revolution through two world wars into the Vietnam era when Britten's music, principally his *War Requiem* with its own settings of Owen, became for some of us part of the 60s syllabus.

I got to know Britten's music myself when living in London in 1966–7 where I had fled from graduate school. I suppose it was during those years that my Stanford contemporary, James McMichael, was living through some of the experiences he writes about in his extraordinary book length narrative/discursive poem, *Four Good Things*. Of all the insomniacs I've known, McMichael is the most tormented, someone for whom insomnia has been a way of life. The whole Wordsworthian catalogue appears in one place or another in this poem—fears gone by pressing like fears to come, conjurings from fictions, mournful calendars of history, dim admonishments, cycles of obsessive worry, damage wrought upon the self—but largely in a domestic context. In a set piece on insomnia, a run of about sixty lines, McMichael has just arrived in London following a transatlantic flight from Maine. After that, he *ought* to be sleepy. With his wife peacefully sleeping beside him as in all those TV ads, he half hears announcements of train arrivals and departures coming from Victoria station below the Grosvenor Hotel, as he waits for "the letting go, forgetting."

> It's rarely that easy. The ease of it has
> little to do with how tired I am. If it's before
> midnight, if there's still time enough to sleep,
> I go to sleep. At two or three, when I wake up,
> I have to be asleep again within an hour.
> I shouldn't let it bother me. Even if I

don't go back to sleep, I shouldn't worry that I haven't
slept enough, that I'll feel it in my eyes. If my
tongue won't work, if it makes me slur the things I
press myself to say, I'll say just that much less.
I should ignore all day in what I do each
thought of myself and how I'm feeling tired.
I work at my breathing for a while, listen to
Linda's and adopt it, a sleeper's breathing.

Like the breathing rhythms of the strings linking settings in
Britten's *Nocturne*, Linda's "sleeper's breathing" draws the poet toward
unconsciousness and dream until he realizes that his own breathing
"would be slower. To breathe the way she breathes, / I'd have to be
awake, and am, have been awake / too long now and have given up
on trying to know / exactly what I should be doing, how I could be /
thinking about it all and changing." He decides not to care that he can't
get to sleep since caring about it is the very anxiety that prevents him
sleeping in the first place, inducing a forced calmness that is "feigned
and crazy." Therefore he won't care. Therefore he'll give up. But

        even the
giving up is trying, a counterfeit that takes me into
someone giving up . . .
                the drowse of
ellipsis, slips beyond it to a second and a third and,
losing count, goes off between the scatter, sleeps,
is someone who's asleep, not me at all, who's only
almost there and pleased to be this close, too pleased,
now coming to my hold again with all the shifts
intact and unrelieved. I've lost my chance.
Having been so close and missed, I can't start over.
Nor can I trust that even now I've given up.
I'm left remembering the times I've gone to sleep,
and what I've done each time is to forget.
It's happened before. I've slept. I was asleep an
hour ago when nothing woke me, when I was simply
awake. I didn't have to see that it was still
too dark . . .
           It might be different if
once for any fraction of that irreversible one

moment I could be unsure. If I had to sort through
where I was and was it time, if there were
sequence or change, some need to tell myself I'd
done it again—that for another night, and here,
again, impossibly, I'd placed myself too soon—
then I'd have doubted, sleep would have given me
doubt, resisted me a little, made me wait,
kept me for just that long from knowing that it's
me who brings this on and can't undo it, who won't
live it as it is, as mine. The certainty that
sleep isn't there is me.

He is sleepless, therefore he is. This René Descartes of an insomniac then tries sexual fantasies to distract himself, contrives "a lustful graphic" and feels in his penis "a proof that things can change." But in the end he goes to the bathroom for his pills. Spilling all fourteen into his hand, he chooses one. It can be, he says, a start. It's "like a tiredness I take inside me. It / weakens and breaks, dissolves inside me in a / gradual prolonged slow carry into sleep." This tour de force of a passage is only half over, but I'll stop with those fourteen pills. Ah, Lunesta, sweet are your entanglements.

The popular sleep-aid Lunesta, however, is nothing to what McMichael probably had in his hand. My own poison was Dalmane. Many years after the scooter accident ended my *Beowulf* movie, I developed a ringing in the ears that kept me awake far longer than those several days at Stanford. When a specialist suggested that he thought he'd better test me for a brain tumor, I was even wider awake. He said we should "give it a couple of weeks" to see if the ringing improved and in the meantime he could "help me with the sleeping problem." The ringing indeed improved but when the couple of weeks extended to a couple of months I was pretty well addicted. When I did sleep before I started taking the pills, I was also having terrible nightmares, and I discovered that Dalmane knocked out REM sleep altogether. One not only slept but one slept without dreaming. Two years later I was still taking the pills. When I didn't take one I didn't sleep. The next night I'd take two, just to be sure. If I woke up in the middle of the night, I'd take a third. At some point I started getting a little crazy. As good or bad luck would have it, someone put Philip Roth's *Operation*

Shylock in my hands, and I read about Roth's experience with Halcyon, benzodiazepine triazolam. One can probably take Roth's account as autobiographically accurate as it appears not only in the novel, narrated by a slippery "Philip Roth," but also in *The Facts: A Novelist's Autobiography*, published five years earlier. At any rate, I recognized my own nighttime horrors immediately

Roth started taking Halcyon for chronic pain following knee surgery. It was not long before he felt his mind beginning to disintegrate. As he writes in *Operation Shylock* "the word DISINTEGRATION seemed itself to be the matter out of which my brain was constituted, and it began spontaneously coming apart. The fourteen letters, big, chunky, irregularly sized components of my brain, elaborately intertwined, tore jaggedly loose from one another, sometimes a fragment of a letter at a time, but usually in painfully unpronounceable nonsyllabic segments of two or three, their edges roughly serrated. This mental coming apart was as distinctly physical a reality as a tooth being pulled, and the agony of it was excruciating." Other, similar hallucinations flooded his consciousness. Several times a day he broke into uncontrollable weeping. He was attacked by both claustrophobia and agoraphobia. His pulse rate shot up to 120 beats while he was just sitting still, staring at the TV news. He had constant panic attacks, especially at night, and became compulsive, doing over and over again "some meaningless procedure . . . as though its meaning went, in fact, to the core of my existence." He dreaded the darkness, the night, his bed. In spite of the pills, he didn't sleep. "My only chance of getting through to daylight without having my mind come completely apart was to hook hold of a talismanic image out of my most innocent past and try to ride out the menace of the long night lashed to the mast of that recollection."

Roth doesn't describe the torments of his eventual withdrawal except to say that they were even worse, "a process that I wouldn't care to repeat a second time and that I didn't think I'd live through the first." In the novel, "Roth" is finally cured of his "Halcyon madness" by traveling to Israel to cover the bizarre Demjanjuk trial—Demjanjuk was accused of being the sadistic Ivan the Terrible of Treblinka—and track down a person who is pretending to be the famous novelist himself while lecturing on 'Diasporism: The Only Solution to the Jewish Problem.' If some of what happens next suggests that "Halcion madness" has somehow been projected onto the external world, at least Philip Roth could sleep, and he was off his drugs. Determined activity in the daylight world has been part of the cure. So has seeking out the man who has impersonated his identity. At the height of his crisis, he would say to his wife: "Where is Philip, where is Philip?"

I once reached that point as well, wandering the house alone at night and thinking, "Where is John?" In my medical files, I have kept copies of the many letters I sent to my doctors in those days. As they didn't have time to listen to the long accounts of my nights, I wrote them down and sent them in the mail. Here is an entry for a night in January 1992:

> A violent event of some kind at 2 a.m., irregular breathing and a sense of buzzing—almost an electrical sensation—in my arms and legs. This is most difficult to describe. I thought it was bad circulation since I had in mind heart symptoms. Now I think it was something else—I don't know what. In spite of the Dalmane, I find it impossible to sleep. As I begin falling asleep I meet pressure, resistance, increased heart rate, irregular breathing and shortness of breath. If I sleep for a moment and jerk awake, I'm tingling all over. I can't move my left arm for fully five minutes. I think I've had a stroke. I get up to walk around but hyperventilate so much I feel faint and get back in bed. The surface of my skin twitches, and there are spasms in my feet.

Like Roth, I also had visual hallucinations connected to language and individual words. The names of various diseases I thought I had appeared before me as neon signs on a marquee—Parkinson's, Amyotrophic Lateral Sclerosis, and others I'd never heard of until I read about them in medical journals trying to diagnose myself—and then would flash, *on off on off on off.* I didn't hear my wife's reassuring breathing beside me—no Benjamin Britten strings—because she had moved down the hall to save her own sanity if she could. In the end, it was she who pulled me out of this.

Given that these days we read all the time about the fine line between acceptable techniques of interrogation and torture, we know from the CIA's experience and the practice of other organizations even more expert than they in the secret prisons of our infamous "renditions," that denial of sleep is more effective than almost anything else in extracting information. Some human rights organizations call it torture, but that hasn't stopped the interrogators, who especially like it when the prisoner has been standing for a long time and has lost all sense of whether it's day or night—indeed has lost his sense of time altogether. In these conditions, one would presumably say about anything. And one would certainly think that he was being tortured. On an obviously less horrendous scale, one thing that happens with chronic insomnia is that you do lose your sense of time. Again and again you check your watch, the clock in the hall. People often begin counting—for some it's the numbers, for others the sheep that matter—and have been known to get into the thousands without stopping. One friend of mine used to do prime numbers and square roots. Another would only count the tin soldiers he played with as a child. You hope you meet no one in the course of the day, because you'll have to speak—and you're likely to say anything, just like the tortured person. That's exactly the state of being where the interrogator wants you, but in the case of the insomniac, he is his own interrogator. Soon enough you also begin to suffer guilt over it all. Everyone else can sleep, why can't you? Because you've somehow made a mess of your life. Now you're messing up everyone else who before you started all this could get a good night's sleep. If you get up and walk around you'll wake up the whole house. And for God's sake don't start to cry. Nearby sleepers hate that most. And if you do drop off and get through the *Delta* waves of sleep stages three and four, then suddenly jerk awake again, you don't just think you're paralyzed, you are.

After giving up the pills and living out withdrawal, what's next? More sleeplessness, on the whole. But perhaps also the slow loss of conviction that one night's loss of sleep inevitably will mean another ten. It might, in fact, help to read (though not at night) McMichael's *Four Good Things*, or the opening pages of Roth's *Operation Shylock*. Eventually, in a Britten sound world of timpani and nightmare, you may drift with breathing strings into an oblivion which, as in his setting of Keats, "the morning blesses." Others have been here before you. And there's even something to be said for counting, though I'm with those who think the objects counted matter most. But heavy day-thinking and sleep don't go together and, alas for the bloody bards, poets can be heavy day-thinkers in the night. You can't both think and sleep. So if you can't stop thinking, what do you do to diminish the pressure of thought? Roth in his desperation was on to something when he lashed himself to the mast of his most innocent early memories. For me, it was children's stories. For a while I willingly submitted to a kind of regression as my wife returned from down the hall and read me *Winnie the Pooh*, all of Beatrix Potter, *Paddington Bear*, and *Jenny*. I could count the honey jars well beyond even Pooh's capacity. In the middle of a story, I was sleeping.

I also had a large monotype on the wall by my artist friend, Douglas Kinsey. I would stare at that picture in a kind of trance. In the end I wrote a poem about it in which my wife appears as the tough friend, who alternated with the gentle friend to pull me out of my insomniac's funk.

> Diana gave me this the morning of our
> Anniversary—the 20th—before the year when
> She believed I had been lost . . .
> A young man with a black beard
> Is lying on a bed. He looks like me
> At twenty-five. A woman bending over him
> Gestures with her arm. Kinsey has
> Done something with the arm I can't explain,
> Some trick with paint and printing
> That has turned the gesture of the arm
> Into an open sweep of brilliant wing.
> That January I was suddenly ill. Everything
> Went dark, and for many months I simply
> Lay in bed trying not to think. The woman
> By the young man's bed was always there,
> Exasperated, hurt, pitilessly loving him.
> *Get up*, she said. *For God's sake get up!*

ᏉᎧ

Robert Pinsky, James McMichaels's close friend at Stanford, also has a poem about insomnia—'An Alphabet of My Dead,' from *Jersey Rain*. Given that Pinsky is the most consistent booster of McMichael's

Four Good Things, one might even guess that it could be a response to the passages I've quoted from that book.

Pinsky's version of fighting "insomnia and its tedium" is a telling-over of the dead, "a game not morbid but reassuring. I tell them over not as a memorial comfort, but as evidence that I may be real." He does this alphabetically, imagining the letters (a little as Roth does the disintegrating word *Disintegration*) inside a "medicine pouch, flapping at my saddle" which function as "tokens of who I have been. Therefore I exist, sleepless." The names "told over" are different each time, but "with recurrences." Like a good traditional meter, there's a constant and a variant. Again, it's a kind of breathing; again, a kind of murmur in the strings. And the game's not morbid, he says. In an interview somewhere, Pinsky remarks that he often recites George Herbert's "Church Monuments" to himself in times of fear or crisis. Even before airplane take-offs in bad weather he recites, this too in his medicine pouch, a poem that admonishes the reader: "Fit thyself against thy fall." Perhaps these ABCs are a version of that. Each name carries a small narrative or anecdote, sometimes funny and sometimes sad. It reminds me also of the title poem from Pinsky's first book, *Sadness and Happiness*, about a bedtime game he played with his young daughter in which they tried to remember together some happy things and some sad things that had happened during the day. Here, except for quotes from George Gascoigne, the memories appear in prose paragraphs of varying length.

> Henry Antonucci, who used to play basketball at the Jewish Community Center, as many Italian kids did, paying five dollars to join the same way a Jewish boy might find it convenient to join the YMCA . . . The night he died, the car he was in and the one right behind it were both full of kids from the senior class: football players, class officers, a blond girl named Cornelia Wooley who was Harry's date. She was bruised and scarred; he was the only one killed.

> Elizabeth Bishop. The last time she was in public was at the Grolier Book Shop, at the afternoon signing party for my second book of poetry. Then afterwards, getting ready for dinner, the sudden stroke . . . A "good death," fortunate,

people called it, but she didn't get to witness the upsurge in her reputation.

Nor Cummings the decline of his . . .

My college friend Henry Dumas, shot dead by a cop . . .

Becky Eisenberg, my mother's mother . . .

This last is the longest of the ABCs. Becky took care of the young Robert when "[his] mother was crazy." She had come from a Jewish settlement in Arkansas where everyone's name was Eisenberg. Becky married a cousin called Eisenberg, gave birth to a daughter, Pearl, then married another Eisenberg, another cousin. His mother barely remembered Pearl, who had been taken to Baltimore and put on a train. What happened to her? His mother is "the spirit of confusion and darkness incarnate. Except for what she says, the story is locked away among the dead forever."

Next come Robert Fitzgerald, Mason Gross, Lynda Hull, Army Ippolito, and grandfather Dave Pinsky, a tough guy with a "hardness" in whom the young Robert "took reflected glory." Then: "A drowsy spell," he says. "It's working." P. is also for Plural dead, like counting sheep: "the exterminated Jews of Europe, the obliviated Kallikaks of New Jersey, the dead Laborers who framed and plastered these bedroom walls threaded by other dead hands with snaking electrical wires and the dendritic systems of pipes and ducts, audible." When he reaches Q, Pinsky realizes that he's singing himself a lullaby, like George Gascoigne does in 'Lullaby of a Lover' anthologized by Arthur Quiller-Couch in the 1900 *Oxford Book of Verse* in which printing, as Yvor Winters pointed out to him in 1963, Quiller-Couch had omitted Gascoigne's stanza written to his penis:

> Eke lullaby my loving boy,
> My little Robin, take thy rest;
> Since age is cold and nothing coy,
> Keep close thy coin, for so is best;
> With lullaby be thou content,
> With lullaby thy lusts relent,

> Let others pay which hath mo pence;
> Thou art too poor for such expense.

This is not at all Gascoigne's (or Pinsky's) version of James McMichael's lines about the "lustful graphic" he contrives to "feel it take" as a distraction from wanting to sleep, but rather the shutting down of lust altogether. Gascoigne will sleep, McMichael won't, and I'm not sure about Pinsky. I'm particularly unsure when we find him at X before "this machine I type at." What, not in bed? Perhaps the mimetic conventions of the poem break down here, and the reference is a flaw in the poem. Still, there he is, in front of his screen. Although Z finds him beseeching Zagreaus, "ancient god of the past, dead one," to give him his "honey measure of sleep," I wonder if the next temptation won't be to surf the Internet or google something. But we don't know as the poem ends with his prayer.

Pinsky might have googled "Funes the Memorious," as I've just done. Borges once called his famous story "a long metaphor for insomnia" in which, instead of falling off a motorbike in Palo Alto in 1963, Funes fell from a horse in the 1880s; and instead of the accident effecting a cure, his fall produced an illness—total and obsessive remembering of everything he wanted to forget, every single particular he had ever observed or heard about. My Google search tells me, in fact, that "googlers are building a digital "Funes the Memorious." As a prototype, Funes remembers endless particulars but cannot think abstractly; his world consists of a frightening assault of hapex legomena. One googler posts on futureofthebook.org that although he's not the first to observe that Borges invented the Internet, it's "important to see that the problems of Funes are increasingly everyone's problems. As humans, we forget by default; maybe it's the greatest sign of the Internet's inhumanity that it remembers." He even suggests that we might "pre-emptively deal with the issues that are sure to spring up in the future by actually building forgetting into the systems that comprise the network." However, in the Borges story, it is too late for Funes: he only remembers; he cannot select, omit, or forget.

For ten years or so I had an office down the hall from Anthony Kerrigan, Borges' first translator. He enjoyed reading Borges aloud to me in Spanish, both the poetry and the prose. He rarely went home, so one could find him in his office in the middle of the night if you happened to be in the building yourself. Another sleepless man, he appreciated the company. He had a reputation as an annoying eccentric among the students who ran the Notre Dame classical F.M. station. He would phone to correct them on every mispronunciation of every composer's, conductor's or soloist's name, on every mispronounced musical term—but always in a wry good humor. I think Borges would have appreciated this quirk. Tony would phone up the drowsy through-the-night D.J. and say, for example, "That opera by Wagner is not called *Die, Mister Singer.*"

Evidently, Borges also suffered from insomnia at the time he wrote about Funes: "I remember that I used to lie down and try to forget everything, and that led me, inevitably, to remember everything. I imagined the books on the shelves, the clothes on the chair, and even my own body on the bed . . . and so, since I could not erase memory, I kept thinking of those things, and also thinking: if only I could forget, I would certainly be able to sleep." I take that quote from an interview, by the way, from an essay on 'Gradsavers.net,' which seems to be one of those Internet sites that sells papers to students so that they, at least, might sleep through the night rather than lie awake thinking. As for Borges, it's possible that his insomnia, like mine, derived from the Anglo-Saxon. In his 'Poem Written in a Copy of *Beowulf*,' he writes:

> At various times I have asked myself what reason
> Moved me to study while my night came down
> Without particular hope of satisfaction
> The language of the blunt-tongued Anglo-Saxons

What moved him indeed? "Used up by the years my memory / loses its grip on words that I have vainly / repeated and repeated," he says. But such would not be the case with Funes who, had he read *Beowulf*, could have recited it backwards and inside out until he died. And his condition did kill him at an early age; he suffocated, says Borges, from a congestion of the lungs—though it is really a congestion of the mind. The narrator fears to speak to Funes in the end, knowing that "each of my words (that each of my movements) would persist in his implacable memory." Was Funes a kind of poet? I think so. Even the skeptical narrator, in his account, admits to finding in Funes "a certain stammering grandeur."

> *I have more memories*
> *Than all mankind has had since the world*
> *Has been the world.*
> *My memory, sir, is like a garbage heap.*
> *My dreams are like all others' waking hours.*
> A circle drawn on a blackboard, a right angle,
> A lozenge—all are forms we can grasp.
> Funes could do the same with the stormy mane of a horse,
> With a herd of cattle on a hill,
> With the changing fire and its innumerable ashes . . .
> He had a system of numbers:
> In place of seven thousand thirteen,
> He would say (for example) *Maximo Perez*;
> In place of seven thousand fourteen, *The Railroad*;
> Other numbers were *Luis Melian Lafinur, Olimar, sulphur,*
> *The reins, the whale, the gas, the caldron,*
> *Napoleon, Agustin de Vedia.*
> In place of five hundred
> He would say *nine*. Every word a particular sign.

I have, of course, lined out some of the prose. And if Funes seems a kind of composite poet, he's not writing *verse* any more than he is escaping prime numbers and hapax legomena. And he does not sleep.

J.V. Cunningham writes verse and claims to sleep. He also believes in abstract language and general ideas. The phrase by Cunningham that I have quoted, along with Borges, as an epigraph, comes from 'For My Contemporaries':

> How time reverses
> The proud in heart!
> I now make verses
> Who aimed at art.
>
> But I sleep well.
> Ambitious boys
> Whose big lines swell
> With spiritual noise,

Despise me not,
And be not queasy
To praise somewhat:
Verse is not easy.

But rage who will.
Time that procured me
Good sense and skill
Of madness cured me.

Cunningham implies that he didn't sleep well when he "aimed at art" rather than mere "verse." I wonder if he would think that Pinsky and McMichael, former students of his friend and mentor, Yvor Winters, have become "ambitious boys / whose big lines swell / with spiritual noise." He would certainly think that Funes, a kind of "Language Poet" in my version, was entirely mad. But I frankly doubt that he slept any better after than before he turned from "art" to "verse." And contemplating abstractions is as dangerous to the wakeful as a parade of discrete particulars. What is "Evil"? What is "Love"? What is "Choice"? What is "Haecceity"?

Evil is any this or this
Pursued beyond hypothesis.

It is the scribbling of affection
On the blank pages of perfection.

Evil is presentness bereaved
Of all the futures it conceived,

Willful and realized restriction
Of the insatiate forms of fiction.

It is this poem, or this act.
It is this absolute of fact.

There's no comfort or lullaby in that. In fact I think for a poet— or, okay, a writer of verse—insomnia comes with the territory. And I suppose those Stanford students who invented both the personal computer and Google slept as badly as Funes and James McMichael when they worried over logarithms rather than verse rhythms. That, too, came with the territory, as it might with thinking too hard about Cunningham's epigram on Calculus: "From almost naught to almost all I flee, / And *almost* has almost confounded me, / Zero my limit, and infinity."

Robert Hass concludes a recent poem called 'Consciousness' in exasperation after contemplating a friend's notion that consciousness consists of "an answering call having brought it into being which was, finally, itself anticipating an answer from itself, echo of an echo of an echo." He quotes his old collaborator, Czesław Miłosz: "Consciousness, 'that means nothing,' Czesław wrote." What it so often means is our great longing to lose it, even at the risk of bringing on our cruel, unanticipated dreams. Better, really, the monster nightmare than the endless recitation of the monster text.

Poetry and Murder

The other day a friend was telling me about an experience he had while taking Richard Elman's fiction writing workshop at Columbia in 1969.[1] A student read a story she had written called 'I Who Am About to Die' about a condemned man at San Quentin during the Depression Era awaiting execution in his cell. My friend told me that the woman's story was atrociously bad, a kind of James Cagney movie script full of clichés and stereotypes of every kind. The other students let the author off easily in their comments and Elman didn't seem inclined to point out the obvious weaknesses himself, muttering more or less in a daze something about "*Morituri te salutamus*," and "poor old Lamson." Eventually, my friend became annoyed at both his fellow students and his teacher for letting off such mediocrity so lightly and decided to let the woman have it. He said he found the story pathetic in its failure to demonstrate that the author understood a thing about murder, prison life, capital punishment, or the Depression. Suddenly Elman appeared to wake up from his reverie. He told my friend that he "didn't know a damn thing about it" himself, took the student author by the wrist, and more or less dragged her out of the classroom and down the hall. The students left in the classroom could hear Elman shouting something about blood on a lead pipe and plagiarism. They looked around at each other and slowly began to leave the building, a former lying-in hospital that Columbia had acquired a few years earlier. By the time my friend got home to his apartment on 8th Street between Avenues B and C, his transvestite neighbor had received on his behalf a large bouquet of mimosas from a florist. When he reached the top of the stairs, the neighbor popped out of his/her apartment across the hall and delivered the flowers. There was a small tag attached saying simply: *Elman*. My friend told me that he'd never really understood what this was all about. I said that, as strange as it might seem, I thought I did.

Coincidence is our circumstantial cousin when we tell tales out of our contingent lives. Once, while judging a book-length poetry manuscript for the Ernest Sandeen Prize, I was surprised to find in an elegy that the author's father was the journalist Paul A. Holmes. In 1961 Holmes wrote a book which had changed public opinion in the case of Dr. Sam Sheppard—accused of murdering his wife—and, a few years later, helped to achieve a new trial. My own father, as it happened, was on the Ohio Supreme Court when one of Sheppard's appeals was heard. I read the briefs myself, studied the photographs of Mrs. Sheppard's bludgeoned naked and pregnant body. The Sheppard case was Ohio's O.J. Simpson trial—or its Lamson case, the much earlier trial for wife-murder at Stanford University that so obsessed, as we shall see, Richard Elman. All three were trials which depended on circumstantial evidence. Another coincidence: Like Richard Elman, I studied at Stanford with Yvor Winters, who had written poems about Lamson and a kind of *précis* of the briefs for his appeal filed by Edwin McKenzie, Lamson's lawyer. Like Paul Holmes' book on the Sheppard case, the published précis, *The Case of David Lamson*, helped to change the climate of opinion about the Stanford murder. Paul Holmes' daughter, Janet, finally won the Sandeen Prize for her book, *The Green Tuxedo*, in which one central poem glosses Paul Holmes' diary. She notes that when, at the age of ten, she looked into her father's notes "it was murder, the first in his long career of lurid front-page stories— Bugs Moran, / mad Ed Gein, Sam Sheppard [...] for once the diarist matched the old man I / remember."[2]

Although I was closer to twenty than ten when I gazed with horrified fascination at the body of Marilyn Sheppard, I was not living with a man who, like Holmes, "could write a book in a couple of days,"[3] but with someone who seemed able to make a "life or death" decision in a couple of hours. My father would read a brief, look up, and say something like "No grounds for appeal." At least Sheppard, sentenced in 1954 to life imprisonment, was not sitting on death row. Lamson had been. So had many whose habeas corpus petitions my father and his court had denied, thereby setting the date of an execution. Long before the Sheppard case, I was repelled by capital punishment and my father's complicity in a legal system which allowed it. On a rotating basis, Ohio Supreme Court justices were on call to approve the actual time of an execution when the routine final appeal had been turned down by the Governor. When it was my father's turn to take these calls—they often came while we were having breakfast—I'd take note of the times. There was no difficulty understanding from his side of the conversation what was going on. In an early poem that I never finished I tried to get my child's sense of family guilt in the court's judicial murders written down:

Unable to speak or eat,
I'd imagine every last appliance in the house
was going cold—the oven, the toaster,
the iron in my mother's hand. The radio turned
to static, the TV picture blurred: all our
electricity, I'd think, was being used downtown!
In a way it was. Energy would drain from all of us
for days. My mother went to bed with headaches,
my father sat and stared; I tried to do my
homework and got nothing right. Exhausted, lethargic,
we'd sit in separate rooms and brood.

While Janet Holmes' father may have been responsible for getting Sam Sheppard a retrial, my own father and his colleagues initially blocked it. (It was later ordered by the U.S. Supreme Court, the majority opinion quoting Ohio's Justice Bell saying that Sheppard had been tried in "the atmosphere of a Roman Carnival.") Yvor Winters was certainly in some measure responsible for obtaining a retrial for David Lamson, having written not only his prose book and his poems, but also portions of the defense team's actual appeal.

ை

One might begin a proper chronology of the Lamson trials with an article in the September 11, 1933 issue of *Time* magazine. It happens to be an issue with Gertrude Stein on the cover, who had just published *The Autobiography of Alice B. Toklas* and thereby made herself worthy of taking a small place in the magazine's pantheon. Elsewhere in the issue, in the "National Affairs" section, there is a piece headed 'The Lamson Case.'

To a neat bungalow on the Stanford University campus near Palo Alto, Calif. Mrs. Julia M. Place, a real estate agent, drove one of her clients last Memorial Day. She had heard that the house was for rent. She rang the doorbell, waited. When no one came she went around to the back yard, found a black-haired young man stripped to the waist bending over a bonfire. He said his name was Lamson and that he owned the house. "There was nothing unusual in his actions or speech," said

Mrs. Place afterwards. "He asked me to come to the front door. I called Mrs. Rass, and we waited a minute or so. As we stood there, we heard a peculiar sound. It might have been an hysterical cry. Then Lamson opened the door and cried: "My God, my wife has been murdered."[4]

The article goes on to describe what happened next. Everyone ran to the bathroom to find Mrs. Lamson's body hanging over the edge of the bath tub with a terrible wound to the back of her head. When the police arrived, Lamson himself, sales manager of Stanford University Press, neighbor of Herbert Hoover's brother and friend of the Stanford President's son, became the prime suspect. When a ten-inch pipe was found in the fire Lamson had been stirring in his back yard, a pathologist's report suggested that traces of blood still adhering to it might be the victim's—or might not, might not even be human. California papers published a seven-column photograph of Mrs. Lamson's body. A possible motive was unearthed in an alleged liaison between Lamson and a woman living in Sacramento. The defendant's friends and lawyers argued that Mrs. Lamson had fallen in the bath and struck her head on the sharp angles of a sink. That's where the *Time* article ends. Five days after *Time*'s publication, twelve San Jose jurors found Lamson guilty of first degree murder and the judge sentenced him to hang at San Quentin within ninety days.

At some point during the preparation of the Lamson appeal by Edwin McKenzie, the novelist Janet Lewis, Winters' wife, was asked to do some typing and also to improve the language of the document. This is when Winters became actively involved in the case. In the end, he took over much of this work himself and became more and more convinced that there had been a gross miscarriage of justice. From his work on the brief itself—a brief in which one can easily find evidence of Winters' prose style[5]—came *The Case of David Lamson*, "a summary of the greater part of the brief for the appeal by Edwin V. McKenzie, [with] some additional material and analysis introduced." The pamphlet was published by the Lamson Defense Committee and contained a list of distinguished academics, writers, journalists, and clergy who approved "the publication of this summary and believe[d] it to be essentially a true statement insofar as they individually have been able to ascertain."[6]

I cannot be certain of the exact dates when Winters composed his three poems about Lamson and his defense, but they must have been written during the appeal process and the retrial. *The Selected Letters of Yvor Winters*, edited by R.L. Barth, includes several letters about the trial and the pamphlet, but none that mentions the poems. They were first published in 1940 and have always appeared in the same order: 'To Edwin V. McKenzie, On his defense of David Lamson'; 'To a Woman on Her Defense of Her Brother Unjustly Convicted of Murder,' subtitled 'after an initial study of the evidence'; and 'To David Lamson,' subtitled 'awaiting retrial in the jail at San Jose.' Lamson was released after thirteen months on the San Quentin death row and returned to the San Jose jail after the California Supreme Court, persuaded by McKenzie's brief, ordered the retrial. By this time Winters can address Lamson as a friend. They remained friends for life.

In a note to the *Selected Letters*, Barth observes that "the three poems are among [Winters'] early occasional public poems. No one seems to have considered in any detail YW as a public poet, and yet it seems to me that he was not only a fine one but that the occasional public poem was important to him and is important to any consideration of his work."[7] It is rather strange, therefore, that the poems do not appear in Barth's *The Selected Poems of Yvor Winters*, published by Swallow Press in 1999 and more or less replacing the by no means complete *Poetry of Yvor Winters*, edited by Janet Lewis and introduced by Donald Davie, which is now out of print. This means that the reader will find the poems in print only in Thom Gunn's American Poets Project volume in the Library of America series. None of these poems deals in any way with the gruesome details of Mrs. Lamson's death.

In the first of the three, Edwin McKenzie is seen as an heroic figure in the courtroom. He is compared with great men of tradition embodying Justice itself, and finally as Odysseus "with the giant weapon bent."

> The concept lives, but few men fill the frame;
> Greatness is difficult; the certain aim,
> The powerful body, and the nervous skill,
> The acquiring mind, and the untiring will,
> The just man's fury [...]

I saw you, mantled in tradition, tower;
You filled the courtroom with historic power;
Yourself the concept in the final hour.[8]

The idealized portrait reminds me of Gregory Peck's performance as the lawyer Atticus Finch in the movie version of *To Kill a Mockingbird*—an embodiment of the abstraction "Justice," but also a particular man in a tradition of men engaged in a professional enterprise. Is Odysseus one of these, or like them? The "giant weapon" in his hands is a bow bending chiefly out of revenge, and the hero's slaying of the suitors is clearly itself a sequence of terrible murders. The title of the book that originally contained this poem was also *The Giant Weapon*. When Kenneth Rexroth received his copy, he wrote a poem to Winters "while troop trains move[d] in the valley below." About the title he asks: "The Giant Weapon? The pattern? / The mind? The obdurate / Flesh? Or is it perhaps Janet / And you consecrate / In duality Plato said / Was the creative source / Of the many? Weapon or Tool—."[9]

Janet here is Janet Lewis, Winters' wife, who in fact received the unexpected tool which allowed her to construct a series of historical novels, most notably *The Wife of Martin Guerre*, when someone sent Winters in connection with his work on the Lamson case a book called *Famous Cases of Circumstantial Evidence*. But the weapon in the historical moment of Rexroth's poem, some years after the Lamson trial when the troop trains were taking men to the battle fields of World War II, is drawn where Rexroth sees "Flesh dead in lethal rain, / And the vain mind dissolved in hate, / Kisses at the dark train, / And children born of dead fathers, / And pressed flowers and blood / Stained snapshots—."[10] A weapon, like a tool, is a neutral thing and can be used either for good or evil. If McKenzie was something of an Atticus Finch, the hyperbolical grafting of Odysseus to his courtroom persona is problematic and even troubling.

The poem addressed to Lamson's sister, a physician working in Palo Alto, is a plea for fortitude and courage—"May God support you, for your brother's sake"—in face of the "evil year" in which she has fought villainy, hatred, stupidity, perjury, pride, the shifting eyes of friends, and "outrage and anarchy in formal mien." What she has confronted, "strong in [her] love and by [her] love made free," has nearly destroyed the poet himself. During the three weeks of the trial "through nervous nights awake, / I learned [what] could break me."[11] From a letter to Howard Baker of March 28, 1934, we get a clear sense of what he was experiencing:

> I am up to my neck in Lamson defense work, and in a worse nervous state than I have been in since my mother broke loose. I have just completed a 108-page ms. survey of all the aspects of the case to be published in booklet form some time next month. I did the survey in less than two weeks and hardly got five hours sleep a night in the period. The thing is a nightmare. Lamson is beyond question innocent and broken-hearted. He was railroaded by the O'Neal political gang in San Jose because the Lamsons refused O'Neal's offer to get him off for $45,000.[12]

That last sentence reflects revelations made in *The Case of David Lamson,* which also contains allegations of jury tampering, judicial misconduct, and Winters' affronted portrait of a prosecuting attorney who "excited the jurors by reading them passages from *Oliver Twist,* describing the murder of Nancy by Sykes, adding lurid comments of his own."[13] He calls McKenzie, consistent with his portrait of him in the poem, "a grand man and probably a great lawyer," though he adds that McKenzie is "a terrible stylist." Janet Lewis once lamented that when she and Winters took over the work of improving McKenzie's style, Winters' drinking increased markedly and slowly became for him the problem it was later in his life.[14] At the same time, this struggle, according to Tom Zaniello, a scholar who has been studying the Lamson case for years, intensified Winters' strong advocacy "of rational judgment in matters of life and art—a position he advanced in his critical works of the late 1930s and early 1940s."[15] There are indeed near-syllogistic passages in both the Lamson pamphlet and the critical classic, *In Defense of Reason.* One might compare, for example, 'Preliminary Problems' in the latter with 'Theories Concerning Motive With a Few Related Rational Processes' in the former. One motive put forward by the prosecution was that Lamson murdered his wife in a fury when he discovered she was not menstruating, as she had said, but was wearing a "clean napkin" as an excuse to "sleep apart." Winters writes in his pamphlet:

> The Prosecution says: there was a clean napkin and the two slept apart; inference 1: the two facts are related; inference 2: Mrs. Lamson deceived Lamson into letting her sleep separately by use of the napkin (this inference is deduced not from the initial data, but from the preceding inference); inference 3 (deduced from 2): Mrs. Lamson thus repulsed Lamson because (a) she was of a frigid nature (there is no evidence of this fact brought forward aside from the two facts with which this chain began), or (b) she was angry; inference 4 (deduced from 3b): she was angry because of Lamson's attentions to other women; inference 5 (deduced from 3a or 3b): Lamson was angry upon his discovery of the deception; inference 6 (deduced from 5): Lamson killed her. We have the murder as sixth inference in a chain, only one of the chain related immediately to the known facts, and that one related to the known facts only by virtue of the exclusion of the obvious interpretation of them.[16]

☙

It is not clear to me at precisely what stage Winters came to know Lamson himself, but it was at some point before he wrote the third, and probably the best, of his poems on this theme. In it, we find the poet visiting an innocent man awaiting retrial in the San Jose jail where "Learning's very name [is] jest / And the wise, like village fools / [are] County politicians' tools." There he

> found a quiet friend,
> Working at the evening's end,
> Far beyond the tongues that rail,
> Hidden in the county jail,
> Who, unchanged amid disease,
> Wrote with power and spoke with ease,
> Who, though human thought decayed,
> Yet the dissolution stayed,
> Gracious in that evil shade.[17]

Like several of the Renaissance plain style poems he so admired, Winters' own is written within a whiff of the gallows. The "gracious"

Lamson not only spoke with ease in this situation, but also "wrote with power." The reference here is surely to what became Lamson's book *We Who Are About to Die*. Though about San Quentin, the book was mostly written after Lamson was transferred back to San Jose. It is a remarkable volume and subject of another fascinating entry in Winters' *Selected Letters*, this time to Maxwell Perkins, the famous editor at Charles Scribner's Sons:

> Within a day or two I will send you or have sent you the ms. of a book (as far as completed) on life in the Condemned Row at the California State Prison at San Quentin. The book is written by David Lamson who over a year ago was convicted of murdering his wife and spent 13 months on the Condemned Row. The verdict convicting him has recently been reversed by the supreme court of California and Lamson has written the book while awaiting a retrial in the jail at San Jose. Lamson's attorneys have advised him that the book must not be published while there is any danger of his returning to San Quentin, because the prison authorities might choose to be irritated and make life unpleasant for him there. But as he is fairly certain of being acquitted within the next couple of months, this difficulty is a very minor one.
>
> Lamson did not murder his wife. He was convicted on perjured testimony in one of the most scandalous trials ever held in the state. The trial was a result of the failure of an extortion plot on the part of the chief political boss of the county. I will send you a booklet [*The Case of David Lamson*] on the trial prepared by myself and one of my older colleagues in the Stanford English Department, Professor Frances Theresa Russell. Lamson is personally a fine and intelligent man. The book is brilliantly written and intelligently conceived. As a social document its value is very great. As a series of narratives and character sketches it is extremely interesting reading. I believe it will be as permanent an addition to American literature as *The Oregon Trial* or *Two Years Before the Mast*.[18]

Although Scribner's published *We Who Are about to Die* in 1936, their lawyers finally persuaded the editors to omit an appendix by Winters. Winters tells Perkins in a letter that "the key to the situation is this: when Lamson was arrested, Dr Lamson [his sister] was advised to hire

Louis O'Neal as the lawyer. O'Neal is chief boss of the county and owner of […] the D.A. He demanded a fee of $45,000. When he didn't get it, he gave Lamson the works. It was foolish to go to him, but the Lamsons knew nothing of county politics at the time, and were utterly bewildered with grief and terror."[19] With this as the background, Lamson was tried three more times. After a hung jury, an incident of jury list irregularities, and yet another hung jury, the prosecution dropped the case and Lamson was free for the first time in three years. It was April 3, 1936—the same day Bruno Hauptmann was executed for the Lindbergh murder.

℘

When Richard Elman arrived at Stanford about twenty years later, Yvor Winters was thoroughly established as an almost legendary presence. He had gone on after the Lamson case to produce much of the work in verse and prose for which he is remembered, and he had acquired a reputation as an alternately stern and generous teacher both of literature and poetry writing—and this long before writing workshops became commonplace at American universities. But he had not forgotten the Lamson case. Elman remarks in an essay that he would still from time to time re-enact the defense's reconstruction of Mrs. Lamson's fall in her bath tub in the same way he would re-enact the decisive moves in championship boxing matches. (He was a former fighter himself— allegedly he had done a few rounds with Dempsey—and often made use of boxing analogies in his classes.)[20]

Elman was a Poetry Fellow specifically chosen by Winters for his graduate workshop. In the same class were Thom Gunn and Allen Stevens, among others. Although Gunn never found Winters to be ferocious, Elman certainly did. Winters could definitely be rough on work he didn't like—I saw this myself ten years later—but Elman's account, which tries to be mostly humorous, nonetheless reads like the tale of a one-time suitor stung by an arrow from "The Giant Weapon." There is nothing in his essay like the quiet and balanced conclusion of Gunn's memoir of Winters, 'On a Drying Hill,' where he acknowledges that Winters "pinpointed a certain irresponsibility, a looseness, a lack of principle—a promiscuous love of experience, perhaps—which I know

I need to keep going, lacking his theoretic firmness."[21] But Elman's position, as demonstrated by his later career, cleaves pretty close to Gunn's final contrast between himself and his teacher:

> He had been right [...] I am still a romantic, thinking with Keats that "nothing ever becomes real till it is experienced— even a proverb is no proverb till your life has illustrated it." Winters rather could believe with Ben Jonson that "Not to know vice at all, and deepe true state, / Is vertue, and not Fate"; that one can evaluate and make choices without physically engaging the actions that one comes to reject: and that the romantic immersion in the life of the senses moreover tends to destroy the power of discrimination, and therefore is to be avoided.[22]

Elman's essay argues that Winters regarded his students' inept poems as "high crimes" and "treasonable acts." Elman seems to have been afraid of his teacher and was made to feel that "every impulse that had impelled one to write poems was counterfeit." He and a fellow "Coney Island Keats" had their poems "savaged." While Winters admired Gunn's "classical imitations, his feeling for historical subject matter, sense of form, and clarity of diction," Elman liked Gunn's descriptions of motorcycle gangs, his hipness to the vernacular, his Ray-Bans and black, silver-studded motorcycle jackets, and cowboy boots." Thom Gunn sometimes thought he had chosen an over-demanding mentor; Elman, like his fellow "Coney Island Keats," thought he'd been flayed in a brutal spectacle by "a kind of Oriental Demon who gained power over one only as one recognized and feared him."[23] (This drawn directly from Winters' only published short story, 'The Brink of Darkness,' about his own flirtation with madness.[24]) When Elman ceased to recognize the demon he might cease to fear him. He *might*.

It's revealing that Elman misquotes Winters' quatrain written for "all enlisted in his campaign against the false coinages of modernism and literary madness":

> A poem is what stands
> When imperceptive hands,
> Feeling, have gone astray;
> It is what one must say.[25]

But Winters doesn't say "must." The line should read: "It is what one should say." If Elman thought Winters had been telling him what he *must* say, his imperceptive hands and feelings had probably already gone astray.

There were those who argued that Elman *should* have said something else in the essay from which I have been quoting, which was excerpted for a feature on Winters in the Stanford alumni journal for November/December 2000. By that time Elman himself was dead and the full-length version of 'Yvor Winters, Thom Gunn, and Others,' along with another essay on David Lamson, had appeared in his last book, *Namedropping: Mostly Literary Memoirs*. In the Stanford magazine issue following the one containing the Winters feature, a student from my own generation—the class of 1966—wrote in sympathy with Elman that he, too, had experienced Winters' "sarcastic cruelty to some students" and called him "Stanford's Bobby Knight of poetry academics," whose "narcissistic tyranny" could make "minor roadkill" of people such as himself.[26] This kind of hurt adolescent response was not uncommon among students whose poetry Winters rejected. But Helen Pinkerton Trimpi probably expressed the opinion of most knowledgeable readers when she wrote in the same issue that Elman's piece was "slanderous and offensive." Speaking to and of the editors, she went on to say:

> Your policy seems to have been to dig up purely for sensational value the malicious, mentally warped, envious ruminations of a man whom Winters had offended by refusing to cooperate in his exploitation of the 1933 David Lamson case [...] Elman took out his anger first in a novel fictionalizing the case and then in the passages you excerpted.[27]

Is this true? And if so, does a quarrel over the Lamson case explain Elman's "slanderous and offensive" treatment of Winters in his essay, and the creation of his surrogate figure, Jim Hill, in the novel, *An Education in Blood*?

Elman's essay on Lamson was written long after his novel and can perhaps be seen as an apology for some of its excesses. Its ostensible occasion is to recommend Lamson's Book, *We Who Are about to Die*. It is clear that Elman genuinely admires the book. He finds the style of Lamson's work accurate, civilized, and somewhat off-hand in manner, and he compares it in its compassion toward other inmates to Chekhov's writing about the prisoners of Sakhalin Island. When he asks why we should be fascinated by tales of confinement, he gives an answer that is almost a paraphrase of Winters' poem addressed to Lamson: "They tell us about our own capacities to remain human and enterprising under the most adverse conditions. They remind us of our most fundamental human resources—intelligence, imagination, the ability to experience ourselves and others in solitude and time without falling into madness."[28]

But there are also some strange things about Elman's essay. He begins by saying that the California Supreme Court overturned the verdict and that Lamson "was released and never retried for his wife's wrongful death," when he must at some point have been told that the Court ordered a re-trial and that in fact there were three of these. He also says that Lamson wrote his book "during the next couple of years" following his release. Acknowledging that Yvor Winters persuaded Max Perkins to publish the book, he also adds that Winters had previously tried to persuade Perkins that he himself should write a book about "the injustice and flagrant disregard for the truth in police work on the Lamson case." Elman may here be confusing references to Winters' Lamson Defense Committee pamphlet in letters in the Scribner files at Princeton with his own desire to write a piece of investigative journalism. He mentions that he "was then doing preliminary research on a book about the Lamson murder trials [note the plural] which I regarded as a prime example of American vigilante justice in the thirties" when he received the news that Lamson had moved back to the scene of his torments in Santa Clara County.[29] The most interesting thing in the essay is Elman's claim that he was persuaded to drop his own *nonfiction* project because Lamson himself "broke a long silence and wrote me a short, careful letter to ask that I not write such a book about the trial. Lamson said the death of his wife "had happened more than three decades before. He had a new wife and grandchildren in and around Palo Alto and simply did not wish to relive such an unhappy event with them and saw no need for it personally. He simply asked me to be compassionate and desist."[30] The Lamson figure in an *Education in Blood* writes early on to the narrator:

If you write your book—even if it flops clear across the country—the reporters and the photographers and the TV men will flock to my house and my daughter's house; you will have succeeded in putting the children through a torture such as might mark them permanently. For God's sake keep your hands off them and me; we have all been through enough. [...] And don't get the idea that you can clear my name, as the saying goes: you will only stir up more old gossip and venom. There is a lot of both left around here; right now they are quiet. [...]³¹

A scholar in the Scribner archives might not be at all surprised to find an actual letter from Lamson on which this fictional letter is based. However, it's surprising and fascinating to find this from Winters in the *Selected Letters* instead:

Dear Mr. Elman:
        David Lamson has shown me your letter to him of May 2. Lamson is now past sixty and his wife is a little older; both are in frail health. A couple of years ago he had a coronary attack. Your letter upset him so that he might easily have another. Lamson went through hell for years; now, when his strength is almost gone, you propose to send him through more. Don't get the idea that you could clear his name, as the saying goes; you would merely stir up old gossip and old venom. There is a lot of both left around here, but it is quiet. Lamson's daughter is married to a very brilliant young engineer; they have four children of grade school and high school age. If you write your book, even if it flops clear across the country, the book will send the reporters and photographers and TV men to Lamson's house in Los Altos, to his daughters house in Palo Alto; you will have succeeded in putting the children through a torture that might mark them permanently. They will probably come to my house also, but if they do, I will meet them with a gun and a bulldog. For God's sake keep your hands off the Lamsons; they have been through enough.³²

It must certainly have been Winters who in the 1950s recommended to Elman *We Who Are about to Die* and introduced him through his own obsession with the case to the entire judicial history. It was no longer, after all, a contemporary event that Elman would have stumbled upon when he arrived at Stanford. The letter I quote above is from May 11, 1967, written only shortly before Winters died. In fact it makes reference to the radical cancer surgery he had recently endured, another verbatim quote that comes up later in Elman's novel. In a second letter written six days later, Winters acknowledges a telegram from Elman and thanks him "for giving it up." He adds that

> You say I exaggerated the local consequences; you are wrong; I have lived here for 38 years. A book of that sort would be news and it would be made news [...] You cannot change these people [...] A couple of years ago I was walking past the open office door of Ackerman, our second-string philologist. His back was to me; he was discussing Lamson and I think my poems with some one else. His shoulders hunched and wiggled; I heard his low-pitched academic giggle; he said: "Of course everybody knows he was guilty as hell." That is it: everybody knows.[33]

An Education in Blood, like *We Who Are about to Die*, was published by Charles Scribner's Sons. Reading at its worst like a potboiler trying to be Dostoevsky, it is often completely over the top and dominated by a species of Sixties zeitgeist. Bernard Eastover is the Lamson figure, Jim Hill is Winters, and Steven Tolmach is a version of Elman himself. By 1971 Elman had published six previous books, but this was his most ambitious and his chance to make a big splash as a novelist. It is fair to say that the book is also, in parts, subtle, perceptive, dramatic, and psychologically acute. It is not a "bad" novel, just a very uneven one which sometimes is in control of its materials and sometimes not.

As the telegram to Winters saying that he was "giving it up" was sent in 1967, it is likely that Elman was already writing the novel at that time. In fact, as I have not seen the telegram or any other letters from this period that may be in the archive but not in Winters' *Selected Letters*, it is not entirely clear whether what is allegedly being given up is the nonfiction book or the novel. R.L. Barth thinks the reference is to the novel, writing in a footnote to the phrase that "Elman did not, in fact, give up on the novel. It was published four years later."[34]

In his Lamson essay, Elman says that when he was asked to drop the nonfiction book, he published a novel "much later" which was set in a different part of the state and "allowed Lamson to keep his privacy that was so awfully and flagrantly disturbed by the police investigations and publicity surrounding his first wife's death. Moreover, he especially credits Lamson's *We Who Are about to Die* for moving him by its "sobriety and decorum" to accede to the request for privacy. Perhaps the strangest thing about the essay on *We Who Are about to Die* in relationship to the novel, in which the Lamson figure is not innocent of his wife's murder, is the very obsession with the Lamson figure's guilt. And after all the sympathy expressed for Lamson and his book, Elman seems to hedge his bets, even in the essay:

> The allegations against Lamson were that in a moment of rage he had struck out against his wife who was in the tub and brought about her fatal injuries. Such moments of rage have occurred all too often with husbands and wives. We're probably all capable of such rages, and afterwards there is remorse, which often takes the form of a heightened awareness of the ordeals of others.[35]

Elman claims that the characters in his novel have "no real resemblance to David Lamson." Psychologically, that may be true. But no one acquainted with the case would fail to recognize its details and circumstance. No one could fail to read it as a novel about "the Lamson case." As for the remorse Elman mentions at the end of his essay, I think he feels a good deal of that himself. He protests too much on Lamson's behalf and congratulates himself too effusively for writing a novel instead of the nonfiction book about the murder and the trial. As he convicts Bernard Eastover in fiction, he has the uneasy feeling—a kind of stifled remorse—that he may have convicted David Lamson in reality.

ॐ

When I met Richard Elman in 1996 he had no hesitation in telling me that *An Education in Blood* was about the Lamson trial. He had come to Notre Dame for a semester at the invitation of his former student, then my colleague—the one who was sent the mimosas after his critique of the Columbia girl's fiction that had so upset Elman in 1969. Once Elman and I got to know one another, we shared a number of Stanford stories. He was particularly eager for me to read his "portrait of Winters" in the novel. Elman by then had been through some very hard times and was moving from one visiting professor's job to another. I found him very genial and intelligent, but he did harp a bit on Winters and especially his sense that Winters had dropped him when he hadn't agreed to stay at Stanford for a PhD and pursue an academic career. He thought of Winters as a kind of arch-academic, though in fact Winters disliked most academics.[36] In a late letter to Ian Watt, chair of the English Department after Winters retired, he asks to be left alone by former colleagues: "I never was an academic man; I merely had scholarly interests—and I had to earn a living."[37] But Elman had him pegged as an academic type and he wanted me to read his "portrait," an aspect of the novel he stressed more than he did the main drift of the narrative.

Jim Hill is an interesting character—or maybe I should say character-trace, or shadow-character, since he is chiefly a memory for both of the antagonists in Elman's academic agon. He appears first by way of a reference in the twenty-six page letter from Eastover to Stephen Tolmach that begins the novel. It is a kind of manic explosion of freely associational prose laying out at great length all of the objections to Tolmach's plan to write a nonfiction book about the death of Eastover's wife and his several trials for murder. Jim Hill is quoted in the letter putting forward his argument—derived from *The Lamson Case* and perhaps Winters' re-enactments of Mrs. Lamson's presumed accident— that Judith Eastover died from a fall.

> I say to you, as Jim Hill maintained all along: *In the close steamy air Jude grew faint, fell or turned or spun about and slipped down hard with the back of her head against the edge of the washbasin, and that the force of the blow was such that it spun her around again and again as she was falling so that there was all that blood everywhere... Or else she was surprised—by a prowler . . . a madman . . . I don't know.*[38]

Parts of the letter are in italics and other parts in caps; Eastover writes like a desperate man, or perhaps a man who has lost his mind. If he were speaking this rather than writing, one would call it raving. The whole aria ends on a familiar note: "I no longer want to be exonerated. I don't wish to meet you [...] I don't even wish to hear from you ever again. I am sorry to spoil your little adventure as a crusader for justice [...] So go away and leave me in peace [...] write a novel if you like, and kindly do leave me in peace."[39]

The "novel" presumably begins in Chapter Two, though "Eastover's letter has arrived too late to deter Stephen." So Stephen is on the trail, not having read what we have read. Very soon we learn that Stephen had written bad poetry in his youth, but had eventually put himself in the hands of a poet-professor of his father's generation. He wonders now, looking back at his own and Eastover's association with this professor, whether the man, tied up in various kinds of self-deluding sophistries, could "excuse murder." "Eastover would and could and maybe did for over thirty years to his friends and supporters who, in their own ways, were made accomplices to his act of horror. Even his former master, James Hill." Hill's poetry is central to Tolmach's obsession with the whole ghastly business, for it was "through the poems of his former teacher [...] that he had encountered the Eastover case." Also, far from exonerating Eastover, this early passage would seem to convict him even before Tolmach's investigation has properly begun. What he really wants, Tolmach says, is to feel what it is like to be in Eastover's skin.

In the course of the novel Tolmach becomes, in effect, Eastover's tormentor. In the process, he also pretty much destroys James Hill's reputation for probity and rational inquiry. Tolmach writes his novel as an aggressive act responding to the attack on his motivation contained in Eastover's original letter, a letter one might read as a manic version of Winters' pamphlet and correspondence with Elman, or as Winters' restrained discursive poems imploding in a mind that then regurgitates them in the idiom of Allen Ginsberg.

While at Stanford, Richard Elman spent his time not only in seminars and workshops conducted by Yvor Winters, but also in the revolutionary atmosphere of the emerging Beats in San Francisco and Berkeley. He attended, in fact, the first reading of *Howl* at Gallery Six, and the whole oppositional ethos of that place and time—a time long after which Winters and Kenneth Rexroth were friendly and exchanging books—stuck with him through the Sixties and can be felt on every page of *An Education in Blood.* When Tolmach finally seeks out Eastover in the nursery he runs in Claremont, having been forwarded the latter's "formidable letter" from New York, Tolmach's side of their initial dialogue is pretty much written in period jive: "Look, baby, I didn't choose you at random"; "the whole academic mentality just whacked me out"; "your whole letter to me is a crock"; "if you don't want to tell me, Daddy, I'll just have to make it up"; "dig it"; "sock it to me"; "you're jiving me [...] cut the shit." Jim Hall is characterized by both Tolmach and Eastover in a number of ways, but Tolmach's admission that he loved Hill and "was one of his most devoted students though it almost killed [him]," quickly devolves to calling his father surrogate "a grandiose bigot."

Then the dialogue turns to suffering. Tolmach repeats that he "read those poems which Hill wrote to you on Death Row. [...] I had to know why a man like Hill [...] would care to rush to your defense." Eastover asks him if he ever stopped to think that Hill [...] believed I was an innocent man?" Then it is revealed that Hill has recently died, and Tolmach asks, "Did he suffer very much?" Eastover is enraged: "WHAT WOULD YOU KNOW ABOUT SUFFERING?" (Elman's caps.)

> You ask, Did Jim suffer? Cancer of the tongue and the right side of the neck which spread through his entire body, his mouth, everywhere. Radical surgery, though performed, did not keep it from spreading until he had no more muscle left on his right side [...] the neck and collarbone [...] couldn't talk, was in constant pain [...] In the end there was this massive scar tissue adhering constantly which had to be torn loose several times a day. *Burning like fire. It actually burned like fire.* Suddenly, just like that, his right shoulder might flip out of control at no provocation. He couldn't drive. Typing that last book was misery. He finally had to give up. [...] He would beg us sometimes to stop the medication and let him die, and then he would say *he wanted to live only just a little longer* [...] *enough to finish the last book.*[40]

Winters concluded his letter to Elman of May 11, 1967 like this, following his plea, "For God's sake keep your hands off the Lamsons; they have been through enough":

> Last Dec. 15 I had an operation for cancer on the side of my neck. It was what they call radical surgery. At present I have almost no muscle on the right side of my neck and right collar-bone; instead I have massive scar tissue which adheres constantly and has to be torn loose several times a day and which then burns like fire. My right shoulder flips out of control at no provocation. I cannot drive; typing is difficult and painful; this letter is an ordeal. This is why I have not answered your letters and cannot correspond with anyone. [...] It horrifies me to think that you are planning to destroy one of my few close friends and damage his family irreparably, when he and I are both so near the end of the line. Please stop and think.[41]

Tolmach says he "loved [Hill] very very much." Eastover replies: "You couldn't love anybody." Tolmach says: "That's what you think. It comes with being exclusive [...] a member of that very very old and exclusive club of fellow sufferers [...]"[42]

And so the novel continues. Tolmach plays a game of good cop/bad cop through the interrogation he conducts at Eastover's nursery which leads eventually, after Tolmach has left for the day, to a suicide attempt by the bullied and manipulated Eastover. A back-story is filled in for both of them, which includes abusive fathers in both families, high ambitions, and their differing relationships with Jim Hill. Eastover— rather amusingly if one is acquainted with the canon of great poems advocated by Winters—has become by the time he is worrying about tenure at his and Hill's university, a Charles Churchill scholar. Eastover's own poetry becomes more serious when he meets a woman in the history faculty at a Jim Hill party and begins an affair with her. Hill had found his early poetry sentimental, awkward, callow, and trite. It now improves, but not much. A motivation for the murder of Judith Eastover begins to develop. Eastover begins a second affair with a student and his wife drives him to jealousy with an affair—either real or vividly imagined by Eastover—of her own. During the conversation that brings this information to light, Tolmach and Eastover also accuse each other of being gay. The poem from the Winters canon that begins to hover over everything in the narrative is not by Charles Churchill, but rather Robert Bridges' 'Eros': "Why hast thou nothing in thy face? / Thou idol of the human race [...] Surely thy body is thy mind."[43] The lines are cited along the careening way as the alternating narrators, rather in the manner of Eastover's prosecutor, talk "like some bad novelist [...] on and on, one incident jamming against the next."

By the time the scene shifts from the nursery interrogation to the hospital where Eastover is recovering from his suicide attempt, Tolmach begins to function like a psychiatrist. Eastover eventually launches into a long monologue at the end of which much of the evidence in Winters' pamphlet accumulates to prove Eastover guilty of pushing his wife in her bath in such a way that her head sustained the complicated and fatal wound. In brief, all of the circumstantial evidence which was analyzed in the pamphlet to prove that Lamson was not guilty of murdering his wife—and this includes relationships with women that the defense and Winters argue were not romantic—is used in the novel to prove Eastover guilty. For his part, Tolmach, searching obsessively for "certainty" where there seemed to be only circumstantial evidence, finds his victory hollow. In an 'Afterwords' he seems to have achieved a kind of Buddhist peace: "He knows now and knows nothing." He feels "cleansed." He "hopes for a poem swelling somewhere to throb into his life."[44]

☙

I wonder what Richard Elman wanted me to find when he suggested that I should look up his "portrait of Winters" in *An Education in Blood*. Certainly nothing as obvious as an unresolved father-complex, though the combination of his essays on Winters and Lamson, together with the novel, suggest that something like that existed. Nor the answer to why he responded to his Columbia student's short story the way he did (which at that time I knew nothing about), though perhaps it explained that as well since Elman had done on a large and sophisticated scale what it seemed the student had done in her small and inept way while drawing on the same materials for her work. Or so I had decided on grounds of the circumstantial evidence provided me by my Notre Dame colleague.

There's a passage in the novel where Eastover refers fleetingly to the trial of a Harvard man analogous to his own, a professor accused of murder and convicted on circumstantial evidence, during the nineteenth century. The reference, never followed up, is to the trial of John Webster for the murder of George Parkman, Francis Parkman's uncle. Judge Lemuel Shaw's charge to the jury that convicted Webster became for many years what Simon Schama calls in *Dead Certainties*, "the classic definition of the requirements of circumstantial evidence."[45] Winters, Elman, James Hill, and Stephen Tolmach all strove for certainty in a situation where certainty is only available in fiction. Schama writes of Judge Shaw's charge to the jury that "when he spoke of circumstantial evidence his chosen genre was poetry." Elman returns several times to his contention that Hill "was making a defense of poetry by coming to [Eastover's] defense," that he "had to pretend it was poetry that was being outraged by [the] prosecutors." I think Elman believed that, but I think the outraged poetry was probably his imagined own—the poetry he never managed to write in what is often an ill-written book which ends with that hope for a poem "swelling somewhere [...] into his life." Eastover felt that when the prosecution found poems he had written to his mistress "they were sure I must be a murderer. [...] I was tried for murder because I dared to write poetry at all." Just more circumstantial evidence, but evidence that outrages Jim Hill because the very act of writing poems was considered suspect by the prosecution. Lamson also wrote poems, as did his alleged mistress, Mrs. Kelly, who sent him one of her own with a note: "Lousy! But you get the idea. Changed rhythm in the middle of the line." Winters comments in his pamphlet: "The incident is not a particularly sentimental one"[46] and Elman gives the observation to Eastover in the novel.

And what if my Notre Dame colleague had misheard Elman at Columbia. Instead of exclaiming about "blood on a pipe," perhaps he said he'd left his "bloody pipe" in his office and needed a smoke; perhaps instead of "plagiarism" he'd said something about the "pages in it" he liked. And perhaps the flowers signed "Elman" were really sent to remind my friend that he should take care to remember the tender sensibilities of fellow writing students when launching into an attack so disproportionate in its vigor to the flimsy story at issue. Or perhaps Elman was having an affair with his student, as Eastover was with his, and reacted as he did to protect her from hurtful criticism. Perhaps . . . Perhaps. My colleague tells me he never saw his former classmate again in Elman's classroom or anywhere else. Did a janitor find spots of blood on a manuscript torn in half and thrown in the trash? I am making things up.

When writing about Justice Shaw's famous charge to the jury in the Webster case as a kind of poetry, Simon Schama cites the judge's reliance on imagery to explain circumstantial evidence: footprints in the snow, a cartridge wad near the scene of a murder that unrolled to reveal a half stanza of a ballad "the other half of which was discovered in the pocket of a nearby suspect," a dead baby known to be a bastard born in a secret place and assumed also to have been born alive; "But [the judge] could not with images alone avoid, in the end, the fine distinctions expected of his charge."[47] In his mature poetics, Yvor Winters came to something of the same conclusion about "images alone." And when Shaw finally explains that where "absolute certainty cannot be obtained, moral certainty must always govern," his charge begins to resemble in uncanny ways Winters' notion in 'Preliminary Problems' of the unique act of "moral judgment" that should occur in a poem and in the assessment of a poem. Shaw's charge to the jury demanded that they should achieve, in a case depending on circumstantial evidence, "an abiding conviction to a moral certainty of the truth of the charge." Otherwise, they must find the defendant not guilty. They found him guilty. So did the jurors in the first Lamson trial find the defendant guilty. And the jurors in Ohio's Sam Sheppard trial that my father thought should not go to re-trial but that Janet Holmes' father in his book and the U.S. Supreme Court in their decision did. It was only when Sam Sheppard's son, even after his father had died, insisted on and obtained a posthumous reconsideration of his father's case, trying to achieve "absolute certainty"—a verdict of "innocent" rather than "not guilty"—that the legal system provided him with the only absolute certainty that it could: the absolute certainty that there was no absolute certainty. Sheppard remained, after his death, "not guilty," but not necessarily innocent.

Have I been trying to prove Richard Elman guilty of something in these pages? That has not been my intention. I began only wanting to connect some dots in a story that has come to interest me, to notice some rhymes. But along the way I've suggested that he may have been an imprudent teacher and a writer with a grudge who took more than he should have from a former master in order to travesty his character in a novel. What did Elman teach at Columbia? What he felt he should? What he knew he must? In the first stanza of the Winters poem, 'On Teaching the Young,' which Elman misquotes in his essay on Winters and Gunn, Winters writes:

> The young are quick of speech
> Grown middle-aged, I teach
> Corrosion and distrust,
> Exacting what I must.[48]

In the same way that Elman misread "It is what one *must* say" for "It is what one *should* say" in the second stanza of this poem, I think he may have felt that it was through "*coercion* and distrust" that he was being taught at Stanford, if I may introduce another typo into this short poem. I don't know what Elman made of the last stanza of the poem, where Winters writes that "The poet's only bliss / Is in cold certitude— / Laurel, archaic, rude." But I think I can hear Stephen Tolmach saying something like, "Man, what the fuck is that? Rude is as rude does."

In his preface to *We Who Are About to Die*, David Lamson speaks of "an air of uncertainty" in the pages we are about to read, and how "a feeling of bewilderment and doubt […] is a true and necessary part of the feeling that a convict knows—the feeling that I hope you too will have in reading this. To be baffled and bewildered and uncertain is an important part of being a con"—as it is an inevitable part of being a human being.[49] In the absence of absolute certainty, amidst the bewilderment and doubt we live in, how is something like "moral certainty" to function? As it does in Winters' pamphlet, poems, and essays? While insisting that such a thing as "moral certainty" exists, Justice Shaw in his charge warns: "On a subject where absolute certainty cannot be obtained, where moral certainty must always govern, it is always possible to fall into error."[50] A distinguished beneficiary of Winters' teaching was J.V. Cunningham, who once wrote a poem on the proposition that *all* choice is error. He also likened human experience to a defendant standing in the dock of his poems:

These the assizes: here the charge, denial
Proof and disproof: the poem is the trial.
Experience is defendant, and the jury
Peers of tradition, and the judge is fury.[51]

Outside the poem, unfortunately, the jury can turn out to be a version of the manipulated motley crew of Santa Clara county, the judge an incompetent man rushing toward a guilty verdict of murder in the first degree, and any choice—the verdict, the presumed act of "moral certainty"—not only error, but also bringing with it to the waking Kafka dream of the defendant absolute and unspeakable terror. Thinking about all that, one might well conclude: What a good subject for a novel, or wonder what "the inclusions of a rhyme" might amount to, misremembering another line by Cunningham. The poet wrote about the "exclusions of a rhyme."[52] But the judge is often in a hurry.

Prince Marko

Marko Kraljević, Kraljević Marko: You can say it either way in what used to be called Serbo-Croatian. Neither way was it my friend's real name, but I started calling him Prince Marko a few months after we began our long collaboration translating what used to be called Yugoslav poetry. We worked both on modern poems and the so-called heroic ballads that were important to makers and shakers all the way from Goethe to Radovan Karadžić, the Bosnian Serb leader who is now on trial at The Hague. It's a pity that Karadžić shares a surname with the man who originally collected the ballads, Vuk Karadžić, for he was a great and distinguished scholar. Radovan, in a sense, eventually came between me and Prince Marko, by which time Yugoslavia no longer existed and all my friends in Belgrade had fled like exiles after the Battle of Kosovo. But I'm well ahead of my story.

The historical Prince Marko, a fourteenth-century ruler of lands that are now in the Republic of Macedonia, became the hero of many ballads in both the Serbian and Bulgarian traditions. A scourge of the Turkish occupation, a trickster figure, a kind of Robin Hood, an all-around roughneck, he's full of contradictions, like my friend and collaborator. Charles Simic, the Serbian-American poet, tells about falling in love with Prince Marko as a child in occupied Belgrade, reading ballads about him under his bedcovers—there was no heat—as Allied bombs fell on all sides. "The stories," Simic notes, "are 'action packed,' as they used to say on movie posters." But the poems aren't just yarns for boys any more than, say, Westerns are. Rebecca West and Marguerite Yourcenar were captivated by the entire tradition. And oral performance of these poems supplied Milman Parry and Albert B. Lord with evidence for their theory of epic composition and transmission, set forth in Lord's *The Singer of Tales*.

At the beginning, *my* Marko was mostly a voice, a performing voice like that of the old *guslari* (Balkan tale-singers). Marko's voice came booming down the halls of the building where we both taught. Though hoarse from smoking and alcohol, it was somehow projected to the extent that anyone trying to teach on the same corridor had to shut his classroom door; it was like hearing the voice of Louis Armstrong amplified by a massive stereo. Marko had been teaching at Notre Dame for years before I arrived and was something of a legend in the math department. Although he'd stopped doing serious research in his field, he was the most popular teacher of the required calculus course—and this despite the fact that, in the early days of radical feminism, he'd routinely flirt with his female students and call them "girlie." (The males were addressed as "sonny boy.")

When I met him, in the late 1970s, he'd just been busted for D.U.I. and, as a result, briefly locked up in the South Bend jail and sentenced to several weeks of community service, which had him mopping the floors of Memorial Hospital, two blocks from my house. When going in for a blood test, a mutual student of ours ran into him there one morning. "Professor Kraljević! What are you doing?" he asked. "Mopping the fucking floors," Marko replied. "What does it look like I'm doing?" Later he told me he'd been in a Nazi jail, a communist jail, and finally a capitalist jail, and they were all just the same. Nor was drinking his only pastime. Once we became friends, he happily took me along to a bar and exotic dance club, the Kittykat Lounge, where everyone seemed to know him. He'd buy drinks on his credit card for all the oglers and lechers while the strippers teased him, sitting on his lap and saying, "Marko, darling, give us a kiss."

Loudness wasn't Marko's only distinctive verbal habit. Every word ending in -ed was pronounced with an extra syllable. One walkèd home with him and talkèd on the way. It could sound both funny and sad: Once he told me over a glass of plum brandy that his wife was "all of the time depressèd." While in the hospital with pneumonia, he called me and said, "John, I almost kickèd the bucket." My own name was stretched to something like Johhhnnnnn. "Johhhnnnnn, I almost kickèd the bucket." Or, remembering one of his many sexual conquests: "Johhhnnnnn, the girlie was absolutely gorgeous and I fuckèd her." Surprisingly, I never knew anyone who took offense at the way Marko spoke. At sixty, he still had much of the charm he'd clearly possessed in abundance in his youth. When he had to spend another few days in the hospital for a hernia operation, he got an erection every time the pretty nurse came into his room. She'd turn to the wall with a blush. Eventually she acquired the kind of spray bottle one might use to get one's cat off the dining room table or stove. She'd lift the sheet, turn to the wall, and spray the offending member with cold water. "Girlie," Marko would say, "I just can't help it. I dreamèd I married you in my sleep."

Marko's early mathematical work—on recursive functions—had won him international recognition, but by the time he washed up at Notre Dame in the 1950s he was less interested in math than poetry and philosophy. "Johhhnnnnn," he'd say, "you can write great poems when you're completely drunk, but you can't do mathematics." Though he was a recognized poet in Serbo-Croatian, his poems in English were less than great, and what he called his "serious poem," a commentary in rhyming couplets on Hegel's *Phenomenology of Mind*, didn't seem to me terribly promising. But he was certainly a spirited translator. As I had a developing interest in many things South Slavic, we soon agreed to join forces. Thus began a collaboration that lasted over a decade. Yet our translation sessions often strayed into personal reminiscence, and before long I was spending as much time listening to Marko's stories as prodding him to get back to our work.

Late one evening, after a translation session, Marko began to tell me about his life during the war years. His stories were told with such a unique combination of mock-heroics and self-deprecation, and were fueled by so much plum brandy, that I can't vouch for their accuracy. At any rate, their main episodes were as follows.

With the German invasion, Marko took to the hills with his friends and joined Tito's Partisans. A key element of Partisan strategy was the elimination of German officers. Whenever an officer was killed, the German reprisal was fast and horrific: Typically, a hundred civilians from the area where the assassination occurred were lined up and shot. It's not clear to me exactly what Marko's role was in these assassinations, but eventually he became so traumatized by the reprisals—which he at least once watched through binoculars from a hiding place—that he decided to leave the Partisans. But you can't just quit a guerilla outfit—you're in for the duration. Summarily tried, Marko was tied to a tree as his friends lined up with rifles. Luckily, the man in charge of the firing squad was his uncle, who, unable to bring himself to shoot his nephew, let him go. After striking out on his own for a week, Marko returned to the Partisan encampment and found his uncle and friends lying dead in a ditch. He pushed up the eyelids of his uncle, stared at him in amazement, and took off again.

After his break with the Partisans, he realized he'd better go underground in a serious way. Stopping at his family home outside of

Belgrade, he found that Ustase hit-men, intent on executing Marko because he was a known Partisan, had preceded him; not finding Marko, they'd contented themselves with shooting his father, whose body had just been buried in the family garden by his mother. She refused to let Marko grieve with her, telling him he must flee and hide. In an agony of fear and remorse, he went to Novi Pazar and began dealing in contraband tobacco, which briefly made him rich. One night he was walking the blacked-out streets with a suitcase full of cigarettes and cash. A car passed him, then stopped, then backed up. The driver was a Gestapo officer. After telling Marko he was in violation of the curfew, the German told him to get in the car, and that he would give him a ride. The German asked where he was going, and Marko desperately made up an address on a street far from his actual destination. The German drove to the street but couldn't find the address. They drove around and around, up and down. The numbers were all too low. Marko finally said he was sure he could find the address if he got out and walked. To his astonishment, the German let him out, reminded him again about the curfew, and wished him a pleasant evening.

Eventually Marko made the necessary connections to buy forged papers for himself, his girlfriend, and his math teacher. The trio headed for Vienna, by rail, foot, and stolen car, following some of the same routes the Turks had taken to the city, at whose walls their westward expansion was checked in 1683. Once in Vienna, the girlfriend and the teacher went their separate ways while Marko looked for a suitable place to wait out the war. Instinct and luck led him to a brothel where he found some fellow Serbs. The girls had done a lot of business in the early stages of the war, but now everyone feared the arrival of the Russians. When they came, the "liberators" trashed the city and raped any woman they saw—"a hoard of barbarian bums," Marko called them. The prostitutes begged the Serbs to protect them, and the Serbs did. They'd arrived well armed and were willing to fight. The house was barricaded. When one of the women, going out to find food, was attacked only a hundred yards away, Marko took up a rifle and ran outside. "He had fuckèd her," said Marko, "and was pulling up his pants. So I shottèd him in the ass." I asked him what happened then. "He trièd to run but kept falling down. He must have crawlèd off in the dark because he wasn't there the next day." After the first wave of

Russians washed into town, the second arrived and arrested almost all the men in the first. Finally the "hoard of barbarian bums" was joined by the three other Allied powers, and life became more civilized. The prostitutes went back to their trade, and Marko sat down to write what would become his Ph.D. dissertation.

As I got to know Marko and to learn something of his past, I found myself connecting him more and more with the Prince Marko of the ballads, who knew how to outfox the enemy and live by his wits under an occupation. One ballad in particular reminded me of my friend, the one sometimes known as 'Marko's Smile.' (A version of it appears in Yourcenar's *Oriental Tales*.) The ballad runs as follows. In order to do reconnaissance in occupied Kotor (in modern-day Montenegro), Prince Marko swims down the coast from Ragusa (modern-day Dubrovnik) and stays with the ugly widow of the Pasha of Scutari, who's in love with him. He manages well with his undercover work, but the work he has to do at night to maintain his safe house exhausts and finally disgusts him. When the widow gives him the thigh of an old goat for breakfast, he calls her a "hell-hag" and drags her around the room by her hair. Then, while he naps, the vengeful widow summons the Turks. Marko dives into the sea, but a fisherman catches him with a lasso and hauls him back to shore, where he plays dead. The Turks crucify him and then build a fire on his chest, but because his body is cold from the swim it burns itself out. The Turks decide to torment him with beautiful dancing girls. Haise, the most beautiful of all, smiles at Marko as she dances, and he can't keep himself from grinning back. She drops a veil over his face so that no one else sees. But now Marko's in love. In order to embrace Haise, he rips his hands free from the cross. He then takes the nail from his feet and stabs it into the widow's neck. The Turks flee, and Marko swims off with his beautiful girlie.

That's my Marko for sure: clever and wily, attractive to women, strong-muscled and tough-minded, possessed of a charming ironic smile, capable of thriving in times of war and rebellion. One of the first arguments we had was over what Marko called "the pleasures of war." He didn't mean that war wasn't terrible in itself, but that there were compensatory pleasures. He knew, he said, that I was an "idiot liberal," and so wouldn't know what he meant. I admitted that I didn't think any pleasure could possibly be compensation enough. He said I'd change my mind if I could see the women he'd met in wartime, all of whom understood that the present day might be their last and were not going to waste it.

Yet the first poem we translated together, one that Marko said he'd recited to himself for months in a Belgrade prison, where he'd been locked up for having written broadsides mocking Tito, was an austere piece by Branko Miljković that contains no hint of a secret smile. "He was a bigshot poet after the war," Marko said. "But his girlie left him and he killèd himself." The poem is called 'While You Are Singing':

> While you are singing
> Who will carry your burden?
> While you alone defy
> The poverty of clarity?
>
> While you encounter bitter fruit
> And the sarcastic dew
> While you are singing
> Who will carry your burden?
>
> Travel. Sing. Defy.
> Only the poem desires you
> And the night reveres you.
> But while you are singing
>
> Who will carry your burden?

Whenever Marko became sufficiently annoyed at me for being an "idiot liberal," not to mention a "modernist aesthete," he'd quote those first two lines at me. Sometimes I'd reply, "While you carry your burden / Who will sing your songs?" He knew perfectly well that his own songs (so to speak) had been sung to Tito's henchmen by stool pigeons whom he'd taken to be friends. And he'd smile his Marko smile.

People are often curious about collaborative translation. On the face of it, the procedure seems odd. But I've found working with Marko and two other collaborators to be an enormous pleasure. It takes some of the loneliness out of writing. Talking through possible solutions with a collaborator, one externalizes what are usually internal processes and articulates things that otherwise never get said. If well matched, the collaborators spark off each other like steel on stone. As a rule, the speaker of the source language cleaves to the literal sense, while the speaker of the target language keeps pushing and pulling and testing, trying to make a phrase, a line, and finally a whole stanza live and breathe.

One could write a strange history of friendships among collaborators—think of Czesław Miłosz and Robert Hass, Leif Sjoberg and W.H. Auden, Daniel Weissbort and Joseph Brodsky, Clarence Brown and W.S. Merwin. When Marko and I really got going—and it took my friend a few glasses of plum brandy to get in the spirit— we sometimes produced drafts that would have horrified their authors. But the process of revision goes on and on, and in some ways it's best to begin with something that's really far out and then rein it in. Making a viable translation of a good poem can be more difficult than writing one, and one's relationship with one's collaborator can come under great pressure. In our case, Marko would bellow and incant, but sometimes forget to tell me about something as crucial as a rhyme scheme.

Now and then a terrible error would creep in because of Marko's splutterings. In an epic fragment about the Battle of Kosovo that Marko and I translated, one of Tsar Lazar's knights boasts that he will kill the leader of the Turkish invasion. Marko stuck on the word "slaughter," which came from his mouth with a shower of saliva and a sound I couldn't make out. Annoyed, he said "slaughter, slauuughter, slauuuughter like a pig." I thought I had it and wrote down "slaughter like a pig." A few years later, in London, having been awarded the Janović Literary Prize, I read from our translations of the Kosovo fragments at a ceremony in a Serbian Orthodox church. In the first several rows were a number of extremely well dressed old people who turned out to be mostly exiled royalty—prince this and princess that. Then there were several rows of priests. Then more old people, lots of them, as threadbare in their dress as the first rows were elegant. It was a bilingual reading, with a London Serb reading the original before I read the translation, which was doubtless only required for the younger folk, second- and third-generation Serbs, at the back of the room. After a while everyone began to weep. We were reading from their national poem, after all, and most of the audience would never set foot again on their native soil—or so they thought at the time. At the end, a very dignified gentleman came up to me and said, "Don't say 'slaughter like a pig.' A Serbian nobleman would never say that." I assured him that it was in the original. The text was produced, and it turned out that Lazar's knight had vowed to "slaughter this foreign Tsar." No pig. Marko had been trying to explain what he meant by "slauuughter": "You know, Johhnnnnn, slauuughter, like you slauuughter a pig."

The London reading was memorable for another reason. Well before the partition of Yugoslavia, I'd been urged by these same London exiles to pay no attention to the current rumors about Serbian atrocities in Kosovo province. Even though at that point I'd heard no such rumors, these conversations put a cloud over my friendship with Marko. But I didn't notice it for quite a long time.

In fact I had a rather starry-eyed view of the old Yugoslavia. A leftie from the 1960s, I had a kind of general notion that Tito's confederation was a form of socialism that worked and protected at least the most basic human rights. And I liked it that Tito stood up to the Russian bear; I thought of him as a more determined Dubček. Marko thought of him as the bloated object of a personality cult, a living parody of Stalin. Admittedly, I experienced something like a manifestation of this cult in Slovenia in the late 1970s, when my wife and I attended a folk festival outside Bled, where Tito had a summer home. Though it was the Slovenian "national" holiday, at least half the entertainment was Serbian, including a performance by a singer of heroic ballads, who wore traditional dress and a fez and was (or pretended to be) blind; playing the one-stringed gusle, he chanted some poems about Prince Marko and some about the Battle of Kosovo. There was also choral singing, dancing, sing-alongs, and so forth. At a certain point, one of the large contingents of soldiers—there were hundreds of them in the audience—stood to attention in their seats and shouted out a kind of cheer. The people seated beside us said they were shouting, "We are the friends of Tito!" Immediately another contingent stood up on the opposite side of the hall and answered back: "We are the friends of Tito too!" And so it went for about twenty minutes. A lot of the locals stood up, and I suggested to my wife that, as guests, we should probably stand up as well to be polite. "Don't be ridiculous," she said. "I've never even met the man." So we sat.

When I first visited Belgrade, I met a young woman with excellent English, Borislava Šašić, known as Beba. She had been assigned to me by the Serbian Writers' Union as a translator for a poetry reading and lecture I gave at the American embassy under the sponsorship of what was then the U.S.I.S. After the reading, Beba organized an impromptu party for me at her sister's apartment on the other side of the Sava River, where the apartments were big Austro-Hungarian affairs, all pretty much untouched by bombing during World War II. Beba's sister's place had good furniture, plenty of art, an impressive library, and a general feeling of prosperity that one might associate with a successful Victorian paterfamilias. When I asked Beba what her sister did, she laughed and said she was "in politics." By the end of the evening, I'd discovered that Beba, in addition to being the daughter of an ambassador who'd formerly been a well-known general, was a gifted student of English literature who was interested in attending graduate school in America. I recruited her on the spot for Notre Dame.

When Beba arrived in South Bend a year later, I persuaded Marko, who was an excellent cook, to prepare a dinner for her and some other guests. When they met, Marko paused over her last name and asked if her father could possibly be General Šašic. Beba said he was, and Marko broke into a kind of mad laughter. "Girlie," he said, "your daddy was the commandant of the prison where I languishèd for months." Blushing, Beba began to say how sorry she was, but Marko interrupted. "No, no, it's OK, it's OK. Your daddy arrivèd one day with the jailer and askèd why I was there. The jailer didn't know, and flippèd through the pages on his clipboard. Your daddy askèd me, 'Prisoner, what did you do?' I said I did nothing at all. Your daddy turnèd to the jailer and said, 'If you can't find what this prisoner did to end up in jail, let him out at once and come see me in my office.' So they lettèd me out. And pretty quick I decide to come to America."

Marko's magnificent dinner—roast pork (or "pig meat" as he called it), vegetables from his garden, something like Yorkshire pudding, twice-baked potatoes, a huge Greek salad, a rich cake topped with home-made ice cream—was all served on paper plates, and the Serbian wine and plum brandy in Dixie cups; Marko loved to cook but hated washing dishes. After dinner, Jovan, Marko's former Chetnik friend, got into his usual spat with Marko about the war years. "If we'd capturèd you,"

Marko said, "I'd have let you go." Replied Jovan, "If we'd captured you, I'd have had you shot." He wasn't kidding. The Partisans, by the time Marko left them, were fighting not only the Germans and the Ustaše but the Chetniks. These royalist followers of Draža Mihailović began as the resistance group favored by Churchill but before long ceased to fight for a unified Yugoslavia and became brutal Serbian nationalists and Nazi collaborators. Jovan, after graduating from a royalist military academy, had joined them. (I met his former colleagues when I gave my London reading.) When Marko and Jovan argued, sometimes giving each other a little push on the shoulder or a mock slap on the cheek, the old wounds bled in spite of the joking around. I could tell that Beba was both amazed and annoyed to hear a recapitulation of all this grief in the dining room of a house in South Bend, Indiana. (It might have been worse in Chicago, where Croats and Serbs sometimes dropped each other into Lake Michigan with weights attached to their legs.) At the end of the evening, Marko, becoming courtly, kissed the hand of the "beautiful Serbian girlie" I'd brought to his house. "Beautiful *Yugoslav* girlie," Beba corrected him.

In the early 1980s Marko's wife had bolted; Marko explained that she couldn't take it anymore when he was "joyous," by which he meant drunk. He placed an ad in the local paper—"Mature intellectual seeks conversation and companionship with like-minded woman, age 25–35"—and got some responses. He also began, now and then, putting up the exotic dancers from the Kittykat Lounge in his house. At a dinner he gave for some faculty friends, one of these dancers appeared to be his "date" for the evening. The poor woman was so embarrassed in that company that she wouldn't say a word and only blushed deeply when any of us addressed her. But Marko's chief anxiety was over the fact that she'd been browsing in some manuscripts on his desk, and had come across a poem of mine dedicated to him that contained the following lines:

> In 1941 when I was born
> > beside a silly field
> Of vegetables
> > that noncombatant types
> Were urged to cultivate—
> > officially they called

Such doubtful husbandry
          a "Victory Garden"—
You at just eighteen
           had taken to the hills
With Tito's Partisans.

Marko feared she'd been doing the math, trying to figure out how old he really was. He'd told her he was forty-three. I noticed her taking a hard look at me (born in 1941) and then at him (eighteen in that same year), the wheels turning as, presumably, she made her calculations. By the end of the evening someone noticed that she'd simply disappeared. Then we all let Marko have it: "There should be limits", we told him, shaking with bourgeois indignation, "to the lifestyle of a mathematics professor." But at some level I envied him—he'd decided to live as he liked. And in another week the relationship between him and the dancer, whatever it was, had been patched up.

One day I arrived at Marko's house and found a strange scene in his back yard. He'd dug a large hole in the ground and covered its bottom and sides with three or four cut-up plastic wading pools, the kind that children splash around in on hot summer days. It was indeed a hot summer day, and splashing around in this improvised version of an Esalen communal bath were two of the Kittykat girls. Marko was busy alternately with the garden hose he used to keep up the water level in the bath and with attending to a second hole, this one filled with hot coals over which he turned a pig he'd impaled on a curtain rod. I'd smelled the rich aroma of the spitted pig right away. So had the neighbors. Brought to their open windows by the smell, they stayed to look at the view. The two girls, naked above the waist, frolicked in the muddy water, into which, now and then, Marko would jump, putting his arms around both girls' shoulders. I helped myself to a Dixie cup of wine from the picnic table and, from a certain distance, joined in the fun. When I asked the more voluptuous of the girls what her name was, she asked if I meant her stage name or her real name. "How about both?" She said her dancing name was Tomtomtitty Caboose. "Like, you know, it's Native American. I wear lots of feathers in various places before I start taking things off." But her real name, she said, was Sally, and her surname was something like Skint. But she made a kind of high squeaking diphthong sound: *Skoouunt.* "My grandfather was German, so that's S-k-ü with an omelet-n-k: Sally Scünt." "Oh my," I laughed. "Why didn't you just use that one for your professional name?" "I know," she said, "but everybody has trouble with the diaclitical remark." I suddenly realized that the omelet/umlaut business was no slip; the girl was smart, a regular Joycean punster. She said she'd seen me around campus, that she was a graduate student in anthropology. But it was more fun working at the Kittykat than in the library, and she had serious bills to pay.

After a while a police car arrived. One of the neighbors had evidently complained about public indecency. Having dealt effectively with the Gestapo and Tito's jailers, Marko had a history of relative failure with the South Bend police department. He didn't dare try a bribe, and he hesitated to offer introductions to the Kittykat girls, or even a cup of wine and slice of pork. "We were just washèd," he said. The unsmiling cop pointed to the second-story window of a house nearly overhanging Marko's garden. "You see that window?" he said. "A twelve-year-old who lives in the house has been charging a dollar at his door for five minutes worth of staring down at your mud-bath and your girlfriends. Every kid in the neighborhood's been through. Now get the fuck in your house and close down the orgy before I haul all of you off to jail." The girls put on their tops, Marko put the spitted pig under his arm, and they all went inside. I'd chosen a bad day to drop by for some work on our translations.

During this period, Marko always seemed to be hurting for money. I think he sold some desperate graduate students basic propositions for their dissertations, though he made them do all the calculations themselves. All his credit cards were maxed out. The summers were a particular problem for him since he needed the money he'd earn teaching a summer calculus course but also needed at least eight students for the course to run. One summer he only had six. Notre Dame offers one free class per semester to faculty spouses, and Marko's solution was that my wife and I, both on the university faculty, should sign up for his class as the spouse of the other. We could drop out mid-term when the class lists became final, or else stay and learn something. I was not only an "idiot liberal" and "modernist aesthete" but a "complete ignoramus" when it came to math, and my wife was perhaps even more hopeless.

Yet we attended the class right up to exams, and were both awarded a D followed by seven minus signs: D - - - - - - -.

Marko had other money-making schemes as well. He was convinced he could write a bestseller if he combined some of his life story with formulaic plot elements from detective fiction. His hero was a "tough operator" and his girlie "drew down her fishnet stockings revealing a delectable thighs [sic]." He wrote the novel quickly, in a couple of months, and gave it to me to "revise and correct" at one of our translation sessions. For years I'd tried to persuade him to tell his life story straight, but to no avail, and all this detective nonsense was ruinous. Similarly, though I loved his delicate watercolors, which had the eccentric charm of primitive painting, Marko needed to be like, he declared, "Jackson Polack." One day I came to a translation session and found the floor covered with large rectangles of plywood, which Marko was covering, splatter-style, with house paint from a dozen large buckets, dripped and slashed and swept with a broom. He did these paintings—I think there were eight—all at once. They dried overnight and went on his walls the next day.

As it happens, South Bend had once been the home of a Yugoslav artist rather more talented and successful than Marko, namely the sculptor Ivan Meštrović, who spent his last seven years, from 1955 to 1962, at Notre Dame. (The university's art museum has a large Meštrović collection and its basilica a famous pietà.) In the late 1970s, after spending a week at Lake Bled (where we'd taken in that folk festival and display of Tito worship), my wife and I drove down to Split to visit the city's Meštrović museum; my wife especially wanted to see work from before and during his Vienna Secession period. The immense museum, which was Meštrović's home before his exile, is made of cut stone (like his best work) and has a distinct neo-fascist feel to it, a kind of Mussolini-modern quality. Though Croatian by birth, Meštrović based many of his early sculptures on Serbian myth, history, and ballads, and I wasn't surprised to find in the museum an equestrian statue of Prince Marko. The odd thing was, it looked just like Meštrović's twin mounted Indian warriors at the entrance to Grant Park in Chicago. When he got the commission—in the 1920s, before he became famous in America—he must have remembered this earlier statue.

When I mentioned the similarity to my Marko years later, he said, "Well, sure, sure, he fuckèd it up. What did that Croat Ustaše know about Indians?" To the best of my knowledge, Meštrović, far from being a Ustaše, "languishèd" (as Marko would say) in a Ustaše prison during World War II, until the Pope intervened to get him out. But Marko had it in for Meštrović. For a while they must have overlapped at Notre Dame, and I can picture Marko, as he walks past the great man's studio, shaking a fist and reciting (as he later did to me) a limerick of his own making that began, "There once was Croat that crowèd..." For Meštrović had indeed become something of a Croatian nationalist. According to Marko, he'd also written some very nasty things about Serbs, which had been preserved in his archival papers but were still untranslated.

Knowing that a dig at Meštrović would please Marko, I'd included in the poem I wrote for him (the one that the Kittykat stripper found on his desk) a reference to South Bend as the place "where Ivan Meštrović petered out his talent / in the awful portrait busts and bland madonnas / of his exile." But I admired Meštrović's earlier work, and in 1987, when Marko and I came to publish a book of the translations we'd done of the Kosovo cycle, I wanted some of the poems to be illustrated by photographs of his sculptures, many of which were based on the fragments. Marko reluctantly agreed, and the illustrations appeared in the first edition of *The Battle of Kosovo*, as we called it. At the time the book came out, the Battle of Kosovo was, to most of the world, an obscure and remote historical episode, of no contemporary relevance. But all that was about to change. Within a few years, our casual mingling of Serbian poetry and Croatian sculpture would be problematic, and our relationship as collaborators and friends cast in shadow.

After Tito's death in 1980, the rotating-presidency system he'd devised to hold together the Yugoslav federation began to fail as the republics became more nationalistic. Meanwhile, Slobodan Milošević sought to revive Serbian hegemony and reduce the autonomy of Vojvodina and Kosovo, the so-called autonomous provinces that had a vote in the Yugoslav Presidency Council along with the six republics. By 1989, trains and buses were pouring thousands of Serbs onto the Field of Blackbirds to hear Milošević thunder, "Once again, six centuries after the Battle of Kosovo, we are in battles and quarrels. They are not armed battles, though such things should not be ruled out."

Strange to say, I'd been invited to attend this now-infamous rally, for the same reason I'd been invited to read at the Serbian Orthodox Church in London a few years earlier: because of my collaboration with Marko on translating the Kosovo fragments. By that point, the rumors I'd been urged to ignore in London were in the international press; horrors perpetrated by both Serbs and ethnic Albanians had been amply documented, and it was feared—correctly, as it turned out—that Milošević's rhetoric, honed on the poetry I'd been translating with Marko, might itself translate into war. Charles Simic thought it wouldn't be wise for me to accept the invitation, which had made the event sound more like a meeting of scholars, translators, and poets than a political rally. A few years earlier, the great Serbian poet Ivan Lalić had translated a poem of mine, 'Friendship,' into Serbo-Croatian, and it was now reprinted in a leading Serbian paper. The "friendship" in question had nothing to do with nations or ethnicities, but the possibility that I might be mistaken as pro-Serbian began to worry me. So I took Simic's advice and stayed home.

By the time blood began to be spilled in Slovenia, Croatia, and Bosnia, I'd written a poem in which I imagine that I had in fact been at the Kosovo rally. It's called 'Into Cyrillic':

I see they've written пријателбство
but it's Greek to me. They sign
it with my name. Something's been
translated, something here is very strange.

They've written цон and метајас
and they say it isn't Greek, they say
it isn't Russian either and I see
my name. I point to Macedonia,

to Leningrad. But everything, they
tell me, points to Kosovo. Everything
they tell me points to Sarajevo too.
For example, пријателбство.

I ask them, did I write that word?
They found it in my poem. They say I stood

with Miloš Obilić in 1389: everybody
heard me shouting LAZARUS!

I tell them I was silent; if there, I stood
aside. They say I stood among
the Yugovići as in 1989 I stood between
Milošević and Karadžić.

I'm tangled in Cyrillic and I cannot
find my way. They'll help me.
They'll lead me on. I say I want to be
led out of this, away.

They say пријатељбство!
The trains have all stopped running and
there is no petrol for the cars.
Everyone is shouting џон, џон, џон!

The Cyrillic words are "friendship" in the first stanza, "John" and "Matthias" in the second, "friendship" again in the third, and "John" (three times) in the final line. Miloš Obilić is the hero of the Kosovo poems and "LAZARUS!" refers to Tsar Lazar. Milošević and Karadžić had yet to become murderous allies, but time was running out on any peaceful solution to the Yugoslav problem. I was beginning to feel "tangled in Cyrillic" in more ways than one, that I'd somehow been conscripted to fight in ancient battles not my own. Shortly after the rally I received an e-mail from Beba telling me that the whole of our *Battle of Kosovo* had been posted on a Serbian nationalist website. It's still there—I've found no way to get it taken down. (Curiously, the book also drew the attention of Ohio's Senator George Voinovich, who asked our publisher for a hundred copies for colleagues in the Senate who didn't understand what was going on in the Balkans. The book's second edition—which didn't include the Meštrović illustrations—was quickly reprinted and sent to D.C.)

By chance, Marko himself returned to Yugoslavia at about the same time I was absenting myself from the Kosovo rally. Though preoccupied with family matters—his brother was dying—he managed to visit the annual Belgrade literary conference and to meet with a mutual friend of ours, the English poet Richard Burns, who was living there with his

Serbian wife. While in Belgrade, Marko also gave an interview with the magazine *Duga* about his part in the falsification of statistics on the number of Yugoslavs killed by the Germans and the Nazi-controlled Independent State of Croatia, statistics that found their way after the war to the International Reparation Commission in Paris. The interview came about because in 1985 Marko had published in *Our Word*, a Serbian émigré journal, an article that revealed his part in Tito's falsifications.

Marko mentioned neither the article nor the interview to me when he returned to South Bend, but about a year later I learned of them from Richard Burns, who, while doing research for his ambitious book *The Blue Butterfly*, about the 1941 Nazi massacre of civilians in the Serbian city of Kragujevac, had come across Marko's article and interview. I phoned Marko and asked about them. It turns out that in 1947, Marko, then a twenty-four-year-old math student, began working for the Belgrade Bureau of Statistics, which had been instructed to exaggerate the number of war victims but to base the figures as closely as possible on real statistics. Marko did the calculations because his superiors, who should have done the job themselves, passed it to a novice. It took him two weeks, after which he was given a pat on the back and a week off. Marko enjoyed his holiday and forgot about the whole thing. "Johhhnnnnn, " he said. "I cookèd the books. What can I say? They askèd me to do this job and I did it. I hadn't yet turnèd all against the regime, and it seemèd at the time as a kind of duty." I asked him why he'd suddenly remembered it all in 1985. Evidently questions about the numbers of Serbs killed during the war had arisen both in the Yugoslav and émigré press, and these had jogged his memory. I didn't know quite what to make of all this. Like Prince Marko in the heroic ballads, my Marko had apparently worked in the system while also working against it.

As Radovan Karadžić emerged as the leader of the Bosnian Serbs, I discovered that he not only shared a name with Vuk Karadžić but was related to him. More than that, he was a poet himself and devoted to the heroic ballads, especially those of the Kosovo cycle, which he used to legitimize his obsessive desire to create a "Greater Serbia." In retrospect, it's almost surreal to imagine him in New York City studying American poetry on a Fulbright, but in fact he did just that. In a TV documentary, I saw him admiring the traditional performance of a *guslar*. My work co-translating the Kosovo poems began more and more to trouble me. This wasn't my tribe, so why was I dancing in its war dance?

Once the "ethnic cleansing" began, Americans watched as Franjo Tudjman, the Croatian leader, drove Serbs out of one town and Ratko Mladić, the Bosnian Serb general, drove Croats out of another. When Bosnia proclaimed its independence, the beautiful multiethnic city of Sarajevo was surrounded by Serbian artillery and the long siege got under way. At Notre Dame, a poetry reading was organized in support of Sarajevo. I phoned Marko to ask if he would be willing to participate. "No, sir!" he said. "No, sir!"

Years earlier, while on a package holiday in Sarajevo, I'd met a bus conductor whose English was so good that I asked her where she was from. "Cleveland, Ohio," she replied. She and her family had moved back to the land of their forefathers because they'd become so frightened and discouraged by the violence in Cleveland. As the siege in Sarajevo dragged on, I found myself wondering what had happened to her. And I wondered as well what had happened to Beba and her family. She'd returned to Belgrade, but I was no longer hearing from her. When Marko had called her a "beautiful Serbian girlie," she'd been quite serious in correcting him: "beautiful *Yugoslav* girlie." The friends I'd made during my visits to Slovenia, Croatia, and Serbia had considered themselves Yugoslav, but they were now beginning to scatter all over the world. Beba eventually made her way to Geneva, while her sister, in whose Belgrade apartment I'd been so well entertained, ended up in New York holding diplomatic papers from a country that no longer existed.

After 9/11 and the years of fighting in Afghanistan and Iraq, Americans have begun to forget the siege of Sarajevo, the atrocities at Srebenica, the U.N. intervention in Kosovo. But for me, at least, certain images and facts are indelible: men and women and children staring through barbed wire, looking like the ghosts of Auschwitz; Elie Wiesel weeping at the Holocaust Museum, the proclamation "Never again" having been given the lie; the use of rape as a military strategy; the thousands shot and buried in mass graves; the intentional shelling of the National Library in Sarajevo, resulting in the destruction of a million books that collectively contained, in the words of Christopher Merrill, "the memory of a precious exception—Serbs, Croats, Muslims, and Jews living as one people."

After Merrill published his book *Only the Nails Remain: Scenes from the Balkan Wars*, he came to Notre Dame to give a presentation. He also brought along a video of the TV documentary I mentioned earlier, the one showing Radovan Karadžić listening with appreciation to a *guslar* singing about Serbian heroes. Next to Karadžić is a Russian nationalist poet, Eduard Limonov, who looks delighted and more than a little drunk. At the end of the performance, Karadžić asks Limonov if he'd like to fire a machine-gun into the city from their encampment on Mount Trebevic. And then the poet fires into Sarajevo. Did he hit a Muslim, a Serb, a Croat, a Jew, the girl from Cleveland? At any rate, the poem was incanted, the offer made. It looked like cause and effect. Sitting in an auditorium at my American university, I thought of our pirated translation out there on some Serbian server and felt complicit. When I asked Marko if he'd like to come to the presentation and meet Merrill, I got another "No, sir!" I was beginning to be embarrassed, or, more than that, afraid to ask him questions I'd once have freely asked. Collaborating had made for a strange intimacy between us, and at one point years earlier, after we'd been working together for many months, he'd declared that we were academic *hajduks* (outlaws) and blood brothers. Yet now we saw little of each other, and I wondered if we were still *hajduks* and blood brothers. Marko was getting old, and I suffered a period of intermittent illness that, with its accompanying depression, kept me away even from friends it was easy to be with—and Marko was never easy at the best of times. But I was often tempted just to drop by his house, or to see if he was at the Kittykat Lounge, or at least to return some of his books.

It was in fact a book that led to our last meeting. In the middle of the Balkan wars, my colleague Gerald Bruns published a book called *Hermeneutics Ancient and Modern*. Jerry is that rare thing, a literary theorist who really loves literature. On campus one day, I ran into him sitting in the spring sunshine and thumbing through his new book. He motioned me over and showed me the epigraph:

But peace, peace
> to all who wander
For whatever reason
> from their stony lands
Bringing all the heavy cargo
> of their legends
Humming in a cipher
> in their lucid, spinning minds!

This is the conclusion to my poem dedicated to Marko. In his preface, Jerry had written, "One could, for reasons that the conclusion will make clear, take this book as a slowly unfolding gloss on the lines from John Matthias' poem that I have quoted as an epigraph." My God, I thought, the whole of hermeneutics, from Socrates and the Midrash through Heidegger and Derrida! But before feeling too honored, I quickly remembered that these were Marko's legends, *his* heavy cargo, and *his* lucid, spinning mind—not mine. I had to show this to him.

Jerry gave me a copy of the book, and I drove out to Marko's house to show him the epigraph. "Marko!" I said. "He means your stories!" Marko was mildly amused, but not at all excited the way I was. He poured me a glass of plum brandy but didn't take one for himself. "The doctor orderèd—no more drinking and smoking." It was as difficult to imagine him not drinking and smoking as not telling his stories. I thought of the Miljković poem we'd translated early on: "While you are singing / Who will carry your burden?" Marko didn't seem in a singing frame of mind, and he certainly looked burdened. When I asked what he'd been doing, he said he'd returned to mathematics. Now that he was sober all the time, he told me, he might as well do something difficult. In fact he'd been trying to figure out string theory.

The visit wasn't really a success. Neither of us said anything about further work on translations. I gave him the books I'd held onto for such a long time. He didn't ask for a copy of Jerry's book, and I didn't offer to get him one. I hugged him goodbye.

In the heroic ballads, there are several versions of the death of Prince Marko. The most famous was performed for Vuk Karadžić by Filip Višnjić, generally held to have been the best of the *guslari* during the period when Vuk was collecting the ballads. In this version, Marko's magical horse, Šarac, begins to stumble, something he hadn't done once in the hundred and sixty years of their career together. Then Marko hears a *vila* (a sort of nymph or fairy) crying from Mount Urvina. She calls him blood brother, and says that he and Šarac both must die, though no man can kill Marko and no man other than Marko can kill Šarac. Still, it is time. It is the will, declares the vila, of "God the executioner." She orders Marko to ride up Mount Urvina, where he will find a well between the two tallest trees. He will look into the water and understand what must be done. "O false world, my lovely flower!" Marko cries. He draws his sword and cuts off Šarac's head. He breaks his sword and spear into pieces and throws his mace from the top of Mount Urvina all the way into the sea. He takes three belts of gold from around his waist and, dipping his pen in an inkhorn, writes out his will. One belt is for whoever finds him and gives him a proper burial; the second is to adorn a church; and the third is for the crippled and blind, who are to go forth in the world singing poems in his memory. Then he takes off his coat, crosses himself, sits down beside the well, and draws the hood of his coat over his eyes.

Grand Old Dirty Old Men

[I began thinking about the following essay when a cutting from the Spring 1997 Sewanee Review, Samuel Hynes' 'How To Be An Old Poet,' fell out of Ernest Sandeen's Collected Poems three years after the latter's death. I was then, as I sometimes do, looking into Sandeen's work for an answer to that vexing question. I had obviously placed Hynes' essay in the book as a kind of extended gloss on Sandeen's poems. Hynes writes movingly contrasting the ways Hardy and Yeats—the way of resignation vs. way of outrage, the way of Prospero vs. the way of Lear—face old age and death in their poems. Sandeen had a Yeats phase and a Hardy phase, but Hardy dominated at the end. I watched my old friend age and die, and I read what he wrote, sometimes only days or hours after he wrote it, right up to the end. He was my own Old Poet, as I am now an Old Poet for some of my younger friends. I think this is perhaps the last moment when I will feel the inclination to publish the rather ferocious argument that follows. It has been resting in a dark drawer for several years. The essay begins with some borrowings from Hynes, along with unavoidable Shakespearian glosses and contrasts to which we both have early recourse. Ernest Sandeen would not have liked this essay and would have been perplexed about the reasons I was drawn to most of the texts, chiefly prose, engaged below. Because of that I dedicate it to his memory. For decades we had long and wonderful arguments through long afternoons and into the night.]

§

Grand indeed. Dirty without doubt: W.B. Yeats, Yasunari Kawabata, Gabriel García Márquez, J.M. Coetzee, Octavio Paz, and Guy Davenport. As it happens, they are all Nobel Prize winners except for Davenport, who called himself "a minor prose stylist" but was much more than that. Eros drove their work. Eros drives the work of anyone with work to do. Especially at the end. Write or die, seems to be the daily mantra. But the writing, in its turn, is erotic foreplay, voyeurism, masturbation, last coming at the first coming of some girl, age of Lolita, age of your daughter, Mr. Jones. My list, of course, could be completely different. Or, starting with these six, could be extended by another six or sixteen or twenty-six. But these will do.[1] I leave aside the Grand Old Dirty Old Women. But that too would make a tale.

Shakespeare's Jacques left a stage out of his famous seven ages of man catalogue in *As You Like It*; we'll call it age six-and-a-half. Six-and-a-halfers pass quickly through age six:

> With spectacles on nose and pouch on side,
> [And] youthful hose, well sav'd, a world too wide
> For [their] shrunk shank; and [their] manly voice[s],
> Turning again toward childish treble

and do not like it. Knowing perfectly well what's coming, the seventh age—"second childishness and mere oblivion"—they pause as long as they can in second adolescence, the much maligned stage six-and-a-half. As in their first adolescence, they gaze and grope and long to know. Instead of dreaming about girls a few years older, those in their second adolescence dream of girls forty, fifty years younger. They earn the mockery of mankind, but they have also a kind of greatness. In spite of shrunk shank, they stride the wide world, they buy their contact lenses, sing their song in treble if they must. Their motto is "Let copulation thrive." They will not "go gentle into that good night." With Cadmus and Tiresias, they adorn themselves with fawnskins and climb the mountain with their Bacchic wands.[2] They scan the porn sites, tell their neighbor's wife at the dinner for emeriti that "Love has pitched his mansion in the place of excrement" and recommend Pan's disco where the Golden Codgers dance with the nymphs where "belly, shoulder, bum / flash fishlike," and then "copulate [with them] in the foam." They mutter darkly that "Saint Joseph thought the world would melt / but liked the way his finger smelt." Overhearing that, another dinner guest might object the way "Sister Kate" does on her amusing web site, 'Dreck of the Greats: How Bad Poems Happen to Good Poets': "A line of astonishing grossness and an image that reminds [one] of a scene in *King Kong*."[3] But Sister Kate doesn't understand what Sister Life (or Crazy Jane) has overheard:

> You think it horrible that lust and rage
> Should dance attention upon my old age;
> They were not such a plague when I was young;
> What else have I to spur me into song?

Yeats is as good a paradigm as any, writing poems like these right up into 1939, the year of his death. One reads old masters differently when one is getting old oneself. When I was nineteen or twenty, I was told by a six-and-a-halfer that I shouldn't bother to read Proust before

I was fifty. I thought my intelligence had been insulted and so began reading Proust at once, but he had a point. One "understands," but doesn't fully feel what is at stake in such a work before a certain age. The young will deny this, of course. For thirty years I lectured on Yeats. I preferred to teach the desiccated Eliot. It is easier to talk about the *Four Quartets* as a late work than to ask students: "What did Saint Joseph's finger smell of, exactly?" Or: "Does he really mean *in* the place of excrement, or merely adjacent?" (Teaching Lawrence, who was dying as he wrote *Lady Chatterley*, one asks the same question.) It is easier to sing along with "all shall be well / and all manner of things shall be well," especially at a Catholic university, than engage the Yeatsian graffiti. Things in fact will not be well. Why not write it on the wall? Six-and-a-halfers will write it desperately even for the daughters of their former girl friends. They're inevitable losers, but their late energy, or tragic ineptitude, is something to behold. It's grotesque, heartbreaking, beautiful, outrageous. Powdered Gustav von Aschenbach in his lipstick and rouge. The dying Benjamin Britten making him sing.

Yeats' infatuation with Maud Gonne's daughter, Iseult, actually came fairly early, well before his Steinach treatment for impotence in 1934. It was still only 1915; she was twenty-one and he was only a year on from having apologized to his "old fathers" in the poem introducing *Responsibilities* that he, "come close on forty-nine," still had no child, which was all the fault of "a barren passion" for the mother whose daughter now caught his eye. Even Lady Gregory thought Yeats still looked young at fifty and if Iseult—the daughter of a "drunken, vainglorious lout" and moreover Yeats's successful rival for the mother's attention—still seemed young at twenty-one, she was a six-foot-tall beauty and, as R.F. Forster suggests, maybe a little in love with him. And there were only thirty years between them then. The "uncontrollable mystery" might manifest itself on more than one "bestial floor" and there was "enterprise in walking naked."[4]

Margot Ruddock, Ethyl Mannin, and Dorothy Wellesley were of course not children nor, except for Ruddock, women in their twenties like Iseult Gonne. But they all offered post-Steinach adventures for Yeats. In his great biography, R.F. Foster says that "what in fact was a simple vasectomy [performed in 1934] intended to increase the production of male hormone, thus arresting the ageing process and restoring sexual vitality . . . convulsed his life and changed his work beyond all expectation." It is by no means clear what, if anything, the surgery did for the master's phallus, but it did a great deal to what many a six-and-a-halfer finds to be the most sexual organ in the body—his brain. Yeats' erotic imagination and the poems he was able to write in his final years were enough to attract the ladies. The manic Margot Ruddock was, in the end, too much even for the Mad Old Man. Wellesley was a lesbian—which seems to have turned him on—and Mannin told Yeats' friend and physician, Oliver St. John Gogarty, that she "did [her] best for him," though the tryst sounds to have been not much more successful than, in his own words, Yeats' first encounter with a prostitute: a little like "trying to get an oyster into a slot-machine." It doesn't matter. His imagination was stimulated by an erotic energy that resulted in his ability to write many of his very best poems between the Steinach procedure and Drumcliff Churchyard, 1934–1939. One is touched and amused by the Yeats who would correct Ruddock's poems, write bawdy verse in collaboration with Wellesley, and put the inept work of both into the strangest anthology ever, his 1936 *Oxford Book of Modern Verse*. "I take thee, Life / Because I need, / A wanton love / My Flesh to feed," wrote Ruddock. What a dotty book it is: sixteen pages of Wellesley and three short poems by Auden (two of them mistakenly run together as one). First adolescence has only some etchings to show; second adolescence can put you in the *Oxford Book*.

Foster quotes a letter from Yeats to Wellesley in which he reveals an erotic self-stimulation "through an exploitation of androgyny": "My dear, my dear, when you crossed the room with that boyish movement, it was not a man who looked at you, it was the woman in me . . . I have looked out of her eyes. I have shared her desire." Wellesley's poems "have the magnificent swing of [her] boyish body. I wish I could be a girl of nineteen . . ." When Yeats revises *A Vision* in 1937, he returns, Foster says, in his 'Phantasmagoria' to a story that had fascinated him for years concerning "impotence and surrogate sex: two friends share a woman, one of them being unable to perform sexually until his friend has preceded him." The watching, perhaps, becomes everything in the end, the deep source of imagining. He wants to look at Wellesley the way he might if he were a nineteen-year-old girl. In his last letters to Margot Ruddock he says he wants only "to look at you." In 'The

Chambermaid's Song,' a man is left on the maid's bed, "Weak as a worm, / His rod and its butting head, / limp as a worm." But Yeats persisted in thinking—persisted *imagining*—as he had when he courted Iseult Gonne, that a young woman, a chambermaid or somebody's beautiful daughter, might like to be initiated into sexual experience by an ageing and ever older man. Or at least might like to be looked at. The necessary delusion of a six-and-a-halfer. The sweet foulness in "the foul rag and bone shop of the heart." Like Crazy Jane, he'd tell it to the Bishop.

The looking is everything in Yasunari Kawabata's *House of the Sleeping Beauties* and in the short novel by García Márquez that derives from it, *Memories of My Melancholy Whores.* Though Kawabata's Old Eguchi might ask with Yeats what he should do with "this absurdity . . ./ this caricature,/ Decrepit age that has been tied to [him] / As to a dog's tail," his imagination is not as "excited, passionate, fantastical" as the poet's. But at sixty-seven, he is still able to distinguish himself as half an age short of his friend Old Kiga, who initially tells him about the secret house where he might go "when the despair of old age was too much for him." When Old Eguchi makes his first visit to the house, he compares himself with Old Kiga, "who was no longer a man." Old Eguchi still is—barely. Immediately, when he is taken into the room with a sleeping girl, he is tempted to violate the rules of the establishment. "He was not to do anything in bad taste, the woman of the inn warned Old Eguchi. He was not to put his finger in the mouth of the girl, or try anything of that sort." For Eguchi, the sleeping girl, not yet twenty, was "life itself." When left alone with her he can not help himself from shaking her shoulder and whispering "Wake up." And he finds he must control his impulse to "arouse her by violence." There are internet sites offering exactly this fantasy. The girl is asleep. A man approaches. He stares at her. He touches her. She does not wake up. He puts a finger in her mouth, in her vagina.

Georges Bataille has argued, as Peter Michelson explains in *Speaking the Unspeakable,*[5] that "without taboo there is no transgression" and without transgression there is no full consciousness of being alive. Nothing is much more transgressive than watching, or reading about, an old man having his way with a young girl. Even Humbert Humbert isn't old. Old Eguchi is sixty-seven, still way short of the virile Clint

Eastwood's age, for example. But García Márquez's narrator in his *Melancholy Whores* is ninety. In *On Late Style*, Edward W. Said, dying himself as he wrote his last book, distinguishes between the kind of late style he admires and the characteristic "reconciliation and serenity often expressed in terms of a miraculous transfiguration," as in *The Tempest*, *The Winter's Tale*, or *Oedipus at Colonus*. Said does not explore in his book what "is assumed to be a general abiding *timeliness*, by which . . . what is appropriate to early life is not appropriate for later stages." The lateness that interests Said is not harmony and resolution, but "intransigence, difficulty, and unresolved contradiction." He looks for "a nonharmonious, nonserene tension, a sort of deliberately unproductive productiveness going *against* . . . where late style is what happens if art does not abdicate its rights in favor of reality." Or in favor of old age and approaching death.[6]

Perhaps it is serenity and reconciliation that a recent *New York Times* reviewer of Gerald Martin's biography of García Márquez had been hoping for in a second volume of García Márquez's own autobiography, *Living to Tell the Tale*, which has not yet appeared and may never appear. Philip Swanson laments that instead of the second volume of autobiography García Márquez chose to write *Memories of My Melancholy Whores*, which he finds "disconcerting" in its "pathetic image of an old man yearning for an adolescent virgin." He also calls it "gloomy," which it is not. The first person narrator is more energetic at ninety than Old Eguchi is at sixty-seven. What he finally experiences in this short novel, outrageous as it may appear, is love.

More disconcerting than that is the degree to which García Márquez recapitulates a good deal of Kawabata (whose *Sleeping Beauties* is fully acknowledged in his epigraph, which consists of the first paragraph of Kawabata's novel). Like Eguchi, García Márquez's narrator gets in touch with an old madam, Rosa Cabarcas, who will supply him with a sleeping girl for his ninetieth birthday. She is fourteen. The man has never slept with anyone for love, and he stopped counting prostitutes when he was fifty and the list had already reached 514. Like Kawabata, García Márquez caresses the girl's body with his language. "She was dark and warm. She had been subjected to a regimen of hygiene and beautification that did not overlook even the incipient down on her pubis. Her hair had been curled, and she wore natural polish on the

---

nails of her fingers and toes . . . Her newborn breasts still seemed like a boy's, but they appeared full to bursting with a secret energy that was ready to explode." He sings to her, calls her Delgadina. Like Eguchi, he touches, then caresses, his sleeping beauty, kisses every part of her body. But she does not wake up. He must always leave before she does.

After several visits the narrator "has [the girl] in [his] memory with so much clarity that [he] could do what [he] wanted with her." He changes the color of her hair, imagines her a parlor whore, the queen of Babylon, a saint. In his imagination, they sing Puccini love duets and Carlos Gardel tangos. He leaves her messages written in lipstick on the mirror because of which, we later learn from the madam, the girl begins learning to read. His weekly newspaper column evolves into a series of coded love letters written to his sleeping beauty. Time passes and she is fifteen. The visits continue until another customer, "an important client," is stabbed to death in one of the rooms and the establishment is suddenly shut down. Delgadina disappears.

In despair, the old man searches the town. He can't recognize himself in his "adolescent's pain." He realizes that he also would not recognize Delgadina dressed and awake, and of course Delgadina has never seen him at all. He goes to the button sewing factory where she had worked and finds three hundred virgins in white blouses. He begins to suspect that Delgadina may have been forced by Rosa Cabarcas to sell her virginity "to one of her big-shot clients in exchange for being cleared of the crime." He experiences jealousy for the first time in his life. Having encountered one of his "melancholy whores" while searching for the girl, he falls into a nostalgic conversation. The former prostitute is herself now in her seventies, but she harbors deep affection for the old man. "Do whatever you want," she says, "but don't lose that child." Find her, she insists. And then, "Wake her, fuck her brains out with that burro's cock the devil gave you. . . . Don't let yourself die without knowing the wonder of fucking with love."

The narrator takes the advice of the melancholy whore. Rosa finds Delgadina, and the old man fucks her with that burro's cock the devil gave him. He buys the madam's house and moves in. According to Rosa, Delgadina is in love with him, although it is unclear if the two of them have ever communicated except through the madam's agency, the lipstick on the mirror, and the Sunday columns' coded love letters. Or whether Delgadina has been asleep or awake when finally relieved of her virginity. No matter. Well beyond Jacques' seventh age of man, though in fact a virile six-and-a-halfer, García Márquez's narrator concludes: "It was, at last, real life, with my heart safe and condemned to die of happy love in the joyful agony of any day after my hundredth birthday." In *Love in a Time of Cholera*, Florentino Ariza is only seventy-six when he tells the captain of the ship in which he and Zenaida have finally consummated their love that they'll keep coming and going on the river "forever." But Zenaida is not fifteen and *Love in a Time of Cholera* is not a work in Edward Said's "late style"; it is not even a late work, though it manifests the harmony and resolution of *The Tempest* and *A Winter's Tale*. It adheres, give or take a decade or two, to the abiding timeliness of natural life. *Memories of my Melancholy Whores* is an outrage against nature, but it sings. It does not abdicate its rights in favor of reality.

Kawabata's *House of Sleeping Beauties* was published in 1961, when he was sixty-two. In the decade that followed he published *Beauty and Sadness* and the story 'One Arm,' among others, won the Nobel Prize, became infatuated with a young girl, and followed his friend Yukio Mishima in suicide. At the end, he was writing with the full knowledge and symptoms of Parkinson's disease.

House of Sleeping Beauties is altogether a more ambitious work than García Márquez's *Melancholy Whores*, in part because of the way that memory functions in Kawabata's novel.

It is also more fully hermetic; almost no action at all, save for the memories, takes place outside the secret house itself. And, unlike the *Melancholy Whores*, it is not about an outrageous love but about outrageous lust. In an Introduction to the work, Mishima writes that "eroticism has not, from Mr. Kawabata, pointed to totality, for eroticism as totality carries within itself humanity. Lust inevitably attaches itself to fragments, and, quite without subjectivity, the sleeping beauties themselves are fragments of human beings, urging lust to its highest intensity. And, paradoxically, a beautiful corpse, from which the last traces of spirit have gone, gives rise to the strongest feelings of life." (And is there not somewhere in Alfred Nobel's bequest for his prize some phrase or another about the deserving works being "of an idealistic tendency"?)

Old Eguchi visits several girls in their drug-induced sleep in the course of the story, not just one. He himself is given a sleeping medication, but not one as strong as the sleeping beauties have taken before he arrives. The girls range from novices to the well-experienced. At each session, before he takes his own medication, he gazes upon the body of the young girl and begins to remember . . . his mother, his wife when she was young, a woman with whom he had had an affair in Kobe. This last, the woman in Kobe, arrives unbidden and from a depth of forgetfulness. He has thought about asking for the same drug that is given to the girls so that he too could "sleep like death," and it is that phrase—"sleep like death"—that jogs his memory. The sex with this stranger had been magnificent, but what Old Eguchi seems to cherish is that afterwards she told him that she had slept like death— "the happiness of hearing her say that had stayed with him like youthful music." Like the older and impotent men who come to the secret house, Eguchi begins to imagine his own death in the arms of a naked girl, a kind of *Liebestod*. He begins to wonder if his real transgression has not been touching naked virgins in their sleep, but his marriage and the fathering of his daughters. "To marry, to rear his daughters, these things were on the surface good; but to have had the long years in his power, to have controlled their lives, to have warped their natures even, these might be evil things. Perhaps, beguiled by custom and order, one's sense of evil went numb."

While the dramatic crisis in *Melancholy Whores* is the murder of a customer, in Kawabata it is the natural death of a man, Old Fukura, in the arms of a sleeping beauty followed by the death of a girl in Old Eguchi's own room. Perhaps Fukura had achieved his greatest desire: "To die on a night like this, with a young girl's skin to warm him—that would be paradise for an old man." But the death of the girl? Had she been given too strong a dose of the drug? Eguchi had been given two girls with whom to sleep during a night shortly after Old Fukura's death, and he feared that one of them had been with Fukura when he had his seizure and died. Eguchi realizes that he has "lost the vigor to take such a girl by force," but he begins to think he might strangle the one he feared had been with Fukura. Sleeping fitfully between the two girls, he has disturbing erotic dreams and suddenly awakens to find that one of them is not breathing. In a panic, he calls the madam, who denies that the girl is dead. As she is removed from the room, Eguchi is told to return to the other girl: "Go back to sleep," she tells him. Although Eguchi feels that he has "not yet entered into the companionship of ugliness," he considers making an end like Old Fukura's: "Would this not be a most desirable place to die? To arouse curiosity, to invite the disdain of the world—would these not be to cap his life with a proper death." Earlier on, Eguchi reflected that since he had not ceased to be a man, it would not be necessary for him that the girl remain asleep. But he has now passed over into the seventh age.

In her essay on pornography, Susan Sontag says that all such writing is ultimately not about sex, but death (a love-death hymned as a kind of necrophilia even in a poem like Yeats' 'Byzantium'—"A mouth that has no moisture and no breath / Breathless mouths may summon").[7] But Kawabata and García Márquez, of course, are not pornographers, not quite. García Márquez remains an erotic comedian in *Melancholy Whores*, a work ending in a kind of marriage, traditional in comedy, and not reaching toward a terminal darkness or emptiness. Kawabata, on the other hand, is perhaps something of a Buddhist toward the end of *Sleeping Beauties*. Old Eguchi has considered the possibility that in remorse and the fear of death the old men surrender to the silent girls more than the girls surrender to the old men. "Might not the sleeping beauty herself be a Buddha of sorts?" he wonders. "He almost thought that, as in old legends, she was the incarnation of a Buddha. Were there not old stories in which prostitutes and courtesans were Buddha incarnate?"

The central relationship in *Beauty and Sadness* is complicated by the fact that Oki Toshio is a novelist and has written about it. He is younger than Eguchi, but Kawabata himself is older as he writes his book The young girl, Otoko, was sixteen when the initial relationship in the novel occurred. Twenty years later she is an artist planning a painting "in the classical Buddhist style" of her student and lesbian lover, Keiko. Keiko is, in a sense, the agent of revenge on the old men of *Sleeping Beauties* if Oki Toshio can be regarded as their surrogate representative. He was younger than they when Otoko was sixteen, and Otoko was a waking rather than a sleeping beauty, but a new and complex issue is raised with the question of representation. Oki Toshio's book, *A Girl of Sixteen*, renders Otoko as passive as the sleeping beauties when in the grip of her former lover's prose. He can do with her what he will. In life, she was made pregnant by the novelist, lost the child, and attempted suicide. In art, all that grief is missing and an idealized version of the sexual union of the aging man and the young girl is itself put to sleep for the reader to behold and that way also kept alive for both Oki and Otoko. Oki's mistake is to awaken his double portrait by visiting Otoko twenty years after the end of the affair.

When the two of them emerge from Oki's novel they must share their world with Oki's son and Otoko's lover, who is jealous on Otoko's behalf and vows revenge on Oki for Otoko's suffering and the death of her baby. The exotic and beautiful lover, Keiko, is meanwhile to be the subject of another idealization—Otoko's nude portrait of her modeled in the classical Buddhist style of depicting a boy saint, in which "some of the figures looked like pretty little girls or beautiful young maidens . . . with a certain voluptuousness." She would "follow the design of the boy saint's portrait, [where there was] the hint of a woman's breasts." But Keiko's acts of revenge intervene between Otoko's intention and act. She seduces both Oki and, soon after, also his son and succeeds in drowning the son in what appears to be a boating accident on Lake Biwa. When Otoko arrives at the hospital where her lover has been taken, Keiko is under a sedative. She had "looked dead when they brought her ashore," says a nurse. "Keiko was sleeping peacefully. Her breathing was calm." Otoko asks: "When will she wake up?"

At the end of *Beauty and Sadness,* Keiko is not a sleeping beauty but a sleeping agent of revenge. She is an unpredictable and predatory character throughout, often engaged in what seem to be unmotivated actions. She is sexually irresistible to both men and women, but she is somehow as incomplete physically as she is psychologically; she will not, for example, allow anyone to touch her right breast. Kawabata lavishes some of his best prose on Oki's fondling of her left breast, to the extent that it seems to have an almost independent existence. The reader thinks that it might even be detached as a fetish object offered as a gift, as indeed the arm of a young girl is detached in Kawabata's story, 'One Arm' that followed *Beauty and Sadness.* In a bizarre and surrealistic instance of synecdoche, the narrator borrows a girl's arm for the night. He fondles it, talks to it, gazes at it while it sleeps, and finally detaches his own arm and attaches the girl's to his shoulder. He puts the fingers in his mouth, caresses his own rounded shoulders which feel like breasts, feels the girl's blood flowing through him, and then rips off her arm and restores his own. The story ends with the man embracing it again "as one would a child from whom life was going. I brought the fingers to my lips. If the dew of woman would but come between the long nails and the finger tips!"

Rather surprisingly, this may be as close as Kawabata comes to pornography, even though his character plays with an arm, not a breast or a penis. Pornography is an art of manipulating body parts, an art of describing, drawing, or photographing the orifice and the finger, the cunt and the cock, and not the whole person, an art of violent dislocation. It disconnects sex from psychology and character, desire from an erotic meeting of minds; and it may well be, as Sontag suggests, as much about death as lust.

As Mishima says in his Introduction to *Sleeping Beauties*, "lust inevitably attaches itself to fragments" and the "fragments of human beings [urge] lust to its highest intensity"—including, in 'One Arm,' a narcissism of self-pleasuring perversity. But this generally despised art of violating taboos can open visions as well as bodies, and great writers often approach its boundaries as they age, driven by an imagination able to conjure socially forbidden encounters as life itself begins to deny the pleasures of ordinary sexual intimacy.

J.M. Coetzee writes a good deal about pornography in his collection of essays on censorship, *Giving Offense*. In a fully nuanced and sometimes legalistic discussion of familiar arguments against pornography by Catherine MacKinnon and Andrea Dworkin, Coetzee also engages Susan Sontag's 'The Pornographic Imagination' cited earlier. He finds Sontag "conflating the ambitions of pornography and the ambitions of sexual desire itself. It is one thing to acknowledge the demonic, another to act it out. There is a deep sense in which Jane Austen finds sex as demonic as Sade does." Because Austen finds sex demonic, she "locks it out." Sade makes use of it as a tool to "break down the bounds of the self," using the "rituals of writing" in what is essentially a metaphysical ambition. MacKinnon, Coetzee maintains, "collapses the distinction between reality and representation." She also "shows a striking . . . absence of insight into desire as experienced by men . . . Any assertion of male desire, and the exploration of the nature of that desire—an exploration that can be conducted only under the aegis of desire itself—will have to be a sexed desire, such as serious erotic art may undertake, [and] must enter the lists in an adversarial relation to MacKinnon's enterprise," which is a censorious one. Much of what Coetzee feels that feminist critics like MacKinnon, Dworkin, and even Sontag fail to understand is intuitively grasped by the sexy typist Anya in Coetzee's novel *Diary of a Bad Year*.

Early on in that work, Mr. C, an aging writer living in an apartment building with Anya and her boyfriend, Alan, reflects that in the 1990s he "published a collection of essays on censorship. It made little impression." Many of the issues discussed in *Causing Offense* are engaged by Mr. C, or Señor C as the Filipina Anya calls him, or Senior Citizen, as the boyfriend likes to think of him. He is writing a series of brief essays called 'Strong Opinions' for a German publication and the initial symptoms of Parkinson's Disease make it difficult for him to write. When he first sees Anya in the apartment building's laundry room, he is more attracted to her lithe and sexy body than to her typing skills. In order to see more of the body, he asks her to type. Anya is well aware of the attraction. "As I pass him, carrying the laundry basket, I make sure I waggle my behind, my delicious behind, sheathed in tight denim. If I were a man I would not be able to keep my eyes off me."

Each page of the novel is sectioned by black lines. At the top of the page are C's formal 'Strong Opinions' written for the Germans and typed by Anya from C's taped recordings; in the middle are C's informal journal-like reflections; and at the bottom are Anya's remarks. Eventually, Alan enters as a third voice. The "strong opinions" are familiar to readers of Coetzee's work and can mostly be taken as his own. The eventual critique of those opinions by Anya, however, achieves an authority that one does not anticipate in the early pages of the book. She is no dummy, however much she sometimes passes herself off as such. As for her sex appeal, she usually seems to relish it. But she also sets her limits for Señor C, and is able to be (rather amiably) grossed out:

> There is a pair of panties of mine he pinched from the dryer. I'm sure of it. My guess is he unbuttons himself when I am gone and wraps himself in my undies and closes his eyes and summons up visions of my divine behind and makes himself come.

Pure Portnoy. However, like the Sade of *Giving Offense*, desire, for C, has its metaphysics:

> As I watched her an ache, a metaphysical ache, crept over me that I did nothing to stem. And in an intuitive way she knew about it, knew that in the old man in the plastic chair in the corner there was something personal going on, something to do with age and regret and the tears of things.

Unlike MacKinnon and Dworkin, Anya understands such an ache, "in an intuitive way she knew about it . . . and the tears of things."

While C writes his strong opinions on subjects like democracy, terrorism, universities, animal rights, probability, and other rather abstract and chiefly political topics, Anya flirts with him, teases him about his know-it-all tone, and suggests that he might write about other topics that would interest people of her generation—women he has been in love with, for example. Alan calls C "a leftover from the Sixties, an old-fashioned free-speech sentimental hippie socialist." But Anya feels sorry for him, understands his "hovering uncertainty about what he actually expects the object of his infatuation to supply."

Alan begins to intervene more and more as he actually becomes jealous of Anya's affection for C. He becomes particularly concerned when Anya wonders if "she will wind up in C's opinions too," and Alan tells her that if C uses her in his book she should sue him. "Maybe that is how he gets his kicks: making the woman read his fantasies about her . . . it is a means of exercising power over a woman when he can't fuck . . . He can't just do what he likes with you. He can't . . . have obscene fantasies about you and then sell them in public for profit."

When C's strong opinions turn to "the erotic life" and even "pedophilia," he considers the inadequacy of his friend Gyula's attempt to maintain outward chastity "in the autumn of his days" by choosing the body of a young woman whom he may have seen or met and imaging an affair "from infatuation to consummation" as intensely as a meditating monk might imagine death with his fingers in the eye-sockets of a skull. But this is not enough for C because "there was the real thing, which I knew and remembered, and then there was the kind of mental rape Gyula performed, and the two were not the same." As for pedophilia, Anya finally objects to what she has all but encouraged herself: "Among Señor C's latest set of opinions there is one that disturbs me, makes me wonder if I have misjudged him all along. It is about sex with children. He doesn't exactly come out in favor of it, but he isn't against it either. I can understand that he should have the hots for a petite number like me. But little girls are a different story."

So is C just a dirty old man after all? Actually the dirty old man turns out to be Alan, and he's up to dirty tricks as well—not only does he try to poison Anya's mind against C, but also to swindle C out of his badly invested money by installing some spyware on his computer hidden in an installment of 'Strong Opinions' typed up as an attachment by Anya. This scheme, together with Alan's drunken and boorish behavior at a dinner celebrating the completion of C's contribution to the German book, leads to Anya's break with her lover and her decision to live for a while with her mother. In their last meeting, Anya asks C if he wouldn't like "a hug" after all his fantasizing, which she tells him later in a letter that she never minded and even encouraged knowing that it "helped him." When they embrace, the music of a line of Yeats comes to his mind, though he cannot pin down the words. "For a whole minute we stood clasped together, this shrunken old man and this earthly incarnation of heavenly beauty."

For the rest, there is a brief correspondence and the composition of what Anya calls C's "Soft Opinions" on questions more personal and intimate than his strong ones, a kind of writing C had promised earlier after Anya went off in a huff after she had to type the entry on pedophilia. These "take up suggestions you let drop. A gentle opinion of birds, for example." And indeed one of C's best pieces at the end of the book has to do with the carryings-on of a magpie in the apartment's garden. After one of the last "opinions," which has to do with the miracle of Bach's music and reminds us that the technique of this novel is essentially fugal, Anya writes to Mrs. Saunders, the apartment's concierge, asking her to phone when—and she is pretty sure this will happen soon—C grows even weaker and begins to die. "I will fly to Sydney. I will do that. I will hold his hand. I can't go with you, I will say to him, it's against the rules . . . but as far as the gate I will hold your hand, I would be proud to do that." And in a last letter to C, she advises him to have a professional go over his computer and clean his hard drive.

From a beginning that seems to promise a refusal of reconciliation characteristic of Edward Said's favored version of Late Style to an ending that appears to embrace it, Coetzee's novel and C's strong and soft opinions—along with his lust, his voyeurism, and his fantasies—probably give a censorious sensibility less offense than some passages in the essays in *Giving Offense*. This is chiefly because Anya's voice is always there to repeat a theme from the fugue and give it a comical turn. And when she imagines a final *Liebestod* duet, it is gentle and touching, and not obscene in the least, as it certainly is in Kawabata. Only when C writes about pedophilia does Anya think she may have misjudged him and takes offense herself. Had Coetzee pursued this theme any further, there would have been no reconciliation with Anya, and probably not with himself as the "pessimistic anarchistic quietist" he finally acknowledges himself to be.

An unsympathetic reader might well dismiss some of Guy Davenport's most characteristic work as verbal pedophilia, or something very akin. When he was dying of lung cancer, he worked almost until the very end revising the posthumously published extended original version of *Wo es war, soll ich werden*, a 100-page (self-censored?) abridgement of which had appeared in *The Drummer of the Eleventh North Devonshire Fusiliers* in 1990. The work, especially in its original form published in an elegant "restored original text" by the Finial Press, might be seen as an example of "late style" in Said's sense, and it tests to the limit any reader's patience for one manifestation of such a style. It's interesting that when Said chooses an example of Mozart's late style, it is not his requiem, but *Così fan tutte*. There are pages in *Wo es war* that one might compare with the gorgeous foolishness of that opera. But there are also pages of what will seem to many readers self-indulgent tedium. Said talks about an "unproductive productiveness" that he finds in late style, and "a form of exile from what is generally acceptable." He finds the style "wayward and eccentric" in Beethoven, whereas Beethoven's work as a young composer was "organically whole." Late style even communicates an impression of "being unfinished" (in opus 111, for example). In Goethe, he finds "a plethora of unmastered material." In Adorno's late essays, Said finds a late style that "abjures mere bourgeois aging and insists on the increasing sense of apartness and anachronism." In a hypothetically academic context, he imagines "an aging and embarrassingly frank former colleague" whose work may have become "unashamedly mandarin," or, as Adorno has it, even "a catastrophe."

Toward the end of his life, Davenport wrote to the critic André Furlani that he "knew [he] was imagining a morality transcending practically all present cultures." The taboos he was breaking imaginatively were the kind that, if actually enacted, land one in prison. I have myself been a great admirer of, and also deeply influenced by, Davenport's essays and modernist historical reconstructions in fiction. But when it comes to some of the longer erotic pastorals in which the ideas of Fourier are superimposed, along with many other familiar Davenport sources, on Plato's *Symposium*, I must actively try not to be offended myself. These long stories and novellas are adolescent in a very literal way, celebrating adolescence in a kind of precocious, and sometimes precious, adolescent idiom. They also celebrate a guiltless childhood sexuality found nowhere else in American literature, and certainly nowhere at all in American life. Their Socrates is easily seduced by Alcibiades—and also by Diotima, Agathon, Aristophanes, Pausanias, Phaedrus, or anyone else who may be hanging around. The children gossip, talk philosophy, masturbate, urinate, fellate one another, fetishize underpants and jock straps, commit incest, form *ménages à trois*, kiss the genitals of a baby, and fuck each other blind while quoting the classics. Long ago I asked Hugh Kenner, Davenport's mentor, what he thought about these longer fictions. He said that the pedophilia made him squirm. I think that must be true for many readers who also, even if schooled by Davenport's essays about narrative form in *Geography of the Imagination*, will find them pretty formless. And the style, which is almost everything for Davenport, they may find simultaneously pedantic in its learning and anecdotal range of reference, and a bit twee, fey, whimsical, or *farfelu* when the kids in the Phalanstery's *nouveau monde amoureux* or Theban Band jack each other off with their teacher looking on or joining in.

After having read a number of Davenport fictions focused on childhood and adolescent sexuality—'The Dawn in Erewhon,' 'Apples and Pears,' 'The Jules Verne Steam Balloon,' 'The Owl of Minerva,' 'The Playing Field,' 'Gunnar and Nikolai,' 'The Death of Picasso,' 'The Bicycle Rider' and both versions of 'Wo es war, soll ich werden'—the reader begins to find the repetitious punctuations in the narrative for a blow job or comparing endowments or a roll in the hay becoming obsessive. Davenport admires the innocent and unconscious beauty of children. He attempts to imagine a new Arcadia in his Danish and Dutch settings, and a new kind of teaching and leadership in the figures of Adriaan van Hovendaal in the earlier stories, Hugo Tvemunding and Holger Sigurjonsson in 'Wo es war.' Taking the part of a "naïve" reader like Coetzee's Anya, one might ask if these bucolic fantasies aren't meant to function as actual social models. After a while, the reader may be likely to emerge from the fictions as Anya does from typing up C's "strong opinion" on pedophilia in Coetzee's *A Bad Year*, wondering if she has misjudged the author in thinking of him as fundamentally a kind and gentle old lecher. Though Anya, who moves too quickly and easily from abstract speculation and aesthetics to the real world of ethical and moral action, is hardly Davenport's ideal reader, someone like Judith Levine would be almost perfect—and she no more hesitates to imagine the actual social effects of ideas like Davenport's at work in the real world than does Anya. When her own book, *Harmful to Minors*, appeared, which argued that educators should encourage rather than pathologize the expression of childhood sexuality, Davenport reviewed it with warm approbation after a commercial publisher had dropped it and the university press that finally took it on was threatened with the loss of funding by members of a state legislature. Against the public hysteria produced by even discussing such an issue, Davenport points out the "biological ignorance" of would-be censors and a taboo transparent "as any known to anthropology."

The various threesomes in Davenport's stories—Bruno, Kaatje, and Adriaan in 'The Dawn in Erewhon'; Sander, Grietje, and Wolfje in 'Apples and Pears'; Franklin, Pascal, and Alexandra in 'Wo es war'— might be compared with the threesome of Simone, Marcelle, and the narrator in the avowedly pornographic classic, *The History of the Eye* by Georges Bataille. Interestingly, Bataille once told Octavio Paz that "eroticism is inseparable from violence and transgression. Eroticism is an infraction, and if prohibitions disappeared, it too would disappear. And with it, mankind, at least as we have known it since the Paleolithic." This position made Bataille against, not in favor of, the kind of sexual liberation characteristic of the 1960s. Davenport, of course, was in favor of breaking taboos, as he makes clear in the review of Judith Levine's book, but the idea that eroticism should involve pain and violence was anathema to him, while pain and violence are the endgame of the pornographer. I once sent Davenport a poem of my own about the composer Percy Grainger called 'The Flagellant.' Grainger in fact was turned on by being whipped, an aspect of his complex character with which I dealt frankly enough in the poem but which Davenport found totally repellent. The sexual antics in Davenport's fiction may violate taboos against childhood sex, pedophilia and incest, but no one intentionally causes pain to anyone else. His children and adolescents are motivated by curiosity, a desire for innocent physical pleasure, and even love—just as healthy adults are.

Although he began publishing fiction only in his forties, Davenport was already known as a critic, scholar, and polymath. He had also been a painter and student of visual art from an early age, and his ideal version of the modernist serial collage which he practiced included drawings. *Tatlin*, his first book of fictions, reproduces in the title story his portraits of Lenin, Stalin and Tatlin, as well as his copies or versions of Russian constructivist art, but does not include drawings in 'The Dawn of Erewhon,' where the world of Samuel Butler's satire is superimposed on a version of Fourier's New Harmony and the legend of Orpheus. Some reviewers were harsh about the explicit sexuality in this story among the younger characters and their mentor, von Havendaal, and would doubtless have objected even more had it contained erotic illustrations. When drawings do appear as part of erotic stories culminating ten years later as part of Davenport's longest homage to Fourier, 'Apples and Pears,' the Greek athletes, boys' portraits, young men in jock straps or tight and low-cut jockey shorts, sleeping nudes, and collaged material including meticulously drawn male and female genitalia, the visual and verbal work would seem to be effectively integrated without a thought of the censor.

With regard to the play element in the verbal and visual collages, James Kincaid has said that it "feasts on its own inventiveness" and "does not lead to anything but its own perpetuation . . . Play eroticizes the whole world—and keeps it that way." On the other hand, Wyatt Mason, acknowledging that Davenport seems able to imagine a space "in which certain received ideas about human interaction and psychological development are revoked, [and] the stories [set there] read as if the Fall never happened and Freud was never there to assemble the pieces of our shame," nonetheless concludes an essay on Davenport like this:

> Davenport's [Edenic] garden, abandoned but pristine, is a world of potential waiting to be seized. Unaware of what befell the prior tenants, innocents fill the house, and each other, with endless stores of goodness [...] That Davenport's boys might forge joyful bonds in nature should be an acceptable alternative of William Golding's version, in which children left to their own devices hack one another apart. Alas, few critics have seen it that way. When a seventy-five-year old man writes about little boys falling in love, describes them admiring each other's dicks, rubbing noses, blowing kisses to each other, it seems his work can't escape the most literal interpretations.[8]

In 1990 Davenport published the short version of 'Wo es war, soll ich werden,' the story with which he eventually decided he was most satisfied, in the volume called *The Drummer of the Eleventh North Devonshire Fusiliers*. It was reprinted in 2003 as the concluding piece in *The Death of Picasso: New and Selected Writing*. There had been, however, a period of doubt when neither this story, 'The Dawn of Erewhon,' or 'Apples and Pears' were being reprinted in retrospective selections and when he was willing to acknowledge what might have been a temporary loss of nerve in a *Paris Review* interview. He called these pieces "shapeless novellas" but reserved his right to "change [his] mind" or "rewrite." In Michael Kalor's *Secreted Desires: The Major Uranians*, the author remarks that the carryings-on in and around the school setting at NFS Grundtvic in 'Wo es war' and the related stories "would certainly be (mis)interpreted by most adults on the outside as maladjusted, psychotic, immoral, sinful, unlawful, fringe, objectionable, and/or intrusive. It would also warrant the idealised Hugo, were he in America or Britain, a stint in prison or a psychiatric hospital; or, at the very least, the forfeiture of his teaching position."

If Davenport's hesitation over the form, or formlessness, of the stories in question disguises what was actually a period of self-censorship, his decision at the end of his life to authorize publication of the extended version of 'Wo es war,' write a 'Circumspectus' for it which explains and defends its form (about which he seems to have "changed his mind"), and deliver it into the hands of a "fit audience though few," lifts the burden anyone might feel at the end of his life that perhaps some of his best work would never be published as originally conceived.

Although Davenport declares in the 'Circumspectus' that he prefers the shorter form he is also—wanting it both ways—delighted that David Eisenman wants to print a limited edition of the restored version. "Books," he says, "are not for everybody. Books are for the readers who can appreciate them." And so Finial Press published an elegant edition of 100 copies, most of which are in libraries. Two copies are designated as "traveling copies" and may be rented for $25.00 from Mr. Eisenman.

Receiving this package in the mail is an interesting experience. Unwrapping it, one feels something of the excitement early readers of *Ulysses* or *Lady Chatterley* must have felt during the ban on those books upon receiving a package from a friend visiting Paris. What a surprise, then, to find the initial pages of the longest and most central restored section sounding like something out of *Winnie the Pooh*:

> —Hey! Friend Holger, you're up, too. But you can pee, and I'm so tight I can't.
> —It'll go down in a bit, but not if you keep pushing your foreskin up to see its elastic snapback.
> —Fun.
> —There's French apple jelly and American blackberry jam for our rolls, and Danish country butter, and what do you say to coffee?
> —Yes is what I say.
> —I imagine a decent theology would look forward to a paradise in which we glup blackberry jam and buttered rolls with a hand in our pants.
> —Whoopee for blackberry jam!
> Holger, in sweater, jeans, and hiking socks, sat beside Pascal, bumping his knee and getting a kiss on the corner of his mouth.
> —Blackberry jam kiss, Pascal said, for friends only. Not even for Franklin. A pascalized jam smack.
> —I hope a psychiatrist never gets wind of any of this.

This dialogue, in fact, begins the crucial seduction scene in which the twelve-year-old sexual and intellectual prodigy, Pascal, seduces Holger, his teacher and mentor on an overnight hike. Like all of Christopher Robin's friends in *Winnie the Pooh*, everyone has a jolly good time, especially once Eeyore and Rabbit arrive, who are as much into making each other come as Pooh and Piglet. No wonder Holger hopes a psychiatrist never gets wind of any of this.

And yet the title is from Freud. Earlier in the story, Holger has seen that his colleague Hugo, the classics master who lives with Mariana and also fucks her brother Franklin, has been "trying to show [him] that [he] needs to be liberated from something in [himself]." Hugo then translates the enigmatic German statement: "Where it was, there must I begin to be." He explains that "Nature compensates. A tree blown over will put out a bracing root to draw itself upright again . . . stutterers write beautifully. That is, one source of strength seems to be weakness." Holger's weakness comes from his austere Icelandic Lutheran conditioning. In 'The Dawn in Erewhon,' Adriaan, the character who most corresponds to Hugo in 'Wo es war,' conjoins Blake and Freud when he explains that "innocence [is] a kind of Herakleitian opposite of jealousy. Jealousy, [Blake] felt, was the awful possessiveness of the selfhood, by which he meant Groddeck's and Freud's Id, the suspicious old snake's brain just under our civilized one. I think Blake meant a spirit jealous of happiness, of benevolence, of freedom love needs for its charming folly." Hugo champions the relationship between Holger and Pascal, and the twelve-year-old, acting on Hugo's weakness, brings forth in him precisely happiness, benevolence, and freedom. Since all of this happens in the thirty pages cut from the short version of 'Wo es war,' the restored text is more than an alternative for a serious reader of Davenport. It is essential.

The eccentricity of Davenport's mannered prose increases after *Tatlin*, becoming in 'Apples and Pears,' 'The Bicycle Rider,' and 'Wo es war,' what Furlani in his book on Davenport calls an attempt to enact Fourier's utopia at the level of form and style, where "language becomes the sonorous equivalent of erotic acts" and approximates the style of Fourier himself "in the service of rhapsodic particularity rather than a postmodernist assault on the stability of the signifier." In Davenport's 'Circumspectus' to the restored version of 'Wo es war,' he addresses his critics directly: "My critics have habitually disregarded my architectonic style (reading around it) and focused on content, subverting my best efforts to transmute content into style. Style is not ornament; it is the mind of the narrative structure." We must take this death-bed proclamation of intention as seriously as we can, but nonetheless we must finally "trust the tale" rather than the teller. The style is a manifestation of the content, even where it is more like Milne than Fourier, and not a song in which the masturbation, fellatio, and cunnilingus are somehow "transmuted" into pure sound. Moreover, the two most moving elements in the collage are probably the long passage translated from Ausonius and the section that explains why the book in which the shorter version of 'Wo es war' appeared is called *The Drummer of the Eleventh North Devonshire Fusiliers*, and neither of these sound anything like the more typical passage quoted earlier. 'Mosella and Bisulla,' a few pages from which text by Asonius appear in translation, has to do with the freeing of a slave, "a child," at the edge of empire in Bordeaux where "the new religion of the imperial family . . . fits strangely into the order of things." Ausonius, more pagan than Christian, frees the girl child and lives with her in a way "poets and peasants can understand, but not the corps of diplomats and soldiers with whom I dine and whose rank I share. She is the spirit of this land." So, in a way, is Holger's Pascal a spirit of the land. And when Holger says "You realize that I will never hurt you or do you an injustice," the reader is moved—and especially so in a school context where Hugo has made up a new Theban Band named for Tom White. Collaged into 'Wo es war' is the sad story of the Drummer Boy White, who was hanged for the crime of sodomy on 7 March 1811 at the age of sixteen.

But Davenport never dwells on tragedy, and he calls his master Fourier "the only philosopher of happiness." In the 'Cadenza' that travels with the restored edition of 'Wo es war,' which was probably the last thing Davenport wrote and which I doubt has been read by more than a few dozen people—in fact, it was written for only one person, David Eisenman, who prepared the limited edition—all of the old boys have returned to celebrate Holger's fiftieth birthday, pooled their resources, and bought him a Paul Klee painting. A school choir sings Bach's 'Sheep May Safely Graze,' and Pastor Tveunding says it would seem that "the love that usually propels [the universe] is all gathered in this room." Again one rubs one's eyes: It's Christopher Robin's party for Pooh where all the animals in the Hundred Acre Wood pool their resources and buy him a Special Pencil Case. But since it's really by Guy Davenport, it also includes Taffy's proud declaration that he has recently gone camping with Holger and Phineas "and got masturbated by one or the other the whole time." These must be some of the strangest last words in the whole of literature.

No one in the Marquis de Sade says anything like "I will never hurt you or do you an injustice." The hurt and the injustice are the work's rage against the universe, and they fascinated Octavio Paz both early in his career and again at the very end. Everything that is innocent in Davenport is *Wo es war* in Sade—born of what Adriaan calls the "old snake's brain . . . intolerant, lethal, the essence of all that's negative." Paz is a poet of love, but he has also always been a poet of the erotic, which is not the same thing. And for him, Sade is a master of the erotic imagination.

Like Davenport's restored 'Wo es war,' Paz's remarkable little book on Sade, *An Erotic Beyond*, is a literary recovery, the result of a late decision to print and reclaim some early work in light of a lifetime's thought and writing. Published in Spanish in 1993, it appeared in the same year as *The Double Flame*, Paz's much longer meditation on love and eroticism. In his preface to the latter, Paz recalls writing fifty pages on Sade in 1960 in an attempt to define the boundaries between animal sexuality, human eroticism, and "the more restricted domain of love." In 1965, he tells us, he fell in love himself and "decided to write a little book about love." Though the book was quickly abandoned, Paz made use of notes for it to write a piece on Fourier, about whom his mentor, André Breton, had written a book-length ode in 1947. The philosopher of harmony and phalansteries is the very antithesis of Sade, and it is interesting that Paz and Breton were drawn to both. Paz was especially taken with the long-suppressed *Le nouveau amoureux*, in which Fourier maintains that "desire is not necessarily deadly . . . society not repressive by nature . . . and pleasure is good." He is attracted, indeed, to exactly the side of Fourier that most appeals to Davenport.

Nearly thirty years passed and Paz grew old. Remembering the abandoned book, he felt, he says, "more than regret"; he felt "shame" and "was gnawed by remorse." But still he waited. "Wasn't it a little ridiculous, at the end of my days, to write a book about love?" What Paz did write while gathering the will and energy required for *The Double Flame* was 'Carta de Creencia' ("Letter of Testimony" in English), which appears last in Eliot Weinberger's bilingual edition of the *Collected Poems of Octavio Paz 1957–1987*. In 'Carta de Creencia' (the title refers to a kind of document one carries in order to be believed by strangers), lines appear that contain diction, themes, and even rhythms that are developed, paraphrased and qualified both in *The Double Flame* and *An Erotic Beyond*:

> . . . it is an accident
> a fever, an aching,
> a struggle, a fury, a stupor
> a fancy . . .
> Desire invents it,
> mortification and deprivations give it life,
> jealousy spurs it on,
> custom kills it . . .
> . . . to hurl down:
> interminably falling,
> the coupled we
> in our abyss.
> The caress:
> Hieroglyph of destruction.
> Lust: the mask of death.
> Transgression
> of nature's fatality,
> hinge
> that links freedom and fate . . .

If *The Double Flame* reads like a last will and testament, *An Erotic Beyond* reads like a codicil. "Shame" and "remorse" are strong and unusual words to describe one's feelings about not having finished a writing project begun thirty years in the past. While those words do not appear in *An Erotic Beyond*, I wonder if they might nonetheless describe something of what Paz felt when *The Double Flame* was finished and he realized that his continuing fascination with Sade had not really been acknowledged in the book. That fascination clearly amounts to an attraction-repulsion response to Sade's texts, but even in Paz's old age the attraction continued to be very strong.

If one reads *An Erotic Beyond* back-to-front, one is observing a fascinating re-birth of the brilliant young poet who arrived in Paris in 1945 and discovered the figure the Surrealists had "turned . . . into an emblem of rebellion." The final section of the book, 'Jails of Reason,' was written in 1986 and is retrospective, including the conversation with Georges Bataille from which I have quoted earlier. Agreeing with Bataille that certain books "lose a great deal of their force if they lose the ambiguous incentive of prohibition," Paz finds that sadly even Sade has now landed in the hands of academics, "on the way to extinction [with] all modern literature, which today howls from its beatings by the sticks of the dogmatists and the canes of professors." Paz understands that works like *The 120 Days of Sodom* and *Philosophy in the Bedroom* depend "precisely on [their] immense subversive power. If prohibitions and anathemas disappear, will not subversion also vanish?" Although he is clearly more circumspect in 1986 than he was in 1945 in his dealings with Sade, he does want to pry the texts from the hands of academics and return them from the academy to the catacombs. Having discussed Sade and Pauline Réague (author of the Sadeian *The Story of O*) with Sade's biographer, Jean Paulhan, Paz concludes:

Sade was an enemy of love, and the hate with which he professed this feeling, which for him was an ill-fated chimera, can only be compared to the horror the idea of God inspired in him. For Sade, love was an idea: the true reality was the pleasure that annihilates everything it touches.

Disagreeing with Paulhan that "the philosopher of sadism was actually a masochist," he argues:

Sadism is a joy in the suffering of others. The sadist's pleasure is dulled if he realizes that his victim is also his accomplice. The voluptuousness of the crime, according to the cognoscenti, is in causing an unexpected suffering in another. In contrast, the masochist interiorizes the other: he enjoys his suffering because he sees himself suffer. The masochist is double: both the accomplice of his tormentor and the spectator at his own humiliation. In sadism the other only appears as an object, a living and throbbing object; in masochism, the subject, the I, becomes an object: an object endowed with a consciousness. Turned into the spectacle of himself, he is the ear who hears the cry of pain and the mouth from which it comes. Sade was consistent with himself: the conduct that has been called sadistic was for him a philosophical and moral exercise. He repeatedly affirms that the ultimate end of libertinism is to reach a state of perfect insensibility, similar to the impassivity or atarasia of the ancients. The exact opposite of masochism.

In 1986 Paz is primarily interested in two matters, his disagreement with Bataille and his disagreement with Paulhan. In contrast to Bataille, he sees the Sadeian theatre as a demonstration that eroticism is inseparable from violence and transgression. This makes it uniquely human, different both from animal sexuality and love, though proceeding from the former and an aspect (contra Sade himself) of the latter. And he is fascinated by his own conclusion, arguing against Paulhan, that libertinism ends in atarasia, a condition not unlike the Buddhist Nirvana.

Written in 1960, the middle section of *An Erotic Beyond* is the title essay, subdivided into four parts: 'Metaphores,' 'The Hospital of the Incurables,' 'The Innumerable Exception,' and 'The Universal Dissolution.' The first part is more or less absorbed into *The Double Flame*, dwelling as it does on the distinction between sexuality and eroticism. Repeating the argument that eroticism is distinctly human, that it encourages and excites sexual activity, and that it is a product of the imagination and "a ceremony that is performed behind the back of society and in front of a nature that never contemplates representation," he now adds that it is also historical. Much of *The Double Flame* traces that history, but *An Erotic Beyond*, aside from its brief discussion of Plato and Freud, leaves the historical to the longer book. The insistence here is that "eroticism is not a simple invention of sexuality: it is its metaphor." It is also language. No matter how outrageous the things done in its name, "action is the child of discourse." Though we know what Paz is reading, what he is imagining, what he sees before his eyes, what kind of stimulation erotic discourse must produce in him, he seldom quotes from Sade's descriptions of sexual acts. There is a strange reticence.

Only once, in 'In the Hospital of Incurables,' is there a comparatively modest citation from *Justine*. In a kind of joke comparing Freud's desire to provide "help" even in a world where a cure is impossible, he cites Sade's notion of human aid: "Some libertines act outrageously toward a young woman. The victim is at the point of succumbing. Realizing it, someone says: 'You are in need of help, madame', he said to Delbére. 'It is sperm that I need,' replied the Abbess."

'The Hospital of Incurables' is basically the world of Freud's 'Civilization and its Discontents.' While Freud, a man of science, finally became a philosopher and a tragic poet, Paz feels that Sade was a philosopher from the beginning: his aim is to aggressively forward his "idea of the human" and his work's main interest is "of a philosophical order." Still, the Abbess wants more sperm; the libertines ejaculate. Sade launches his weapons from his prison or asylum and they explode a century and more away, in Paz's own time. The coherence of Sade's vengeance on the world has the logic of a catapult. His work is "impeccable and implacable." In his attempt to "isolate and define the unique principle that is the source of eroticism and of life itself . . . it must appear as a plurality hostile to all unities." Before the Internet made magazines like *Playboy* and *Penthouse* superfluous, intellectuals used to buy them "for the literary interviews," or, in the case of *Playboy*, even for Hugh Hefner's "philosophy." The comparison is, of course, unfair, but I'm pretty sure that Paz first read Sade for the porn.

In 'The Innumerable Exception,' Paz investigates the nearly infinite plurality of instances in Sade: "with a cold-blooded patience that provokes both horror and admiration, Sade collects example after example. Each negates the one that preceded it and the one that follows." His kingdom, his theatre, may seem incomprehensible, but "it is still not unmeasurable; if we can't understand it, we can describe it." But our description "is condemned never to end" as "classification degenerates into enumeration." We are caught up in a delirium as nature destroys itself and creates itself. An obsession which looked at first to be linear turns out to be circular. We are dizzy with nausea discovering "the interdependence of pleasure and pain." Paz speaks of the Spanish monosyllable "ay!" when he examines the "cruel pleasures": "an exclamation of both pain and delight,[it] expresses this well: it is both a verbal arrow and the target it strikes." When Paz first read Sade in the Paris of the middle 1940s, he wrote the poem that is published as the first part of *An Erotic Beyond*. Addressed to Sade, it is enthusiastically Sadeian:

> Imagination is the spur of desire,
> its kingdom is as inexhaustible and infinite as boredom,
> its opposite and twin.
> Death or pleasure, flood or vomit,
> autumn like the fall of the days,
> volcano or sex,
> puff of wind, summer that sets fire to the harvests,
> stars or teeth,
> petrified hair of fear,
> red foam of desire, slaughter on the high seas,
> blue rocks of delirium,
> forms, images, bubbles, hunger to be,
> momentary eternities,
> excesses: your measure of man.
> Dare to do it:
> by the bow and the arrow, the string and the "ay!"
> Dream is explosive. Explode. Be a sun again.

Although it mainly comprises reprinted prose and verse, *An Erotic Beyond* can be read as new work as of 1986 and an example of Edward Said's preferred version of late style by virtue of its re-emergence and re-contextualization as a collage of pieces functioning as a strange codicil to *The Double Flame*, a testament that says something very different. The final part of the title essay, 'The Universal Dissolution,' makes one feel the power of what Paz calls "a *No* as enormous as St. Augustine's *Yes*." But, among the alternatives offered in the book, which position does "Octavio Paz" affirm? That of the circumspect and distinguished poet soon to win the Nobel Prize of the last essay that we have read first? Or that of the erotic old man leering through the eyes of the young disciple of André Breton whose poem is printed first and that we have read last? Both; either/or; neither/nor. That is the way with attraction-repulsion. Paz imagines Sade's libertine as the superman who must self-destruct in his repeating circle of contradictions. "He is the degree of incandescence that destructive energy must attain. The libertine vanishes. His annihilation proclaims the superiority of inanimate over living matter. A circular thought that tirelessly repeats itself and that, repeating itself, infinitely destroys itself. Its task is the annihilation of itself. The vital principle, the generating root of eroticism, is universal dissolution." This dark vision exercises a continuing fascination.

The very thing that is missing in Edward Said's posthumous and unfinished book on late style is any extended consideration of the erotic as perhaps the most volatile expression of the phenomenon that he found more compelling than anything else at the end of his life. He touches on the erotic in several pages on Proust and Genet, but it is generally a subject he seems disinclined to engage. The late erotic work of certain writers like the six I have discussed—and certainly also of painters; think of Picasso, for example, in contrast to Matisse—makes the case better than anything else for a style that involves, as Said says, "a nonharmonious, nonserene tension" manifesting intransigence . . . unresolved contradiction . . . [and] what happens if art does not abdicate its rights in favor of reality." Octavio Paz is a powerful figure with whom to conclude because he really has two late styles—the one investigated by Said, but also the one which he sets his preferred style against: the voice of Prospero instead of Lear, and the expression of harmony, reconciliation and serenity against . . . well, against *against.*

In *The Double Flame*, Paz establishes love as a far more radical term than eroticism alone, and the passionate embrace within a freely chosen union—the "free union" of Andre Breton's famous poem to his wife—as a "sensation of infinity" and the only momentary "victory over time" available to mortal persons, "a glimpse of the other side, of the there that is a here, where nothing changes and everything that is, truly is." His long history of ideas and expressions of love—from Plato to Provence, from Petrarch and Dante to Flaubert and Joyce—concludes with two enraged chapters, 'The City Square and the Bedroom' and 'Digressions on the Way to a Conclusion,' which lament the passing of a traditional notion of what constitutes a human person in the thought of prominent neurologists and computer scientists bent on "the mass production of androids." He calls in the end for a new Kant "to carry out the critique of scientific reason" and this rescue of "one of the great human inventions—love." In these chapters one certainly hears the voice of Said's "aging, disobliging, and even embarrassingly frank former colleague who, even though he has left one's circle, persists in making things hard for everyone." One may even begin to hear the "increasing sense of apartness and exile and anachronism" of Said's analysis of late style when Paz foresees "the twilight of love" in a technological barbarism, the expropriation of eroticism by the power of money, the crime of modern revolutionaries who reduce "the revolutionary spirit to its affective element" and of the liberal democracies where votes are cast in an atmosphere of "moral and spiritual misery" and "affective insensitivity." It is in the spirit of these chapters, perhaps, that Paz assembled his codicil and published *An Erotic Beyond*. "Dare to do it: / be the bow and the arrow, the string and the "ay!"/ Dream is explosive. Explode."

A Double Flame could have ended with these chapters, but it does not. The last chapter returns, by way of recapitulation, to the basic proposition of the book: that love is the intersection of accident and choice where erotic attraction leads to an embrace in which object becomes subject and yields a kind of poetic clairvoyance stimulated by the imagination and consummated in time which simultaneously creates and destroys the transfigured couple. Like Breton, Paz believes that love is finally more subversive than the nihilism of the libertine, and so, like his mentor, finally abandons Sade (where the erotic object is always and only that) as much as he does "the Communist determination to ignore private life and its passions" and "the old prohibitions of the Church and the bourgeoisie." Love, seeking nothing beyond itself, is not immune to rivalry, spite, fear, jealousy, or hatred. Catullus wrote: "I love and I hate." It can die before the body dies. Existing in time, even with its unique permission of "a glimpse of the other side," love is always tragic. It does not aspire either to Platonic or Tantric disincarnation. And it is always as much about death as it is about life. In the way that poetry eroticises language, love eroticises the world. Imagination "turns sex into ceremony and rite, language into rhythm and metaphor." Choice makes love exclusive; it has nothing to do with charity. Nor with politics. One of the most moving moments in the book occurs when Paz, a veteran of ideological wars, remembers Pasternak's *Zhivago* and its "description of the ecstasy of lovers isolated in a cabin on the steppe as men slit each other's throats over abstractions."

And so, a double flame: domination/submission, submission/ domination: a "transformation of the erotic object into a person immediately makes that person a subject who possesses free will." By way of the bridge of mutual desire the object becomes desiring subject and the subject becomes desired object . . . a knot made of two intertwined freedoms," bewitched, transubstantiated, subversive to any order but its own. Paz proclaims this again and again. But what about the old?

Wanting to hear Octavio Paz reading his poems, I recently dusted off an old video tape of a 1987 presentation in Chicago in which I was privileged to read the translations in the usual format of a bilingual poetry reading. I had never watched the tape before. 1987 was the year *A Tree Within* was published, which is the last book included in Weinberger's edition of the *Collected Poems*. Paz was then 73. It would be six more years until, in two months, he wrote *The Double Flame*, but perhaps he was already beginning to feel the "shame" and "remorse" to which I alluded earlier. Reading his poems, he seems mellow. The audience is large, and largely Latino. I can see my friend Anthony Kerrigan, the great Spanish language translator, beaming in the back of the hall. Since the book was still very new, I had been sent a copy by the organizers with a note saying only that Señor Paz wished to conclude with 'Carta de creencia,' from which I have quoted some lines suggesting that both *The Double Flame* and *An Erotic Beyond* might be read as competing glosses on that poem. Its conclusion, however, is unambiguously resigned, reconciled, yielding to time and not any longer seeking, as Said says, to demand its rights against the claims of reality. Reality brings death. Paz is fascinated and haunted by Quevedo's sonnet 'Amor constante más allá de la muerte' (Love faithful beyond death). He finds it wonderfully blasphemous and an uncanny manifestation of Blake's notion that "eternity is enamored of the works of time." The dust of two lovers is poured together, but attraction does not cease. The mixture is animate, the dead matter still full of longing: "Ash they'll be, yet still aware; / they will be dust, but dust in love."

Paz does not go that far in his own poem. He is still alive and still talking, though we have the sense that the last lines of his poem may be the last thing that he says. On the tape I hear him read the 'coda,' and then watch him look over at me. I read it in English:

Perhaps to love is to learn
To walk through this world.
To learn to be silent
Like the oak and the linden of the fable.
To learn to see.
Your glance scatters seeds.
It planted a tree.
        I talk
Because you shake its leaves.

The fable Paz has in mind is the Ovidian tale of Philemon and Baucis in Book VIII of the *Metamorphoses*. He discusses it at the very end of *The Double Flame*. Although he acknowledges that youth is the time of love, he also believes that old people fall in love, and, however ridiculous or pathetic they may appear to others, "eroticism is singular and finds no anomaly contemptible." When Baucis and Philemon see their hut transfigured into a temple as Jupiter destroys the impious Phrygians, the god asks the lovers he has spared for their greatest wish. They wish to become guardians and priests of the temple, but they wish for something else even more. They might have asked for immortality, but they do not. It is their place to surrender to time; they are old. "Because we have lived together since we were young, we wish to die together at the same moment," says Philemon. "May I not see the funeral pyre of Baucis nor she bury me." This wish Jupiter grants. "Worn out by time, each saw the other become covered with leaves. They said at the same moment, 'Farewell, my spouse,' and bark sealed their mouths. Philemon and Baucis had turned into trees: an oak and a linden."

Erotic love, Paz concludes, can not defeat death, even though it is "a wager against time and its accidents. Through love we catch a glimpse, in this life, of the other life. Not of eternal life, but, as I have tried to say in several poems, of pure vitality."

Amanece	Day breaks
en la noche del cuerpo	in the night of the body.
Allá adentro, en mi frente,	There within, inside my head,
el árbol habla.	the tree speaks.

Young Mendelson's Young Auden

[After the death of W. H. Auden in 1973 Edward Mendelson immediately emerged as the leading Auden scholar. As executor (appointed while still a student), bibliographer, editor, and critic, Mendelson has worked with devoted and indefatigable energy from 1973 onward. He has given us the later Auden's version of Auden by editing the Collected Poems *(first edition, 1976) in accordance with the poet's final instructions regarding inclusions, exclusions, and revisions. But also, by editing* The English Auden *(1977) he has made the poems from the 1930s accessible in their entirety and in their original versions.* Early Auden *(1981)—which was followed by a second volume on the later Auden in 1999—studies the poetry of the 1930s from a perspective that is largely sympathetic to the work that follows. Meanwhile, in Humphrey Carpenter's* W. H. Auden: A Biography *(1981) we still have the best biography we are likely to get unless Mendelson eventually decides to write one himself. Carpenter stresses in his book that Mendelson's cooperation and support make him virtually "an active collaborator." This essay is part of a review of several books on Auden that appeared in* The Southern Review *in 1983. It is placed here in part as one side of a dialogue with the essay on Carpenter's biography of Benjamin Britten, which follows. The best way to bring all of this up to date would be to take in a performance of Alan Bennett's* The Habit of Art, *in which Auden, Britten, and Carpenter all appear as characters. It should be directed by Edward Mendelson.]*

§

Early Auden is many things, and one of the most interesting (and sometimes irritating) of them is a sustained polemic against modernism, postmodernism, and structuralist and post-structuralist theories of literature that Mendelson takes to have their sources in Romanticism and ultimately in the vatic, as opposed to the civil, tradition of poetry. As such, *Early Auden* takes its place alongside such books as Robert Pinsky's *The Situation of Poetry* and Gerald Graff's *Literature Against Itself*, and assures for its author a place in an important debate well outside the limits of Auden criticism. It is almost as if Auden and Mendelson had made a deal: Mendelson would defend the later Auden while attacking much of the poet's early work in almost exactly the later Auden's own terms on condition that Auden would help Mendelson "get that lot" in Paris and at Yale.

Beginning in his Introduction with Homer's Achilles singing to himself in his tent, and ending 350 pages later with a resonant footnote on Heidegger, Mendelson makes Auden into the poet who successfully "challenged the vatic dynasty" and found a way out of his artist's isolation and "the imprisonment of a reflexive personal voice" into "the context of civil poetry that extended from Chaucer through Shakespeare, Dryden, and Pope." Arguing that the vatic and civil traditions "perennially divide literature" and have done so since before Aristophanes' Dionysus presided in the underworld over the contest between the civil Aeschylus and the vatic Euripides in *The Frogs,* Mendelson rejects an art of inner vision made of a deliberately invented poetic language which, in isolation from an audience and with the "breakdown in what might be called the symbolic contract" joining both poet and audience to the subject of the poet's poems, becomes virtually autistic. Instead of Achilles singing for himself alone, Mendelson wants a Phemius or a Demodocus singing "in service to their audience" and responding to "a specific occasion." Rather than the "extravagant modern fictions" of Euripides, Mendelson (like Dionysus) chooses the moral teaching and traditional gods of Aeschylus. Rejecting the "dislocation of language" required by Rimbaud, Pound, and the early Eliot, Mendelson looks to the formal conventions, meters, and parabolic didacticism in Hardy, Kipling, and Brecht. If later generations in the vatic/modernist line "understood the self to be constituted *by* language, and the wordless unconscious to be organized *like* a language" then "no community seemed possible except the centerless, contradictory, unstable community of language itself." Auden, whose own earliest poems brought him up against this dead end, abandoned a poetics "that would be occupied by an avant-garde thirty years afterwards."

When he turns to Auden's earliest poems, Mendelson appears to be well aware—which he is not always later on—of John Bayley's admonition that "critics of Auden have always appeared to find it difficult to talk about his poetry, as opposed to the borrowed materials in it, and its nominal preoccupations." Mendelson succeeds in large measure in talking about the poetry, about its essential nature. He finds that nature to be of an "intensely isolated and reflexive character" which has long "been obscured by the more public character of [Auden's] later work." Auden's early poetic language, a language theoretically justified in the early essay called 'Writing' with its "insistence on the antagonism and difference between language and its objects," is "nonsymbolic" and "noncommunicative." When gathered together in his first volume, however, the poems nonetheless seemed to suggest that they were "fragments of a larger whole," and yet, when they are read in sequence they do not "provide enough data to identify that whole."

By "noncommunicative language," I think Mendelson really means "nonparaphrasable language," for even when one reads the poems as he suggests—on balance, a thoroughly good idea—one finds that they communicate with extraordinary energy their rhythms, images, tones of voice, and fields of force—the unique, jagged, and mysterious linguistic universe that Auden's early style creates. They communicate their *sound* as they engage the silence around them. In the end, in order to make certain key points about the central early poems, Mendelson must contradict himself to a degree by attempting to paraphrase and interpret quasi-referentially what he takes to be reflexive and "noncommunicative," and then indeed there is some talk about the "borrowed materials" and "nominal preoccupations" that John Bayley speaks of, rather than about the processes that transfigure, say, the psychological, political, or moral content of such materials and preoccupations into the non-symbolic content of the poems themselves. Also, there is the problem of sequence and structure in Auden's individual volumes to be dealt with.

By arguing that the individual pieces in *Poems* are fragments which do not cohere to form a larger whole, Mendelson is absolved from having to make anything much of the sequence of poems that seemed, by sporting Roman numerals rather than titles, to insist on its sequential nature. His refusal to discern a pattern where he feels none exists recalls the early refusal by I. A. Richards to find "a coherent intellectual thread" upon which the items of 'The Waste Land' are strung, and a more recent refusal by Donald Davie to look any longer, as he had looked before, for either narrative or patterns of personae in 'Hugh Selwyn Mauberley.' Finding the chronological order of composition usually more instructive than the order of poems in Auden's published books, Mendelson not only organizes his own topical discussion to take up the poems chronologically, but also publishes the numbered sections of *Poems* (as well as the poems in *Look, Stranger!* and *Another Time)* in the order of composition in *The English Auden.*

This is my one strong objection to an otherwise fine editorial job. Although it is useful to know that the poem beginning "Will you turn a deaf ear" was written immediately before the one beginning "Sir, no man's enemy," it is disconcerting to find them numbered XXII and XXIII in *The English Auden* when they were numbered I and XXX in both the 1930 and 1933 editions of *Poems*. In *Early Auden,* Mendelson does find the first poem to be an appropriate opening for *Poems* since it is "a rebuke to Auden's literary and personal isolation" while the other is a formal, although unsatisfactory, conclusion in its "appeal to some external agency to impose from without the change he could not make from within." As he also finds the poem which Auden later entitled '1929' the "centerpiece" of both editions of *Poems,* we have at least a beginning, a middle, and an end.

When it comes to the chronology of composition, Mendelson is a master of the facts. With the executor's privileged inside view, he can tell us about Auden's development almost down to the hour, as the poet worked slowly or hectically through poetic contradictions and personal reversals of fortune toward what Mendelson regards to be the achieved, mature, civil poetry of the American period. Thus, Auden wrote one poem "within a few days or weeks of his first meeting with John Layard"; certain speculations had "outgrown the confidence in which they began a few months before"; "the dire sense of evolution's indifference . . . yielded, for a month or two, to a meliorative faith out of the woozier pages of Gerald Heard"; and so on. After an impressive and elaborate interpretation of *The Orators* made possible by the fact that this book, unlike *Poems,* actually does possess a key to its obscurities in the unlikely shape of John Layard's anthropological paper 'Malekula: Flying Tricksters, Ghosts, Gods, and Epileptics,' Mendelson traces the emergence of a poetry in search of an audience aiming at accessibility and communication where public references replace private ones, inner divisions take outward forms, and an attempt is made to overcome personal isolation and employ a language which can be shared and which can illuminate and affect "a physical and ethical world whose order and events are not only verbal ones." This development corresponds with a decision, in 1932, "to write larger and more coherently patterned poems . . . that recommend a large social unity by embodying a large poetic unity."

Since the publication of *The English Auden,* Mendelson's biographical approach to Auden has made the second poem from the sequence *Look, Stranger!* (which Auden later called 'A Summer Night') the most significant single poem of the English period if not the most significant one in the entire canon. He reads this piece in the context of Auden's 1964 essay contributed to Anne Fremantle's anthology, *The Protestant Mystics,* in which Auden describes "a fine summer night in June 1933" when he experienced what he calls "a vision of Agape." Mendelson's assumption, and the burden of his argument in the eighth chapter of *Early Auden* as well as in the introductions to *The English Auden* and Auden's *Selected Poems,* is that the poem and the relevant paragraphs in the essay are about the same experience. By the time 'A Summer Night' has received its fullest treatment in the present book, it appears almost as a sacred text, with lines numbered down the left margin as if it had just stepped out of *The Norton Anthology.* The chapter title, taken from the poem's second stanza, 'Lucky this Point,' reminds us at once of Mendelson's observation in his introduction to *Selected Poems* that "luck eventually acquired in Auden's vocabulary almost the force of religious 'grace'." In *The English Auden,* he says in a sentence what in *Early Auden* he expands upon and explains in the book's remaining two hundred pages: "It is possible to read almost all his work during the rest of the thirties as a series of attempts to learn—or to evade—the meaning of that summer night in June 1933."

While it is certain that 'A Summer Night' does indeed represent Auden's transitional style at its strongest, the poem has never seemed to me to be about the same experience treated in the 1964 essay, but always to have been more sympathetically than antithetically related to a range of poems that cluster around it in *Look, Stranger!,* some of which Mendelson, following the judgment of the later Auden, thoroughly regrets.

Although I have never experienced anything like a "vision of Agape," I have experienced the cozy sense of warm well-being—"lazy and ardent," as Barbara Everett calls it—that I think 'A Summer Night' half celebrates and half condemns, in terms of the class guilt attaching to privileged complicity in an unjust social system, where other people's suffering, even nearby and on an enormous scale, does not move us to act or change or even ask "what doubtful act allows / Our freedom."

Mendelson's reading of the poem (which does not, incidentally, ignore the guilt or complicity) is lovingly detailed, deeply committed to its central hypothesis, and almost convincing. It needs, however, to be absolutely convincing, given its utter centrality to the argument of *Early Auden* as a whole and the place 'A Summer Night' has assumed in Auden's work as a result of Mendelson's editions and introductions. 'A Summer Night' is one of the poems Auden extensively revised for inclusion in the 1945 *Collected Poems*. In the revised version, the concluding flood imagery is largely depoliticized by the loss of three stanzas, and the guilty recognition that a wall conceals the self-indulgence and petty charity of "Our metaphysical distress, / Our kindness to ten persons" from the wretchedness of gathering multitudes is lost. An attempt to clarify pronoun references and antecedents in the final stanzas alters the meaning of the poem while not entirely eliminating ambiguity. 'A Summer Night' seems to have given Auden more doubts than it does his critic as he attempted to save it from the wreck of *Look, Stranger!*

All other doubts which Auden eventually had about poems from this period, however, Mendelson shares. Taking Auden more or less at his word that he never "attempted to revise [his] former thoughts or feelings, only the language in which they were first expressed," Mendelson finds that, when Auden writes badly in the mid to late 1930s, "it is generally a sign that he cannot make himself believe what he is making himself say." As a result of this, a later stylistic revision is likely also to be an ideological revision. The chief indication of a "dishonest poem"—a poem that "expresses beliefs which the author never entertained"—is found to be significant internal contradiction. Auden's attempt "to learn—or to evade—the meaning of that summer night in June 1933" involved, according to Mendelson, five essential "projects" which, after the momentary triumph of a single poem, sought permanently to resolve his divisive loneliness and overcome the frontier between himself and the world of others through a language now committed to accessibility and reference. The problem is that the new, accessible language often betrayed Auden into what he later took to be rhetorical dishonesty and what, revealed in its contradictions, Mendelson resoundingly condemns. These were the projects which occupied Auden until his departure for America in 1939: *"Erotic—* joining two worlds through sexual love and personal growth;

Redemptive—saving mankind from its divisions by personal example and direct cure; *Didactic*—teaching an audience, through parables, to unlearn hatred and learn love; *World-Historical*—allowing the problem to be solved by determined forces working on an international scale; and *Escapist*—abandoning the problem altogether and finding comfort on an island of refuge."

Behind the incidental contradictions in many of the best-known poems of this period lies the fundamental one, which Mendelson again attributes to Auden's inability to make a clean break with modernist poetics. Now determined to write "in a tradition that engaged the problems of choice and action, and performed a didactic function in society," the poet continued to apply "the formal and rhetorical methods of a tradition that claimed to be independent of existing society [and] superior to its vulgar concerns." Like the critical methods of the schools Mendelson dislikes—formalist, structuralist, deconstructive, and so on—his own approach "thrives on the internal contradictions of the texts," even though its ultimate aim is to bring us—in another book— before poems in which the techniques of modernism are no longer adapted "to contexts unsuited for them."

As contradictions are revealed and rhetorics explained, Mendelson's moral assessment of particular poems (as well as certain key essays) becomes more pronounced than it was in the first half of the book. Sometimes it is leveled with a vehemence exceeding Auden's own in later years. Auden was "violating his gifts . . . Perhaps at moments he convinced himself he actually believed this wretched stuff . . . All that is missing is the vibrato of massed violins . . . The poem takes so much pleasure in its witty images of crisis that it manages to avoid saying what is to be done . . . The new final stanza is the crudest and clearest example of Auden's historical double-think . . . This contemptible idea [is] brought into the poem for the sake of a paradox . . . This inept stanza says that what the poet's voice can do . . . is proclaim that individual acts and lies make no difference."

There are, to my mind, two rather problematic chapters and two especially successful ones in the second half of *English Auden*. The particular successes are Mendelson's treatment of Auden's love poems of the middle 1930s discussed in chapter X which, together, make up the first of those five "projects" following on the heels of 'A

Summer Night'; and his treatment of *Spain* and 'September 1, 1939' in chapter XIV which, along with a few related poems, make up the fourth such "project"—"project," by the way, being the one annoying term Mendelson borrows from his adversaries among the currently fashionable schools of criticism. Chapter X includes persuasive readings of Auden's best love poems of the period—'A Bride in the Thirties,' 'Lullaby,' the ballad 'As I walked out one evening'—and a fascinating if overconfident reading of 'Our Hunting Fathers' which, like the reading of 'A Summer Night,' is almost, but not quite, convincing.

Dating the love poems with his usual precision from the "vision of Agape" in 1933—"by the following spring [it had] altogether faded"; "six months had passed since Auden's vision of Agape," and so on—Mendelson sees the Audenesque Eros of the period offering "a brief refuge from political chaos" but "giving no relief from the difficulties of choice." The major poems, which are really *about* choice, are seen to be largely successful in kind with their "double subject of sexual success and emotional failure." Mendelson's treatment in chapter XIV of Auden's briefly held belief in a determined and purposeful History, along with the collapse of the notion in the self-contradictions of 'Spain,' is masterful. He claims persuasively that there are two sustained and mutually exclusive arguments in 'Spain,' one expository (insisting on human freedom and human choice), and the other figurative (suggesting that the central actions of the volunteers in Spain are determined rather than willed); and that, when Auden came to revise the poem, all of his changes tried to rid it of the figurative argument for a determined history. In the process, he also provides the best answer I have ever seen to George Orwell's famous objection to the poem.

Less successful on the whole, but interestingly problematic, is Mendelson's treatment of Auden's third "project," the one he calls "Redemptive," in chapter XI. My doubts here turn on the use made of an unpublished poem in regular unrhymed triplets in which Auden evidently indulges certain messianic temptations and redemptive ambitions. Written just before Poem XVII from *Look, Stranger*—which Auden later called 'The Malverns' and eventually eliminated from the canon—the poem in triplets casts the poet in the role of prophet and aims to warn and to save an entire generation. Six stanzas from the unpublished poem became that part of 'The Malverns' beginning "And out of the turf the bones of the war continue," while other parts found their way into yet another unpublished poem in triplets. Transcriptions of both unpublished poems finally ended up in Michael Ransom's "most self-important and sometimes hysterical . . . speeches" in *The Ascent of F-6*, which is pretty much where Mendelson thinks they belong.

Mendelson often makes use of unpublished manuscripts and drafts in his book, and there are moments when one feels that Auden should have left instructions that these, rather than his letters, be destroyed after his death. Early revisionary processes, which involve these drafts, are usually seen, unlike the later revisions, as a sign of confusion and contradiction rather than clarification. In the case of the messianic triplets and 'The Malverns,' Mendelson feels 'The Malverns' to be virtually contaminated by the presence of borrowed material. Monroe Spears has written of J. W. Beach's shock at Auden's "use of the same passage in different contexts." Mendelson could hardly be more different as a critic from the literal-minded Beach, and his rather melodramatic revelation about the source of these borrowed stanzas, like his later revelation that Auden cribbed passages in *The Dog Beneath the Skin* from Anthony Collett's *The Changing Face of England*, sounds somewhat disingenuous. 'The Malverns' does not say the same thing the poem in triplets says, even though it manages to incorporate six of its stanzas; and Auden, in his published work, never took on the role of messianic poet/prophet/savior. But Mendelson's real interest is in the unpublished poem itself, and for now predictable reasons: "Having begun with the purpose of saving his generation, Auden ended by writing a poem concerned reflexively with its own composition, and ultimately with preventing itself from being written."

Of the two remaining "projects,"—the "Didactic" and the "Escapist"—Mendelson's treatment of the "Didactic" is, I think, the less engaging mainly because he is obliged to provide a narrative account of theatrical and film history during the 1930s in which he does not appear to be very interested. Humphrey Carpenter's version of Auden's involvement in the hectic activities of Rupert Doone's Group Theatre and John Grierson's GPO Film Unit is a good deal livelier. Mendelson's discussion of the plays and films—poetic drama being Auden's main didactic vehicle—is chiefly important for what it has to say about *The Ascent of F-6*. Although Christopher Isherwood is given all due credit for his contributions to three of the plays—and also chided for being so silly as to think the subject of *F-6* was really T. E. Lawrence—Benjamin Britten's work on two of them is only just acknowledged. Mendelson feels that Auden solved more of the problems of writing modern poetic drama than anyone but Brecht, although the plays are seen to be full of imperfections. *The Ascent of F-6* is taken to be the appropriate focus of our attention among the plays and films for two related reasons, both of which give it the same kind of biographical prominence Mendelson attributes to 'A Summer Night.' As he has told us twice before in his introductions to *The English Auden* and *Selected Poems,* Mendelson takes the creation of Michael Ransom to be a kind of simultaneous externalization and exorcism of Auden's secret (because unpublished) self-deluding messianic fantasies. "The implied equation between Ransom the redemptive climber and Auden the redemptive poet would have been entirely lost on the play's audience," but there it was nonetheless. Mendelson explains that Auden understood for the first time that he would have to leave England for good while he was at work on this play. This is the second reason for its particular significance. Read with a full knowledge of Auden's subsequent career, *F-6* becomes "a parable of the fate Auden . . . avoided, the fate of the indifferent redeemer destroyed by a public role his private terrors tempted him to accept." (Humphrey Carpenter quotes from the interview, which Mendelson only refers to regarding this sudden realization. The fate Auden was *conscious* of trying to avoid was not the redeemer's: "I knew that if I stayed [in England] I would inevitably become a member of the British establishment.")

Perhaps my final hesitation about this important study is suggested by the phrase "with the full knowledge of Auden's subsequent career." As we read Mendelson's excellent concluding chapter which treats the final "project" in terms of the island imagery which replaced the border "as Auden's geographical sign of entrapment and enclosure," we begin to wonder if Mendelson hasn't himself been tempted by a characteristic of the modernism which he rejects—I mean its particular rage for order, its obsession with pattern, its view of things from a very high altitude, its "hawk's vision," in fact. The modernist critic, perhaps a good deal more conspicuously than the modernist poet, is inclined to impose a grid on the material he studies—and is attacked, in fact, by the postmodernist critic for doing so. Everything must cohere; nothing can be out of place; the territory is mapped; and the mapmaker, like Stephen Dedalus' dramatic artist, sits above it all paring his nails. An *oeuvre* is somehow already read, already understood, rather than encountered or engaged in the critical prose. There are moments when I think the structure of this book is much too neat to accommodate the chaotically explosive world of Auden's early poetry. Mendelson criticizes a form that "can accommodate *all* experience within itself, and can do so on its own formal and aesthetic terms." He criticizes "content ruled by pattern." And yet reading and re-reading his book gives me the sense that Mendelson himself is guilty of allowing pattern to rule content. The desire for coherence always threatens to take over, and it makes one worry about various fixed points always already on the map—especially the summer night and the decision that came with the composition of *The Ascent of F-6*.

The present volume moves toward its conclusion with a deeply appreciative reading of *In Time of War*, the sonnet sequence, which Mendelson feels to be "Auden's most profound and audacious poem of the 1930s," and "perhaps the greatest English poem of the decade." It recovers, in his view, much of the ground lost since 'A Summer Night' and suggests that Auden is now ready to learn, rather than evade, its meaning. The discovery already alluded to in Sonnet XXVI that will "release him from his private island" is, not surprisingly, "the amazed discovery of love's consistency and strength," and the sequence as a whole which, like 'Spain,' surveys all of human history, makes a "first gesture toward finding the ground of ethics in religion." In his discussion of what he takes to be the central sonnet (XIV), Mendelson at last concludes his debate with modernism, postmodernism and "certain schools of literary theory" in a lengthy footnote. Auden, like Heidegger, makes use of Hölderlin's line *"dichterisch, wohnet der Mensch auf dieser Erde."* But, while Heidegger (inspiring those certain schools) uses the line to argue that "Being itself is founded by poetic language, with the implication that there can be no absolutes beyond the fiats of verbal imagination," Auden uses it "to expose the corruption of any system of thought that regards the ethically neutral powers of language or nature as the measure of all things."

The mountains cannot judge us when we lie;
We dwell upon the earth; the earth obeys
The intelligent and evil till they die.

For the rest, Mendelson praises the poems Auden wrote in Brussels immediately before his departure for America as precursors of the later work, of the mature orientation and style. In 'Musée des Beaux Arts' in particular, Auden gives notice that he has begun not only "to accept in himself the dull ordinariness of suffering," but also "responsibility for others' suffering" and, in following Breughel's example, he refuses to be awed by the "grand rhetoric of History" or "appeals to the autonomy of art." This, according to Mendelson, was to the bafflement of critics— the ones Mendelson so dislikes—"who prefer bright colors and loud noises."

The Haunting of Benjamin Britten
(Reflections on Humphrey Carpenter's *Benjamin Britten: A Biography*)

[A good many years ago I reviewed Humphrey Carpenter's biography of W.H. Auden in The Southern Review *(Winter 1983), along with two books treating Benjamin Britten's collaborative work with Auden and Ronald Duncan—Donald Mitchell's* Britten and Auden in the Thirties *and Duncan's autobiographical* Working With Britten. *Because Carpenter's subsequent biography of Britten draws both on his own earlier study of Auden as well as on the Mitchell and Duncan volumes, I needed to repeat a few things I had said more than a decade before. Most of all, because Carpenter makes of the Auden letter which I quoted from Mitchell's notes the key to understanding Britten's life and work, I needed to quote and comment on that strange and prophetic document once more. The situation is still the same as I print these reflections for the first time in a book.]*

§

During the comparatively brief phase of their collaborative work, W.H. Auden challenged and dominated Benjamin Britten like no one else in his life. Having followed Auden to America in 1939, Britten and Peter Pears decided in 1941 to return to England, a decision which Auden regretted and which led him to write in his characteristically intimidating way about the dangers he foresaw for his friend. "Goodness and Beauty," he began, "are the results of a perfect balance between Order and Chaos, Bohemianism and Bourgeois Convention. Bohemian chaos alone ends in a mad jumble of beautiful scraps; Bourgeois convention alone ends in large unfeeling corpses." It becomes clear that Auden is really talking about the artist's need to locate and release potentially destructive energies in himself while simultaneously controlling, making intelligible, and indeed domesticating them through the imposition of form.

> Every artist except the supreme masters has a bias one way or the other. The best pair of opposites I can think of in music are Wagner and Strauss. (Technical skill always comes from the bourgeois side of one's nature.)
> For middle-class Englishmen like you and me, the danger is of course the second. Your attraction to thin-as-a-board juveniles, i.e. to the sexless and innocent, is a symptom of this.

167

And I am certain too that it is your denial and evasion of the demands of disorder that is responsible for your attacks of ill-health, i.e. sickness is your substitute for the Bohemian.

Wherever you go you are and probably always will be surrounded by people who adore you, nurse you, and praise everything you do, e.g. Elisabeth, Peter (Please show this to P to whom all this is also addressed). Up to a certain point this is fine for you, but beware. You see, Bengy dear, you are always tempted to make things too easy for yourself in this way, i.e. to build yourself a warm nest of love (of course when you get it, you find it a little stifling) by playing the lovable talented little boy.

If you are really to develop to your full stature, you will have, I think, to suffer, and make others suffer, in ways which are totally strange to you at present, and against every conscious value that you have; i.e. you will have to be able to say what you never have had the right to say—God, I'm a shit.

Carpenter's long examination of the life and work plays variations on this letter again and again for more than six hundred pages. Britten's prodigious technical skill—the speed, ease, and complexity of his composition rival that of Mozart—which produces work after work on the single obsessive theme of lost innocence; his negotiations with "the demands of disorder" which lead him to build around himself a protective and nurturing community at Aldeburgh—his Bayreuth on the Suffolk coast—while suffering out a series of illnesses and repressed longings for young boys finding oblique or direct expression in his operas from *Peter Grimes* to *Death in Venice*; his development from charming provincial prodigy—a curly-haired Lowestoft teenager who had composed from the time he first sat down at the family piano—to the tormented and dying Lord Britten whose "full stature" is reached in part by "making others suffer"—these are the stories Carpenter has to tell. Many works, especially the operas, are weighed on the Audenesque balance—this one tending to bourgeois order, that one to bohemian chaos. And Auden himself, as Britten once said, is in all of them.

If Britten's sense of personal guilt was necessary for the full musical realization of his theme of lost innocence, Auden, Carpenter insists, predicted the nature of his mature work with the last full text he provided for his friend, 'Hymn to St. Cecilia,' arguing (as Carpenter has it) "that loss of innocence must be celebrated, must itself become the subject of music":

> O dear white children casual as birds
> Playing among the ruined languages,
> So small beside their large confusing words,
> So gay against the greater silences
> Of dreadful things you did: O hang the head,
> Impetuous child with the tremendous brain . . .
>
> O weep, child, weep, O weep away the stain
> That what has been may never be again,
> O bless the freedom that you never chose,
> O wear your tribulation like a rose.

These lines, written for the composer actually born on St. Cecilia's Day, were set for unaccompanied choir on board the ship returning him to England in 1942. They anticipate with great accuracy just what it was that Britten's work would do. But if Britten was able in his music to celebrate the loss of innocence and acknowledge darkness or the demands of disorder by setting words, writing operas, introducing the impurities of "ruined languages" into what might otherwise be pure articulations of sound, in his life he sought to be a kind of Peter Pan, to live as only music—pure and utterly gratuitous—can live:

> I cannot grow;
> I have no shadow
> To run away from,
> I only play
>
> I cannot err;
> There is no creature
> Whom I belong to,
> Whom I could wrong.

This middle section of Auden's 'Hymn' describes pure music, not human life. Britten was such a profoundly musical being that to many he appeared almost to embody it, to be music. But, unlike music, he had to grow; he had a shadow that darkened and lengthened; he could err; there was a creature to whom he belonged and many he could wrong. He played beautifully, but he played in a fallen world of ruined languages, confusing words, great silences and dreadful acts where, as Cecilia says in her italicized response to Auden's supplicant in the final section of his 'Hymn,' lost innocence may even wish its lover dead.

When I first reviewed the Carpenter, Mitchell, and Duncan books, I was brought up short by Duncan's claim in his memoir that he was "not fooled by Britten's diffidence, knowing his ruthless ambition; nor impressed by his gentleness, having observed his cruelty. If he embraced anybody, it was to strangle them eventually . . . No man had more charm . . . but behind the mask was another person, a sadist, psychologically crippled and bent." I wondered at the time, and I asked, if Duncan's account could possibly be true and accurate; it seemed more like the bitter and jealous exaggeration of a librettist suddenly replaced by Eric Crozier. But similar accounts of Britten's humanly crippling yet musically enabling contradictions multiply in Carpenter's biography to the extent that one has no alternative but to take Duncan at his word, to realize that Britten earned the dubious right to say, as Auden hoped he might, "God, I'm a shit."

II

All this makes Carpenter's biography very painful reading. One would rather hear the music itself, take out all the old recordings. Doing so, however, it becomes difficult after reading Carpenter to hear the work the way one did before; everything seems to be autobiography, even an opera about Queen Elizabeth.

Carpenter has been criticized for musically unsophisticated and essentially literary readings of Britten's works, but these works, many of them, belong to literature as well as music—they are settings, in several languages, of some of our greatest poetry and treatments of stories, myths and liturgies that define our culture. It is for this reason that Britten, above all other British composers, is of importance to literary as well as musical history and why his biography demands consideration by literary scholars. But it is true that Carpenter, who can effectively quote from poetry to demonstrate a thesis in his biographies of Auden and Pound, often attempts to do the same in his biography of Britten, and never once reproduces a passage from a score. Instead, substituting a rudimentary description and analysis of the music which he hopes will be accessible to laymen, he risks the charges of reductiveness and superficiality brought against him by reviewers like Robin Holloway and Nicholas Spice, who feel, as the latter wrote in the *London Review of Books*, that insofar as Carpenter analyzes the music at all, he treats it "as just text in another form—in short, as code." Although it is clearly difficult to discuss music, as Spice says, "in terms of texts and narratives without reducing [it] to crude and schematic verbal paraphrases," Carpenter takes his risks on behalf of the general audience for whom his book is written. How many readers would be able, even with expert guidance, to read a passage—to hear a passage—from a Britten score? Besides, many books on Britten of great musicological sophistication already exist, and the expert or musician will want to seek them out. I don't myself feel that Carpenter damages the music by reading it, through the lens of the texts it often sets, as autobiography. He does, however, make us conscious of uncomfortable dimensions in it which, knowing little of Britten's life, we may never have considered.

Before Auden, the chief influences on Britten's life were clearly his mother, the sound of the sea breaking on the beach at Lowestoft, and the music, example, and teaching of Frank Bridge. Mrs. Britten provided the first "warm nest of love," adored Britten, nursed him, sang with him, and praised everything he did—which included, by the age of fourteen, twelve piano sonatas, six string quartets, pieces for violin, viola and cello, a tone poem, a symphony, an oratorio, and many songs. Early on, she conceived the notion that Britten would be the fourth "B," after Bach, Beethoven, and Brahms. A fifth "B," Bridge, provided the training in technique and attention to sincerity, clarity, and professionalism which Britten later failed to find at the Royal College of Music. By the time he got there, he was rapidly advancing beyond the abilities of his teachers. Bridge's *The Sea* echoed the sound which Britten had heard from birth on the Suffolk coast, introduced him to modern music, and provided a source for the brilliant 'Sea Interludes' in *Peter Grimes*. In an early draft of the *Grimes* libretto, Montague Slater wrote: "I have a father in the sea / Scolding from the tides . . ." Britten's actual father, a dentist, remained rather remote and slightly sinister; Bridge scolded and encouraged, and Mrs. Britten cheered, comforted and, perhaps, made the nest of love, in Auden's terms, "a little stifling." But the early years seem to have been remembered as a time, as Hardy wrote in the poem which Britten set last in *Winter Words*, of "primal rightness . . . when all went well."

If there was a violation of the rightness and innocence of Britten's early life, it was a profound one. Carpenter makes much of Eric Crozier's claim that Britten once told him "he had been raped by a master at school," a version of which story Beata Mayer remembers more generally from long talks during Britten's illness and fever at her mother's home in 1940 as "a traumatic sexual experience" of some kind. Donald Mitchell wonders if Britten was "fantasizing" when he told the story, and warns against "building some enormous superstructure of speculation" on it. "We shall never know," he says, "what he meant by 'rape', if he used the word. Nor can we summon back to life the inflection of tone or voice in which the claim was uttered." After investigating all of the possible circumstances at South Lodge School in which such an event might have occurred, Carpenter appears, in the chapter where he first brings it up, to drop the idea as perhaps "fantasy sparked off while [Britten's] imagination was at work on his operas." However, it is a hypothesis to which he returns from time to time in a tentative way throughout the book, particularly when Britten's homosexuality is at issue.

Whether the incident actually occurred or not—and it seems to me unlikely on the evidence provided in Carpenter's text—Britten was clearly behaving like a sexually repressed, rather than a sexually traumatized, young man when he met Auden. Determined to "bring him out," to make Britten admit his homosexuality and "throw aside all repression," Auden wrote 'Underneath the Abject Willow,' with its invitation to "Walk then, come / no longer numb / into your satisfaction." This is a poem which Donald Mitchell feels Britten "parried," as it were, in his setting of it "as a kind of brisk—jaunty, even—impersonal and highly mannered polka-like dance."

Carpenter follows the strange dancing with Auden all the way from *Our Hunting Fathers,* a major but still infrequently performed song cycle from 1936 with texts either written or chosen by Auden; collaborations on plays and films before the sojourn to America; *Paul Bunyan,* a musical theatre piece which seems part Broadway, part Kurt Weill, and part anticipation of the proper operas that would come; to Auden's place, as Carpenter would have it, in most of the operas themselves either in their treatment of the tension between "Bohemian Chaos" and "Bourgeois Order," or in some version or other of a more specific presence—as The Tempter, for example, in *The Prodigal Son*, whose injunction to the son to "Act out your desires" echoes "Underneath the Abject Willow," or in Owen Wingrave which concludes "as if Auden had suddenly returned and had again thrown down his 1942 gauntlet" when Kate accuses Owen of cowardice and "challenges him to spend the night in the haunted room" where he dies. There were not to be many polkas. Donald Mitchell finds as early as 'The Dance of Death' in *Our Hunting Fathers* "a ferocious transformation of music hitherto associated with the hunt" brought to "the very brink of chaos and disintegration."

The break with Auden, when it came, was permanent. Perhaps Britten sensed that further collaboration would be a kind of dance of death; in any case, he required more compliant librettists. He had also, shortly before his mother's death, met Peter Pears, thus beginning one of the most remarkable collaborations in the history of music.

Carpenter says that Pears' singing voice had an uncanny resemblance to Mrs. Britten's. If this is so, it only reinforces what is obvious—that Pears took over the job of providing "the warm nest of love," that he presided at the festivals of adoration, nurture, and praise. In Auden's terms, at any rate. But Pears also seems to have seen that Britten would not "develop to his full stature" if he remained under the intellectual and emotional domination of Auden, whom he thought of as a kind of bully. After three years in America where Britten and Pears had gone at the outbreak of World War II in part for professional reasons— Britten felt he might have a bright future in the country—and in part because they were conscientious objectors, they returned with a suitcase full of compositions and plans for *Peter Grimes*, the opera that would establish both of them as permanent features on the British cultural map. Although often unhappy and ill in America, Britten nonetheless managed to write a good deal of music, including *Les Illuminations*, *Sinfonia da Requiem*, and the first string quartet. He also composed the first of endless pieces specifically for Pears, *Seven Sonnets of Michelangelo*, which, Carpenter says, has "been taken as a declaration of love between composer and singer" even though "its storyline portrays a restless and largely unsatisfied desire."

While they were still in America, Auden referred to Britten and Pears as "a happily married couple," and so they appeared to be to most people who knew them. But both were also clearly attracted to young boys, and in Britten's case even a repressed pedophilia was a source of terrible anxiety and guilt. Those "thin-as-a-board juveniles" of whom Auden wrote moved him in a way that was neither "sexless" nor "innocent," and had nothing to do with any evasion of "the demands of disorder." Quite the contrary, the attraction was the greatest temptation in Britten's life to surrender to disorder, to bohemian chaos. "Chaos and sickness," Aschenbach mutters to himself in Myfanwy Piper's libretto for *Death in Venice*, and then to Tadzio: "What if all were dead / and only we two left alive?" Ronald Duncan, Norman Del Mar, and Donald Mitchell even feel that Britten was a reluctant homosexual in adult relationships, and Duncan says he was "a man in flight from himself, who often punished others for the sin he felt he'd committed himself. He was a man on the rack."

After Britten's death, Pears maintained that "Ben never regarded his own passionate feelings . . . as anything but good, natural, and profoundly creative." The evidence, however, seems to suggest that Pears' account of Britten's sexuality comes closer to describing his own relaxed and uninhibited feelings than it does those of the composer. But even if Duncan's extreme account is accurate and Britten was "a man on the rack" who felt that his most secret and powerful longings were "sinful," there is no doubt that his emotions were, in Pears' terms, "profoundly creative." He understood from the inside both innocence and the desire to destroy it, and was therefore able to embody musically both a Billy Budd and a Claggert, both a Miles and a Quint. Especially in *The Turn of the Screw* is the temptation to surrender to "bohemian chaos" expressed at its most seductive possible pitch. In Quint's melismas on the single syllable of Miles' name, we hear the uncanny voice of an unfulfilled desire.

Carpenter sees the *Serenade* for tenor, horn and strings, with its setting of Blake's 'The Sick Rose,' as a pivotal work. "Nowhere else," he says, "had Britten conveyed 'the sense of sin' so graphically." Not only the setting of Blake, but also that of the fifteenth century 'Lyke Wake Dirge' that follows it as a kind of *dies irae* in which "the tenor's grotesque sweeps up the octave [suggest] mortal terror of judgement," are written, Carpenter feels, directly out of an experience of "dark, secret love" which terrified the composer even as it attracted him. But if *Serenade* prefigured certain aspects of *Peter Grimes*, it is also clearer in its implications.

Grimes has fascinated and puzzled critics ever since its premier. Is Grimes a psychopath, a poet, a pedophile, a visionary, or some combination of these? Is he utterly at odds with his community, or does he seek to become a part of it? Is he in love with Ellen Orford, his apprentice, or the sea? Britten and Pears had read an essay by E. M. Forster on George Crabbe's 'Peter Grimes' while still in America, and the poem, the essay, and the notion that there might be an opera were factors in the decision to return to England. *Grimes* is set in Aldeburgh, a small town on the Suffolk coast near Britten's native Lowestoft, and the future home of his now-famous music festival. Was *Grimes* to represent a homecoming, or the impossibility of ever being at home in the world—even in one's native place? It is also worth remembering that the war had just ended, and that Britten and Pears were well known as conscientious objectors. Edmund Wilson, who attended an early performance, wrote that "at first you think that Peter Grimes is Germany. But, by the time you are done with the opera . . . you have decided that Peter Grimes is the whole of bombing, mining, machine-gunning, ambushing humanity which talks about a guaranteed standard of living yet does nothing but wreck its own works, degrade or pervert its own moral life and reduce itself to starvation."

There are two famous tenors, not just one, who have made the part of Grimes their own—Peter Pears and Jon Vickers. Their interpretations are very different. Pears, who had a hand in writing the libretto and whose early notes on the plot included lines that were never set for Grimes to sing to his apprentice—"you are sweet, young . . . you must love me"—plays the fisherman, in Pears' own words, "as an ordinary weak person who, being at odds with the society in which he finds himself, tries to overcome it and, in doing so, offends against the conventional code, is classed by society as a criminal, and destroyed as such." Edmund Wilson's remark about "a guaranteed standard of living" is more than a bleak post-war jest, for Grimes is also motivated, and encouraged by Ellen Orford, to make himself respectable, make money, become acceptable to the Borough, and set up in a household. Peter Conrad has deprecated Pears' Grimes as "an ineffectual dreamer, beseeching the pity of his fellows" in order to praise Jon Vickers' "barnacled prophet, a pathological martyr who defies the community rather than imploring its aid." Interestingly, Vickers has said that he could play the "totally symbolic" figure of Grimes "as a Jew," or "paint his face black and put him in white society," but that he could not play Grimes as a homosexual because this "reduces him to a man in a situation with a problem." But that problem was part of Britten's "situation" as he moved back to Grimes' own Suffolk, living first in Snape and later in Aldeburgh itself, intending to celebrate a homecoming with his first opera, but also, as Conrad feels, "confirming an outlawry from which he [was] seeking to be pardoned." According to English law before 1967, Britten was, of course, a criminal. Living as an open, if discreet and largely domestic-minded homosexual, he could perfectly well have been prosecuted.

After the next two operas, *The Rape of Lucrecia* and *Albert Herring*, were written and taken on tour, Britten and Pears conceived the idea of creating the festival in Aldeburgh. Not only did Britten establish a household with Pears where even Ellen Orford might have been a contented guest, but from this point on Aldeburgh would also be his Music Center, the place where a man in many ways at odds with society—as pacifist, homosexual, and obsessive artist—would attempt to integrate himself and his work by "imploring aid" and seeking to "make himself acceptable" to his community, but also by challenging that community to pardon outlawry by, as it were, legalizing and licensing its fullest artistic expression. It is a strange paradox; it is as if Peter Grimes had been elected mayor.

The festival provides a setting in which Carpenter can portray, over the years, the actions and attitudes of those two sides of Britten one might call "Good Ben" and "Bad Ben." "Good Ben" charmed and delighted everyone, especially in the early years of the festival, and some who knew him well—Janet Baker and Mstislav Rostropovich, for example—seem only to have seen this side of him. "Bad Ben," on the other hand, appeared, in Auden's terms, determined "to make others suffer." Joan Cross, an early colleague says, "He just used people, and he finished with them, and that was that." Stephen Reiss, perhaps Britten's most conspicuous victim, felt that Britten's cruelty was linked in some way to sexual frustration.

The early days of the Aldeburgh festival must have been remarkable. I began to attend it myself only in the 1960s after the concert hall had been built at the Snape Maltings, but even then one got a sense of what the initial excitement, informality, and charm of it all must have been like at performances that were still being given in the old Jubilee Hall and the local churches. Britten, of course, was not only a director of the festival but an active participant. He made much of his impact as a performer and conductor, and both his virtuoso skills as Pears' accompanist and his brilliant conducting of his own and other composers' works were always part of the Aldeburgh experience. The local community—and later on a range of wealthy patrons—supported and attended some events that were easy to understand and aimed at giving listeners uncomplicated musical pleasures, but also new and demanding works by Britten himself and other contemporaries. Britten, Pears, and the musicians who came to perform were accessible and eager to please, and by all accounts people experienced something magical in Britten's presence. Janet Baker talks about a sensation "almost like [that] of being in love," and Robert Tear remembers "those times when Ben was so wonderfully charming that when he spoke to me the world seemed to stop." And it was not only fellow musicians like Baker and Tear who felt this; people who were employed by Britten, ordinary Aldeburgh residents, children, even fishermen like his friend Billy Burrell report, in the early days, similar reactions.

Carpenter says that those who worked with Britten thought that a change in the nature of the festival, and perhaps in Britten himself, could be felt from about 1953, which was the year in which *Gloriana* was first performed. Although Carpenter's reading of that opera as a "continuing private debate, an examination of the choices an artist has to make . . . and a self-portrait and examination of the stresses experienced by a public figure such as [Britten] had now become" seems at first a bit far-fetched for a story, after all, about Elizabeth and Essex, such an interpretation should not be dismissed out of hand. Janet Baker, for all her affection for Britten, says that she could not ever be put entirely at her ease, that "being with Britten was a bit like being with the Queen"; and Stephen Reiss, speaking of his forced resignation as Aldeburgh Festival general manager in 1971 remarks chillingly "that had it been in Elizabethan times, he would quite happily have had me murdered."

The catalogue of cruelties committed by "Bad Ben" while "Good Ben" continued doing his best to compose, perform, conduct, and be a responsible citizen rather than an autocratic monarch is depressingly long. To begin with, his musical standards were extremely high and he would frequently find that a colleague, often one who had been a close friend, was no longer meeting them. Musicians were dismissed, soloists not invited back, former protégés dropped without a word, singers cut dead in the street, an ailing member of the orchestra verbally abused from the podium. Librettists, in particular, had a rough time—Auden, Montague Slater, Ronald Duncan, Eric Crozier, E. M. Forster, and William Plomer all being replaced in their turn with little thanks and no warning. In a book on Britten carefully supervised by the composer himself, Imogen Holst omits any reference at all to Slater, Duncan, or Crozier. Crozier, not only a librettist, but a founding father of both the English Opera Group and the Aldeburgh Festival, felt that Britten always had "a particular favorite upon whom he would lavish affection, while foreseeing with a grim kind of pleasure the day when that special friend would be cast off." Britten told Crozier that Montague Slater was "one of [his] corpses," adding that Crozier himself would "be one, too, one day." Even Auden, to the end of his life, referred to Britten's break with him as "a permanent grief."

Instead of the sense of generous inclusion that most people appeared to feel in the early years of the festival, there was now a sense of exclusion. George Malcolm speaks of "an organization called The Club. It consisted of people who used to sing or play for Ben." The old feeling of community diminished both among those who came to play or sing and those who came to listen. Meanwhile, Britten, Pears, and whoever was temporarily part of the entourage sometimes looked, as Robert Tear caricatures them, like "Pope, King, a couple of sycophantic academics and perhaps a handmaiden or two strewing palms." Tear sums up the atmosphere of Aldeburgh as he found it in the later years as "weird, personal, unhealthy, obsessive, perhaps incestuous, but above all these seductive." He remembers a place characterized by "waspishness, bitterness, cold, hard eyes . . . cabalistic meetings . . . secrecy." Of Britten, he says, "there was a great, huge abyss in his soul." It is in the context of these accounts and others like them that Carpenter takes up in great detail Britten's infatuation with boys—with David Spencer, Ronald Duncan's son Roger, Jonathan Gathorne-Hardy, David Hemmings, Ronan Magill, and others. He quotes Gathorne-Hardy, now an author who has written much about the complexities of sexual experience, to explain that in spite of Britten's devotion to Pears, his greatest passion may have been for these boys: "It's a common homosexual situation," Gathorne-Hardy argues, "when their passions are in one place, and their hearts and affections in another." And so it becomes a central thesis of this book that Britten's passion, although never acted on beyond the hugs, pats, and goodnight kisses which the boys, grown up, have been happy to describe to Carpenter, was for children; and that desire, deeply felt but in the end repressed, produced the contradictions in Britten's character and determined the nature of his work.

The passion twisted, yet also sustained, Britten's Peter Pan characteristics which Auden reflected in the second part of 'Hymn to St. Cecilia,' and in a strange way may actually have made possible the remarkable music which he wrote for children, without, as Nancy Evans has said, ever writing down for them. In works like *The Little Sweep*, *Noye's Fludde*, *The Golden Vanity*, and *Children's Crusade*; in parts like Miles' in *The Turn of the Screw*, Isaac's in *Abraham and Isaac*, and the boy's spirit in *Curlew River*; and in writing for choirs or small groups of boys in *Spring Symphony*, *War Requiem*, and *A Midsummer Night's Dream*, the repertory of music written for young voices is expanded beyond measure. Britten, says Donald Mitchell, "does not cheat by writing music for [children] that is isolated from the music he writes for adults. He skilfully takes account of their talents as performers...but his real respect for them shows in his insistence on being no less himself in [works like] *Vanity* than in a work of grander proportions."

Both Eric Crozier's unpublished memoir quoted extensively by Carpenter and Tony Palmer's television film about Britten, *A Time There Was*, suggest that the boy whom Britten most passionately sought was perhaps ultimately always himself as a child—"a kind of idealized

[self] at the age of ten or twelve, the gay, attractive, charming young Lowestoft boy," as Crozier says. The treatment both of innocence and the compulsion to destroy it in many of the works of his middle and later years may well reflect Britten's sense both of what he had done to himself by the life he had led, and the singing child still alive in him and father of the man who found its image in choristers, boy trebles, prodigies, poets who died young, midsummer dreams, ghost stories, plays, parables, and the children of his friends. If this was fundamentally a kind of narcissism, his relentless examination of it in his work made it socially responsible and, finally, essentially religious. He did not, after all, abuse young children; instead, he wrote great music. His last Canticle, the fifth, is a setting of Eliot's 'Death of St. Narcissus':

> By the river
> His eyes were aware
> of the pointed corners of his eyes
> And his hands aware
> of the pointed tips of his fingers
> Struck down by such knowledge
> He could not live men's ways,
> but became a dancer before God . . .
>
> Knowing at the end
> the taste of his own whiteness,
> the horror of his own smoothness
> . . . he became a dancer to God.

The journey from the polkas with Auden to dancing before God was a long and exhausting one. Along the way, there were moments when the youthful exuberance of the Piano Concerto and *Les Illuminations* returned, notably in the *Spring Symphony* and *The Prince of the Pagodas*, and there were some fine compositions that are not amenable to autobiographical readings—the cello suites, sonata, and *Cello Symphony* written for Rostropovich, the *Harp Suite*, the *Metamorphoses* for oboe. But Britten's most characteristic work remained driven, in one way or another, by language, and the texts he found among the poets and required from his librettists produce a sequence of major works in *The Turn of the Screw*, *A Midsummer Night's Dream*, *War Requiem*, *Curlew*

River, Death in Venice, and several of the song cycles and Canticles in which Carpenter is able to follow the theme of innocence and its loss to an autobiographical resolution in music which grows increasingly austere in its economy of means, and increasingly direct in its treatment of Britten's engagement with the demands of disorder.

Peter Quint in *The Turn of the Screw* and Oberon in *A Midsummer Night's Dream* represent a similar temptation. Donald Mitchell has said that beneath the etiquette of the court and the "escape from the carnal enchantments of the wood" in *A Midsummer Night's Dream*, we are beckoned by the music's covert life—its "audible sexual delirium." Quint tells Miles that he is "all things strange" in whom "secrets and half-formed desires meet," and so indeed is Oberon—a counter-tenor with a coloratura soprano for a consort—who, like Quint, is a supernatural being who desires to possess a human boy, whose home key is E flat and whose characteristic singing is melismatic. By the time Britten wrote *Curlew River*, however, the glissando recalling Miles' response to Quint is the disembodied voice of a madwoman's dead child telling her to "go her way in peace" and that "the dead shall rise again." That is also what the choral settings of the mass in *War Requiem* tell the baritone and tenor singing Wilfred Owen's poems: *Requiescant in pace*. Even Tadzio says as much—although he neither speaks nor sings—dancing before Aschenbach, but also before God.

I happened to attend the première of *Death in Venice* at Aldeburgh in 1973. At the time, I had no idea how ill the composer had been as he worked on his opera, that he had delayed surgery on his failing heart in order to complete it, that the operation had not been successful, or that he turned off his radio that night, unable to listen to the BBC broadcast in his house a couple of miles from the concert hall in Snape. He lived for three more years and wrote a few more works, including a valedictory string quartet, his third, that quotes extensively from *Death in Venice*. Was he himself Tadzio as much as he was Aschenbach? Was he Billy Budd, Miles, Isaac, the Madwoman's son, Owen's doomed youth? In *Winter Words*, his Thomas Hardy cycle which I mentioned earlier, he concludes with a setting of 'Before Life and After':

> A time there was—as one may guess
> And as, indeed,

earth's testimonies tell—
Before the birth of consciousness,
When all went well.

None suffered sickness, love or loss,
None knew regret,
starved hope, or heartburnings;
None cared whatever crash or cross
Brought wrack to things.

"But," the poem concludes, "the disease of feeling germed, / And primal rightness / took the tint of wrong." Like Grimes, like Claggert and Quint, like Aschenbach, Britten experienced the germing of his feeling, and followed in his way, and up to a point, its logic. During the composition of *Death in Venice*, Pears told Sidney Nolan that "Ben is writing an evil opera, and it's killing him." At the end of it, recalling Plato's dialogue between Socrates and Phaedrus, Aschenbach delineates Britten's dilemma in his life and work:

Does beauty lead to wisdom, Phaedrus?
Yes, but through the senses.
Can poets take this way then
For senses lead to passion, Phaedrus?
Passion leads to knowledge
Knowledge to forgiveness
To compassion with the abyss.
Should we then reject it, Phaedrus,
The wisdom poets crave,
Seeking only form and pure detachment
Simplicity and discipline?
But this is beauty, Phaedrus,
Discovered through the senses
And senses lead to passion, Phaedrus,
And passion to the abyss.

Although it's Myfanwy Piper's libretto, the basic terms of Auden's letter written to Britten so many years before would still seem to be relevant.

I should conclude by addressing a final point, the common objection to Britten's later work anticipated earlier when I mentioned its austerity and economy of means. With the *War Requiem* excepted, we observe a tendency in his music analogous to that in Auden's later poetry—a determination to hold prodigious virtuosity in check, chasten the expression of emotion, narrow the focus of attention, eschew the inessential, and counter the romantic expectations of an audience. The small orchestras of the chamber operas shrink to seven or eight musicians in the church parables; Grimes' robust singing in his meditative moods becomes Aschenbach's *recitativo secco*; rich instrumental writing grows severe, abstemious, ascetic. "Too many notes," complains Peter Schaffer's Joseph II upon hearing Mozart's *The Abduction from the Seraglio*; Britten's critics said there were too few. But Britten's response, I feel sure, would have been exactly that of Mozart in *Amadeus*: "There are just as many notes, neither more nor less, as are required." Although both biographical and musicological arguments have been advanced to explain, lament, or (sometimes) praise the later work, one finally reaches the point when it is necessary to say—Go and listen to it. Nicholas Spice in his review of Carpenter convicts the mature style of anemia: "The bloodlessness of fear, on one hand, and the bloodlessness of idealized innocence, on the other." T. W. Adorno was the cruelest of all, calling Britten's music "the apotheosis of meagerness." But go and listen to it.

When Britten died, I wondered for a day or two what sort of elegy Auden would have written had he been alive to write it. Then I wrote my own, for a program on the BBC, trying to answer Adorno and trying to make it seem at least in some respects, in Auden's absence, Audenesque. I'd like to put it in the record.

> Operas! A feast for burghers, said Adorno.
> And of your work: The apotheosis
> Of meagerness, a kind of fast. That's
> A cruel case against you
> And it may have weight, in time.
> But let's call meagerness
> Economy today
> And call the bourgeoisie the people
> Who like me have (barely) what it costs
> To listen and who like to hear
> These songs, but who will pay a price.

Economies of living soon enough
Make meager even music of the spheres!
To be of use, you said.
Directly and deliberately I write
For human beings. And not
Posterity—for which the general outlook
Isn't very bright.

A tenor mourns. And you lie down in Aldeburgh
One last time. But you have work to do
In spite of what the two of us have said.
A tenor sings. When you
Get out there over the horizon
This December morning with the likes
Of Peter Grimes,
Row your shining boat ashore
And be extravagant in song:
Leave economy to the ungrateful living
Who will need it, whose Justice
And whose History have multiplied unendingly
Expenses by Apotheoses by Sublimes.

From 'Mauberley' to Middagh Street:
Ways of Meeting the British

For a long time we needed a successor poem to 'Hugh Selwyn Mauberley'—something by a British or Irish poet that would reverse the direction of E.P.'s immigration and place a Brit or an Irishman in a cultural context as weirdly American as Mauberley's was weirdly British. The poem needed to be written by someone who delighted in the comedy of cultural collision, who was a prosodic virtuoso, and who wanted to probe the significance of what Stephen Spender thirty years ago called "immigration in reverse," an immigration initiated by Auden and Isherwood that ended the age of American literary exile in Britain or Europe—that of a James, an Eliot, a Pound. Such a poem would need a cast of characters as interesting and representative as the figures who people 'Mauberley', a concern with the disorienting and conditioning effects of World War, a preoccupation with the function of art, and a traditional form stretched to the breaking point analogous to the 'Mauberley' quatrain, a stanza very rarely imitated but, as Spender noted, "having a catchiness which makes one wonder it has not been exploited like the limerick or clerihew."

It was in the middle of trying to read Paul Muldoon's *Madoc*, that ambitious book-length sequence treating the apocryphal journey of Southey and Coleridge to the banks of the Susquehanna to found their Pantisocracy, that I remembered '7 Middagh Street' from *Meeting the British*. If *Madoc*, for all its fun and games, is as demanding and confusing as some species of mock-*Cantos*, 'Middagh Street' is Muldoon's 'Mauberley'. If *Madoc* is his American myth, 'Middagh Street' is his comic history of literary immigration in reverse—a 'Hugh Selwyn Mauberley' for the 1990s (although written in the previous decade).

Another Irish poet, of course, had taken Spender's suggestion that it might be interesting to exploit the 'Mauberley' stanza as one does the limerick or clerihew, and in *A Kensington Notebook* Derek Mahon writes a 'Mauberley' pastiche with a full cast of E.P. contemporaries—James, Lawrence, Yeats, Lewis, Ford, and Gaudier-Brzeska. But it's only an elegant exercise, a demonstration piece. With a fine ear, you can produce the goods:

The operantics of
Provence and Languedoc
Shook the Gaudier marbles
At No. 10 Church Walk

Where 'Ezra Pound, M.A.,
Author of *Personae*',
Twitched his nostrils and
Invisible antennae . . .

Muldoon writes quirky quatrains too, but they are usually the component parts of sonnets—sonnets both Shakespearean and Italian which are as idiosyncratic and flexible in their own peculiar way as is the 'Mauberley' quatrain in the hands of Pound or Derek Mahon. '7 Middagh Street' begins and ends with recognizable sonnets. Sometimes they are upside down—the Shakespearean couplet or Italian sestet coming *before* the quatrains or the octave rather than after—and sometimes they are rightside up, but they are immediately recognizable as sonnets. Less recognizable, but still sonnets of a sort, are the runs of couplets that have a way of counting out in groups of fourteen lines, and then the sections of the poem that look to be written in longish stanzas—but stanzas of either seven or fourteen lines where the seven line stanzas come in even pairs. The mutating and flexible sonnet, then, corresponds to the 'Mauberley' quatrain. The most traditional of forms is stretched at points *almost* beyond recognition. Also, as in 'Mauberley', there is a doubling effect, or a mirroring. The first poem begins with an inverted Italian sonnet followed by two inverted Shakespearean sonnets followed by a run of seven couplets. The last poem *ends* with a proper Italian sonnet preceded by two proper Shakespearean sonnets preceded by a run of seven couplets. And so on, through the sequence. The last poem, 'Louis,' stands the first poem, 'Wystan,' on its feet, the rightside-up sonnets answering the upside-down sonnets; the second poem, 'Gypsy,' is written in fourteen line stanzas and is answered by the second-to-last, 'Carson,' which appears in double sevens; the third poem, 'Ben,' and the third-to-last, 'Salvador,' are written in couplets; and between 'Ben' and 'Salvador,' at the center of the cycle, is 'Chester,' an Italian sonnet. There is also an echoing of phrases from section to section in such a way that all or part of a final line in one poem becomes all or part of the opening line in the next; and the entire sequence begins and ends with the same words.

My point is that Muldoon plays with the sonnet tradition in ways that are far more purposeful than is Mahon's simple imitation of the 'Mauberley' quatrain; also, that he plays with the sonnet in order to achieve at the end of the century something quite similar to what Pound achieved at the beginning, but reversing the transatlantic route. Instead of E.P. in London, we have Wystan in New York.

> Quinquereme of Nineveh from distant Ophir;
> a blizzard off the Newfoundland coast
> had, as we slept, metamorphosed
>
> the *Champlain's* decks
> to a wedding cake,
> on whose uppermost tier stood Christopher
>
> and I like a diminutive bride and groom.
> A heavy-skirted Liberty would lunge
> with her ice-cream
> at two small, anxious
>
> boys, and Erika so grimly wave
> from the quarantine-launch
> she might as truly have been my wife
> as, later that day, Barcelona was Franco's.

Allusive in the 'Mauberley' manner, these lines begin with a quote from Masefield which serves to introduce Auden and Isherwood as immigrants on the deck of the *Champlain* about to be met by Erika Mann (with whom, to keep her out of Nazi Germany, Auden had made a marriage of convenience) on that decisive day in the Spanish Civil War when Barcelona fell to Franco. Auden and Isherwood had recently finished their third collaborative play and *Journey to a War*, a book about the Sino-Japanese conflict in which Isherwood wrote the journalistic prose and Auden the sonnet sequence with verse commentary called 'In Time of War'. Before China, of course, Auden had been in Spain, and Muldoon's next two sonnets continue Wystan's monologue by narrating events from his experience in both wars and setting up the

run of couplets about W.B. Yeats in which Wystan takes a position on
the political function of poetry which he was in fact to take in his elegy
to Yeats and in related essays written shortly after his arrival in New
York.

> As for his crass, rhetorical
>
> posturing, 'Did that play of mine
> send out certain men (*certain men?*)
>
> the English shot . . . ?'
> the answer is 'Certainly not.'.
>
> If Yeats had saved his pencil-lead
> would certain men have stayed in bed?
>
> For history's a twisted root
> with art its small, translucent fruit
>
> and never the other way round.
> The roots by which we were once bound
>
> are severed here, in any case,
> and we are all now dispossessed;
>
> prince, poet, construction worker,
> salesman, soda fountain jerker—
>
> all equally isolated.
> Each loads flour, sugar and salted
>
> beef into a covered wagon
> and strikes out for his Oregon,
>
> each straining for the ghostly axe
> of a huge, blond-haired lumberjack.

Auden's problem, unlike E.P.'s in 'Mauberley', was that he had
been too much *in* key with his time; he had observed the mottoes on
sun-dials very closely; he was deeply affected by "the march of events."
Further, he had given the age exactly what it demanded—"an image of

its accelerated grimace," "something for the modern stage"; born not in a "half-savage country" but on the "obstinate isle" itself, he now looked west to half-savage Oregon and the campy Paul Bunyan he was about to imagine for an operatic collaboration with Benjamin Britten. Just about in *l'an trentuniesme de son eage*, he was about to shake things up in New York City. He had no intention of passing from men's memories, only of passing from England, of passing on the dubious honor of being laureate of the blitz to someone else.

Are they now tempted to rechristen

their youngest son
who turned his back on Albion

a Quisling?
Would their *chaise-longue*

philosophers have me somehow inflate
myself and float

above their factories and pylons
like a flat-footed barrage-balloon?

No, he has "leapt with Kierkegaard/out of the realm of Brunel and Arkwright/with its mills, canals and railway-bridges," fallen in love with Chester Kallman, "learned to play softball with Robert Frost," and moved into 7 Middagh Street—with Chester, Erika, Gypsy Rose Lee, Benjamin Britten, Peter Pears, Salvador Dalí, Carson McCullers, Louis MacNeice, Paul and Jane Bowles—and, Muldoon assures us in a note, a trained chimpanzee. A far cry from No. 10 Church Walk in Kensington.

I am assuming that my reader is well acquainted both with 'Hugh Selwyn Mauberley' and the various critical problems surrounding it, especially as they have been confronted over the years by Donald Davie's attempts first to discover a coherent pattern of personae and narrative in the sequence and later, in great frustration, to argue that no such pattern exists and that the individual sections should be read as a series of discrete lyrics modelled on the quatrains of Théophile Gautier. Although Vincent Sherry has recently discovered an unlikely source for

'Mauberley' which will oblige everyone to restore a reading based on plot and personae, it is also true that questions remain: Who speaks in 'Siena Mi Fe; Disfecemi Maremma'? Who is Mr. Nixon talking to? Who "awaits the Lady Valentine's commands"?

Muldoon makes similar questions about 'Middagh Street' easier to answer by writing each section as a monologue—we are never, except perhaps in the case of 'Ben,' in any doubt about who is speaking, only now and then about what is being said and alluded to. E.P.'s engagement with poetics, intellectual history, war, cultural forbears and contemporaries (the Pre-Raphaelites, the poets of the Rhymers Club, Brennbaum / Beerbohm, Nixon/Bennett, Ford the stylist, and the rest) all have their approximate parallels in 'Middagh Street'. But the poem coheres more rapidly than Pound's because Auden, Gypsy Rose Lee, Kallman, McCullers, MacNeice (and possibly also Britten) speak in monologue. What these voices speak *about* ranges from Auden's account of visiting MacNeice in a New Hampshire hospital, through Gypsy's reminiscence of the circumstances in which she became a stripper, Britten's (possible) echoing of Big Ben chiming for his and Pears' return (along with other voices calling from home: Cyril Connolly's baritone in the pages of *Horizon*, Harold Nicholson's, the Dean of St. Paul's, an M.P.'s in the House), Kallman's revelation that he searches out hard trade in a Sands Street bar, Dalí's dreams and memories and surrealistic visions of Chamberlain, Hitler, Lenin, André Breton, and his first American one-man show, McCullers' description of what the daily routine is like for all of them in the old Brownstone in Brooklyn Heights, to MacNeice's wide-ranging associations touching his journey to Iceland with Auden in 1936, his Ulster childhood in the context of his father's ministry (a Protestant, but arguing Home Rule), the early career of Delmore Schwartz, the death of Lorca, and a response to Auden's elegy for Yeats: "For poetry *can* make things happen—/not only can, but *must*—/and the very painting of that oyster/is in itself a political gesture." MacNeice exits, and 'Middagh Street' concludes, from "the back door of Muldoon's" (perhaps the bar on Sands Street where Chester found "Jack Tars"), which is also the back door, the last poem, of the book called *Meeting the British*.

Although Muldoon's historical distance from the figures and events of 'Middagh Street' is approximately the same as Pound's from

Beerbohm and the poets of the Rhymers' Club, his distance from the Spanish Civil War, World War II, and the moment in which his monologuists speak is much greater than Pound's to World War I and the moment in which the chief events of 'Mauberley' unfold, 1919–1920. This is one reason why there is no equivalent in 'Middagh Street' for Pound's famous lines on World War I in which Bion replaces Gautier as the formal model and the tone suddenly changes from irony to outrage. Pound lost friends in World War I whereas Muldoon wasn't even born until after the end of World War II. Still, 'Middagh Street's monologues are deeply conditioned by wars and troubles—by what has happened in Spain, by what is happening in the early stages of World War II, and by the whole history of troubles in Ireland from Parnell to Muldoon's own time. Indeed the whole treatment of "Immigration in reverse" in 'Middagh Street' may turn on the implicit relationship between Auden's decision to leave England in a time of war and the decision of a good number of Ulster poets to leave Ireland in a time of Troubles. If the quasi-historical E.P. and the fictional Mauberley fail in their respective ways to "resuscitate the dead art/of Poetry" in an England conditioned by post-war trauma and "neo-Nietzschean clatter," the quasi-historical Wystan and Louis at least suggest the manner in which the fully historical Paul Muldoon is determined to practice his art as a poet who grew up in Ulster but who now, like many of his contemporaries, spends much of his time in America.

Seamus Heaney, who also spends much of his time in America, wrote in his Richard Ellmann Lectures of 1988 that "Muldoon absconded, like Auden, from a native audience's expectation that he would play 'the war poet' and act as a kind of home guard on the domestic front." When Wystan says, "For History's a twisted root/ with art its small, translucent fruit/ and never the other way round," Heaney feels justified in hearing an expression of Muldoon's point of view. These lines paraphrase, in fact, the speech of Auden's Defence Council (who represents his own position) in an essay called 'The Public vs. the Late Mr. William Butler Yeats': "Art is a product of history, not a cause. Unlike some other products, technical inventions for example, it does not re-enter history as an effective agent, so that the question whether art should be propaganda is unreal." But is this to imply that art may abscond from history as artists may from the expectations of their native audience? Wystan goes on to say in his monologue that "roots by which we once were bound/ are severed here," and it is one function of Louis' monologue to provide a critique of Wystan in a phase when he appears to "set himself up as a stylite/ waiting for hostilities to cease, a Dutch master/ intent on painting an oyster/ or lemon." Muldoon himself is neither a maker of still lives nor of Mauberleyesque silent heads in medallion. His series of curious heads are *talking* heads, and as soon as they speak they reveal their historical conditioning. But his own American sojourns may have made it easier to imagine a response to sectarian Ulster not unlike Dalí's response to the Anarchist taxi driver's demand with respect to sectarian Spain: "Which side [are you] on?" Dalí says: "Not one, or both, or none."

The artist goes into exile looking for artistic freedom, for new experiences, new friends and colleagues, perhaps even a new self. He also, if he is Ezra Pound, goes looking for what he takes to be a living literary culture (although at first he finds only Edwardian poets). Along the way, he invents E.P. and buries him beneath the residue of war, the detritus of failed literary movements, and the maudlin confessions, faint susurrus, and subjective hosannahs of Mr. Mauberley. For a moment, it might have looked as if England could mean Wyndham Lewis, Gaudier-Brzeska, Ford Madox Ford, W.B. Yeats, and T.S. Eliot. Suddenly it seemed to mean Mauberley. It was time to move on—Joyce was in Paris, Yeats would visit Rapallo.

Pound never liked or understood W.H. Auden's poems (nor Auden Pound's). In the 1930s, Auden became the licensed *enfant terrible*, a role which Pound had played without the license. And it was the licensing that made the difference. Having satisfied all too well the expectations of everyone besides himself and F.R. Leavis, he went into exile looking for artistic freedom, new experiences, new friends and colleagues, perhaps even a new self. Instead of Lady Valentine in a stuffed satin drawing-room, he met the stripper—Gypsy; instead of wringing lilies from the acorn, he plucked his new found Orchid—Chester; instead of the Burne-Jones cartons at the Tate, he had Dalí lobsters propped against the wall on Middagh Street; instead of Raymonde Collignon singing Lawes or the songs of Provence, he had Peter Pears to sing the songs of Britten; instead of Mauberley and his like for colleagues, he had Frost and Delmore Schwartz; and instead of Mr. Nixon, he had the chimp. His true Penelope was about to become Reinhold Niebuhr, and his tin wreath eventually the Pulitzer Prize.

Auden, of course, stayed in New York and became an American citizen—as did Isherwood in California. Stephen Spender, a close friend of both, wrote in 'Immigration in Reverse' that "just as the pattern of Eliot's [and let us add Pound's] literary migration[s] to Europe repeated that of Henry James . . . so the younger writers suggest a repetition of the Auden pattern when they go to America." Since Spender published his essay in 1961, however, many of these younger writers have been Irish rather than English and, as one of them said to me once, "We are no longer exiles, we are commuters." Among the English, there have been some of both types—Davie was a commuter from Vanderbilt and Stanford, Thom Gunn a San Francisco exile—but it's true that most of the Irish, teaching in the east and in the west, do fly home from work once the academic year is at an end. Whether Muldoon himself turns out to be at last a commuter or an exile, Heaney (a commuter) is certainly right to find his situation reflected in 'Middagh Street' (as indeed it was in earlier poems with American settings or sources).

I have always regarded 'Middagh Street' to be a poem of great intrinsic interest, but I think it gains in stature when read as the successor to 'Mauberley' treating reverse immigration which, rather surprisingly, no one else seems to have written. It responds, in ways that *both* Pound and Auden might have appreciated, to the voice which Isherwood, in *Christopher and His Kind*, remembers hearing in the wind and driving snow as he stood with Auden on the deck of the Champlain staring at Manhattan "aggressively flaunting its rude steel nudity."

> We're Americans here—and we keep at it, twenty-four hours a day, *being* Americans . . . Don't you come snooting us with your European traditions—we know the mess they've got you into. Do things our way or take the next boat back . . . Are you quitting or staying? It's no skin off *our* nose. We promise nothing. Here, you'll be on your own.

As Isherwood left for California he had no way of knowing that there was at least one address in Brooklyn where being on one's own was about to become impossible or that an Irish poet would make it his coracle for an Atlantic voyage more than forty years later.

The Poetry of Roy Fisher

One cold evening in the winter of 1980 I drove with Roy Fisher through a landscape of abandoned factories, empty warehouses, and uncollected refuse past the ruins of the railway station in South Bend, Indiana. He was in town to give a reading at the University of Notre Dame and, as I discovered to my considerable surprise, was about to spend the first night of his life outside of Britain. As we talked about cities— Birmingham, Chicago, London, Indianapolis—lines and phrases from his work surfaced in my mind which led me, partly in jest and partly with a fascinated sense of what I took to be a near identity between the setting of a poem and the scene in which we found ourselves, to label, as it were, things and places that we passed along the road by quoting bits of *City*. At the same time, I had the odd feeling that I was looking at familiar objects, not through the windshield of a moving car, but through the glass above some labelled trays exhibited for an ambiguous purpose in an industrial museum of the mind—one like Fisher would later, in actual fact, imagine in a section of 'Diversions' where the works of a foundry pattern-maker—shapes for "drains, gears, / furnace doors, [and] couplings"—mime "the comportment / of the gods in the Ethnology cases." As we passed the station, coming on it just exactly as one does upon the station in *City*—"suddenly in its open prospect out of tangled streets of small factories"—I had the uncanny sense that Fisher had, his first night out of Britain, fallen from the sky directly into his best known poem.

Because the language of *City* seems sometimes to describe the decayed industrial topography of Studebaker Corridor in South Bend— an area where auto manufacturing produced at first a prosperous, small Detroit and then, following the bankruptcy of Studebaker in the 1960s, a few square miles of hulking, empty buildings and unlighted streets—one's memory of the poem could make it for a moment an example of the realism many seek to find in it and which two other early Fisher poems, 'For Realism' and 'The Memorial Fountain,' might seem to validate. The remembered language seemed to match, or correspond to, aspects of the bleak urban landscape through which we drove in many of the same ways it might have had we been driving through the streets of Birmingham instead, leading me to point and quote (though also to hallucinate the glassed, sealed, and labelled trays in that industrial museum of the mind). But Fisher has talked about confronting a topography as "an indecipherable script with no key" when he went to work on *City*, about "a perceptual environment for which no vocabulary needed to exist," about "floating real things into a fictive world" and "exploring inner space rather than in any way attempting to do justice to a place as itself." More than the actual city of Birmingham, Fisher thought of Rilke's Paris and Kafka's Prague, towns in paintings by Kokoschka and Paul Klee, the tiny hilltop cities in the backgrounds of paintings by Italian primitives.[1] This does not suggest the imagination of a realist. Perhaps Fisher was more the poet of the glass case—or even the Large Glass—than he was the Laureate of postindustrial Birmingham.[2] And maybe his urgent desire to *construct* complex configurations out of language aligned him with assumptions absolutely antithetical to realism—those of the philosophers and cognitive psychologists who believe, as one of them says, that "knowledge does not reflect an 'objective' ontological reality, but exclusively an ordering and organization of a world constituted by our experience," and who agree with Piaget when he says that "Intelligence organizes the world by organizing itself."[3] Fisher's "indecipherable script" had found its key when he had made from his perceptual environment a vocabulary and conceptual construction by floating real things into a fictive, inner space. This, by his account, was *City*. And yet the critics talked of it as if it were a photograph—or even a place that one could go and visit. And I myself was pointing to it out the window as we drove to Fisher's reading in a place where he had never been.

Fisher was in town partly because I had included *City* in *23 Modern British Poets*, an anthology which appeared in 1971. My intention in that book was to demonstrate the existence of an indigenous British modernism by anthologizing work by David Jones, Hugh MacDiarmid, and Basil Bunting (all of whom were still living in the early 1970s) and following that up with selections from the poetry of, among others, Fisher, Charles Tomlinson, Christopher Middleton, Ian Hamilton Finlay, Gael Turnbull, Christopher Logue, Matthew Mead, Ken Smith, Peter Whigham, Lee Harwood, John Montague, Nathaniel Tarn, and Tom Raworth. Some of these poets, and perhaps Roy Fisher himself, would now be called postmodern rather than modern by many critics.

But in 1971 the term postmodern was just beginning to rear its head, and I thought of my twenty-three as representing an extension and development of mainstream Anglo-American modernism.

I had come to *City* as to a kind of demythologized *Waste Land* and wanted to see it as a link between the fully mythologized work of David Jones and the nominalistic constructions of Lee Harwood and Tom Raworth. Toward the end of *City*, Fisher writes that "each thought is at once translucent and icily capricious," calling this "A polytheism without gods," and I also liked to think of my reader remembering the polytheism *with* gods of Christopher Logue's *Patroclia* and *Pax*, his versions from Homer which appeared in the anthology, where Apollo, dressed as Priam's brother, strolls with Hector for a while, and Logue writes in amazement (or Homer matter-of-factly): "Think of it: They stand like brothers, man and god, / Chatting together on the parapet that spans the inner gate." From living gods to icily capricious and translucent thoughts. It defined a kind of range.

When Fisher read at Notre Dame, however, celebrating that initial night away from Britain, he did not read from *City*. More than a decade had passed since the publication the Fulcrum Press *Collected Poems* of 1969, and after *Matrix*, *The Cut Pages*, and *The Thing about Joe Sullivan*, one began to wonder if the radically hermetic *Ship's Orchestra* mightn't have prefigured more in the later Fisher than did *City*, and without forcing the choice of whether to toss that herring *realism* from one's analytic net or eat it for hors d'oeuvres. Still, *City* had begun the critical discussion, and by 1981 it had already led to something of a critical debate. While I return to an early moment in that debate into which I was drawn by virtue of having included *City* in *23 Modern British Poets* and then go on to look at certain key poems of the 1970s which anticipate *A Furnace*, I should leave Roy Fisher where I best remember him—playing jazz piano at a party following his reading—"jamming sound against idea / hard as it can go," as he says about Joe Sullivan—while another guest of the university, also in town to read, watched and listened and smiled enigmatically, making the rest of the audience, though not the pianist, about as uncomfortably conscious of a perceptual environment as possible. It was John Cage.

Although even John Cage may ultimately be seen to have more in common with Roy Fisher than have Thomas Hardy and Philip Larkin, Donald Davie's polemical *Thomas Hardy and British Poetry* of 1973 attempts to secure Fisher's work for a native British tradition stemming from Hardy and leading to Larkin which, civic-minded and politically responsible, involves "an apparent meanness of spirit, a painful modesty of intention, and extremely limited objectives."[4] There has been little avoiding Davie's influential book in discussions of Fisher, and nearly every commentary on his work addresses it at one point or another. It is particularly difficult for me to pass it by since my anthology is the one which Davie has in mind in his 'Afterword for the American Reader' when he talks about "anthologies of British poetry since 1945" which are "now on offer to the American reader" but which leave out Philip Larkin and are hostile to the native, Hardyesque tradition.[5] There was, in fact, no conspiracy of anthologies in 1970, there was just my book, still (as I write this in 1992) the last anthology of exclusively British poetry published in the United States. And however inadequate it may have been in some respects, I *do* think it placed Fisher's work in the proper context—with poetry by those whose names were listed earlier that is modernist, experimental, and wide open to a range of influences from abroad.

Davie finds Fisher's concerns to be "social" rather than "human," his sentiments to be anti-Lawrencian in their derivation from a realism which "sees intensities and ecstasies . . . only as so many dangerous distractions," and his work through the Fulcrum Press *Collected Poems*, and particularly in *City*, to be a kind which excludes tragedy in favor of pathos. Facing a real world in the real Birmingham, Fisher, Davie feels, tells hard truths: "One responds to [a section of prose quoted from *City*] as one responds to Larkin's 'Whitsun Weddings': "This is how it is!" And like Larkin, Davie's Fisher is fully aware of the bargain he is striking [in denying tragedy to render pathos], and he agrees to its humiliating terms."[6] But Fisher's concerns are almost entirely cognitive and aesthetic. Both tragedy *and* pathos seem beside the point, as does the distinction between content that is social and content that is human. And while Fisher is no D.H. Lawrence—a mistaken affinity invalidating much of J.D. Needham's initial response to Davie in an article of 1975[7]—he has intensities of his own and is not a Larkinesque poet of defeat, settling for what Davie calls a "hobbit-world of reduced expectation."

Thomas Hardy and British Poetry was written before the publication of *Matrix*, *The Cut Pages*, *The Thing about Joe Sullivan*, or *A Furnace*. But Davie did have *The Ship's Orchestra* and 'Three Ceremonial Poems' before him, and he didn't like them at all. Here perhaps we arrive at the crux. While Davie is willing to admire the technique of "making strange" in a poem like 'As He Came Near Death,' he recoils sharply when "the full battery of resources" which Fisher has derived from Russian modernism is deployed. Fisher has called himself at various times a "1920s Russian modernist," and Davie's point is that Fisher's allegiance to a non-discursive poetics in *The Ship's Orchestra* and 'Three Ceremonial Poems' is, in his view, "mannered, wasteful, and perverse." Specifically, in the case of 'Three Ceremonial Poems,' such a poetics deriving, Davie supposes, chiefly from the practice of Mandelstam and Pasternak, prevents Fisher from making definitive judgments.[8] But Fisher is not, whether in 'Three Ceremonial Poems,' *The Ship's Orchestra*, or *City*, in the business of making definitive judgments. He is in the business of building fictive verbal structures, sometimes definitive and sometimes indeterminate. And if we are to invoke the poetics of Achmeism or the theories of Victor Shklovsky[9], we should also consider that other Russian modernism—the modernism of Constructivists like Malevich and Tatlin, together with their Bauhaus contemporaries and assemblagist successors—for Fisher has always been deeply influenced by visual art, and, when he describes his work, it is more frequently by way of an analogy with painting, printmaking, or music than by way of comparison with the practice of other poets. Instead of viewing *City* as a discursive mix of verse and prose that seeks to arrive at a judgment about life in Birmingham, it would be better to see it as Fisher does himself—as an assemblage in which a fictive world is made from the signs and names of real things.[10] Both assemblage and constructivism use materials out of the real world to make an object which has never existed in that world before, an object which does not reflect or represent it, but takes its place in it, fits beside or among the very objects from which it has taken the materials out of which it has been made, but as a thing apart.

Although the dominant idiom of the several at work in *City* differs substantially from those of *The Ship's Orchestra* and 'Three Ceremonial Poems,' nonetheless passages from all three works could be interchanged in such a way as to severely test a reader's sense of how strange "making strange" can get before it grows to be "mannered, wasteful, and perverse" or seems to crop up in an inappropriate context.[11] (Had Fisher played in a ship's orchestra for twenty years without ever setting foot on land and had only seen photographs of Birmingham in a book, which of his two major early works would critics confidently call mimetic, and which hermetic?) Fisher's assemblage in *City* is made from a wide range of English idioms—from the sharply denotative to the weirdly surrealistic—and not, of course, from things. The figures gathering objects and materials in the section called 'Starting to Make a Tree' are making a *physical* assemblage in an irregular, radial form (like *City* itself) from "a great flock mattress," "two carved chairs," "chicken-wire," "tarpaulin," "a smashed barrel," "lead piping," and "leather of all kinds," while Fisher is making an assemblage out of those words (the words in quotes), along with others. More than that, some of the parts that comprise the larger assemblage of *City* as a whole are themselves, as parts, discursive. But the final effect of the work is neither that of discourse nor of a form, as Davie insists, with a center, nor indeed of a judgment being rendered or a message being delivered about the politics or social history of British urban life. The effect is stranger, finally, than much in Mandelstam and Pasternak because *City* really does have the *feel* of assemblage in visual art—as described, for example, by Lawrence Alloway.

> Its source is obsolescence, the throwaway material of cities, as it collects in drawers, cupboards, attics, dustbins, gutters, waste lots, and city dumps. Objects have a history: first they are brand new goods; then they are possessions, accessible to few, subjected, often, to intimate and repeated use; then, as waste, they are scarred by use but available again . . . Assemblages of such material come at the spectator as bits of life, bits of the environment. The urban environment is present, then, as the source of objects, whether transfigured or left alone.[12]

Fisher's objects, whether imported from Birmingham, other cities, literature or works of art,[13] are usually much larger than those identified by Alloway or those collected in 'Starting to Make a Tree'—they are typically buildings, street lamps, statues, oil drums, viaducts, cisterns, girders, buses, and windows—but the mind moves among them as the eye moves among the objects of a Louise Nevelson sculpture—or, to return to my drive through Studebaker Corridor, among objects under glass in an assemblage as defined by anthropology, "a group of artefacts found together in a closed context of association."[14]

I think Roy Fisher had probably read *Thomas Hardy and British Poetry* by the time he gave his interview to Jed Rasula and Mike Erwin in the year of its publication, 1973. More recently, he has objected to Davie's treatment of his work in an interview with Robert Sheppard and a letter to John Ash,[15] but even in 1973 he must have had Davie in mind, or at least a critic of the same temperament, when he referred to "quite skilled readers who will very characteristically go at my work from the representational end or the end which appears to have morality in it . . ." (*GI*, 25). It is extremely interesting that in the same interview Fisher reveals that an earlier book by Davie, *Ezra Pound: Poet as Sculptor*, provided a source for the very aspect of his work that these skilled readers are bent on exaggerating—the representational or the realist (*GI*, 32). Now I have not intended in what I have written thus far to suggest that a mimetic impulse does not exist in Fisher, only that its job is usually the production of parts that take their place in configurations in which the effect of the whole is non-mimetic, as in assemblage or constructivist art. But it is necessary now to qualify this claim by considering the nature of the subject in Fisher's work, the "I" which perceives, creates, moves among his images, and, finally, becomes itself an object in an overall design.

I mentioned at the outset the titles of two early poems, 'For Realism' and 'The Memorial Fountain.' In the latter, the speaker looking at the fountain describes himself as "a thirty-five-year-old man,/ poet / by temper realist . . . / working to distinguish an event from an opinion." In the Grosseteste interview, Fisher tells us that he was looking at two things when he wrote 'The Memorial Fountain'—"a very vulgar thing," the fountain, which was "an actual reality which looked fictive," and passages in Davie's book on Pound in which Davie "makes a good deal of play with ideas about realism," saying that "there's something of a joke going on." The joke had to do with the fact that "what I was portraying was already rendered, that the rendering was real" (*GI*, 32), and certainly too with the fact that this realist, looking at passages in Davie, was not, or not any longer, the sort of representational writer whose realism Davie might want to sponsor—and later would think he had in the chapter on Fisher in *Thomas Hardy and British Poetry*. In a recent article, John Ash describes the speaker of the poem as "a realist for whom realism is no longer adequate," quoting from an earlier moment in the *Grosseteste* interview where Fisher says, "I find it a bit of an irritation to make fictive things which look fictive in order to show that I am not merely a brute documentary writer." And so he "plays with" a landscape that "didn't need to be rendered fictive since it WAS so."[16] But the interest here is really in the subject, the speaker, the observer who in the companion poem writes about what is required 'For Realism.' And I think the orientation of this observer is best approached as Fisher suggests we approach a passage in 'Five Morning Poems from a Picture by Manet,' taking it as a "sort of sortie or sally from which I've withdrawn, or withdrew pretty quickly" (*GI*, 22).

All of this is to say that the observer in the early poems, including *City*, is a less stable figure than we might suppose. Davie takes the speaker in *City* to be the poet himself speaking in his own voice, finding there to be no grounds "for thinking that the 'I' of the poem is a persona behind which the poet conceals himself."[17] Fisher, on the other hand, sees the observer as "dramatized" and "wedging himself into a Byronic posture" in which he "speaks as if afflicted in his sensibilities" (*GI*, 36). Peter Barry has said that neither in *City* nor in 'The Handsworth Liberties' (the first sections of which were published in the same Grosseteste pamphlet that contains the interview) does Fisher avoid turning people into specimens, or things.[18] But Fisher does not attempt to avoid this, and indeed the subject—the "I" which is responsible for the process—is the most conspicuous specimen in the poem, correctly identified by Barry as the Romantic solitary, the "I" as an "eye," looking (as it does, disembodied, from the cover of Fisher's *Collected Poems*), but also seen, objectified, thinged (as it also is on the cover).

> I . . . see no ghosts of men and women, only the gigantic
> ghost of stone . . . (21)

I . . . see people made of straws, rags, cartons . . . kitchen
refuse . . . (23)
I stare into the dark . . . (27)
I see . . . as it might be floating in the dark . . . (28)
I have often felt myself to be vicious, in living so much by the
eye . . . (28)

I want to believe I live in a single world. That is why I am
keeping my eyes at home while I can. The light keeps on
separating the world like a table knife: it sweeps across what
I see and suggests what I do not. The imaginary comes to me
with as much force as the real, the remembered with as much
force as the immediate. The countries on the map divide and
pile up like ice-floes . . . I feel only a belief that I should not
be here . . . (29)

But being "here"—there, in the assemblage—is the condition required
for arriving at what may be *City*'s most radical, and of course unforeseen,
anticipation of *A Furnace*: the implication that we cannot know
objective reality at all; that we inhabit our minds and know what they
have built; that we are the process of our building and also all the bricks.
That is why "each thought is at once translucent and icily capricious."
And if Pound thought the gods were eternal states of mind and that
they manifest themselves when such states of mind take form, then
Fisher's "polytheism without gods" is a remarkable way to describe the
transience of his observer's thoughts which partly form the multifaceted
assemblage in which he is himself assembled, the parts of which—if
something must be imitated—may yet mime, like the works on exhibit
of that foundry patternmaker in 'Diversions,' "the comportment of the
gods" whom the observer's polytheism does without.

But Fisher is not entirely happy with the speaker/observer in
City because, although not identical with the autobiographical, social
self—what Fisher calls, following Michael Hamburger, the "empirical
self"[19]—he "hasn't got the discontinuous self . . . which I would claim to
have portrayed in later writing" (*GI*, 36). Also, of course, the experience
of the dramatized speaker/observer overlaps with—doubtless through
exaggeration—certain aspects of Fisher's own experience. While Fisher
wishes, in retrospect, that he had not created such a romantic/dramatic

presence in *City*, he does not want his poems spoken by the voice of the empirical self either. Of 'The Entertainment of War,' that section of *City* in which the speaker probably comes closest to reproducing specific details of Fisher's autobiographical past, Fisher says that these stanzas "about some of my relatives getting killed in an air raid" are "the thing most untypical of anything I believe about poetry that I ever wrote" (*GI*, 25). And in 'The Poplars,' he writes of needing "to withdraw/ From what is called my life / And from my net / of assembled desires" both in order "to know" adequately the objects, represented here by the poplars, that he would engage in his writing—he will learn that he cannot "know" them, although he can fit them into his constructions well enough—and also to avoid becoming "a cemetery of performance" in his life outside his art.

One way of "withdrawing from his life" is to create a dramatic persona and externalize it in his poetry, something which Fisher feels he has done, if not in 'The Entertainment of War' and 'The Poplars,' then in most of the rest of *City*. Another way is constantly and consciously to probe away at the empirical self in an attempt to locate a cognitive self, as it were, buried beneath it and then "try to steer a sufficiently agile course [that you] may be able to see the back of your own head" (*GI*, 33). This is a matter, in Rimbaud's terms, of locating the "I" that is being thought, rather than the I that is thinking. In 'Of the Empirical Self and for Me' Fisher writes:

> In my poems there's seldom
> any I or you—
>
> > you know me, Mary;
> > you wouldn't expect it of me—

and many of the shorter poems on this subject are almost jokes, poems which Peter Barry has called the poet's "wry explanations of why he must remain in the corner he has written himself into."[20] But I'm certain that Fisher regards this corner not, as Barry implies, to be one that constrains him as a poet, but rather to be the very corner which he must inhabit to be free to understand constraint itself and write the kind of poems which he wishes to compose. As he has said in the *Grosseteste* interview, "[it] seems to me a very honorable thing to try

. . . to catch time or the limits of the perceptive field at [their] tricks of limiting consciousness of the world" (*GI*, 33). But how, exactly, is this to be done, and what new kinds of forms emerge from the processes adopted after *City* and the *Collected Poems* of 1969? The journey to *A Furnace*, Fisher's masterpiece and his revision of *City*, is a long one, with major stages on the way recorded in 'The Cut Pages,' 'Stopped Frames and Set Pieces,' 'Metamorphoses,' 'Matrix,' 'Handsworth Liberties,''Diversions,' 'New Diversions,' and 'Wonders of Obligation,' the eight cycles that I think comprise Fisher's most important work after *City* and *The Ship's Orchestra*, and before *A Furnace*. It will be useful, however, before looking at three of these cycles, to consider a very recent poem about the empirical self in order to understand why Fisher's later constructions are so bent on excluding it.

Often it will start without me and come soon to where I once was
whereupon I am able for a while to speak freely . . .
                              I have never chosen
to speak about what I have
myself said, seldom of what I have done.
Though these things are my life
they have not the character of truth I require.

. . . .

Often it will start without me. More truthfully
other than without me it wouldn't, I have to be away . . .
                              taking that walk is compulsory, for
there's something about me
I don't want around at such moments—maybe
my habit of not composing . . .

. . . .

Whatever I start from
I go for the laws of its evolution,
de-socializing art, diffusing it
through the rest till there's no escaping it. Art talks

of its own processes, or talks about the rest
in terms of the processes of art; or stunts itself
to talk about the rest in the rest's own terms
of crisis and false report—entertainment,
that worldliness that sticks to me
so much I get sent outside
when the work wants to start

For the poetry, the work of art, to begin, the empirical self must be somehow gotten round, sent on a walk, outwitted. Otherwise, it will take over the process of writing and talk about itself, socialize art, grow worldly, discuss the evening news. 'Lessons in Composition,' the poem from which I have quoted that appears among the most recent work in *Poems 1955–1987*, echoes the notion that "the poem has always/ already started" from 'If I Didn't' in *The Thing about Joe Sullivan* and anticipates a key passage from the beginning of *A Furnace* .[21]

Something's decided
to narrate
in more dimensions that I can know
the gathering in
and giving out of the world on a slow
pulse . . .

What is involved here, I think, is a freeing of poiesis in the cognitional self through a kind of Heideggerian openness to language which augments Fisher's openness to perceptual stimulation, even to the point of hallucination, leading to an art which goes about its proper work, which "talks of its own processes, or talks about the rest / in terms of the processes of art," and to the effacing of the autobiographical, social, empirical "I" which does not know, to borrow the conclusion of Fisher's poem for Michael Hamburger, "the language / language gets my poems out of." What "will often start without me," what "has always already started," the "something" that "wants to narrate," is an active process which Fisher seeks to enter in various ways, and, moreover, one which leads him to a place in which his experience of the process is intensified and deepened—a place first discovered in the isolation and fear of a youthful illness which he now identifies as the location of his imagination, combining "a sense of lyrical remoteness with an apprehension of something turbulent, bulky, and dark." [22] The methods of entry into the process—and through it to the place—vary from work to work, but they may be seen to begin afresh after the 1969 *Collected Poems* in the rapid association of improvisation and to end in the high artifice of Vorticist construction.

It was through an improvisational piece, *The Cut Pages*, that Fisher managed to work his way through a severe writing block that had cut off composition entirely between 1966 and 1970. In some ways, the practice of improvisation is related to the automatic writing with which he had experimented as early as 1956 after having been introduced to the work of Americans like Zukofsky, Creeley and Olson, the effect of which was intended "to get me out of my own way." In an introductory note to *The Cut Pages*, Fisher tells us that the improvisations in the book are intended "to give the words as much relief as possible from serving in planned situations; so the work was taken forward with no programme beyond the principle that it should not know where its next meal was coming from. It was unable to anticipate, but it could have on the spot whatever it could manage to ask for. This method produced very rapid changes of direction"—and certainly also got rid of the empirical "I."

The method in *The Cut Pages* suggests not only an analogy with Fisher's experience of playing jazz in which, when one musician takes over the improvisation from another or begins to work variations on a known theme, the music "has always already started," but also Heidegger's notion of language speaking through our listening when, as Gerald Bruns has said, "nothing gets signified . . . but things make their appearance in the sense of coming into their own." [23] It is difficult to quote effectively from *The Cut Pages*, but this is the way the work begins:

Coil   If you can see the coil hidden in this pattern, you're colour-blind

            Pale patterns, faded card, coral card, faded card, screen card, window fade

Whorl   If you can see this word and say it without hesitation you're deaf

Then we can get on with frame

Frameless   Meat rose, dog-defending, trail-ruffling

Once the improvisation, the listening which has given access to a process, produces materials out of which to build a form, serial construction gets under way, a construction which Fisher regards to be methodical and systematic—"self-branching and self-proliferating," he calls it (*GI*, 34)—but different from the "additive" technique first explored in *The Ship's Orchestra* and developed in 'Matrix,' 'Handsworth Liberties,' and other cycles.[24] But in *The Cut Pages*, as in these other works, Fisher characteristically creates a model of certain precincts of the place to which the process leads and in which it continues to unfold, that mental space discovered in his illness—and later identified with very early memories unlocked by words—characterized by "lyrical remoteness and an apprehension of something turbulent, bulky, and dark."

The way this works will become clearer by looking at 'Handsworth Liberties,' a poem that at first glance would seem to have much in common with *City*. It represents a process analogous to the one in full view in Fisher's recent 'Home Pianist's Companion' in which, in the course of actual piano improvisations, what appears to be "a disorder of twofold sense"—visual images asserting themselves as the pianist concentrates on his playing—turns out in fact to be "an order thinking for me as I play." The act of listening to his own playing projects "an image trail" for the pianist across "what looked like emptiness . . ." all the way to "the utterly forgotten," a vestigial figure from a lost time who resurfaces also in *A Furnace*, "primitively remembered, / just a posture of her, an apron, / a gait."[25] But the analogous process is hardly in full view in the 'Handsworth Liberties.' For some time, in fact, it was deliberately hidden.

Fisher described his method of composition in the Handsworth poem only after it had been in print for five years.[26] It derived, it seems, from a sequence of associations which developed between certain recorded performances of music and the mental images which, in

each case, came into his mind when he first heard them. All of the
images are associated with various locations in the Handsworth area of
Birmingham as it existed in his youth. Eddie Condon's 'Home Cooking'
produced "a pleasant sunny morning on the stretch of grass outside
what was then Holmes' Garage at the junction of Church Lane and
Grove Lane"; Billy Banks' 'Spider Crawl' had its existence somewhere
in the air of a leafy and peaceful suburban street called Butler's Road,
viewed from the north-east"; Beethoven's 'Arietta' and its variations
from the piano sonata Opus 111—for not all the music consisted of
jazz improvisations—was "tucked up under the branches that used to
overhang a long-disappeared set of railings" a little way along the same
road that elsewhere contained Ralph Vaughan Williams' 'Fantasia on a
Theme of Thomas Tallis.'"[27] And so on. In the poems, Fisher provides a
small gallery of sixteen mental snapshots, the process which has "always
already started" when he hears the music having given access to one
precinct of his mental space—call it 'Handsworth, Birmingham'—out
of which the images, not quite of "places," more like "the backgrounds
and marginal details of photographs and postcards,"[28] issued as language:
on Butler's Road, at the junction of Church Lane and Grove Lane,
tucked under the branches that used to overhang a set of railings. The
character of the listening is different here from what it amounts to in
'The Cut Pages,' but it is still listening. And the individual scenes lead
downwards toward the penultimate, all of them pointing finally toward
that zone which is "turbulent, bulky, dark, and lyrically remote."

> No dark in the body
> deep as this
>   even though the sun
> hardens the upper world.
>   A ladder
> climbs down under the side
> in the shadow of the tank
> and crosses tarry pools.
>   There are
> metals that burn the air;
> a deathly blue stain
> in the cinder ballast,
> and out there past the shade
> sunlit rust hangs on the still water.

Like 'Matrix,' which preceded it, 'Handsworth Liberties' has to do with "getting about in the mind" and locating there materials in a visual memory which is, Fisher says, "hallucinatory to a stupefying degree" (*GI*, 21). The scenes in the cycle, cut off for the reader from a music which the poet does not cease to hear, arrange themselves in silence. But we are involved, without our fully knowing it, with Fisher's listening, his "diffusing of art through all the rest [of experience] till there is no escaping it," his "talk about the rest in terms of the processes of art," and his search for a self that is thought by language which "will start without me and come soon to where I once was."

'Matrix,' the title sequence of Fisher's 1971 volume, is as deceptive in the initial impression it makes as the 'Handsworth Liberties,' and grows even stranger than the later poem when we understand the manner in which the poet enters a process which has already begun when he starts to write. On first glance, the ten sections look like brief descriptive pieces treating a costal area which seems to include islands, inlets, shingle, gardens, paths, and so on—a kind of seaside parallel to one's first impression of the urban "scenes" in 'Handsworth Liberties.' But again we are dealing with a mental rather than an actual physical place, and again also with a configuration which involves "the diffusing of art through all the rest [of experience] till there is no escaping it." This is how Fisher describes the work's origin:

> The sequence of ten poems called 'Matrix,' from which the book takes its name, is probably the most developed piece of work in verse I have done, a comparatively rich mix of allusions and sensory imagery. Some while ago, without warning, I had one of those curious near-hallucinatory experiences in which one is able to stand outside one's mind and watch its oddly assorted memories quickly re-programming themselves to make new forms. On this occasion there was a rain of images which seemed to be joining one another according to some logic of their own. They were nearly all to do with works of art; and I could see impressions from Böcklin, Claude Monet, Thomas Mann and lurid tourist souvenirs from Japan, among many others, forming up into relationships which I should never have presumed to try to impose on them consciously. The complex collective image they made was still present after

some months had passed, and the poems of the sequence are a
sort of tour of its interior.[29]

The looking (as from the outside) at the mind's display becomes
a listening when the language of Mann's *Dr. Faustus* mingles with the
names of things in Manet, Böcklin, and postcards from Japan in the
dictation of Fisher's muse as mental-programmer and tour guide. There
is, that is to say, an element of automatism once again implicit in this
process. But 'Matrix' is also, according to Fisher (writing of course before
the composition of *A Furnace*), "the most developed piece of work in
verse I have done," and the development involves the construction of
individual units from the "complex collective image," what he describes
elsewhere as the breaking up of—or separating out of details from—
something like an immensely complex color slide or stained glass
window (*GI*, 21).[30] There is an externalization, through language, of
the mental images, and an objectification of them through austerities of
form that once again recall the Russian Constructivists and anticipate
the Vorticist affinities of *A Furnace*. As Marjorie Perloff writes about
an early Malevich, quoting Roman Jacobson on Khlebnikov, Fisher's
cycle manifests characteristics of *nanizyvanie*, "the conjoining of motifs
which do not proceed on the basis of logical necessity but are combined
according to the principle of formal necessity, similarity or contrast . . .,"
and has the effect "of dispelling the autonomy of the lyrical 'I'," a version
of the self no less problematic for Fisher than the despised empirical
"I".[31] (One could also apply the notion of *nanizyvanie* to the work of
Fisher's frequent collaborator, Tom Phillips, whose illustration appears
on the cover of *Matrix*.) In 'Matrix,' the lyrical "I" which otherwise
might speak—or, God help us, even sing—is effectively dispelled in
favor of an implied cognitive self whose perceptions are broken down,
sorted out, and labelled through the agency of Mann, Böcklin, and
Monet. In the 'Handsworth Liberties' a version of the "I" appears twice
(in sections 12 and 13), but in the most equivocal way possible, where
"Travesties of the world / come out of the fog / and rest at the boundary"
leading (in 12) to the conclusion that "I shall go with them / sometimes
/ till the journey dissolves under me," and where Fisher writes (in 13) of
a slope in the mist: "I / never went there / Someone else did, and I went
with him." Through various contortions in the poems of the 1970s and

early 1980s, Fisher seeks to see, through the eyes of this equivocal "I"
and through the agency of art works, "the back of [his] own head" (as
he has it in the Grosseteste interview) and, in a manner analogous to
that of *City*, to make the perceiver a fundamental property of the thing
perceived even as the thing perceived becomes a fundamental process
in the perceiver's act of writing, always already begun. As he writes in a
poem to Tom Phillips:

> Caught sight of myself
> in the monitor
>
> The world looked like itself
> I looked like it too
> not like me
> as if I was
> solid or something . . .
>
> It's not hard to look busy
> from behind . . .

In what is perhaps the most impassioned moment in the *Grosseteste*
interview, Fisher returns to the sources of his art in jazz, painting and
printmaking, saying that "I very often turn to people who do a very
small thing and do it again and do it again and do it again and vary and
vary and vary." He cites the musicians Pee Wee Russell, Jess Stacey, and
Eddie Condon, and also the three minutes available to such musicians
on one side of a 78 rpm record—brief takes and re-takes, music that
"fills and exhausts, fills and exhausts," something that becomes "a life"
(*GI*, 31). And he turns again to the printmakers and illustrators—
ultimately to Paul Klee—for what can surely be taken as an analogue to
the "additive method" in the cycles which I have examined as typical of
his work leading from *City* to *A Furnace*:

> Again you do a thing, and you haven't exhausted it, you haven't
> inflated it, and you do it again, same size. You do a thing which
> is slightly different, you turn it backwards, do it again, nothing
> is wasted. You stick to what you first thought of, you do it again.
> This appeals to me enormously. The idea of Klee working away
> at things, having a theory, and doing many variants, many

alphabets, many grids, and having an apparently inexhaustible source of statements and restatements which are like frames, like hours, like days, very simple conceptions. I like that.

This would also seem to describe Fisher himself at work. And the artist's rage "to make visible with charged energy," as Klee wrote from the Bauhaus, rather than merely seeking "to render the visible," is Fisher's rage.[32] It takes him just about as far from the poetics of Philip Larkin as it is possible to be.

Fisher has said that he seeks to avoid allowing his cycles to "solidify" or "turn into a collection of colour slides" by stalking up on "a perceptual field jammed solid with sensory data" and breaking it up into mobile, unstable parts (*GI*, 21). Nonetheless, if I were to posit an analogy for the cumulative effect of typical Fisher sequences and cycles consistent with his statement about Paul Klee, it would be something like a slide show—the 'Handsworth Liberties' he called "a gallery of 16 mental snapshots"—or an exhibition of prints that would come to mind. In a very early poem, Fisher wrote of looking out a window "that holds what few events come round / like slides, and in what seems capricious sequence," and there is something of that feeling in an initial reading of the 'Glenthorne Poems,' 'Matrix,' 'Handsworth Liberties,' 'Diversions,' 'New Diversions,' and, in a rather different way, the earlier 'Stopped Frames' and 'Seven Attempted Moves.'

But repeated readings show us that these sequences are far more systematic than capricious—sufficiently systematic in the poet's convoluted treatment of cognition that we might even be reminded of the subject-object relationship in a work of M.C. Escher's such as 'Print Gallery,' an etching in which the observer—a man at an exhibition of prints—is ultimately found to be standing inside the same work of art he is looking at. About this etching Francisco Varela has drawn the following conclusions—conclusions which it is tempting to apply to Fisher in his sequences and cycles:

> We find ourselves in a cognitive domain, and we cannot leap out of it or choose its beginnings or modes . . . In finding the world as we do, we forget all we did to find it as such, entangled in the strange loop of our actions through our body. Much like the young man in the Escher engraving 'Print Gallery,' we see

a world that turns into the very substratum which produces us, thereby closing the loop and intercrossing domains. As in the Escher engraving, there is nowhere to step out into. And if we were to try, we would find ourselves in an endless circle that vanishes into an empty space right in its middle.[33]

"No system describes the world," Fisher writes of a projected film at the end of 'Metamorphoses,' and one must be consistent on this point turning from his poems which can be thought about as if they were a run of slides or prints lining up to form an Escher loop to the "system" of the double spiral in *A Furnace*. But Fisher's vortex in this magnificent poem, like the works of the foundry patternmaker in the 18th section of 'Diversions' from which I quoted very early in this essay, *engages* the world it cannot describe by virtue of fulfilling analogous "conditions of myth":

it celebrates origin,
it fixes forms for endless recurrence;
it relates energy to form;
is useless in itself;

for all these reasons it also attracts
aesthetic responses in anybody
free to respond aesthetically;

and it can be thought with . . .

One thing that Fisher wants to think about in *A Furnace* is time, and he tells us in a preface that the sequence of the poem's movements "is based on a form which enacts, for me, the equivocal nature of the ways in which time can be thought about. This is the ancient figure of the double spiral, whose line turns back on itself at the centre and leads out again, against its own incoming curve."

Were there space left to do so, I think we might profitably extend the several connections made thus far between Fisher's work and the Constructivist-Bauhaus-Assemblagist aesthetic by listening to the turning of the double spiral in *A Furnace* as an elegiac backward-looking version of the forward-striding double spiral of Tatlin's famous Tower, the wooden model for his 'Monument to the Third International' and answer to Eiffel's engineers, which looked with such optimism into the industrial-communal future, but which was never built and which, as much now as in the time of his Icarus glider, is an emblem of something archaic in the way of human aspiration. Of Tatlin too, as of the foundry patternmaker, Fisher might have said: "*Everything cast in iron / must first be made of wood.*" And that such casts might mime "the comportment / of the gods in the Ethnology cases."

What there is just space enough to do is to indicate that Fisher's examination of the subject-object relationship in the context of a process that has "always already started" reaches its fullest development in this book. It would take an essay the length of what I have already written to explain the workings of so complex a poem, but I can suggest a few continuities by glossing the titles of the first two parts, 'Calling' and 'The Return,' by way of extending for a few lines a passage from the 'Introit' quoted earlier:

> Something's decided
> to narrate in more dimensions than I can know
> the gathering in
> and giving out of the world on a slow
> pulse, on a metered contraction
> that the senses enquire towards
> but may not themselves
> intercept. All I can tell it by
> is the passing trace of it
> in a patterned agitation of
> a surface that shows only
> metaphors. Riddles. Resemblances
> that have me in the chute
> as it meshes in closer, many modes
> funnelling fast through one event . . .

From this passage the subject (the speaker, the "I") which is clearly part of the process under observation—those "resemblances that have [him] in the chute" of the vortex—emerges "having eased awkwardly / into the way of being called" in Section I. At the level of narrative, this calling comes to an urban man from Gradbach Hill, a mysterious corner of North-West Staffordshire which includes Lud's Church and its legendary connection with *Sir Gawain and the Green Knight*, and thus suggests initiation and change. I also take this calling to suggest both the perfectly traditional notion of a poet being called to practice his craft, as well as the calling into existence of an internal energy externalized in the figure of the vortex and of the impulse to "make identities" which Fisher says in his preface acknowledges "a primary impulse in the cosmos."[34] In cosmological terms—and the poet has gone to school for this poem on the visionary novels of John Cowper Powys, to whom it is also dedicated—Fisher's Heraclitean cauldron through which all lines of his vortex pass explodes the matter of what was Birmingham into something like a verbal analogue to an expanding universe. *City*, in comparison, is a steady state.

In a brilliant and so far unpublished essay on *A Furnace*, Andrew Crozier makes some observations which will help me to conclude.[35] He remarks that while philosophically Fisher is not a realist, neither is he a nominalist, "for he is not concerned with real existences as such but with the signs they make by which they can be evoked. His interest in knowledge concerns cognitive modes rather than positive knowledge, and he sees its boundary fluctuating with intention. The laws of the Newtonian universe—the laws of the heavy industrial processes, and the commerce they served, that lie in ruins throughout *A Furnace*—fail to describe the involution of time and space in the mind's conjunction with the world." Where I disagree with Crozier—and where I must end—is in his contention that the mind's conjunction with the world in this poem does not "arrive, finally, at a heterodox mysticism." It seems to me that it does. 'The Return,' which no one, to my knowledge, has traced back to Ezra Pound's early poem of the same title, or to Yeats' use of it in *A Vision*, is uncanny in its dealings with the dead. If in 'Calling' the subject moves outward on the double spiral, in 'The Return' the dead—the objects in this section of the subject's thought—return to earth along the incoming curve, grounded in the present by the act of being "called" into the memory of the subject, himself "called" into the infinite reaches of the cosmos by the objects of his thought. The poem is about the return of the dead, as Yeats thought Pound's poem was.[36]

John Matthias

Whatever breaks
from stasis, radiance or dark
impending, and slides
directly and fast on its way, twisting
aspect in the torsions of the flow
this way and that,
                              then suddenly
over,
          through a single
glance of another force touching it or
bursting out of it sidelong,

doing so
fetches the timeless flux
that cannot help but practise
materialization . . .

and it fetches
timeless identities . . .

like dark-finned fish embedded in ice
they have life in them that can be revived...

Something always
coming out, back against the flow,
against the drive to be in,
                              close to the radio,
the school, the government's wars;

the sunlight, old and still,
heavy on dry garden soil,

and nameless mouths,
events without histories, voices,
animist, polytheist, metaphoric,
coming through . . .

Although these mouths, beings and voices—including Fisher's own
dead among his family and early neighbors—have "no news," they have
a life in this poem in the poet's memory as disturbing as the politics

216

of the dead in the life of the living in journeys to the underworld in Homer, Virgil, and Pound:

> They come anyway
> to the trench,
> the dead in their surprise,
> taking whatever form they can
> to push across.

It may seem ironic, given the way I began this essay, that I want to end by saying that it was probably Donald Davie, more than any other critic, who was equipped to grapple with both the function of the vortex and the metaphysics in *A Furnace*. Davie the Poundian was not the same critic who wrote *Thomas Hardy and British Poetry*, and his approach to 'Ideas in *The Cantos*' in his Modern Masters series volume on Pound could have been usefully applied to analogous issues in *A Furnace*. His reluctance to write about the later Fisher—there is nothing on his work in Davie's *Under Briggflatts: A History of Poetry in Great Britain 1960–1988*—is a loss for Fisher's poetry, Fisher's readers, and for Davie's last book engaging the work of his own important contemporaries. Donald Davie died in 1995 at about the time this essay was initially published. The dialogue, insofar as there is a dialogue going on in the piece, has been with a living critic. Davie's loss to British poetry and criticism was a very great one.

Left Hands and Wittgensteins

For Roy Fisher at Seventy and, inter alios, *Leon Fleisher, Blaise Cendrars*

Paul's brother Ludwig the philosopher had said
the world is everything that is the case
in case you lost your arm. In case you could not play
for all the world. *No left hand*
we used to say as glib precocious critics of the young
Ahmad Jamal, one of us the southpaw pitcher
on the high school baseball team who struck out every
right hand batter in the junior league.
But Paul was *all* left hand who bitched at both Ravel
and Sergei Prokofiev but nonetheless
performed their music no right hand would ever play.
The world was everything that was the case
when Blaise Cendrars also lost his arm. In that same war.
In that same war where everything that was the case
exploded in the world. My friend the southpaw pitcher studied
in the end with Leon Fleisher who awoke one day
with no right hand as a result of carpal-tunnel stress. A syn-
drome: drone, his repertory was diminished but he played
Prokofiev he played Ravel, and all thanks due to Wittgenstein
whose world was everything that was the case.

Left hand, left wing? Roy, are all right-handers Tories
in their bones? They'd case your joint as if
they'd lost most everything left in the world.
(Or would you pack them in your case with all the world
except for B and exit in that key?) I weep
for your right arm, your stroked-out days of therapy,
your egging on your brain to find a few more millimeters
of its limb. But what's permission but commission
to a left-hand poet, left-hand pianist at seventy?
You might well go ask Wittgenstein, might well ask Cendrars.
Then go ahead—put the piano at risk, put the poem
in jeopardy: Millennium's a comin' after, Roy:
If anything could be the case
the world is everything that is the case.
Are those iambs, da-dah da-dah? Is that in 4/4 time?

Longs and Shorts

And will a photograph save us? We're old enough
To have had a temptation to think
That the old cliché about *ars longa* had some
Actual merit. What's long
Are the drifting sands as we plod to the
Music of *vita brevis*. But it *is* a music, tra-la.
It seems but a moment ago you were only 70
And we urged you in your words to
Put the piano at risk, to left-hand us a poem.
But photography's the democratic art.
I just saw a snap of you in South Bend, Indiana
The very night of your reading in 1980.
It was also the first night you'd spent outside
Of Britain: Not in Paris, not in Rome, but
South Bend, Indiana. I can't even say it's the
Midwestern Birmingham, although you
Liked and found familiar the "abandoned workings,"
As W.H. Auden would say, of the old
Studebaker auto plant. After the reading we
Travelled out to the house of a prof
In the same car with another guest of the school
Who seemed even more laid-back
Than you, though also a bit incongruous.
He too both wrote and put the piano at risk. He too
Had a cosmopolitan soul. At the party
You sat together on a sofa—clearly someone
Would play. As you jazzed the *vita brevis*
Out of the upright, *Ars Longa* himself
Appeared with his camera. And here in
A short book is the picture long after the music
Has fled. I can see it's my friend Roy Fisher
Fishing for the right notes in a riff.
But the caption grasping at by god immortal life
Declaims like Caesar's newsboy: *John Cage*
Plays four minutes of silence
While on the opposite page Harold Brodkey's
Mislabeled *Joseph Brodsky*.
Irreversible, Roy. But what the hell?

219

British Poetry at Y2K

[*This long survey of British poetry at the turn of the century has, of course, aged by now, along with the 2000s. I have no desire, however, to bring it up to date a decade and more after it was written. Though new poets have emerged and older poets have done some surprising work, my opinions about the general scene as represented in the anthologies and critical books under review remain basically the same. Although a number of good poets of my own generation—Richard Berengarten, Jeremy Hooker, Ken Smith, Alan Halsey, Peter Robinson—are missing from this discussion, my original brief was to draw a map connecting certain established encampments and solitary homesteads generally recognized, or at least recognizable, by the last decade of the twentieth century. I should also note that I was unable to discuss much of the experimental work by British women just then coming within view of a general poetry readership. I would like to have written about Denise Riley and Caroline Bergvall, in particular.*

It is important to make very clear that I was writing at a time when the table of contents of Keith Tuma's Oxford Anthology of Twentieth-Century British and Irish Poetry *still included poems by J.H. Prynne. Having been given the contents before publication of the book itself, I wrote as if Prynne's work were included, as it should have been. However, at some point between Tuma's final preparation of his vast manuscript and Oxford's printing of the text, J.H. Prynne withdrew his poems. The reader of this survey is encouraged to imagine the Oxford anthology containing a substantial group of Prynne's poems while also understanding that they are in fact not there. Somehow this seems exactly right.*

Originally intended for Parnassus, *my essay turned out to be far too long at fifty pages for even a journal famous for giving its authors space to have their say.* (Electronic Book Review *eventually published it online.*) *The books I initially agreed to consider were the following: Simon Armitge and Robert Crawford, eds,* The Penguin Book of Poetry from Britain and Ireland; *Richard Caddel and Peter Quartermain, eds,* Other: British and Irish Poetry since 1970; *Ian Sinclair, ed.,* Conductors of Chaos; *Keith Tuma,* Fishing by Obstinate Isles: Modern and Postmodern British Poetry and American Readers; *Sean O'Brien,* The Deregulated Muse: Essays on Contemporary British and Irish Poetry. *I also consulted a dozen other books in significant ways, and these are listed at the end of the survey.*

Re-reading the essay now, I also see that I would have said some rather different things about these poets, their contexts, and the whole tradition of transatlantic dialogue between British and American writers had I been writing a year later, after September 11, 2001.]

§

I: Penguins, Conductors, and Others

*Some blessed Hope, whereof he knew
And I was unaware.*

Thomas Hardy, 1900

*. . . Wrong from the start—
No, hardly . . .*

Ezra Pound, 1920

*Britannia's own narrow
miracle of survival
was gifted to us by cryptanalysts . . .*

The Bletchley magi!

Geoffrey Hill, 1999

My attempt in this essay will be to conduct a survey of some British poetries at the turn of the millennium. Any number of books besides the five listed above might also have provided an occasion or excuse for the undertaking, but these five—three anthologies and two books of criticism—will serve. It is perhaps a propitious moment for Americans to look again at British poetry. (I will only glance at the Irish. America is in love with Irish poetry and does not need to hear anything more at the moment about Harvard's Heaney, Stanford's Boland, or Princeton's Muldoon.) One does have a sense that the smoothly running machinery of the post-Movement, post-Larkin, Oxbridge-London establishment has finally broken down, that in spite of the recent appointment to the Laureateship of Andrew Motion, Larkin's biographer and co-editor of the Penguin anthology the three anthologies under review seek to displace, even the Palace and Prime Minister have recently had to consider the merits of poets as diverse as Carol Ann Duffy, Geoffrey Hill, Tony Harrison and Benjamin Zephaniah. The ghost in the machine, the Y2K virus of modernism and postmodernism, has been mutating largely undetected for quite some time. Finally it threatens to kill off its host.

Not, however, without some resistance. I suppose it's unfair to characterize the Armitage/Crawford anthology as a book that represents the mainstream in its derivation from a kind of Hardyesque ethos epitomized by Philip Larkin in his poetry and by Donald Davie both in his early critical writings and in his polemical *Thomas Hardy and British Poetry* of 1973. Among other things, there are too many Scottish eccentrics in its pages. Too many Irish and Welsh poets as well. And yet not only does one fail to find any of the younger experimental poets included in Iain Sinclair's *Conductors of Chaos*, but the selections which overlap with the poets represented in *Other* are chiefly those from Guyana and Jamaica: an attempt to achieve a racially diverse table of contents following an Introduction called, importantly, 'The Democratic Voice.' And democratic it is, in a serious sense to which we will turn in due course. But the book also has the disconcerting feel of a democratic document of an almost Clintonesque kind—a book that might have resulted as much from reader polls and focus groups as from fiercely independent editorial judgment.

My first epigraph above, taken from Hardy's 'The Darkling Thrush,' is meant to suggest, without irony, that the native bird is indeed still singing its song. But it's also meant to remind us what an "anthology piece" is, whether in 1900 or 2000—a poem which, as Davie said in his Hardy book, cannot possibly give offense, whether a bird or a dog. In spite of the importance of certain unexpected selections to which I will return, Armitage and Crawford have edited a book more than half-full of anthology pieces—from Muir and Auden to Motion, Duffy, and Fenton. But I do not mean to characterize the inoffensiveness of anthology pieces in Davie's sense of innocuous composition. I mean inoffensive entirely with regard to over-familiarity and reader expectation. Ted Hughes' 'The Thought Fox' is hardly innocuous writing, but in a strange way it cannot possibly any longer give offense.

It is not the same poem in this Penguin anthology that it was in *The Hawk in the Rain* in 1957. Larkin's 'This Be the Verse,' Heaney's 'Punishment,' and even Plath's 'Daddy' have suffered from a similar anthological domestication over the years: all these former foxes are now wagging their tails by the hearth. The reader, having encountered these poems in a dozen other anthologies or studied them in school, expects to find them here; he opens the book and there they are.

I in fact respect Armitage and Crawford highly, and I like their refusal of the typical editorial vice of making their anthology a showcase for their own work, which indeed is not in the book and which, in the case of both poets, is much better than a lot of work that is. But where they say their book "is the kind of anthology in which [they] might have liked their work to appear," I find myself thinking how much more interesting it would be to find it in a volume like Keith Tuma's forthcoming *Oxford Anthology of Twentieth Century British and Irish Poetry*, where it would be read with a wide range of poetries written from aesthetic assumptions wholly different from their own—alongside, in fact, the work of many poets appearing in *Other* and *Conductors of Chaos*.

While it is still too early to examine more of the Oxford anthology than its table of contents kindly sent me by the editor, Tuma's book will clearly attempt to establish a dialogue, if not a reconciliation, among pre-modern, modern, anti-modern and post-modern poetries generally assumed to be antagonistic to one another in the three anthologies under review while rescuing from oblivion certain foundational works of British modernism which will tilt the volume, which covers the entire century, in a direction favored by the American angler who fished by obstinate isles rather than the one upon the shore with arid plains behind him. Tuma's critical volume attempts to do something similar. Neither the Caddel/Quartermain *Other* nor the Iain Sinclair *Conductors of Chaos* are interested in anything like a dialogue with the majority of poets appearing in the Armitage/Crawford Penguin. Of the 144 poets appearing in the Penguin, which covers poetry from both Britain and Ireland since 1945, only three poets appear also in *Conductors* and only eight in *Other*. While *Other* includes British and Irish poets only since 1970, *Conductors* gives itself a longer memory by the innovation of making room for personal selections of poets from an earlier generation made by five of the younger contributors: J.F. Hendry by Andrew Crozier, W.S. Graham by Tony Lopez, David Jones by Drew Milne, David Gascoyne by Jeremy Reed, and Nicholas Moore by Peter Riley. This is to my knowledge a wholly original idea and constitutes the particular genius of this very odd book. Interestingly, two of the three poets in *Conductors* who are also in the Penguin are David Jones and W.S. Graham. The third, the only poet to appear in all three books—a perhaps unenviable distinction—is Denise Riley.

What is familiar, and perhaps over-familiar, in *Other* and *Conductors* is not a range of anthology pieces or a large group of famous poets. In fact, aside from some few readers who make it a point to consult British small press publications and journals, most Americans will be encountering these poems and poets for the first time. The familiar aspect of these books has to do with their editors' aggressive presentation of a self-consciously avant-garde agenda and their selection of poems and poets working in international modernist and postmodernist modes that share many evolving and often contradictory assumptions with several generations of American experimental writing: the early modernists, the Objectivists, the New York School, the Black Mountain poets, the Beats, and the Language Poets. Other affinities which these poets variously share are mostly continental or Russian: Rilke, Celan, Rimbaud, Tzara, Apollinaire, Pessoa, the Futurists, and the Constructivists. In his critical volume and, implicitly, in the contents of his Oxford anthology as well, Keith Tuma takes a qualified stand— qualified by his understanding that one must remain alert to local contexts—in favor of this lingua franca of internationalist poetics which "seeks to either transcend (momentarily) or resist all cultural practices that gather identities too quickly and rigidly into the nation." Deriving his title from 'Hugh Selwyn Mauberley', he finds the resistance among many in Britain to the poets included in these anthologies to be a form of "obstinance." "Wrong from the start," said E.P.'s London critic...

"No, hardly . . ." And yet one does worry a bit about the continuing authenticity of an aggressively avant-garde stance at the turn of the new century. Ezra Pound, as Davie has shown, is sometimes at his most attractive when, in his private correspondence, doffing his hat along with his public role as impresario of the new, he seeks to make accommodation with Hardy himself: "I don't think mere praise is any good—I know where I can get it . . . Forgive me if I blurt out this demand for frankness." So let it be said that, frankly, although my own sympathies, like Keith Tuma's, are generally attuned to much of the work in *Other* and *Conductors,* there is something almost silly about the way in which the work is presented, beginning even with the titles of the books. These lightning rods and creatures from the black lagoon! The editors of both volumes, like Armitage and Crawford in their different way, narrate a version of cultural history intended to favor the work they present, a story told at greater length and with greater nuance in Tuma's critical volume and given a thoroughly different focus and moral in O'Brien's *The Deregulated Muse.*

The *Other* and *Conductor's* version of this oft-told tale goes something like this. After the war an exhausted Britain was only able to launch that nominally challenged movement called The Movement. Enshrined in Robert Conquest's anthology *New Lines,* Philip Larkin and his friends held the high ground unchallenged until A. Alvarez, in *The New Poetry,* attacked them for gentility and prefaced his selection of postwar British poets not only with a fighting Introduction but with poems by Lowell and Berryman and Plath and Sexton as a kind of lesson in intensity for the anaemic Brits. But Alvarez got it wrong. The real stateside news was not to be found among the confessional—or, as Alvarez called them, "extremist"—poets, but from Donald Allen's *The New American Poetry,* itself in mortal battle against the academic-oriented Hall/Pack/Simpson anthologies of the period, with its New Yorkers and Projectivists and Beats. By the late sixties and early seventies, centers of opposition to the mainstream had established themselves around J.H. Prynne in Cambridge and Eric Mottram in London. While Mottram briefly opened up *The Poetry Review* and The Poetry Society itself to innovative and experimental work, Prynne influenced (or actually taught) an entire generation of poets including Andrew Crozier, John James, Wendy Mulford, Peter Riley, Rod Mengham, John Wilkinson and Tony Lopez. Journals such as *The English Intelligencer* and *Grosseteste Review* were established, and presses actually edited by poets among the *Other*s and *Conductors* briefly flourished. Late work by indigenous British modernists like David Jones, Hugh MacDiarmid and Basil Bunting was published and even more fully marginalized figures like the English Mina Loy and the Irish Brian Coffey began to be noticed again. While multicultural, multiethnic and feminist influences began to make themselves felt as part of the alternative poetry scene, the establishment regrouped. The Arts Council purged Eric Mottram from *The Poetry Review*, Andrew Motion and Blake Morrison edited the *Penguin Book of Contemporary Poetry* (which promoted the work of all the wrong Irish, working class, and feminist poets and which thoroughly misunderstood postmodernism); Craig Raine took over at Faber and Faber while also launching The Martians, and Bloodaxe published the deceptive Hulse/Kennedy/Morley *New Poetry* anthology (which, like the Motion and Morrison, also backed the wrong Irishmen, working stiffs, and ladies, and which possibly misunderstood postmodernism even more thoroughly). This book more or less coincided with the arrival of the *New Generation*, with Simon Armitage as the point man, and a good deal of vulgar but commercially effective media hype on behalf of the lads.

Caddel and Quartermain oppose their anthology to "the narrow lineage of contemporary poets from Philip Larkin to Craig Raine and Simon Armitage" and to their attendant "collectives" (the Movement, the Martians, and the New Generation). They oppose the typical poems by these poets because they find them to be "a closed, monolineal utterance, demanding little of the reader but passive consumption." Iain Sinclair, who manages to mock and deride almost as many of his friends as his enemies in his Introduction, ultimately finds only Donald Allen's book and the 1987 Andrew Crozier/Tim Longville anthology of mostly Cambridge-based and Prynne-influenced poets, *A Various Art,* to be in any way models for his own. He rejects a "politically correct scorecard" of race, sex, or educational status and anthologies with anything other than an aesthetic agenda. The New Generation poets, he says, "have arrived in our midst like pod people." The work he values "is that which seems most remote, alienated, fractured." In his selections, he admits only to "registering a prejudice, not essaying an historical survey." If Sinclair's and Caddel/Quartermain's reading of recent poetry wars seems to an outsider verging on paranoia, it's worth noting that Caddel and Quartermain report that it's "no accident, in this adversarial context, that when Rupert Murdoch's media empire News International took over the Collins publishing group, an early priority was to close the Paladin Poetry series (in which a number of the most innovative writers featured here had appeared), destroying much of the remaining stock."

If there is something legitimately embattled in these two Introductions and in the contents of some of the poetry itself, there is also something disturbingly exclusionary, self-protective, and maybe even deluded as well. When Keith Tuma first mentions *Conductors of Chaos* in his book, he does so in the context of worrying the bone of authenticity as it is debated by theorists of the avant-garde like Peter Burger, Renata Poggioli, and Charles Bernstein. Willing in the end to accept a "neo-avant-garde" with its "traditions alongside other [competing] traditions," he questions Burger's rhetoric of genuineness and Poggioli's insistence on avant-garde "agonism" and "alienation." The poetry among the *Conductors* and *Others* that Tuma likes to read can be read as well in the seminar room as on the battlements. It can also instructively be read beside valuable poetries deriving from "other traditions." The problem with many among the *Others* and *Conductors* is in part their unwillingness to understand that Simon Armitage and Robert Crawford are not Rupert Murdoch and Bill Gates, that a late stage in an art's development might legitimately produce an atmosphere of accommodation and catholicity of taste, that, as Tuma says, avant-garde traditions now exist alongside other traditions and that the work itself might properly "leave its first coterie audience behind and enter the public sphere" without pretending that "radical subversion of institutions or large-scale social change is likely to result." If J.H. Prynne really ought to read Geoffrey Hill and if Hill should really read Prynne, certainly those of us who buy these books need to read both of them. It says something about the stage which the avant-garde tradition has reached, even in Britain where the going has admittedly been difficult, that anthologies published by a major university press like Wesleyan and a commercial press like Picador can even exist. And at this writing it is Oxford (OUP in Britain rather than OUP in New York, which will indeed publish Tuma's anthology)—owned by Oxford and not by Rupert Murdoch—which has recently scuttled its poetry list, a list not known for poets among the remote, the alienated, or the fractured.

My last epigraph above is from Geoffrey Hill's *The Triumph of Love*, certainly one of the great books of British poetry published during the century's last decade. It may be a symptom of an oversimplified oppositional tactics, of pitting "them" against "us" and "their" notion of a unitary culture against "our" ideas of pluralism and diversity reaching back to a fourteenth century plain full of Saxon, Norman, and Cymric folk, that Geoffrey Hill is seen in *Other* only as a poet of "stylized anglophilia" like Philip Larkin. His poetry could not, any more than Paul Muldoon's, Peter Reading's, and any number of others' in the Armitage/Crawford Penguin, possibly be characterized as "closed, monolineal utterance." Without engaging the question of who might be more remote, alienated, and fractured than thou, it's worth noting the polyvocal strategies and oblique encodings of Hill's recent work at this millennial moment of cultural dis-ease that might, in its sometimes almost autistic soundings, be read inside, rather than outside and against, the context established by work appearing in *Other* and *Conductors of Chaos*. Did Hill and Prynne know each other at Cambridge? Do they even now read each other's work with any sympathy? My guess is that the answer to both questions is no. But it is these two ferociously difficult and demanding poets who seem to me to have produced the most challenging work to come out of Britain in the last twenty years. Hill's brief evocations of *Bletchley Park* during the war in *The Triumph of Love* move me enormously. Here was a moment when the remote, the alienated and the fractured—all those mathematicians, linguists, chess grand masters, crossword-puzzle addicts, proto-computer nerds, misfit musicologists, men and women of every conceivable arcane and dubious passion—sat down together to break the Nazi codes and save the world. I like to think of Hill and Prynne and certain related poets in these books among them—*Penguins, Conductors,* and *Other*s—born again as Bletchley magi working on a common poem in common cause.

II: Island Fishing and Deregulation

Ah, as Hill's heckler from *The Triumph of Love* might say, isn't that a pretty fantasy. It's even a fantasy to assume that my American reader knows the work of more than two or three of the twenty or so poets I have alluded to thus far. That's why Keith Tuma's *Fishing By Obstinate Isles* is such a necessary and timely book.

Tuma sets himself the task of reading modern and post-modern British poetry in terms of its reception, or lack of it, by American readers and institutions. He begins the historical section of his book by arguing that British poetry—with a few important exceptions—was by the late sixties and early seventies virtually erased from the American literary consciousness by "a combination of benign neglect, ordinary ignorance, and casual half-truths of a critical journalism cognizant only of the narrowest field of extant poetry." Interestingly, this was also the very moment that Prynne in Cambridge and Mottram in London were becoming magnets for many of the poets appearing in *Other* and *Conductors*. A very few Americans—Donald Hall in a number of essays and reviews, M.L. Rosenthal and Calvin Bedient, I myself in *23 Modern British Poets* (1970)—and two or three British commuters or exiles like Donald Davie and Thom Gunn, pointed out some of what was happening or had already happened in Britain: the late work of Jones and Bunting, the early Prynne, Mina Loy's forgotten poems, the Stevens- and Williams-influenced work of the early Tomlinson, Christopher Middleton, Roy Fisher's *City*, and maybe the first books of Tom Raworth and Lee Harwood. In spite of these several voices arguing for the value and interest of certain British poets—and it's important to remember that among the younger Irish poets who had any real affinities with the modernist-influenced Brits only John Montague at this point was really visible—no one, on the whole, seemed to be paying any attention. Americans during the Vietnam and post-Vietnam period read North Americans, Latin Americans, and East Europeans. What little modern and contemporary British poetry was read or taught in the universities—Auden, Dylan Thomas, Larkin, Hughes and sometimes Gunn or Stevie Smith—suggested very little of what was beginning to happen in London or Cambridge or the North of England (where Neil Astley was soon to establish Bloodaxe Books), while effectively obscuring those foundational works of an indigenous British modernism still in the process of being rescued by Tuma himself and the five contributors to *Conductors of Chaos* who select and introduce work by their predecessors.

Tuma somehow manages to be at the same time both attractively modest and passionate in his advocacy. Since he regards his book as essentially a loosely-connected series of essays, it is probably best to avoid any implication that it can be regarded as a complete account of any kind or seeks an Archimedean point from which to survey the field. It aims, instead, to enact the tentative probings toward both a nearly forgotten British modernist poetry and a British postmodernist poetry still in the process of being written by coming again and again at its material in bits and pieces, and from first one angle and then another. The jagged pattern achieved is intellectually stimulating and aesthetically satisfying. While Tuma is definitely out to open up the transatlantic route once more to two-way traffic, he pessimistically assumes the odds are heavily against him. His strategy, however, may in the end be more successful than he supposes. He wants "to present enough poetries not to map the whole field but to erode established [American] caricatures [of modern British poetry] and prevent new ones from solidifying"; and he wants "to ventriloquize from enough perspectives to prevent discourses of national identity from emerging, as they have in the past, with the blunt force that inevitably distorts and interrupts the reading of poems, or just makes whole areas of poetic practice disappear."

Writing, then, chiefly for American readers, Tuma believes that "one reason for reading British poetry, and for reading as widely in it as possible, is to combat narrow views of that poetry that emerge in premature and reified accounts of American identity." And if the typical American characterization of British poetry is indeed "a monolithic source of all that is obsolete, standardized, and ruled by timid conventionality," the most effective method of combating such a view will be through the close examination of particular poets and particular poems that contradict it: work that is experimental, formally innovative, radical. While Tuma seeks to defend the academic study of contemporary poetry in his book, he also argues that "one good reason to study British poetry, especially British 'experimental poetry,' is to see what happens to a poetry which more often [than American] has had to go it alone, as it were, without being able to depend quite so heavily on the artificial economics created by the academy and other institutions."

Actually, I find the book a good deal less fragmentary and impressionistic than I expected after first reading the Introduction. The literary-historical chapters are extremely thorough and will be of enormous use to American readers who are, as Tuma reiterates, unaware of almost everything that has happened in British poetry for the past fifty years, while his considerations of work by Joseph Gordon Macleod, Mina Loy, Basil Bunting, and Edward Kamau Brathwaite are among the best I have read on these poets. The essays are short, but they say a great deal. They involve both analysis and advocacy. This last, again, is important. As Tuma says, he writes about work he admires. He wants to find readers for this poetry, and his discussions persuade us that the work will reward our attention. He is a critic who opens books rather than one who closes them. So I find the volume, in the end, something much more than "a series of essays." It stakes out territory and establishes priorities with critical insight and imaginative energy. And the balance between the literary-historical chapters and the studies of major figures is aesthetically very satisfying. I very much admire, for example, the strategy of focusing sharply in Part One on the old Hall/ Pack/Simpson *New Poets of England and America* anthologies in order to set up the recovery of British modernists like Macleod, Loy, and Bunting by way of extended readings of their best work. (I am reminded here of certain moments in M.L. Rosenthal's *The New Poets* of 1967, a very useful book in its time and one that, in its way, also tried to find American readers for British poetry.) And I am deeply impressed, while sometimes also amused, by the sixth chapter on "Alternative British Poetry" that manages to maneuver through a difficult terrain—the very terrain occupied by many among the *Conductors* and *Others*—that has never before been mapped at all, a chapter that investigates contending camps of the British avant-garde with the scrupulosity of a fastidious anthropologist among newly-discovered tribes.

Because my own orientation with regard to British poetry is somewhat different from Tuma's, I do lament the exclusion of several important poets from his discussion. David Jones, for example, seems to me even more central to the story he has to tell than Bunting, Loy,

231

or Macleod. Tomlinson and Middleton are missing. So are J.H. Prynne and Geoffrey Hill and Christopher Logue's versions from Homer. But Tuma's reading both of his chosen major figures and the contexts out of which they emerge is fascinating, authoritative, and compelling. He knows the British poetry scene about as well as any American I can think of and his position is independent of fashion, original, and well-considered. Tuma's frequent interjections of the personal, and his defence of the eclectic and the lapidary against the systemic and the theoretical, should prepare the reader for his reluctance to sum things up. Even without a summation, however, *Fishing by Obstinate Isles* is the best possible introduction for American readers to a range of British poetries and poetic histories long neglected here.

Sean O'Brien's *The Deregulated Muse* stands in relationship to *Fishing by Obstinate Isles* in about the same way the Armitage/Crawford Penguin stands in relationship to *Conductors* and *Other:* it frames the group photograph of avant-garde fraternity in both predictable and unexpected ways by exploring the work of an increasingly democratized, pluralist, and sometimes even experimental mainstream. While all thirty-six poets discussed by O'Brien can be found in the Penguin anthology and only one—Roy Fisher—in *Conductors* or *Other,* or discussed at any length in *Fishing by Obstinate Isles, The Deregulated Muse* nonetheless shares certain similarities with Keith Tuma's book.

O'Brien says at the outset that he is in no position (any more than Tuma is) to write a comprehensive account of contemporary poetry in Britain, that his approach will be non-theoretical, and that his notion of deregulation—a word in his title deliberately entangling his essays with the public world of Thatcherite and post-Thatcherite history—acknowledges the notion that "it is not clear where authority in poetic matters resides." Since Tuma laments that part of the blame for American neglect of recent British poetry might be extended to the British themselves for their failure to produce much serious critical writing on their recent poets, one imagines him welcoming a book like O'Brien's even though it privileges such a radically different range of talents from those he himself would like us to read. Both critics, in fact, appeal to a non-specialist reader by writing in lucid, lively, memorable (and sometimes even aphoristic or epigrammatic) prose.

Tuma says he wants no part of "the power of systematic, theoretical language" and feels lucky and grateful to have the reader's attention at all. O'Brien says his essays are written "in the conviction that criticism had better be readable" and not something written in "the interior code of a class or professional cadre." If Tuma's audience might be imagined as a class of bright undergraduates or graduate students, O'Brien's is the somewhat more endangered species of common readers who favor the tough, argumentative pub-talk of Grub Street reviewing whose journalists and professional writers are not much influenced by the terms of either British or American academic criticism. O'Brien, the British poet-journalist from Philip Larkin's *Hull,* argues that "the very variousness of contemporary poetry seems to prevent the emergence of a dominant line." Tuma, the American academic from Oxford (Ohio!), would clearly dispute that claim, feeling that the majority of O'Brien's thirty-six poets *are* the dominant line (if that in fact means the line that has long sought to dominate). O'Brien acknowledges that "for some readers [his] idea of variety will be their idea of homogeneity," and looks forward to reading their accounts of the matter.

O'Brien's account of the matter begins with essays on Larkin, Hughes, and Hill that lean rather heavily, as does the Introduction to the Armitage/Crawford Penguin, on Seamus Heaney's excellent essay, 'Englands of the Mind,' in *Preoccupations.* This opening section of the book, 'The Ends of England,' is more or less predicated on Heaney's notion, cited in O'Brien's later remarks on the Irish poet's prose, that "English poets are being forced to explore not just the matter of England, but what is the matter with England." In general, O'Brien finds "the confidence of Irish poetry of the last two generations to be "in part an oblique commentary on the exhaustion and anxiety of Englishness." But while insisting on the manner in which history impinges on these poets, and describing their responses—he is harsh on Hill, ambivalent about Larkin, and focuses rather surprisingly on Hughes's Laureate poems in *Rain-Charm for the Duchy*—he would also seem to share the conviction he attributes to Heaney "that experiences and things in themselves have meaning and value, over and above those bestowed by institutional and class history, when made into poetry." Indeed Heaney's short and elegant literary essays seem in many ways to be a model for O'Brien's approach—modified perhaps by the vitriol he finds in Tom

Paulin's prose and the concision he finds in Neil Corcoran's—and he pays one of them the highest compliment one could well imagine when saying that Heaney's argument "becomes the embodiment of its own justice."

Finding the Englands of Larkin and Hughes in the process of vanishing, O'Brien in his second section, 'Different Class,' looks sympathetically at a large body of work by Tony Harrison, Douglas Dunn, and Ken Smith both in terms of its working class origins and its poetic achievement before going on to separate chapters dealing with two groups of Irish poets—Heaney-Mahon-Durcan and Carson-Paulin-Muldoon—which are divided by his discussion of feminist poets Fleur Adcock, Carol Rumens, and Carol Ann Duffy and the first of what I think are the two most interesting chapters of the book, 'A Daft Place,' which examines work by Roy Fisher, Peter Reading, Peter Porter, and Peter Didsbury. The work of these four poets, together with that taken up in the amusingly titled final section—'Postmodernist, Moi?'—makes the most interesting contrast with the poetry discussed by Tuma and anthologized in *Conductors* and *Other*.

The first thing one notices about the poets discussed in O'Brien's chapter on postmodernism is that not a single one in this group warrants a mention by Tuma, Sinclair, or Caddel/Quartermain among poets assumed to be sympathetic to postmodernism in *Fishing, Conductors,* and *Other,* except insofar as they are perceived to completely misunderstand it. O'Brien's notion of postmodernism is both inclusive in a one-of-the-lads sort of way and, as the title suggests, simultaneously skeptical. And it includes in its selection of representative post-modern poets both those identified as such in the Motion/Morrison *Penguin Book of Contemporary British Poetry* and the Hulse/Kennedy/Morley *New Poetry* anthology which in some ways opposed it and helped to launch New Generation poets like Armitage and Glyn Maxwell. Most interesting of all, perhaps, it traces the post-modern spirit in England not to Prynne at Cambridge or Mottram in London, but to the influence of John Fuller at Oxford; and it traces Fuller's own sources not to Charles Olson or John Ashbery, but to W.H. Auden.

O'Brien argues that postmodernism is now so ubiquitous that definition has become increasingly difficult, especially as he finds that attempts to theorize it are both profligate and contradictory when both avowedly experimental and seemingly mainstream camps claim for themselves a piece of the action. Among the mainstream postmodernists (eux?) he discusses, the only common ground he's much interested in establishing has to do with "a deliberate awareness of and curiosity about poetic devices [which are] often allied to the redeployment of familiar kinds of poem, particularly narrative." He believes, "contrary to what some critics may claim," that "theory is always belated," and that abstract ideas about uncertainty, for example, are much less interesting than an impulse in any practicing poet which "relishes flying blind across the page" or peculiarities of a poet like Peter Didsbury which are as much innate as acquired, leading "less to an aesthetic program [than an] inclination to write poems." He is not willing to add much more in general terms save the observation that "the concern of these poets is less with immutable truth than with the means [they] employ, and by which [they] are led, to construct ideas of it or to question the possibility of doing so." Poets like James Fenton, O'Brien's favourite poet of the group, may have learned from John Fuller's teaching and example "a curiosity about the poem's status and the workings of language which makes the frame of reference and the means of construction into part of the subject." Although much of this could apply to just about any poetry at all, one can also see the interest in O'Brien's attempt to retrace the emergence of a particularly British postmodernism emerging from Auden (whether early in *The Orators* or later in *The Sea and the Mirror*), and the reasons for his frustration with certain theorists' disinclination to see that "the unwritten moment-to-moment history of poetry accommodates mess and disorder, chance and distraction, just as much as the determination to make it new and see the picture whole." He complains that John Osborn, a postmodern critic of Didsbury, reveals a paradox that troubles him: "if the old Big Picture myths and explanations have given way to uncertainty, what grounds has uncertainty to be so peculiarly sure of itself?"

Although one could easily imagine the answers to these questions that Osborne or J.H. Prynne or some of the critics O'Brien jokingly calls Muldoonologists might put forward, it is more interesting to look at what O'Brien says about some of the poets who appear in the Armitage/Crawford Penguin to see if any common ground actually exists between their work and that of the poets in *Conductors of Chaos* and *Other.* O'Brien complains about antitheses reproducing themselves from generation to generation—modernity versus tradition, avant-garde versus mainstream, establishment versus rebels—even to the point where poets who probably write from a similar impulse but inherit these binary echoes would, if given the chance, "go back and run each other over twice to be certain."

III: Mainstream Postmods

Taking James Fenton as the representative student of Fuller and Auden, O'Brien in fact discusses 'The Pitt-Rivers Museum' from the cycle 'Exempla' in *Terminal Moraine* in ways that might almost satisfy N.H. Reeve and Richard Kerridge, authors of *Nearly Too Much: The Poetry of J.H. Prynne.* Fenton's use, both here and elsewhere, of a range of technical languages to displace the lyric subject and its point of view, along with whatever consolations such a limited perspective might provide, recalls not only the use of scientific knowledge—anthropology and geology, for example—in Auden or David Jones, but also what Reeve and Kerridge call in Prynne's work "the presence of discourses [which challenge] the humanist paradigm and its place in late-capitalist culture by imposing shifts of scale which immediately disrupt any sense of personal, unmediated perspective," reminding us that we are in fact ourselves the products of infinitely large and infinitely small processes—cosmic, geological, molecular—to which the human subject may properly be subordinated in a poetry seeking an expression for these processes themselves.

   In its sixteen sections and sub-sections, Fenton's *Exempla* draws on such sources as Smith and Miller's *Developmental Psycholinguistics,* Lyell's *Principles of Geology,* Raymond Bush's *The Fruit-Growers,* an Oxford billboard, an article on frogs' eyes, and the museum labels and other materials from the Pitt-Rivers Museum. O'Brien calls the poem's fragmentary narrative elements "residually Audenesque," but so too, certainly, is the strange hodge-podge of bookishness recalling Auden's own use of W.H.R. Rivers himself, John Layard and other anthropologists, psychologists, and neurologists in *Paid on Both Sides* and *The Orators.* While the stanza O'Brien quotes echoes Auden even in the rhythms—"All day, / Watching the groundsman breaking the ice / From the Stone trough, / The sun slanting across the lawns"—the decisive point made about the poem as a whole in relation to Fenton's work in general might well lead us back to Reeve and Kerridge on Prynne:

> This is an early example of Fenton's interest in interfering with, or removing, the interpretative frame through which readers may at first believe themselves to be viewing a poem . . . The poem is a 'museum-piece', whose random inventory gradually ushers us towards the realisation that to excerpt and categorize items from the world and encase them in a building does not enable us to stand outside the world from which we have removed them. The poem in fact makes an elaborate fetish of the museum, in order to view this place of learning or idle contemplation as the embodied unconscious of a culture . . . Fenton clearly gains in the relative indirectness of his approach, which enables the psychic strains of amnesia ('A German Requiem'), displacement and class/cultural exhaustion ('A Vacant Possession', 'Nest of Vampires') to become matter for poems rather than rhapsodies on themselves, as they might in the hands of inferior writers in the confessional mode.

Reeve and Kerridge argue that "in order to survive, poetry has to collide with the powerful discourses of our culture (smashing them to pieces), rather than dodging into alley-ways while they pass, or lingering in safe places like gardens." Although readers of Fenton and Prynne seem no more interested in talking to each other than do most *Conductors* to most *Penguins,* the manifesto-like passage of Prynne's 'L'Extase de M. Poher' ought to find the author of 'Exempla' sympathetic to his tirade:

> No
> poetical gabble will survive which fails
> to collide head on with the unwitty circus:
> no history running
> with the french horn into
> the alley-way, no
> manifest emergence
> of valued instinct, no growth
> of meaning & stated order:

we are too kissed & fondled,
no longer instrumental
to culture in "this" sense of time:
   1. Steroid metaphrast
   2. Hyper-bonding of the insect
   3. 6% memory, etc
any other rubbish is mere political rhapsody, the
gallant lyricism of the select.

No doubt the most obvious Audenesque aspects of Fenton's work exist in his early and explicitly political poems about Indochina in the early seventies, like 'Cambodia,' 'In a Notebook,' and 'Dead Soldiers.' But no one would have called those poems post-modern when they were first published and I doubt that anyone is inclined to now. Of the Fenton poems that appear in the Penguin selection, it is in particular 'A Staffordshire Murderer' that O'Brien finds, together with 'England,' among the "most truly radical . . . most impressive varieties of English postmodernism to date." Noting that Fenton is again in Auden's debt as he draws on ritual elements of the detective story in 'A Staffordshire Murderer,' O'Brien goes on to describe with appreciation what he calls "its cubism," which offers a series of menacing digressions without supplying a narrative or establishing any sense of novelistic "real time." He quotes Alan Robinson to the effect that Fenton's poems often exhibit "a recalcitrant fragmentation [which is] characteristic of much of an emergent tendency in Postmodernist writing which parallels the deconstructive preoccupations of much contemporary literary theory" and concludes his essay by saying that Fenton—and John Fuller as well—has undertaken an "unwriting" of England in which "the linguistic representation of 'otherness' encounters an experiential otherness so extreme that it subverts representation itself." O'Brien imagines Fenton having "trained under hothouse conditions a type of poem that might have been glimpsed in Auden's 'Bucolics,' to the point where it brings in question our capacity to grasp its internal contradictions, and where the only evidence of its own coherence and relevance to itself lies in the poem's insinuating tone."

   I belabor all of these attempts to identify Fenton as a post-modern poet who can find his own radical sources in such a mainstream figure as Auden simply to suggest that, if this characterization is even remotely correct, Fenton—Oxford Professor of Poetry and anathema to many of the *Conductors* and *Others*—could without contradiction himself appear in *Conductors of Chaos* represented by cycles like *Exempla* or poems like 'A Staffordshire Murderer' while also making a choice from early Auden—choruses from *Paid on Both Sides*, parts of 'The Airman's Journal' or 'The Initiates' from *The Orators,* certain pieces from *Poems* (1930) that would parallel in interesting ways the actual five contributors' sponsorship of work by Gascoyne, Moore, Hendry, Graham, and Jones. Since O'Brien is rather stubbornly unwilling to discuss any of the poets in *Conductors* save Roy Fisher, he is not quite the critic Robert Pinsky called for some years ago in *The Situation of Poetry* who would be able to take up the work of particular poets without being distracted by the quasi-political divisions into groups or camps or parties with which they are superficially identified or superficially identify themselves. In part because he categorically groups and excludes "neo-modernists," "language poets," and "performance poets" from his discussion, it is necessary to consult a book such as Tuma's to complete the account of recent British poetry in somewhat the same way one needs, in the American context, to read Marjorie Perloff after reading Helen Vendler. Nonetheless, O'Brien is generally more impressed by poets and poems than by movements and groups. Many of the poets he discusses are as much a challenge to avant-garde pieties as the really innovative work of British experimentalists—neo-modernists, language poets, and performance writers among them—is a challenge to mainstream literary conventions.

It may be easier to claim Fenton's work for a kind of mainstream post-modern canon than that of Glyn Maxwell and Simon Armitage. Although as co-editor of the Penguin anthology Armitage does not include his own work in the book, American readers should know that he has been paired with Maxwell—who now teaches at Amherst and is published by Houghton Mifflin—in journalistic accounts of the New Generation at least since the 1993 publication of the Bloodaxe *New Poetry* anthology. He has even played MacNeice to Maxwell's Auden in *Moon Country,* a collaborative book about Iceland reminiscent of the Auden/MacNeice *Letters from Iceland* of 1937. O'Brien grants Armitage the distinction of being "perhaps the first serious poet since Larkin to achieve wide popularity" in Britain, but he finds the "everyday postmodernity" of his poetry, in which a younger readership has clearly come to recognize its own image, to consist mainly in "a kind of linguistic automatism, or echolalia—like language running around with its head cut off." Clearly Maxwell is the more interesting poet.

Although I am pretty certain he would dislike some of the jargon, it's possible that O'Brien might be willing to extend his provisional description of mainstream postmodernism to include certain terms and formulae that Hulse, Kennedy and Morley used to introduce Armitage, Maxwell, Didsbury, Reading, and even O'Brien himself as a poet in 1993. The editors of *The New Poetry* asked us to observe in their poets a "relish for cumbersome cultural props for their totemic presence alone," a realization that "ideas of meaning, truth and understanding are in themselves fictions determined by the rhetorical forms and linguistic terms used to express them," a "mixing of registers, idioms, and thematic provenances," and "doubts about authenticity of self and narrative authority" where "the pronominal act is itself a risk." Reading Maxwell's work specifically as a response to the questions which they took to be implicit in many of the younger poets in their anthology—How does the new poet "escape the negative inheritance of British poetry: its ironies, its understatements, its dissipated energies?"—they pointed to Maxwell's exploitation of "an untrustworthy I and a passive narrator," his "self-conscious wit and an attack that came . . . from a relentless conceptualizing of language that plays with misreadings, tautologies, insecurities and qualifications," and his "re-emphasized and re-directed syntax that, in mimicking the evasions and non-sequiturs of everyday speech, reminds us that language is always debased currency." Maxwell, who does indeed manifest some of these characteristics in some of his work, also, like Fenton, simply sometimes sounds like Auden and, fleeing as he might "the negative inheritance of British poetry," cleaves with some tenacity to its positive inheritance in formal verse written with an ease that might have impressed the master himself. His range, like Auden's, is very wide—from light verse to narrative to elegy to satire. Derek Walcott has spoken of his ability "to orchestrate asides, parenthetical quips, side-of-the-mouth ruminations into verse with a bravura not dared before." And Joseph Brodsky has said that "he covers a greater distance in a single line than most people do in a poem. At its best, the poetry sounds like this (from 'Drive to the Seashore,' a poem that David Kennedy thinks of as a response to Geoffrey Hill's sequence 'Of Commerce and Society'):

> We passed, free citizens, between the gloves
> of dark and costly cities, and our eyes
> bewildered us with factories. We talked.
>
> Of what? Of the bright dead in the old days,
> often of them. Of the great coal-towns, coked
> to death with scruffy accents. Of the leaves
>
> whirled to shit again. Of the strikers sacked
> and picking out a turkey with their wives.
> Of boys crawling downstairs: we talked to those
>
> but did this: drove to where the violet waves
> push from the dark, light up, lash out to seize
> their opposites, and curse to no effect.

Maxwell's boisterous metrical exuberance in congenial forms employed elsewhere, such as the Burns stanza, not only recalls Auden but also, in 'Don't Waste Your Breath,' playfully invokes his name before asking critics such as myself not to waste our own breath "telling me / my purpose, point or pedigree." Fair enough, one says, while still insisting on how frequently the Auden trick is turned, the pedigree displayed, in something such as 'Just Like Us':

> It will have to be sunny, so these can marry,
> so these can gossip and this forgive
> and happily live, so if one should die
>
> in this, the tear that lies in the credible
> English eyes will be sweet, and smart
> and be real as blood in the large blue heart
>
> that beats as the credits rise, and the rain
> falls to England. You will have to wait
> for the sunny, the happy, the wed, the white. In

the mean time this, and the garden wet
for the real, who left, or can't forget,
or never meant, or never met.

At this point, some of the questions O'Brien raises about the
Audenesque become important. He wonders, for example, exactly what
it is that Maxwell is after in Auden—his "air of knowing [his] way
about," his "cultural assurance and power of synthesis," his diagnostic
abilities, his "tricks with articles and syntax," his "formal gifts," his
"air of secrecy and conspiracy," the "various personal myths," his self-
appointed role as the age's representative, or some combination of
these. What O'Brien doesn't consider as a perhaps unintended result
of Maxwell's schooling himself on Auden is what Keith Tuma calls in
Maxwell's work "a pervasive air of diminished ambition," the "desperate
or campy futility" which vitiates some of Auden's later poetry. And
one might well associate these characteristics with the dangers of a
"rhetorical imagination" that David Kennedy in fact celebrated in the
New Generation poets he anthologized with Hulse and Morley as "a
change of emphasis from the latencies and nuances of language to its
forms and surfaces." O'Brien sees in such a change of emphasis a sign
of possible decline or impoverishment, a decadence of sorts which
he associates with British cultural activities fueled by Thatcherism.
Kennedy's enthusiasm for the paradoxes of a poetry "in which carefully
husbanded resources of containment and circumspection go hand in
hand with exuberant enjoyment, prolific output, and a wide range of
occasion and inspiration" strikes O'Brien as itself curiously Thatcherite,
and he makes an unexpected connection between Maxwell's poetry,
Kennedy's editing and criticism, and Neil Astley's Bloodaxe Books—
publisher of both *The New Poetry* and his own *The Deregulated Muse*.
I'm sure Maxwell wasn't thinking of postmodernism, the Y2K virus
itself, in his Audenesque parable 'We Billion Cheered' included in the
Penguin anthology. Nonetheless, the obscure "threat" in the poem
which seems to disappear when "currencies dance" only to arise again
and, like one of Auden's external "enemies" in *The Orators*, turn inward
"like a harmless joke / Or dreams of our / Loves asleep in the cots where
the dolls are," is as real as the radical methods of invading *Conductors*
and *Others* making mutants of mainstream poets who may seek to

domesticate them in their work. Although "We miss it where / You miss my writing of this and I miss you there . . ."

> We line the shore,
>   Speak of the waving dead of a waving war.
> And clap a man
>   For an unveiled familiar new plan.
>
> Don't forget.
>   Nothing will start that hasn't started yet.
> Don't forget
>   It, its friend, its foe and its opposite.

Surprisingly, O'Brien finds Peter Reading also to be a species of Audenesque post-modern (anti-Thatcher sort of) Thatcherite. If this is surprising given the ferocity of Reading's specific mockeries of Mrs. Thatcher, one nonetheless understands what he means. Focusing on the journalistic side of Reading's work, its relationship to what he calls the "urgencies of its period," the dangers of "whoring after relevance," its determination to reveal the garbage of what Tom Paulin calls "Junk Britain" and make the poet "the unofficial laureate of a dying nation," O'Brien finds "a huge hole where causality ought to be" and a kind of political exhaustion. He thinks the Swiftian contempt sometimes noted in Reading's poetry is often only a "sclerotic posture" such as one associates with the late work of Kingsley Amis, and that Reading projects a self-loathing onto the general public with his castigations of the generic Beckettian "H.sap" and the "pangoids" and "morlocks" that populate his writing. He believes that the poems are finally complicit in "a cruelly Manichean rationalization which lies behind Thatcherism" with its "use of effect (brutalization) to justify cause (impoverishment)." Reading is seen as a poet of the Coleridgean Fancy rather than the Imagination whose chief formal device is "juxtaposition," and whose poetry, like much journalism, "shrinks its subjects to fit the requirements of its rhetoric." This strikes me as a harsh and very one-dimensional view of a remarkable poet who even more than Fenton, and certainly more than Maxwell, can be profitably read in the company of poets appearing in *Conductors* and *Other*.

Armitage and Crawford make a good effort to represent Reading in the Penguin anthology, but ultimately the poetry is not amenable to any kind of selection at all because Reading's best work appears in through-composed books, many of which need to be read dialectically in relationship to other through-composed books. But the eight pages taken from *Ukulele Music*—only Muldoon's 'Incantata' occupies more space in the book—is a gesture in the right direction. American readers should know that Reading's two volume Bloodaxe *Collected Poems* is available from Dufour Editions and that Northwestern University Press publishes separately his *Ukulele Music* and *Perduta Gente* in a single volume. This last is certainly the best introduction to his work.

The editors of 1993 Bloodaxe *New Poetry* anthology claimed Reading—older than most New Generation Poets having been born in 1946—as an important participant in their postmodernist agenda. Reading was seen as a poet who in his "mixing of registers, idioms, and thematic provenances" was happiest when he could "manipulate reader expectation by contrasting tonality and subject, lofty style and squalid nastiness" both in his "socio-political work [and his] writing on everyday human pain." The "lofty" style has much to do with Reading's choice of forms and meters—classical hexameters, the elegiac distich, the alcmanic, the alcaic, the choriamb—scansions of which sometimes appear in the texts themselves. The effect of these scansions is often very unnerving—two dactyllic feet cancelled with an X at the end of *Final Demands,* a fully scanned stanza emerging from a drawn skull's mouth in *Evagatory,* the counting out of distichs in the "plinkplinka plinkplinka plonk" that accompanies and concludes the weird counterpointing of voices in *Ukulele Music.* Neil Corcoran has written that "one of the paradoxes of [Reading's] work, of which he is lucidly self-aware, is that its grim occasions provoke it into greater and greater feats of 'prestigitial' invention, particularly in his adoption of resolutely unEnglish classical verse forms." If Auden is sometimes present behind Reading's work as he is in Maxwell's, it is not only the Auden who imitated the falling meters of Tennyson's 'Locksley Hall' in "Get there if you can and see the land you once were proud to own" and whose social satires had, for a while, a Swiftian rage; it is also the later Auden whose obsessive subject in his talky, intricate syllabics was the ultimate frivolity of art and the inability of poetry to say very much that would disenchant and disintoxicate either the word-drunk poet himself or the self-enchanted reader.

For the same reason that it is difficult to anthologize Reading's work, it is difficult to quote it adequately in a review. In her Introduction to volume one of the *Collected Poems*, Isabel Martin argues for the "absolute unity" of volumes like *Evagatory, Stet, Ukulele Music, Perduta Gente,* and *Going On* achieved by "antithetical or polyphonic plotting, highly sophisticated structures, continual cross-referencing of narrative, imagery, motifs, voices and verbal echoes . . . [which constitute] an interweaving more commonly found in novels." A very good way to begin hearing Reading correctly is in fact to watch the widely available Lannan Foundation video in which he reads both *Evagatory* and *Diplopic* in their entirety. In this tour de force of a performance there is no missing what Neil Corcoran has described as the "intermittent Bakhtinian polyphonies, the voices seeming to emerge from a buzzy radio static, the hiss of permanent interference, the cacophony of crossed signals." Perhaps the following excerpt from *Evagatory* (which is brilliantly read on the video) will give some idea of a few of Reading's effects, along with a sense of his famous "mordant humour"—a quality that saves his bleak vision, like Samuel Beckett's, from at least some of the charges levelled against it in O'Brien's account of his work. The characteristic falling meter of the centered passage introduces, with appropriately Anglo-Saxon trappings, a bard who will sing, in a made-up language, the praises of Mrs. Thatcher herself. The "patois" of his encomium appears in the left column; the translation (in "translationese") appears on the right.

> Snow-haired, an elder, dulled eyes gum-filled,
> tuning a sweet-toned curious instrument,
>   gulps from a goblet of local merlot,
> sings on a theme whose fame was fabled,
> that of a sad realm farctate with feculence
>   (patois and translationese alternately):

| Gobschighte dampetty, | Wonderful little Madam |
| gobby Fer-dama, | self-mocking Iron Lady, |

getspeeke baggsy,   who some said was a windbag
getspeeke parly   some said talked
comma cul, comma   like an arsehole, like
spmalbicker-bicker,   a termagant—why,
porky getspeeke?, porky? why did some say that?

Pascoz vots clobberjoli, Because your pretty frocks,
vots chevvy-dur dur,   your permed-stiff hair,
vots baggsymainchic,   your smart handbag, your
vots collier-prick,   tight-sharp necklace,
cuntyvach twitnit,   satrapess so marvellous,
iscst pukkerjoli—   were so beautiful—
illos jalouz dats porky! they were envious, that's it!

Ni iscst vots marrypappa Nor was your spouse
grignaleto, ne.   a pipsqueak—far from it!
Mas vots pollytiq   But your many wise policies
saggio sauvay   were saving your islet,
vots salinsula,   your filthy isle, and
insulapetty,   made all equal with nil
et fair tutts egal mit-nochts.

After viewing the Lannan Foundation video, the new reader of
Peter Reading might have a go at *Ukulele Music* and *Perduta Gente*.
The latter poem, dealing chiefly with a Dantesque hoard of urban "lost
people," many of them lying among their rags and cardboard hutches
under Royal Festival Hall during a performance of Sibelius, recalls the
world of Tony Harrison's *V* and Ken Smith's *Fox Running*. These *gente
perduta* are the subject of Reading's grim elegy for the "insulate ranks
of expendables, eyesores, / winos, unworthies, / knackered-up dipsos /
swilling rasato- and meths," the dispossessed subjects of the 'Wonderful
Little Madam,' the Iron Lady whose praise-poem was sung by the
snow-haired elder in *Evagatory*. Here, too, the Anglo-Saxon hammers
the reader into the poem.

 Don't think it couldn't be you—
  bankrupted, batty, bereft,
huddle of papers and rags in a cardboard
  spin-drier carton,

bottle-bank cocktails and Snow soporifics,
    meths analgesics,
beg-bucket rattler, no-hope no-homer,
    squatter in rat-pits,
  busker in underground bogs
  (plangent and harp-twang, the *Hwaet!*
Haggard, the youthful and handsome whom I
    loved in my nonage;
    vanished, the vigour I valued;
    roof-tree and cooking-hearth, sacked).
Bankrupted, batty, bereft—
don't think it couldn't be you.

The four voices speaking in the companion poem counterpoint a poet's elegiac distichs with the prose of Viv, his daily help whose comments on her own life and on the poet's manuscripts left around the house sound like Dickens via Monty Python; the archaic-heroic-imperial verse of an aging Captain who, also employing Viv and living in the same building with the poet, can no longer tell the difference between his own life on the sea and the "yarns" he has heard or read; and a series of goofy, high-spirited instructions quoted from a beginner's manual for the ukulele. We are meant to understand that Reading regards the poet's fulminations at the urban violence and ecological destruction all around him to be about as significant as "the man in the music Hall song that goes he play his Uku uker Youkalaylee while the ship went down," as Viv has it in one of her notes. The four voices are kept separate in the first third of the poem, but in the last third, following the Captain's account of voyages that include a time aboard the Lucky Dragon when it sailed too close to an atomic testing ground, they begin to merge—Viv and the Captain first appear in, then begin to write, the poet's poems, while all three are accompanied by the banalities of the ukulele manual. Thus the poet's versions of tabloid horrors are constantly played off against the Captain's seafaring swagger, Viv's Mrs. Gamp-like persistence, and the plinkaplinkaplinks of the Uke. It is at once a deeply upsetting and strangely exhilarating performance.

It's the exhilaration that O'Brien seems unwilling to recognize. His desire that poetry must preserve "something of itself from the general wreck—not optimism or hope, necessarily, but the power of imaginative production"—is surely met by the logopoeia in Reading's "feats of prestigital invention" that Neil Corcoran finds in the Bakhtinian polyphony of voices. *Ukulele Music* is much closer in its verbal energies to a novel like Burgess's *A Clockwork Orange* than to the "sclerotic posturing" of the later Kingsley Amis, and it communicates a similar simultaneous pleasure in language and horror at the perpetration of gratuitous violence. It is also, like some of Fenton's work, worth contrasting again with J.H. Prynne as read by Reeve and Kerridge in *Nearly Too Much.*

If poetry, as Reeve and Kerridge believe, must, like Prynne's, "collide with the powerful instrumental discourses of the culture," and if, as Prynne writes in 'L'Extase de M. Poher,' "any other rubbish is mere political rhapsody, the / gallant lyricism of the select," what is to be made of the bits and pieces that result from the collision? Is some of the junk in Junk Britain "rubbish" in some positive sense? Prynne's poem, quoted in part earlier, continues:

Rubbish is
pertinent; essential; the
most intricate presence in
our entire culture; the
ultimate sexual point of the whole place turned
into a model question

This rubbish, Reeve and Kerridge argue, "is what results from the smash-up, when different discourses do not occupy the cultural places to which they have been directed, but cross the tracks and collide." They also associate it with Julia Kristeva's notion of "the abject": "the expelled and used-up parts of the self which signify that the self is not separate and unitary, but involved in constant processes of dissolution and exchange with the world." One does not need to read Reading with the full machinery derived from Bakhtin, Kristeva, Lyotard, and Habermas, brought to bear on Prynne by Reeve and Kerridge, to argue that one *might* read Reading that way, and that one might once again find some common ground between a mainstream postmodernist discussed by O'Brien and anthologized in the Penguin, and the poets in *Conductors* and *Other.* "Leider's no art against these sorry times" writes the poet in *Ukulele Music,* and his heckler-critic answers a few lines later: "Reading's nastiness sometimes seems a bit over the top." "No / poetic gabble will survive which fails / to collide with the unwitty circus," wrote Prynne. Reeve and Kerridge take their title from a pair of lines in his 'Down where changed,' the second of which is the more important: "Nearly Too Much / is, well, nowhere near enough."

Poets more congenial to O'Brien's taste are Peter Didsbury and Roy Fisher, in part because of the way they use their native cities to "think with." As Fisher says of Birmingham, "it's not made for that kind of job / but it's what they gave me." In fact, O'Brien admires Didsbury's work almost as much as he does Fenton's—largely, I think, because Didsbury does such interesting things with O'Brien's (and Larkin's) own native city of Hull, a place brought to almost preternatural life in some of Didsbury's oddest and strongest poems in a manner recalling the paintings of Stanley Spencer in which biblical stories are re-enacted in the village of Cookham. Not only does O'Brien argue that "it is as a celebrant . . . that Didsbury should be celebrated" who, unlike Reading, has "sustainable positives to set against the dismal, de-historicised character of contemporary life," but he also takes his work as the site where he can contend with theoretical critics like John Osborne, quoted earlier, whose "linguistic materialism" and "Post-religious enlightenment" sound feeble "compared with the grandeur and terror of what [they] seek to replace" in the genuinely religious imagination of poems like 'Eikon Basilike' and 'A Winter's Fancy,' where fiction "crosses over into belief." And yet, although Didsbury himself expresses distaste at being described as a postmodernist, believing himself to be "engaged in tasks and duties and pleasures which are nothing if not ancient," his work is clearly related to that of the poets discussed above and to American models such as Kenneth Koch and John Ashbery — poets, incidentally, who must also be celebrated as celebrants.

Didsbury's poetry is characteristically self-conscious and self-reflexive in the manner of these other poets and it frequently meditates on language and the versions of the self that speak it. Walking in "the empty heart" of his home city, a speaker finds it suddenly like "a level Baltic town," its canal emptying "into a turbulent German Ocean" with "dereliction on one side of the stream" and "an Arctic kind of

Xanadu on the other." Shivering, he thinks of his hip-flask and realizes he "hadn't actually invented it yet" but knew he "wouldn't be leaving it very much longer."

> If this was what linguistic exercise meant
> then I didn't think much of it. The deep structures
> I could cope with, but the surface ones
> were coming at me in Esperanto, and fragments of horrible
> Volapük.

In 'Back of the House,' in an English garden, "Language, fat and prone beneath her fountain, / idly dispenses curling parchment notes, / her coveted, worthless, licenses to imitate." And at the end of 'A Winter's Fancy':

> The cattle squelch past beneath a sodden sky
> below my windows and before the eyes
> of Peter Didsbury, in his 35th year.
> I consider other inventions of mine,
> which rise before me on the darkening pane.

The American reader may feel he has seen enough of this sort of thing in the native product, but Didsbury's British cultural context makes it all a little more distinctive than short quotes can illustrate. In a blurb taken from the *Observer* on the back of Didsbury's recent book, *That Old-Time Religion,* Alan Jenkens says that "some of his invention . . . hints at a rich humane vision of England which yields a kind of surrealism all of its own: estuaries, farms, country estates, city streets and bed-sits, a kind of tatty or compromised pastoral are detectable in Didsbury's oblique, desperate celebrations." This strikes me as a fine characterization of a body of work that is difficult to characterize. About the long passage he quotes from 'The Hailstone,' O'Brien says that memory functions, not as in Reading always to yield only images of something lost, but as something held in store, a "granary of the imagination." He finds a Lockean association of ideas provoking "a momentary experience of the uncanny, as if the mind wakes up to its own presence and contents, refreshed and restored to the original vividness of relations with local and domestic culture." It is a poetry in which an extremely literary poet "tries to show us a world before literature gets at it."

> We ran by the post office I thought, 'It is all still true,
> a wooden drawer is full of postal orders, it is raining,
> mothers and children are standing in their windows,
> I am running through the rain past a shop which sells wool,
> you take home fruit and veg in bags of brown paper,
> we are getting wet, it is raining.'
> It was like being back
> in the reign of George the Sixth, the kind of small town
> which still lies stacked in the roofs of old storerooms in schools,
> where plural roof and elf expect to get very wet
> and the beasts deserve their nouns of congregation
> as much as the postmistress, spinster, her title.
> I imagine those boroughs as intimate with rain,
> their ability to call on sentient functional downpours
> for any picnic or trip to the German Butcher's
> one sign of a usable language getting used,
> make of this what you will. The rain has moved on,
> and half a moon in a darkening blue sky
> silvers the shrinking puddles in the road:
> moon that emptied the post office and the grocer's,
> moon old kettle of rain and idiolect,
> the moon the sump of the aproned pluvial towns,
> cut moon as half a hailstone in the hair.

If Didsbury's poems recall Stanley Spencer's painting, Roy Fisher's urban art is a curious amalgam of figures like L.S. Lowry and Edward Hopper on one hand, Tatlin, Malevich and Paul Klee on the other. If there frequently seems to be a low mimetic convention at work in his poetry, his serious joke about being "a 1920s Russian modernist" is in fact a key to his work and, as I have written elsewhere, even the seemingly realist *City* needs in the end to be read in a context of constructivist and assemblagist innovation as its fictive world emerges from the signs and names of real things. Although O'Brien, like Donald Davie before him, underplays and possibly misunderstands this aspect of Fisher's work, his affection for, as it were, the Hopper-Lowry in Fisher clearly goes very deep for some of the same reasons he admires Didsbury. But we have now come to a point at which—with Fisher's work as a bridge both between the Penguin anthology and *Other* and between O'Brien's reading of contemporary poets and Keith Tuma's—we must look at a few of the "alternative" poets discussed in *Fishing by Obstinate Isles*. There is no great mystery why Fisher can, in fact, function as a bridge by producing work that can be admired by both camps, appear in both anthologies, and be sympathetically discussed by both critics. He is an extremely reader-friendly post-modern (or "1920s Russian modernist" who has moved on), and often he is very funny. As O'Brien says, "he has the artfulness to support the radicalism of his aesthetics and to invite readers into the complicated landscape of his work." He is as good a poet—all schools and movements aside for a moment—as Hill or Tomlinson, Douglas Dunn or Paul Muldoon. Which means he's one of the best alive. But it is, as O'Brien says, his inclusion of consciousness in his poems in such a way that "the poetic imagination has, as it were, no back wall to rest against" and where "the mind itself is continually becoming part of the picture," that aligns one side of his work with the epistemological concerns of Tuma's Cambridge poets, just as a certain affinity with Language poetry (in *The Cut Pages* especially) aligns another side of his work with Tuma's Londoners. But his austerities and self-imposed constraints are all his own. Six short lines allow us a transition and sound a warning:

> Because it could do it well
> The poem wants to glorify suffering.
> I mistrust it.
>
> I mistrust the poem in its hour of success,
> a thing capable of being
> tempted by ethics into the wonderful.

IV: Adjuncts to the Muses' Diadem?

Tuma's chapter on 'Alternative British Poetries' begins by sketching the continuities he perceives between Movement poets, middle generation poets like Harrison, Dunn and Heaney, and the New

Generation poets celebrated by David Kennedy who receive the qualified support of Sean O'Brien. The chapter ends with brief but close readings of one book each by Peter Riley, Allen Fisher, Geraldine Monk, Tom Raworth, and Roy Fisher, all of whom, along with Maggie O'Sullivan whose work is considered earlier on, figure as major contributors to *Other* and/or *Conductors of Chaos*. Along the way, Tuma fine-tunes his distinction between the Cambridge and London branches of his favored alternative poets, and indeed makes clear that the quarrel between a Cambridge-based poet-critic like Drew Milne and a London-based (at least initially) poet-artist like Allen Fisher is both interesting and quite substantial. But the chief service Tuma provides in this chapter is to foreground work by six poets whose poetry does not appear in the Penguin anthology, who receive no mention at all in O'Brien, who are very little known in this country, and who have written books which he clearly prefers to those by Fenton, Armitage, Maxwell, Reading, and Didsbury. I will focus here on Riley, Raworth, and the Fishers while also quoting a few of the others both to broaden contexts and simply to exhibit some unusual work.

Peter Riley (no relation to John or Denise; there are three Rileys as well as the two Fishers on Tuma's "alternative" team) is a poet whose work can be read with profit either in the context of Cambridge-based writing by poets like Prynne, Milne, or Mengham, in the context of British modernists like David Jones or Basil Bunting, or indeed, as he would seem to prefer, in the full context of English poetic traditions stretching back to Renaissance songs, lyrics, and madrigals. Riley is rather suspicious of American poetry and in fact argues that the influence of American experimentalism on British poets had run its course by the mid-1960s. Some of his more general statements about poetry, including the excerpts from an interview printed in *Conductors,* seem, outside any context of avant-garde militancy, both accommodating (in ways I have described and implicitly endorsed above) and aesthetically conservative. He argues that "we need a stronger emphasis on the poem as a beautiful object," that contending camps in modern poetry ought to open a dialogue with each other, that one can no longer confidently divide "modernist and traditionalist" in terms of a politically "dichotic metaphor" nor be certain that "advanced poetic praxis" will employ only open forms—and indeed one of Riley's best known poems, 'Ospita,' is a sonnet sequence. Still, the poems in *Distant Points,* the book discussed by Tuma, twelve sections of which also appear in *Conductors,* look like this:

1.   1
the body in its final commerce: love and despair for a completed memory or spoken heart *enclosed in a small inner dome of grey/ drab-coloured* [river bed] *clay, brought from some distance* (from the valley bottoms) and folded in, **So my journey ended** moulded in the substance of arrival **I depart** *and a fire over the dome and a final tumulus of local topsoil* benign memorial where the heart is brought to the exchange: death for life, relict for pain/double-sealed, signed and delivered— under all that press released to articulate its long silence, long descended * tensed wing / spread fan / drumming over the hill.

2   C39
folded in river clay, the boat on the hilltop */lying East-West facing upwards the right hand on the right shoulder, the left arm across the body* gradients of sleep, to die, to dream, to mean / *Beyond his feet to the East a row of three small circular pits or stake-holes* dawn trap as the compass arc closes southwards and the heart is secured by azimuth, all terrors past: **She only drave me me to dispaire** /dead child, cancelled future in a satellite cloak hovering to SE. Yet the loss, folded into history, sails adroit in the clay ship over commerce and habit, bound for (to) this frozen screen where [cursive] we don't live, but do (love) say, and cannot fail.

If this is a species of British postmodernism that has any kind of commerce with the five poets discussed by Sean O'Brien on whose work I have focused above, the most obvious connection would be with James Fenton in his use of documentary materials in *Exempla.* Expanding on Riley's own notes to *Distant Points*, Tuma examines the poet's sources for these prose poems in his use of nineteenth century excavation accounts by J.R. Mortimer who worked on human burial deposits of the Neolithic/Bronze Age culture in the Yorkshire Wolds. Juxtaposed with quoted, modified, rearranged, and condensed texts taken from Mortimer (mostly in italics), are passages in boldface deriving chiefly from early English song and madrigal verse along with passages in Roman type linking, mediating, questioning, or reconciling elements among the "found" materials in what Tuma calls a "collision of discourses" that creates "a post-pastoral, post-lyric space" where "lyric emotion" and "brute facticity" contend and struggle for some kind of harmony or accord. The effect of the sequence as a whole—and even of the twelve sections printed in *Conductors*—is deeply elegiac and reminiscent of David Jones in passages from 'Rite and Foretime' in *The Anathemata* and 'The Sleeping Lord.' Collectively, these poems also seem to incant with Jones (although above the graves of later "adaptable, rational, elect / and plucked-out otherlings" of Tellus):

> By the uteral marks
> That make the covering stone an artifact . . .
> By the penile ivory
> And by the viatic meats . . .
> *Dona ei requiem.*

Riley's prose poems manage, Tuma concludes, "to confuse or invert the relationship between one and the other genre of writing, so that the deathly description undertaken in the italicized fragments over the course of the series . . . can seem to gain an affective weight one would think to be reserved for the fragments from the English lyric archive." He agrees with John Hall that the final effect, as in Riley's earlier *Tracks and Mineshafts,* is a kind of "hesitant self-contradictory and doomed transcendentalism."

Although *Distant Points* is not necessarily typical of work which Tuma identifies with Cambridge, Riley's poetry and his statements about the art are nonetheless associated in particular with the group's "regard for the artificial status of the poem as a resolved and 'finished' object." Riley has asserted that the poem exists "as an object between poet and reader which is both a means of communication and a barrier to communication" and that even individual units in a poetic sequence need to achieve an "utter completion." He also affirms a notion of impersonality in ways that again recall David Jones (and T.S. Eliot), while extending his notion of the work as both a means of and a barrier to communication by saying that it is "constructed out of paradoxical or conflicting motivations within a tradition: desire crossed with fear, envy crossed with confidence, the need to say and be revealed crossed with the need to remain silent and secret." Without wanting to attribute Riley's views to other poets, these characteristics can, I think, be seen in work by other Cambridge poets associated in various ways with J.H. Prynne whose poems appear in *Conductors* or in *Other* and which I would like to quote if only to provide a glimpse of some important writing most American readers are entirely unaware of. Here, for example, is Drew Milne:

> Clamour for change, with this to plough on
> even though fresh mint, under a flat
> climate, borders on wisteria
> buoyed and flushed in a slogan too far,
> or wills no attempt to portray what palls
> as in every body flirts, don't they?
> So minting, some feel like death over it
> whose only sin is unlikely grist,
> wit and wag this sizzling raunch bears all,
> wailing wall to boot, and now we're told
> due more to Herod's engineering,
> nature not withstanding, as a fly
> passes on withering western winds,
> and all the bold sedge goes hand in fist,
> spent in forage round other and earth.

This is John Wilkinson:

> To his seeming true the apothecary turns about,
> padding between his plastic rows, maintenance of
> plant & smits of government subsidy will make
> his garden grow with Scotch Tape, barrier cream,
> grids of planting shunt the energy where tactful.
> Divert it to the maidens asking for slow horses
> to woa at a residential door swings like gunsmoke—
> words drain their faces, violent ballet means
> decided something from a treatment they accustom
> to draw out of a particular chair by details so
> yielding, Alzheimer's mutates to a contact disease . . .

And Andrew Crozier:

. . . see them flash by, time unit
continuous for two frequency cycles, heart
stutter, one travelling fast round another's
light pulse, delayed burst, in the sequence and
out, remnants of colour displayed, falling
away on the curve of its tangent, out of
the corner, scattered before its return swept
into the bay as a double beat counted twice,
its point in the line divided and dotted
back where, see what, time rushing past
your one body, small corner and one little eye,
time rushing ahead through its gaps, meeting
its markers and dying away as you pass,
snatched up to the stars, sideral passenger
so many vertices plotted, invisibly now
across the celestial sphere, so much infinity
sectioned, such stories foretold, fixed a word
for them, call it out of luck, or under what sign,
or on what base are they struck, short use life,
weather beaten, fallen, degraded, one on its own
if not lost must have been stolen.

Here certainly is a poetry that, just eluding paraphrase, foregrounds the materiality of language in a kind of Heideggerian withholding of exactly what is offered. The atmosphere of all three passages, claustrophobic as Riley's Neolithic graves, is nonetheless alluring: Milne's poem derives from the verbal world of newspapers (the reading of which G.F. Hegel, quoted in the epigraph, once called "the realist's morning prayer") and, later in the sequence, recalls the use of tabloid journalism found in Peter Reading's work; Wilkinson's apothecary-shop-cum-horse-show-and-doctor's-office-of-a-stanza somehow begins to answer the question more or less raised by the title, why do 'City Scientists Grow Magic Skin'?; Crozier's lines apparently describe a hospital monitor—cardiogram or encephalogram or both—where scientific fact and human terror simultaneously register their graphs. All of the poems are stanzaic (Crozier's unit is 30 lines and therefore has been excerpted), two are sections from cycles, and some effort has been taken in each case to give the parts as well as the wholes a formal integrity. Elements of narrative appear in all the poems, but, as Reeve and Kerridge say of Prynne's 'A Night Square' (eleven poems each containing eleven lines), "energizing forces are traced as they run up against obstructions." In Prynne's case, as Reeve and Kerridge observe, the layout on the page resembles the walls of a maze, but the other poems have maze-like qualities as well. Here is Prynne:

> But is
>   the small ensign of love a
>   street by
>   the docks past
>   the screen past
>   the lithograph is fixed so desperately
>   the screen past
>   when he sets his wheel by the form
>   of a per
>   fected nail in
>   structed second part

Although Crozier's sequence may come close to positing the existence of something like an empirical self, there is great suspicion among these poets of the first person singular, which is probably best regarded in their poems as an entity entirely constructed by linguistic convention rather than something like a psychological identity with a state of mind. In this they resemble Roy Fisher, who has spoken of his attempt to "steer a sufficiently agile course [that he might] be able to see the back of [his] own head" while locating the "I" that is being thought rather than the "I" that is thinking. In fact, the claustrophobic atmosphere is also like the world of certain Fisher poems which point the reader finally to a zone that is, as he says, "turbulent, bulky, dark, and lyrically remote."

It is significant that Tuma's group of Cambridge poets, more than other contributors to *Conductors,* are interested in establishing something of a genealogy for their work by making the selections from David Jones, J.F. Hendry, Nicholas Moore, and W.S. Graham. Milne's choice of Jones' 'The Narrows' and the remarkable passage on 'The Zone' from *The Book of Balaam's Ass* reveals an Eliotic High Modernist coming apart at the seams whose "antisocial critique needs to be read against its overtly affirmative claims"; Crozier's Hendry is a one-time New Apocalyptic poet of the Blitz whose work "broke through structures of language and social convention" and whose poem on the air raid that killed his wife should be read beside better-known poems on the raids by Dylan Thomas, Edith Sitwell, Stephen Spender, and Eliot in 'Little Gidding'; Riley's Nicholas Moore reveals a poet "in the full throes of his argument with language as power" while Tony Lopez (not discussed by Tuma, but a Ph.D from Prynne's Gonville and Caius College) introduces W.S. Graham's work as the link, via 'The Nightfishing,' between Eliot's *Four Quartets* and Bunting's *Briggflatts* which demonstrates the continuity of British modernism in spite of the greater visibility of The Movement and its successors. Graham's later work is seen as poetry whose explicit subject, like that of several Cambridge poets, is language itself. However, this writing about writing—taken up by John Wilkinson and Denise Riley, among others—is no mere formalism. Its "language games [are] concerned with damaged and lonely people, with political propaganda, with coercive oppression, with the effects of torture and warfare on local communities."

The American reader will doubtless be asking by now whether or not these Cambridge poets who draw on this particular archive ought to be read as British colleagues of North American Language writers like Ron Silliman, Charles Bernstein, Steve McCaffery, and Susan Howe. It is a question which Tuma addresses directly and at length while making a transition to Allen Fisher and the London-based alternative poets on his list.

While Tuma finds little interest per se among his Cambridge poets in notions like Ron Silliman's "new sentence," Bernstein's "antiabsorptive" techniques, or the utopian program of Steve McCaffery's poetics, he also suggests that specific and sometimes hostile critiques of Language writing which emanate from Cambridge sometimes mistakenly "read what are in fact performative critical texts intent on re-directing contemporary poetic practice as a series of truth-claims and/or 'theoretical' propositions about language, reading, politics, and so forth." Perhaps this is better understood, he implies, by his London poets, who certainly share an enthusiasm for parataxis—the title, incidentally, of one influential Cambridge journal—with both U.S. Language writers and Cambridge poets, but whose experiments with concretism and performance texts, engagement with everyday life, interest in improvisation, chance operations and disruptive techniques that violate what Drew Milne calls "the persistence of lyric," make them a kind of edgy and anarchic urban foil to the hyper-literary, reflective, radical pastoral poets from Cambridge and more receptive (vulnerable?) to Language writing on the one hand, American Black Mountaineers, Beats, and New York School poets on the other.

At this point another run of I hope fairly representative passages may again be useful as these poets, seen in contrast to the five quoted above from the Cambridge group, suggest at once both the interest and the risk in pressing poetry as far as possible toward an endgame of incoherence while maintaining an ability, as Tuma says of Maggie O'Sullivan, "to baffle all critical languages or 'theories' that would seek to 'explain' [the work] or bring it back into the discipline and decorum of . . . hermeneutics." Here is a passage from Allen Fisher's 'Mummers' Strut' which Tuma will include in his Oxford anthology, along with its notes and what is perhaps a send-up of notes in his notes written in the third person. I quote it from the journal *Westcoast Line:*

So much so difficult to take in
Mule driver holds to

a raised path
in case of submersion.

Even as dew drops through
a window space the driver

can be seen holding the ropes' natural lubrication.
What was once cracking has become squeak

and then whistle
before the buckles rust.

Sodium ions are represented by two children
in the skins of nylon bears

dyed fluorescent blue
or ultramarine cut with steel and oil.

Naturalists exchange informations on the relation
between bog bush crickets and the sound of dried grass

The footnote to this section refers the reader to Helmuth Plesner, *Laughing and Crying: A Study of the Limits of Human Behavior,* while the note on the notes to the whole reads in part: "In summary it may be said that, if 'Mummer's Strut' was exemplary of Allen Fisher's poetics in action, then the poetic strategy is one of slow discomposition, disruption of autobiographical voice through the use of many voices, aspiration to multiple and collage form through the pasting of many sources, many space-times, and a subversion of collage form through a use of re-narration, a simulation device evident elsewhere in this poet's work." Well! In the same issue of *Westcoast Line,* Maggie O'Sullivan's 'riverrunning (realisations' includes a passage which is also a kind of note on her notes, saying that she celebrates —like Fisher and Raworth, one concludes—"Origins / Entrances—the/ Materiality of Language: its actual contractions &/ expansions, potentialities, prolongments, assemblages—/ the acoustic, visual, oral & sculptural qualities/ within the physical: intervals between; in & beside." The O'Sullivan text which Tuma says we need to hear in performance to sense its "bardic" quality, along with the way it seems to hover between a pre-literary and post-literary existence, reads in part on the page:

Plage,
Aqueous,

> YONDERLY—
> lazybed of need—
> CLOUD-SANG
> Tipsy Bobbles, Dowdy
> wander. Halt upon

Grinned jeers, gin's note
Someone's in the leading
    of small & pitch meander eares
tune me gold
Dulthie pods

And although Tom Raworth is not specifically grouped with the London poets, certainly his most characteristic moves are much of a piece. He can make them very rapidly indeed, like this:

> stranger. A curious hand touches the snow raising pigeons
>
> they want us to compete so they need only read 'the best'
> next line
> this beautifully carved hand is for scratching the ice to attract the
> seal's attention
> come, take my place in the long hibernation dream of the hamster

Or this:

> what quintessence as she walked to the door
> it is a privilege we allow to the meanest and most despicable of
>   our criminals
> the terminal buildings will be out of sight
>
> the hand has calluses as you shake it

> no doubt she did it with my blessing.

These two early poems from *Lion Lion*, 'Jungle Book' and 'Unease,' read in retrospect like sections frozen in a kind of permafrost from Raworth's more recent process poems like *Catacoustics,* which Tuma quotes and discusses at some length.

> should I begin again
> almost with a capital
> i catch to memory a car
> seen from the back seat
> moving past stone walled fields
> lambs
> a cheval glass, beveled at a bend
> showing nothing
> but depthless shadows
> i knew his motionless eyes

meant he was paying attention
but things look slower
in peripheral vision
something is thinking back to me
enjoy those relegated motors
that is your thumb
it feels for you
it is you
pay it some attention
bell rings
so a current
is running through the circuit
up a stair
round by a window
your car
is a very advanced baby
don't get any ideas

Tuma compares the "disjunctive gaps" in Raworth's syntax with the "white spaces cut between Peter Riley's fragments" in order to argue that a poetics based on "bafflement" has replaced Riley's poetics of the sublime. "Our attention," he explains, "devolves not into a terrifying 'real' altogether beyond the unknowable, calling for our inevitably desperate and failed efforts to acknowledge if not grasp it, but rather into the abundance of material particulars which obstinately refuse any effort to gather them, positively or negatively, into depth or coherence." If this distinction between a poetics of bafflement and a poetics of the sublime among these poets makes any sense, then Roy Fisher can be seen as a poet who has explored both possibilities. The former is predictably represented in the selection in *Other,* and, while the Fisher sublime (rare, but very real) is not exactly on exhibit in the Penguin selection, every attempt has been made to exclude the side of his work that might baffle the casual reader while printing the one and only Fisher chestnut-of-an-anthology-piece (which the poet dislikes and regards as unrepresentative of his work), 'The Entertainment of a War' from *City.*

Following *City*, and en route to his revision and radical reconception of that poem in *A Furnace*—it is as if Eliot had written *The Waste Land* after rather than before *Four Quartets*—Fisher wrote a series of sequences such as 'The Cut Pages,' 'Stopped Frames and Set Pieces,' 'Metamorphoses,' 'Matrix,' and 'Handsworth Liberties' that make use of improvisation, chance methods and automatism, the congruence of subjective musical associations with objective visual imagery, constructivist procedures reminiscent of the Russian formalists, and a treatment of semi-hallucinatory mental spaces in a manner recalling M.C. Escher's *Print Gallery* in which the world we see, as Francisco Varla describes the etching, defines a cognitive domain "we cannot step out of," where we are "entangled in the strange loop of our actions" since there is "nowhere to step out into." It should be clear by now why such poems by Fisher might be respected by poets from both the Cambridge and London groups, and indeed there are moments when he might be thought of himself as a member of one group—

Coil	If you can see the coil hidden in this pattern, you're color-blind
	Pale patterns, faded card, coral card, faded card, screen card, window fade
Whorl	If you can see this world and say it without hesitation you're deaf
	Then we can get on with frame
Frameless	Meat rose, dog-defending, trail-ruffling—

or the other—

No dark in the body
deep as this
         even the sun
hardens the upper world
        A ladder
climbs down under the side
in the shadow of the tank
and crosses tarry pools.
        There are
metals that burn the air;
a deathly blue stain

in the cinder ballast
and out there past the shade
sunlit rust hangs on the still water.

But it is precisely with a poetics of the sublime—and Keith Tuma's original fisher by obstinate isles thought he might "maintain 'the sublime' / in the old sense . . . Unaffected by the 'march of events'"—that I want to leave this Fisher of the latter-days and all but conclude this essay.

I am not alone in thinking that *A Furnace* may be one of the two or three great long poems by an English poet written in the last quarter century. Deeply resonant of modern traditions reaching back through Pound, Yeats, and John Cowper Powys to journeys to the underworld in Homer, Virgil, and Dante, the poem invokes a Heraclitean fire "to persuade," as Fisher says in his preface to the poem, "obstinate substances"—like obstinate isles themselves?—"to alter their condition and show relativities" in a context understanding that "the making of all kinds of identities is a primary impulse which the cosmos itself has; and that these identities can only be acknowledged by some form or another of the poetic imagination." *A Furnace*, as much as Geoffrey Hill's *The Triumph of Love,* is a poem that seeks to bring whatever blood the poet has to offer as libation to the dead, fishing not among the Cantos' "souls out of Erebus," but nonetheless for "timeless identities" like "the one they called Achilles . . . or like William Fisher" who are guided by a syntax Tuma rightly calls conjunctive (as opposed to the disjunctive syntax of Raworth or *The Cut Pages*) to "enter Nature . . . animist, polytheist, metaphoric, coming through." In their way, Geoffrey Hill's Bletchley Magi (with their syntax of grids, probabilities and recursive functions) also half-created what they half-perceived in a situation where initially, as Hill writes, "unrecognized [was] not unacknowledged . . . unnamed [was] not nameless" and "bad faith . . . rest[ed] with inattention." Fisher's attentions are to codes as difficult as DNA and as ancient as the figure of its double-spiral, in terms of which he tries to think about time. Possibly tempted at last, if not by ethics then by metaphysics, into "the wonderful," the poem seems to find their miracle of survival perhaps just miracle enough.

Whatever breaks
from stasis, radiance or dark
impending, and slides
directly and fast on its way, twisting
aspect in the torsions of the flow
this way and that,
    then suddenly
over,
through a single
glance of another force touching it or
bursting out of it sidelong,

doing so
fetches the timeless flux
that cannot help but practise
materialization,
the coming into sense,
to the guesswork of the senses,
the way in cold are
ice-crystals, guessed at, come densely
falling from where they were not;

and it fetches
timeless identities
riding in the flux with no
determined form, cast out of the bodies
that once they were, or out of
the brains that bore them . . . .
. . .
They come anyway
to the trench,
the dead in their surprise,
taking whatever form they can
to push across.

V: Unfinished Business, Current Events

So why is there no anthology of British poetry that represents both
Prynne and Hill, both Raworth and Fenton, both Riley and Maxwell,

both Allen Fisher and Peter Reading, both Roy Fisher and C.H. Sisson? At this writing, Keith Tuma is trying to edit such a book for OUP, a book which will moreover recognize the sources of various contending traditions discussed above by reaching all the way back (with long and sometimes surprising selections) to Hardy and Eliot, Edward Thomas and Mina Loy, Robert Graves and David Jones, Basil Bunting and W.H. Auden. Along the way, the book will recover work by Joseph Gordon Macleod, Charles Madge, Nicholas Moore, John Rodker, Lynette Roberts, Rosemary Tonks, F.T. Prince, and David Gascoyne, while going on to print Gael Turnbull with Thom Gunn, John Riley with Tony Harrison, Andrew Crozier with Craig Raine, and Maggie O'Sullivan with Carol Ann Duffy. Instead of giving the reader the almost meaningless tiny selections common to most anthologies, Tuma will print, for example, all of Bunting's *Briggflatts,* all of W.S. Graham's *The Nightfishing,* all of Tony Harrison's *V,* the whole of 'Introit' and 'The Return' from Fisher's *A Furnace,* and fifteen sections from Hill's *Mercian Hymns.* Such full-scale generosity to long works has in the past mostly been accorded only the likes of Eliot and Pound. Although Tuma is acutely conscious of the strengths of Britain's multicultural poets—E.A. Markham, David Dabydeen, and Benjamin Zephaniah are in the book—the anthology will not strive to implement things like gender balance, affirmative action, or other kinds of politically correct pieties in formulaic ways. It will not assume that skill is democratic, even though the muse may be deregulated. Political equality does not mean that people are given an equal ability to write good poems. But the anthology is also willing to risk including radically experimental poems where aesthetic standards like those confidently put forward by O'Brien and Armitage/Crawford must be willingly suspended. When we are truly entering the unknown—as we do in some of the poems that Tuma will print by poets who appear in *Conductors of Chaos*— we must acknowledge the difficulty of placing value on unprecedented experiences which we are in fact having for the first time. Along with the work of many fine Irish poets whose poetry I have excluded from this discussion in order to focus on at least some of the Brits, American readers will at last be able to compare a range of poetries generally antagonistic to one another and decide for themselves if some kind of dialogue between them is possible or interesting without having to subscribe to six or eight small press catalogues, or surf the Web for distributors of books and pamphlets published in tiny editions across the water.

Until Tuma's anthology appears, we seem to be left with the Armitage/Crawford Penguin, the Caddel/Quartermain *Other*, and the news (just in) that *Conductors of Chaos* is not only permanently out of print but also—no doubt intensifying the British alternative poets' sense of exclusion by and hostility toward the mainstream—that it has in fact been replaced at Picador by *The Firebox,* an anthology much like the Penguin, edited by Sean O'Brien without as high a degree of openness to experimental work as one had sensed in *The Deregulated Muse.* O'Brien's Introduction, like Armitage/Crawford's, makes much of notions of pluralism. So does the Introduction to *Other* and that of the 1993 Hulse/Kennedy/Morley *New Poetry* anthology. Ideas of pluralism are extended in these books to race, religion, region, class, language, gender, sexual preference—to everything, in fact, except poetics. There each book pretty much draws its own particular line. O'Brien's new Picador includes even fewer of the younger poets who appeared in the Iain Sinclair anthology it has just displaced than the Penguin, and the Penguin includes just one. I suppose Keith Tuma will be attacked in some quarters on the Obstinate Isle as an American interloper willing to extend pluralism to poetics. But he has the blessing of this reader. He sails in a big ship and will land a big and various catch.

Finally, rereading this essay, my own omissions disturb me. While discussing British poets, I have intentionally written only about the English, not making it sufficiently clear that the editors and authors of all these books, and Armitage and Crawford in particular, are clear that much of the most interesting poetry being written off the mainland of western Europe is written at a time of political devolution by poets from Wales and Scotland, some of them not writing in English. And my earlier contention that American poetry readers already know enough about the mainstream Irish poets certainly ought not to imply that I think they know anything at all about poets in *Other* like Randolph Healey, Billy Mills, Maurice Scully, or Catherine Walsh, whose work derives not so much from Yeats, MacNeice, and Kavanagh as from Coffey, MacGreevy, and Beckett, or that they are any better acquainted with the poems in Irish by Nuala Ni Dhomhnaill than they are with the poems in Scottish Gaelic by Sorley MacLean. The best way, under the circumstances, that I can make a sudden exit from an essay that has grown very long through wanting to quote at length some work I know my reader will not have seen, is to quote yet one more time. The poem by Peter Finch, a Welshman, appears in *Other*. It is called 'Why Do You Want to Be English?'

> You can't do English much
> a lot of them
> really don't have much to do with English
> I'm English they are going to steal my cattle
>
> Does doing an English
> overlaid with a false English
> mean you are not British
> English is a straw dog, a real dilemma
>
> I am interested in English as one blossom
> one hundred percent English free of guilt
> not my ancestors ran the Roman Empire
>
> The choice:
> Cambridge English
> Elgar
> Hardy
> English Bengali like the remnants of Bosnia
> I could go on
>
> English disjuncture like a blind stick
> please speak clearly after the long tone
> archipelago consensus no longer a land mass
> do not write anything down

John Matthias

Some Works Cited

Acheson, James and Romana Huk, eds. *Contemporary British Poetry: Essays in Theory and Criticism.* Albany: SUNY Press, 1996.

Corcoran, Neil. *English Poetry Since 1940.* London: Longmans, 1993.

Fisher, Roy. *A Furnace.* New York: Oxford University Press, 1986.

Hill, Geoffrey. *The Triumph of Love.* Boston: Houghton Mifflin, 1998.

Hulse, Michael, David Kennedy and David Morley, eds. *The New Poetry.* Newcastle upon Tyne: Bloodaxe Books, 1993.

Kennedy, David. *New Relations: The Refashioning of British Poetry 1980–94.* Bridgend: Seren, 1996.

O'Brien, Sean, ed. *The Firebox: Poetry in Britain and Ireland After 1945.* London: Picador, 1999.

Prynne, J.H. *Poems.* Newcastle upon Tyne: Bloodaxe Books, 1999.

Quartermain, Peter, ed. *Westcoast Line: New British and Irish Writing* 17 (Fall 1995).

Reading, Peter. *Collected Poems.* Vols. I and II. Newcastle upon Tyne: Bloodaxe Books, 1996.

Reeve, N.H. and Richard Kerridge. *Nearly Too Much: The Poetry of J.H. Prynne.* Liverpool: Liverpool UP, 1995.

270

Modernisms: Five Poems

Modernato Pizzicato

O Lynx keep watch on my fire he had written in Pisa
and *Dryad* he'd called her a long time back
and she thought the *new subtlety of eyes* was probably hers
dove sta memoria when she read it in his prison poems
in her Küssnacht sanatorium . . .

                           E.P. loves H.D.—it could
have been encircled with a heart, carved by a couple of kids
on a tree. From the wreckage of Europe they groped their way
toward what they remembered and loved.
And at Küssnacht that clinic was fine for filming
a bust: Dick and Nicole at Dr. Brunner's healing-place,
Scott loves Zelda carved by actors on the widest conifer.
Pound had put a eucalyptus seed in his coat when
the partisans marched him away from hills above Rapallo.
It had the face of a cat: *O Lynx keep watch on my fire.*
And she was herself a feline, an eidolon Helen to boot.
As Freud's analysand she watched the local extras in halls,
a rich girl taking the talking cure talking and talking. Change
the movie to *Borderline* and she is the star, a demi-monde
neurotic with her dipsomaniac beau. Who knows why
they're here? Or Jason Robards and Jennifer Jones who
drive each other's Dick & Nic around town; Jill St. John
is no *San Juan with a belly ache writing ad posternos,*
but she squeaks like a ditsy mouse and shows her pointy tits.

What all fits this case? A pretty face, of course,
a march to the line, a dance to the rhythm, the time.
Rhyme it with mime and bring in the rest of the cast:
Tom and Viv, Gertrude and Alice, Nora and Jim—
Billyam Williams and Freytag-Loringhoven the mad.
Ulysses loves Penelope they carve on yet another tree.
Helen's at the door of Dr. Brunner; Paris is a patent fiction
she complains. Let's to Lake Geneva for a sail. P. Pudovkin
writes in *Close-up*, Bryer's cinema mag, regarding the art

of the cut, but who has the knife any more or the nail?
It's closing time at the jail, the privileged asylum,
contagious hospital, letterpress printer's, the ruined town.
Close up the closet of cut-up text & cut out hearts & heroes
cut down to size. Some guy on TV is singing pizzicato lies.
Someone's baby sits right down and cries.

Their Flims

films, that is. A typo just as easy
an *essai* as William Faulkner's standing
on the set with Howard Hawkes
charged with coming up with something quick to
spice the dialogue in Hem his rival's
Have or Have Not, moved from Florida and Cuba
all the way to Martinique, Hawkes saying
Well well well well   try something
here. And the novelist's response: *Was you*
ever bitten by a dead bee? All for Walter Brennen,
Bogart and Bacall gone off already for
a drink with Scott who'd not have bothered with the big
film of 1939 (because by then *The Last*
Tycoon was on the fire) if he hadn't had a contract still
to honor even if he was fifteenth and not the first
to have a go at Miss Leigh's Miss Scarlett.

Their films. Their fame consists of something else,
a flame and flame-out, both. How to have
both haven for a talent in your palm and payment
in your fist to gobsmack anyone who'd
make you write in anagrams derived from text by
Margaret Mitchell? Not a bloody word
you haven't picked with tiny forceps out of Tara's
Torah, mate: When you're bitten by
a dead bee you'll know the nature of a sting-
ing cut, an improvisation by the broad: *You know*
how to whistle, don't you? What's the difference
between Vichy cops and Southern gents
or officers in Rebel uniforms wrapped
like mummies in the Stars and Bars? Bogy's luck
with Miss Bacall and Gable's reassurances
that he was never gay didn't trouble pages adding up
in *Absalom* or point of view adjusted in
the fictive life of Irving Thalberg, movie mogul, when

the daughter saying I, I, I has got beyond her depth
and can't produce *Producer's Daughter* as a
college girl at Bennington. What added up was
adding up: the debts. To whom however ask the question:
Now I owe you one? The actress on her knees
in some lost outtake in the pre-coded days in Hollywood
saying *Bet you don't believe I ever read your book?*

The Baronesses

It's a pity that William Carlos Williams couldn't have met
The Baroness friend of Thelonious Monk instead of
His own Baroness Elsa von Freytag-Loringhoven. No doubt
About it, Baroness Pannonica de Koenigswarter would have
Been a better bet. Although she dug jazz rather then poetry,
Williams would surely have warmed her heart with
His poems about pure products of America, metric figures,
The gold 5 on a fire-truck, lonely streets. He could have
Read them to her in that room with the terrific outlook over
The Hudson where a baby grand and a night of coffee and
Good conversation were always ready for Monk & his friends.
But alas he instead had for his mediumlong-suffering self
The unwanted attentions of Elsa von Freytag-Loringhoven, a
Baroness Thelonious Monk might have liked. She was
No rich patron, exactly—in fact not at all. Down and out as a
Pure product of America, she might have cadged a drink from
The Baroness Pannonica de Koenigswarter, or just a dime.
Or she might have asked to spend the night in her flat
Or Weehawken house. Lots of people did—and listened to
Records of Horace Silver's 'Nica's Dream,' Gigi Gryce's
'Nica's Tempo,' Kenny Dorham's 'Tonica,' and of course
The tune by Thelonious Monk, all composed for the former
K.A.P. (for Pannonica) Rothschild who married the pilot
And banker Jules de Koenigswarter (later Minister Plenipo-
Tentiary from France) who himself became embarrassed enough
By her night life to leave her forever when Charlie Parker
Died on her sofa and her "good name" got in the tabloid press.
But in fact they never met, mostly because the poor and crazy
Baroness Elsa von Freytag-Loringhoven died in the gas
That she or her lover allowed to escape in her dingy Dada digs
In Rue Barrault on 14 December of 1927, a year when the
Barroness Pannonica de Koenigswarter was still only a girl
Of twelve out in the fields with her gifted father Nathaniel
Charles Rothschild hunting bugs for his entomological pastime
Which etymologically led, said Monk, to her name: Pan-
Nonica of Eastern Europe's Pannonian plain, a butterfly her

Father had found and liked. As for Elsa von Freytag-Loringhoven,
She was hot not for Monk—who after all was only six at the time—
But for William Williams, doctor and poet, thirty-eight in 1921.
She wore a coal-scuttle as a hat, tin cans on her breasts, and
Exhibited with Man Ray and Duchamp in circa those days
A plumbing-pipe she called "God." Williams followed her
Home from the show where she offered to give him
The very thing that he, as a doctor, treated for free in half
His artist friends in New York—a case of the clap.
He withdrew, but she followed. All the way to Williams' house
In New Jersey. At that point everything's right out of
Somebody's travesty of Restoration excess on a Provincetown
Stage: she arrives, he runs, she pursues, he calls for help from
His wife, she curses in German, he shoves her away, she punches
His face, he punches her face, she hides in a tree, he shakes on
Her branch, she falls and stumbling recovers, his wife throws a
Rolling pin in the air, she laughs, he cries, she disappears in the night
With police in hot pursuit and Mrs. W.W. singing out something
A bit like "Well, you needn't" or "By-ya," "Off minor,"
Or "Nutty"—all tunes by Theolnious Monk. Round about midnight
Monk would arrive at Baroness Pannonica's place. There he would
Play the piano for hours, for days. Mostly he didn't talk.
Sometimes he sat and stared at the keys. In the end the Baroness
Took on the jobs that Monk's exhausted wife no longer performed.
She got him to eat, got him to take his pills, got him now and then
Out of the house to perform. She must have loved the man.
He fell at last into a silence deep as Ezra Pound's in Venice.
He no longer played. She let him behave as he liked, dressing up
In his natty way in the morning but lying all day in bed in his
Crisp clean shirt with a coat and tie. That went on for three years.
If Baroness Elsa von Freytag-Loringhoven and William Williams
Had come for a visit or house-call, they would have learned
A thing or two about the pure products of America and respect
Verging on awe. It would have been quiet there as the grave
And tending to the sublime. With Baronesses keeping guard on
Either side of the bed, the doctor poet might have picked the
wet hair from the pianist's eyes and watched him with compassion.

Asheville Out
i.m. Charles Olson and Thomas Wolfe

so you've only a museum now
and not a college at all
although I understand the buildings still exist near the town
where religion has reclaimed the real estate that
John Rice took for the muses after he scandaled at Rollins
lecturing on the classics in his jock. *What . . . ?* she says—
but she's in Asheville here at the Black Mountain Museum
with Annie Albers and Ruth Asawa and M.C. Richards
Women of the College up on walls
their paintings and prints and stills from documentary films
works and days from the place
where poets, if not painters, were so macho they hadn't the time
to read, for example, Hilda Morley's delicate poems.
Who . . . ? she says, young and pretty docent, and I think
of docile women among genital toughs out there
but also of dear Hilda when I met her, Yaddo in the 70s, when
still she was unpublished, getting really old, still telling
all those stories about Stefan Wolpe's Parkinson's—
little paper-wads of poems slipped under my door at night,
her Dickinsonian habit of abasement followed by abrupt display
of weirdly-offered & prodigious genius—
Wolpe her great lover and her husband and the reason why
she didn't publish for so long.
I think the most erotic photograph I've ever seen
was of Hilda once in *Ironwood* where the young and lovely girl
bites into an apple smiling with her eyes at Wolpe
middle-aged and briefly eminent composer
while he grins longing back at her on the Lee Hall front porch
and the grand love between them
positively shimmers in the air, in the lake behind them,
in the green mountains above—

and Tom Wolfe only

wanted out

of all this, the hills, the little town, the boarding house
managed by his mum: *Just off the car line;*
Large Lawns, Reasonable Rates, Newly furnished Throughout.
Our Auto Rides You from the Station for Free
No Sick Folks Here. Did I know, she asks,
any of the really *famous* poets? Dorn, yes; Creeley, yes;
Robert Duncan, yes & for a while & in a way.
'Twas as if I said I'd seen Shelley plain.
Days of *Idaho Out.*
Days of *Gloucester Out.* Asheville out beyond and
south I used to drive on family holidays
my father stuck it in reverse on mountain curves because
our Plymouth—1948—couldn't manage the climb
except by backing up. Scott Fitzgerald didn't meet Tom Wolfe
in 1936 because the six-foot-seven native was
in Germany for the Olympics in a U.S. diplomatic box just west
of Hitler on the day that Owens won his first gold.
He exploded in a raucous Rebel cheer that drew the Führer's ire:
Who's the big oaf with their ambassador?
And who's the man in Asheville with the crazy wife
whose books were all the rage before the crash and all
the unemployed, for who cared in 1936 about those flappers
in East Egg or was it West those rich idlers on the Riviera?
I don't know, she says, *but . . .*
nor did the two giants ever meet – had you
asked Wolfe to climb on Olson's shoulders they'd have
been together something getting onto fourteen feet tall
and a useful human ladder for a second-story man breaking
into Biltmore place. But what's the first story
and she says *Did you teach out there yourself?* Of course
Maximus & Eugene Gant never walked along the Blue Ridge Highway
but they might have done it just as my father
might have gotten round that turn and backed the car
to Cherokee where nothing much is going on
beyond the poverty, casino gambling, Indians playing Indians
for some snotty gringo's snotty children now. But then
there was the first story. It's about three bears.

Alas it's true that some men forgot their obligations and
their clan's rites and found themselves with long hair on their bodies
and without their thumbs
and on their hands and knees, the kinsmen still of Hanging Maw
and Double Head and even John Ridge
they assumed names like Jackson Johnson Jefferson
and knew they must be hunted as they hid
until they had to hunt themselves. What kind of creatures
walk together on the road from Asheville out
of caves and down from trees and into talking leaves
inscribed in signs for eighty-six sounds
borrowed by Sequoia from the Greek and Roman and Cyrillic?
What? She says. *Days of Gloucester Out,* I say.
Days of what? she says. *Those*, I say, *were the days.*

John Matthias

Xoanon

Gunnar Ekelöf

I possess, in you, a wonder-working Icon
If possessing something is to possess nothing
As she possesses me. Thus I possess her.
She was given me on the very day she 'appeared'
At a pre-ordained time, at an appointed place
And the same *Panayía* is revealed again
Whenever the heart so desires. Leaning on her arm
Stands, in ceremonial robes, on an inversely
Perspectival stool, a grown-up infant in arms
Who is the last prince of my line
I lift him away, for every attribute
Belonging to this *Panayía* can be lifted away
As a plunderer dislodges a silversmith's *basmá*
From a picture kissed so much
The hands have darkened and fallen apart
I lift the crown and the two criers of joy
From their cloud and golden ground in the upper corners
I disengage the ornamental clasp from the *Maphorion*
And lift the veil from her hair and from her neck
I free the folds across her right breast
And carefully the folds across her left
Aching with pain. I lift like a spider's web
The thin undergarment, which leaves the enigma
At once resolved and unresolved, and she looks at me
With brown irises in the blue white of the eyes—
Keeps looking at me . . . I disengage her arms
Her brown hand with its rose, the brown breasts
The right one first, the left one carefully last
Aching with pain, and then the girdle after kissing it
I lift her forehead, her hairline and her cheeks
And finally her big eyes which look at me
Keep looking at me, even after they are gone
I lift the golden ground and the priming

Until the wood with its thick graining is bared:
A bit of an old olive plank, sawed off
A tree felled by a storm, in a time long ago
On some northern coast. There, in the tree,
Almost overgrown, appears the eye of a sprig
Broken off when the tree was still young—
You keep looking at me. *Hodígítria, Philoúsa.*

Translated with Lars-Håkan Svensson

Pleasures and Situations:
The Prose of Robert Hass and Robert Pinsky

I – Robert Hass' *Twentieth Century Pleasures*

It's a little difficult for me to write about Robert Hass' *Twentieth Century Pleasures* because so many of the essays began for me as conversations going back as far as graduate school at Stanford. I want to write this essay from the point of view of an old friend, and you'd think that might be easy. But reading these conversations back into the texts, which is something that I find I cannot keep myself from doing, I am acutely aware that other readers are not doing this, although some are doubtless reading different, even contradictory, conversations back into the texts. Should my account include the conversations or restrict itself to the texts? If I am to be the autobiographer of my reading, as Robert Hass often is of his in this volume, I must risk talking about a book that no one else can read. For example, there is a point in Hass' essay on Robert Lowell's 'Quaker Graveyard in Nantucket' where he deprecates "the slough of poetry" engendered by *Life Studies* beginning typically "Father, you. . . ." I remember his making that point in a coffee shop across from Trinity College when we were both spending a year in Cambridge, and I remember saying: "Yes, but your father is still alive." Then he said—but it doesn't really matter what he said; he went on to qualify or modify the remark by saying something else. What began in conversation and was open to the natural processes of conversation becomes a telling point, decisively made, in an essay where I still hear the resonance and backwash of an exchange which occurred ten years ago. This conditions my reading and my response and, while both can be communicated, the second probably cannot be fully shared. It also suggests that it may be more difficult to talk about work by someone you know than by someone you don't.

Then there is the question of voice, or, as the theorists like to say, the question of presence. The related questions of voice, conversation, and presence are taken up by Denis Donoghue in his 1981 book on contemporary theory and ideology called *Ferocious Alphabets*. This has suddenly become a very useful book to me precisely because the form of language which Donoghue wishes to privilege, which in fact he thinks is privileged, is conversation. Arguing that conversation is so radically different from the notion of communication proposed by such early twentieth century theorists as Jacobsen and Richards that we should regard it as communion rather than communication, Donoghue writes that conversation is made memorable "by the desire of each person to share experience with the other, giving and receiving."

> All that can be shared, strictly speaking, is the desire: it is impossible to reach the experience. But desire is enough to cause the reverberations to take place which we value in conversation . . . the words enact desire . . . the "I" and "you" are constantly changing places; not only to maintain the desire of communion but to keep it mobile. The two voices are making a music of desire, varying its cadences, tones, intensities.

When you separate these two communing and fully embodied voices in such a way that one becomes a writer and the other a reader, certain kinds of compensation must occur. The writer's compensation for the lack of conversation's true communion is style. The reader in his turn "makes up for the tokens of absence which he finds in written words. . . . He is not willing to leave words as [he] finds them on a page [but] wants to restore words to a source, a human situation involving speech, character, personality . . . We read to meet the other. The encounter is personal, the experience is satisfying in the degree of presence rather than knowledge."

If this kind of reading, which Donoghue has an ugly word for—he calls it *epireading*—commits one not only to the epos of speech but to the logocentrism attacked by the kind of reader engaged in an activity for which he has an even uglier word—*graphireading*—the objections of the graphireaders might be summarized in the most severely reductionist terms by a bit of graffiti appearing in a recent *Times Literary Supplement* that looks to have been written by a deranged graduate student:

> D'ya wanna know the creed 'a Jacques Derrida?
> Dere ain't no reada
> Dere ain't no wrider
> Eider.

I don't know if I can be an "epireader" in general, but I think I am unavoidably and inescapably an "epireader" of my friends. I hear their voices and I feel the pleasure of their presence in their words. At the end of *Ferocious Alphabets*, Donoghue says that he detests the "current ideology which refers, gloatingly, to the death of the author, the obsolescence of the self, the end of man, and so forth . . . To be sure that I exist, all I have to do is catch a cold or stumble on the pavement. Pleasure achieves the same effect more agreeably . . . Knowledge is debatable, pleasure is not." Robert Hass calls his book *Twentieth Century Pleasures* and, I think, shares most of Donoghue's basic assumptions about the nature of literature and language. Still, he writes in his essay on Robert Creeley that underneath some of the typical pleasures of our time are uncomfortable things "which the mind must, slowly, in love and fear, perform to locate itself again, previous to any other discourse." And in his best known poem he writes:

Longing, we say, because desire is full of endless distances.

In reading the work of friends, something of desire's communion in the pleasure of familiar voices is very present and very real; but so, of course, is the longing, and so are the distances. We fall asleep in the middle of a conversation and awake with a page of prose in our hands.

I am surprised that Helen Vendler in a review of *Twentieth Century Pleasures* and some other books about contemporary poetry feels that Hass fails to engage some of the questions and assumptions touched on or alluded to above. Taking the part of the theorists in the 7 November 1985 issue of the *New York Review of Books*, she argues that all practical criticism "assumes positions silently taken" about basic premises and says that she would like to see Hass and the others consider first principles or at any rate make the reader confident that "the theoretical questions had been silently put, and satisfactorily answered, before the writing was undertaken." Vendler is also worried about the autobiographical element in Hass' writing—its familiar tone, its "determined effort toward the colloquial," its attempt through what she calls "interpolated narratives" to communicate the idea that the texts under discussion have some connection with his own sensual life and the life of the times, that the books have literally been lived with for a while and not just read and rapidly reviewed to meet a deadline.

Actually, Hass engages the fundamental premises of the theorists and implies his own in any number of his essays. The piece on Creeley, for example, deals in Lacanian and Derridian terms with a poetics "which addresses the tension between speaking and being spoken through language," but also makes clear through some "interpolated narratives" why such an "austere and demanding" poet as Creeley could communicate with a large and often uninstructed audience during the 1960s. The "interpolated narratives" imply a "premise" as fundamental as anything in Lacan and Derrida—namely, that art unfolds both in individual lives and our collective history, and that factors which only narrative can reveal condition our response to it. But, of course, there is no systematic statement of principles, no prolegomenon to any further study of contemporary poetry, in a book like this. It achieves its unity and authority from the manner in which art is shown to intersect with life. It is an autobiography of sorts.

Epireader of this text that I must be, the first thing I am conscious of in *Twentieth Century Pleasures* is a voice. It is a familiar voice, and it sounds like this:

> I've been trying to think about form in poetry and my mind keeps returning to a time in the country in New York when I was puzzled that my son Leif was getting up a little earlier every morning. I had to get up with him, so it exasperated me. I wondered about it until I slept in his bed one night. His window faced east. At six-thirty I woke to brilliant sunlight. The sun had risen.
>
> Wonder and repetition. Another morning I was walking Kristin to her bus stop—a light blanket of snow after thaw, the air thick with the rusty croaking of blackbirds so that I remembered, in the interminable winter, the windy feel of June on that hill. Kristin, standing on a snowbank in the cold air, her eyes alert, her face rosy with cold and with some purity of expectation, was looking down the road. It was eight-fifteen. Her bus always arrived at eight-fifteen. She looked down the road and it was coming.

Helen Vendler objects to what she feels marks a difficulty in controlling tone in a passage similar to this one taken from the final and most fully autobiographical essay in this book, which I am going to quote a little later on. It is an intentionally vulnerable passage and functions, along with others like it, to make clear exactly what elements, insofar as Hass is conscious of them, combine to condition his reading and his response, to make it his reading and his response rather than mine or Helen Vendler's or someone else's. It tells us some of what we need to know in order to understand his perceptions, his reactions, and his judgments. And it is especially in passages like it, and like the one quoted above, that I hear the familiar, amused, vigorous, disarming voice often touched with a Chekhovian irony and sadness that I know. I sense the presence of a friend and not a difficulty in controlling tone.

One function of the passage about Hass' children is, of course, to get an essay about form begun in a relaxed and graceful way. No academic categories introduced, no pedagogical solemnities. But we are also persuaded by this kind of writing that his coincident experiences of "trying to think about form" and remembering the power of repetition in the lives of his young children yield the surprised perception out of which the essay grows, that "though *predictable* is an ugly little word in daily life, in our first experience of it we are clued to the hope of a shapeliness in things . . . Probably, that is the psychological basis for the power and the necessity of artistic form." But let me take an example from the first essay in the book to demonstrate more fully the usefulness of narrative and autobiography.

On these terms, Lowell's prayer moved me.

What are "these terms," and what conditions them? The prayer which Hass is moved by occurs in Part V of 'The Quaker Graveyard in Nantucket'—"Hide / our steel, Jonas Messias, in Thy side"—and the terms of his being moved are conditioned by the way in which his own inherited Catholicism has been modified or transmuted by a range of experiences and some important reading by the time it meets the intense but unorthodox Catholicism of a convert's poem.

At the beginning of his essay, Hass says that it's difficult to conduct an argument about the value of music in favorite poems once it's gotten into the blood: "It becomes autobiography there." But so does the meaning of favorite poems become a kind of autobiography—so conditioned is it by the times and places and the circumstances of initial or repeated readings—and only narrative can really show us how this happens. After explaining the "enormously liberating perception" found in Robert Duncan's prose that "the mistake of Christianity was to think that the soul's salvation was the only human adventure" and, Christ seen therefore on an equal footing with the other gods, Pound's idea that they all were "forms of consciousness which men through learning, art and contemplation could inhabit," Hass writes this paragraph:

> I got my Catholicism from my mother's side, Foleys from Cork by way of Vermont who drank and taught school and practiced law on the frontiers of respectability until they landed in San Francisco at the turn of the century. My father's side was Protestant and every once in a while, weary probably with the catechisms of his children, he would try to teach us one of his childhood prayers. But he could never get past the first line: "In my father's house there are many mansions . . ." He would frown, squint, shake his head, but that was as far as he ever got and we children who were willing to believe Protestants capable of any stupidity including the idea that you could fit a lot of mansions into a house, would return to memorizing the four marks of the true church. (It was one, holy, catholic, and apostolic.) But that phrase came back to me as a way through the door of polytheism and into myth. If Pound could resurrect the goddesses, there was a place for a temple of Christ, god of sorrows, desire of savior, resting place of violence. I could have the memory of incense and the flickering candles and the battered figure on the cross with the infinitely sad and gentle face and have Aphrodite as well, "the fauns chiding Proteus / in the smell of hay under olive trees" and the intoning of Latin with which we began the mass: *Introibo ad altare Dei.* On these terms, Lowell's prayer moved me: "Hide our steel, Jonas Messias, in thy side."

The essay on Lowell is important for a lot of reasons. It is the generative essay of the volume, written in England in the cold winter of 1977 when Hass and his family were living in the Cambridgeshire village of Little Shelford in a huge house owned by the master of St. John's College, which I had lived in two years before. The essay may be as personal, as autobiographical, as it is in part out of compensation for not being able to write, there in Little Shelford, the poems he had hoped to write in the course of the year away from his familiar turf in Berkeley and San Francisco.

Actually, I feel vaguely guilty about this. I persuaded Hass to go to Cambridge for the year rather than to York where his Bicentennial Fellowship was really supposed to take him, thinking that it would be good to spend the year near one another—I was once again to be in the area—and that the big house in the little village would be as productive a place for him to live and work in as it had been for me two years before. Once the weather turned, all the poems were frozen out of his system—the house "has central heating," but the system is in a permanent state of disrepair—and he wrote very little poetry until the San Francisco sun had warmed his blood and spirit again eight or nine months later. He did, however, write a lot of prose, and he wrote this first essay of the present book which, I think, led to his wanting to write the others and established their characteristic tone and point of view.

It begins and ends with recent and more distant memories of voices—that of a mild-looking schoolteacher in the Shelford pub who, when the subject of favorite poems came up one night, treated the locals to a recitation of Kipling's 'Gunga Din,' and the surprise of Robert Lowell's when Hass finally got to hear it at a reading, which sounded "bizarrely like an imitation of Lionel Barrymore" or "like a disenchanted English actor reading an Elizabethan sonnet on American television." So much, perhaps, for the possibility of being an epireader of poets whom we haven't heard give readings or of those we don't or cannot know. Hass' own poems returned to him again once he was back in the world where he and his brother, as he remembered in the pub, had also, like the Shelford teacher, loved as children reading Kipling aloud "on summer nights . . . in our upstairs room that looked out on a dusty fig orchard and grapevines spilling over the wooden fence." I suppose it would have been even colder in York than it was in Cambridgeshire. Anyway, the one piece in *Twentieth Century Pleasures* actually called a memoir returns Hass to "the San Francisco Bay Area as a culture region." It is a rich and evocative autobiographical essay, and it connects with the important reading of Miłosz that comes just before and the remarkable 'Images' which comes afterward.

In his Bay Area memoir, Hass is dealing in the most delicate and often amusing and ironic way with the fundamental mysteries of our common world as they were given a local habitation and a name in the area where he grew up. The memoir glosses his desire, in the Lowell essay, to have "the battered figure on the cross . . . and Aphrodite as well," and provides a context both for the way in which he deals with the Gnostic side of Miłosz and his celebration of the image in the final essay of the book.

It begins, in fact, by recalling Hass' attempt to write another essay—for one Sister Reginald to enter on his behalf in a competition sponsored by the National League for Decency in Motion Pictures about how fine a film could be made from a book called *Stranded on an Atoll*. In his comical account of the revisions and reversals of attitude while working on this junior high school project, Hass' memory connects Sister Reginald's austere Dominican habit first with the order itself, "founded in the twelfth century as a kind of Papal CIA to root out the Gnostic heresy of the Cathars," and then, to his surprise, with the modest dress of the Cathar women who had been burned alive at Montségur and elegized, as he had found years later, by both Pound and Robert Duncan. Hass' essay, revised at school but recopied at home before his favorite radio show came on—*I Love a Mystery*, heard ritually each night against the family rules but with his father's visible acquiescence—won a ten-dollar money order from a local bookshop where he bought, dizzy and confused by all the possibilities, *A Comprehensive Anthology of American Poetry*. Unable to understand any of the poems, he stumbles onto Stevens' 'Domination of Black' with its cry of the peacocks.

Although the young Hass does not at first remember the cry of the peacocks from the front yard of his Portuguese babysitter, the reader does at once, having read about them "trailing their tails in the dust" under a palm tree in the first paragraph of the memoir. Stevens' peacocks seem to announce the existence of another world. Hass read the poem again and again: "I read it exactly the way I lined up for a roller-coaster ride with a dime tight in my fist at Playland across the bay." It made him, he says, "swoon"—and it made him "understand what the word swoon meant" a year before he found himself actually riding the Playland roller coaster beside a girl in his ninth-grade class whom he thought to be "the most beautiful being I had ever come close to in my life, which may also account for some of the previous year's swooning."

Mysteries, then. The young boy's fascination with the Sister's habit and her "long beautiful hands which she waved in the air like doves when she conducted us at Mass in the singing of the *Tantum Ergo* and *Pange Lingua*," the Cathars at Montségur, the theosophical and Gnostic writings standing behind the poetry of Robert Duncan later given association with these early memories, the hypnotized amazement at the sound of peacocks crying in what seemed to be an incomprehensible poem read over and over again like a mantra nevertheless, the similarity hypnotized amazement at the existence—at the otherness—of a beautiful girl, a radio program called *I Love a Mystery* mysteriously allowed to be heard even though it violated family rules, and the sound of peacocks crying in a babysitter's yard unconnected with the ones that cried in the poem, even unnoticed.

In the same year he won the essay prize, Hass and his friends were playing baseball on teams sponsored by businessmen's clubs and insurance companies with hilarious names, especially when seen stitched on players' uniforms in competition, like *Optimists* and *California Casualty*. Playing center field, he heard the "irritated, prenocturnal cries of the peacocks" in the yard of the Portuguese babysitter. And the grown man writes:

> I never once associated them with the Wallace Stevens poem. Art hardly ever does seem to come to us at first as something connected to our own world; it always seems, in fact, to announce the existence of another, different one, which is what it shares with Gnostic insight. That is why, I suppose, the next thing artists have to learn is that this world is the other world.

Beside the baseball field ran a creek called "Papermill." By the time Hass reads a poem by Kenneth Rexroth, who published "the first readable book of poems by a resident" of San Francisco in 1941, he is a little older. But reading that "Under the second moon the / Salmon come, up Tomales / Bay, up Papermill Creek, up / The narrow gorges to their spawning beds in Devil's Gulch" moves him deeply, and in a way very different from that in which he had been moved by 'The

Domination of Black' before. It is the presence of Papermill Creek in the poem that provides the final jolt and makes it "seem possible that the peacocks in Wallace Stevens and the scraggly birds under the palm tree could inhabit the same world."

These are some of the factors that condition the mind—the being-in-the-world—of the man who will read Miłosz for us (and Rilke and Wright and Tranströmer and Brodsky) and tell us about the nature of images, the music of poetry, and a poetic form which is "one body." We learn to trust his voice because he does not seek to mute its characteristic tones and intonations in the idiom of critic-talk or theoreze, and because, as they used to say in the 1960s, we know—we are specifically told—where he's coming from.

One of the places he is coming from is the 1960s, and Helen Vendler is right to point this out in her review. But she is wrong to stress the notion that Hass' aim is to rehabilitate the familiar essay. The familiar essay may be rehabilitated along the way in some of these pieces—and very winningly so at that—but the aim of the autobiography and "interpolated narratives" is to dramatize as vividly as possible the inevitable historical conditioning of both the texts to be read and the perceptions of the reader who intends to talk about them. Hass does not attempt to clear his mind of everything that's in it before turning to the poem on the page; instead, he gives us an account of what is in his mind when he begins to read and how it comes to be there. He does not stop living while he struggles with intractable profundities in Miłosz or in Rilke; he shows us daily life as an illumination of the struggle.

Even poems that do announce the existence of another world must be perceived in this one, and the history—both personal and social or political—which shapes the circumstances of their being read by this particular reader in this particular time in this particular place becomes, in Hass' writing, essential to the work at hand. The premises for which Helen Vendler is looking are found, essentially, in the narrative and autobiographical passages of the book. And not only premises, but a whole implied poetics. There is a moment—and Vendler doesn't like it; it is the passage she objects to in terms of what she regards to be a descent into bathos and a failure of tone—when Hass the particular reader becomes for a brief moment the perfectly average American of his time and place, which is one aspect of his existence as person and poet and reader of poems which he knows he must acknowledge.

> I am a man approaching middle age in the American century,
> which means I've had it easy, and I have three children,
> somewhere near the average, and I've just come home from
> summer vacation in an unreliable car. This is the *selva oscura*.

That is the passage which Vendler quotes. But it goes on: "Not that it isn't true, but that it is not the particular truth. It is the average, which is different from the common; arbitrary, the enemy of form." And Hass is the friend of form.

In the Miłosz essay, the Berkeley native, conditioned by a life that makes him in some ways a hostage to what he calls "the seemingly eternal Saturday afternoons of *l'homme moyen sensuel*" and in others a gifted and utterly displaced member of the diaspora of poets and readers of poems still half listening for the peacock's cry that announces the existence of another world, must deal with the fiercely isolated and visionary Berkeley immigrant from Lithuania who refuses "in the privacy of his vocation as a poet to become an accomplice of time and matter." This last, says Hass, is a difficult step for the American imagination to take.

Hass' imagination as a poet does not take that step, but his imagination as a critic follows with deep sympathy and understanding the voyage of Miłosz as he takes it. The essay on images which ends the book probably comes closer than anything else to being Hass' *Ars Poetica*. The essay on Miłosz, to use a word borrowed I think from Robert Duncan in these essays, gives "permission" for its affirmation of the world—of time and matter—by testing the most typical manifestations of the American poetic imagination against Miłosz's "leap into dualism or gnosticism" seen against the full history of the poet's life and thought and, again, the factors conditioning the critic's reading. "It might be useful," he says, "to begin by invoking a time when one might turn to the work of Czesław Miłosz."

The time turns out to be the later 1960s, and the first scene recalled is a protest march to the napalm plant in Redwood City which I remember very well participating in. Bearing our pathetically inadequate signs and listening to the hopelessly inane or merely rhetorical speeches, we did indeed "feel sheepish between gusts of affection for this ragtag army of an aroused middle class." In three pages of narrative and description as good as anything in *Armies of the Night*, Hass evokes the atmosphere of guilt, commitment, generosity, illusion, disillusion, cynicism, and craziness culminating in what he calls "a disease that was on me." He remembers the World War II veteran who shaved his head, smeared himself with red dye, and began attending Quaker meetings carrying an American flag; the careerist professor who returned from a European antiwar demonstration "to wear jeans, T-shirt and a Mao cap to teach his course in Victorian bibliography"; a friend arrested with dynamite in his trunk driving off to blow up a local air base. On his way home from the Redwood City demonstration, he even catches a glimpse of his loathed double twenty years before its time, a version of "the man approaching middle age in the American century" from the essay on images in the form of a vacationing paterfamilias driving his wife and somewhere-near-the-average-number-of-children off to enjoy dinner "on a deck from which you can admire green pines, grey granite, blue sky . . . thousands of miles away [from] fear, violence, brothels, villages going up in an agony of flames." He thinks about myth and decides that "myth is about eating each other . . . man's first tool for sanctifying the food chain. . . . The world was a pig-out; or the matter-universe was a pig-out. As if there were some other universe to distinguish this one from."

The disease that was on him had various names—philosophy, theology, eschatology—and the one thing he felt he knew about them "was that they were the enemies of poetry." But they were the enemies of a poetry inherited from Williams and Pound, an American modernism which sought to render things rather than ideas, to build a poetry out of natural objects or pictographs "as if no one had ever thought before and nothing needed to be thought that was not shot through with the energy of immediate observation." The problem was that the things and objects and pictographs of an imagist or imagist-derived poetics threw "the weight of meaning back on the innocence and discovery of the observer, and something in the dramatic ambivalence of that gesture rhymed with the permanent unconscious of the man with the boat," the vacationing paterfamilias noticed while returning from Redwood City. Hass felt "vaguely ashamed" when he saw this in the poems he was reading. "I wanted to read a poetry by people who did not assume that the great drama in their work was that everything in the world was happening to them for the first time." He finds such a poetry in the work of Miłosz, but also a poetry willing to postulate a universe different from this one, different from the pig-out matter-universe of Hass' eschatological disease which the medicine of American poetry didn't seem to cure.

Hass discusses or alludes to twenty-nine books by Miłosz in his long and loving consideration of the full career, and I haven't space enough to outline the entire argument. For my own purposes, I want to focus on the end of the piece, the pages where Hass' poetic imagination sidles up most closely to Miłosz's own, but where—because Miłosz really does locate the disease Hass was suffering from in the matter-universe itself, and not in a particular subjective aberration caused by a particular objective moment in a nation's history—the two imaginations also must part company.

Hass argues that Simone Weil's lesson to Miłosz that "contradiction is the lever of transcendence" gave the poet, who had also taken Eros as one of his teachers, permission to dwell in contradiction: "and once that happened, Eros—in the form of dream, memory, landscape—comes flooding back into his work" after the years in Paris during the 1950s. But since erotic poetry "is usually intense because it is narrow and specific, mute and focused," when the focus of Miłosz's work "widens through a terrible and uncompromising love of his own vanished experience, the poetry, refusing to sacrifice the least sharpness of individual detail to that wider vision, makes a visceral leap into dualism or gnosticism." Hass writes three closely argued pages explaining exactly how this happens, concluding thus:

> If you do not want one grain of sand lost, one moment lost, if you do not admit to the inexorable logic of the death or suffering of a single living creature, then you might, by a leap of intuition, say that it is *all* evil, because then nothing could be judged. Because it all dwelt in limitation or contradiction or, as Blake said, in Ulro. But the universe could be saved if you posited a totally independent but parallel universe of good in which each thing also had an existence. Thus, when the matter-universe fell away, the good universe survived.

Again, if you like, the cry of peacocks. But for Hass himself the other world announced must be this very world he's living in—the other universe, the only universe we know.

In the final essay in the book—and I am passing over a brilliant reading of Rilke which falls between the Miłosz essay and the essay celebrating images, not to mention half a dozen others of enormous interest—Hass becomes "an accomplice of time and matter." To praise things is not necessarily, as it comes to be in Miłosz, "to praise the history of suffering; or to collude with torture and mutilation and decay." The American will out (with a little help from the Japanese), his illness purged perhaps by contemplating all the implications of the gnosis vouchsafed to the Lithuanian. But the most extraordinary thing about this essay is that it requires from life a vision as remarkable as any given to a Catholic mystic or a Gnostic prophet, and that life cooperates with all the urgency that literature could possibly require of it.

It's difficult to know even what to call the essay on images. Like other essays in the book—but maybe here more fully achieved—it may invent a new nongeneric form of writing in its combination of vivid anecdote, personal reminiscence, literary history and analysis, meditation on life and death and imagery found in poetry, fiction, painting, sculpture, mythology, and ordinary quotidian experience.

Hass begins by gathering some images from his recent domestic life and running them through his mind along with others found in Chekhov, Buson, and Issa to demonstrate their power and the extent to which we may be haunted by them. He examines the nature of "the moment, different for different memories, when the image, the set of relationships that seems actually to reveal something about life, forms." Then he picks out such a moment: a woman camping with him and his family in a canyon about to tell a story of early sorrow: a frying pan in one hand, a scouring pad in the other, a Stellar's jay perched in the tree above her, Hass' son playing card tricks, a long granite moraine behind them, a meadow in the distance. Then Issa, then Buson, then Tu Fu who said of the power of images: "It's like being alive twice." Neither idea, nor myth, nor always metaphor, images do not explain or symbolize: "they do not say this is that, they say this is."

Hass walks through the rooms of his house feeling his life to be in part "a long slow hurdle through the forms of things." It is a sensation he resists because it implies a kind of passivity, but he would doubt the absence of the sensation because he knows his life is lived among the forms and facts and objects of the natural world. "The terror of facts is the purity of their arbitrariness. I live in this place, rather than that. Have this life, rather than that. It is August not September." Then comes the sentence about being a man approaching middle age in the American century having come home from a summer vacation. The true haiku of his recent domestic life would have to go, he says, something like this: "Bill and Leif want to climb Mount Allac and Karen and I are taking the Volkswagen to go fishing, so can you and Mom walk to the beach now and pick up Luke at Peter's later in Grandma's car?" Collecting images, beginning his essay, these distracting twentieth century pleasures had begun to eat him up. He felt "a means to a means to a means" and longed for a little solitude in which to think about poems as arresting as Basho's haiku written just before his death: "Sick on a journey, / my dream hovers / over the withered fields."

At this point, Hass breaks off writing. The second part of his essay begins by unexpectedly incorporating an experience which has just occurred. "Because it is summer," he says, "I have been in the mountains again and am now back at the typewriter." The experience in the mountains has been shattering. Walking a path in 'Desolation Wilderness', Hass began to feel the prickly sensation and notice the rash of an allergic reaction which he sometimes gets. He ignored it and kept walking until the inside of his mouth began to swell, the sign of a generalized reaction which can end in one's throat dosing up. He took two antihistamines, but the reaction intensified nevertheless, and he began to feel dizzy and frightened. He thought of the worst that might happen: that his son would have to punch a hole in his trachea with a knife; no, that he would die. The images and attendant memories that he had been collecting passed through his mind, including Basho's dream that "hovers over the withered fields." Then his legs gave way and he was on his back looking at the hillside and the sky. "Everything green in the landscape turned white, and the scene flared and shuddered as if it were on fire." Later, after the antihistamines had taken hold and he had recovered, he felt as if he had been granted a vision of death. "White trees, white grass, white leaves; the snow patches and flowering currant suddenly dark beside them; and everything there, rock, tree, cloud, sky, shuddering and blazing. It was a sense, past speaking, past these words, that everything, all of the earth and time itself, was alive and burning."

This is an amazing passage to encounter in the middle of a literary discussion, and it ought finally to make clear that phrases such as "interpolated narratives" or categories like "familiar essay" don't begin to say enough about how Hass' writing works on us. After the death vision—and it is a vision of death, not resurrection, not the vision of Czesław Miłosz where "the demiurge's workshop will be stilled . . . / And the form of every single grain will be restored in glory"—Hass returns gratefully to time and things and human beings to celebrate the world of the peacocks in the babysitter's yard, the other world which is this world, and the sensation which great art and image-making give us of marrying that world, of living in the grain at the permission of eros and "in the light of primary acts of imagination." He doesn't give up the idea from the Miłosz essay that many things bear thinking about that are not "shot through with the energy of immediate observation," but he does, here, affirm that energy as one of the supreme values in poetry.

In spite of this, or maybe even because of it, the essay is death-haunted to the end, and this is one of the things that makes it so exceptionally memorable. "The earth turns, and we live in the grain of nature, turning with it. . . . When the spirit becomes anguished or sickened by this cycle, by the irreversibility of time and the mutilation of choice, another impulse appears: the monotheist rage for unity. . . ." One sometimes finds this rage in Hass' work both as poet and critic, but not very often; not, at any rate, unless it appears as the "fuel" which he says can power "the natural polytheism of the life of art." Remember the essay on Lowell's monotheistic rage in 'The Quaker Graveyard' and the terms according to which Hass was able to be moved by the prayer at the end of its fifth part. For the rest, the essay delicately builds a collage of images from the haiku masters, from Pound and Williams and H.D., from Whitman and Chekhov and Cezanne, and comments on them, bringing life's experiences—his own and those of the artists whose work he loves—to bear upon that commentary. If we are lucky, he says, the images in terms of which we live our lives "are invisibly transformed into the next needful thing." (The danger is in clinging just to one, to the exclusion of yet others which should naturally compose themselves.)

Although there is something of Basho's spirituality and a lot of Issa's humanity in the prose of *Twentieth Century Pleasures*, I associate the author of these essays most of all with the spirit of Buson whose "apparent interest in everything that passed before his eyes and the feeling in his work of an artist's delight in making" provide a sense of "something steadying and nourishing" for Hass. I am similarly steadied and nourished by his own work here, and by the sound of a voice that I think I know. Concluding his book by quoting a final Buson haiku about whale-watching, Hass remembers his own participation in a West Coast version of that ritual and says: "We go to glimpse being." And of the poet himself, whose whale-watchers in the haiku find no whales: "Buson is not surprised by the fullness and the emptiness of things."

II: Robert Pinsky's *The Situation of Poetry*

[Among the graduate student poets who were my contemporaries at Stanford University in the 1960s, the most prolific author of critical prose has been Robert Pinsky. During 1976–77 when Robert Hass was writing some of the first essays that appear in Twentieth Century Pleasures, *Pinsky's critical volume,* The Situation of Poetry, *appeared nearly simultaneously from Princeton University Press with his first book of poems,* Sadness and Happiness. *In the winter of 1976, I argued with Ian Hamilton, editor of* The New Review, *that Pinsky's critical book was important enough that it should be reviewed alongside John Berryman's* The Freedom of the Poet *under the title 'Poet-Critics of Two Generations.' Hamilton was skeptical, saying that it seemed to him that Pinsky was "just an academic." In the end, I persuaded him to let me include Pinsky's book with my review of Berryman's by showing him the brilliant passages in it about the latter's* Dream Songs. *When the review appeared, Pinsky wrote me a surprising letter saying that once he realized his poems were going to be accepted, he very nearly withdrew the book of prose, which was basically "propaganda for the poetry."*

Hass, Pinsky, and I had all been students of Yvor Winters. Of the three of us, Pinsky was, at this stage, the only practicing Wintersian. After Sadness and Happiness *and his book-length discursive poem,* An Explanation of America, *his style changed. Because Hass and Pinsky are now very well known, and because as former US Poets Laureate their work is often read comparatively, I have detached the pages that follow from my piece on Berryman in order to print them here with some pages on Hass. When I wrote the original review, I was doing everything that I could to write sympathetically about Pinsky's position and its sources in Yvor Winters. But my heart is with Robert Hass in any comparison between these two old colleagues. When I imagine "another kind of critic" who believes that a poem is not "a statement in words about a human experience," but "an object made out of words that provides a human experience," I might have been talking about the Robert Hass who later that year wrote in a prose section of his poem 'The Beginning of September': "The dangers are everywhere. Auxiliary verbs, fishbones, a fine carelessness. No one really likes the odor of geraniums, not the woman who dreams of sunlight and is always late for work nor the man who would be happy in altered circumstances. Words are abstract, but 'words are abstract' is a dance, car crash, heart's delight. It's the design dumb hunger has upon the world."]*

Robert Pinsky's book overlaps in many respects with John Berryman's *The Freedom of the Poet*, also published this year. When Pinsky begins his defense of discursive poetry, he quotes a snatch from a Berryman interview about the difficulties of finally abandoning "Henry" and the Dream Song idiom, and remarks that "Henry and the special manner of *The Dream Songs* are 'marvellous' and useful to the poet because of what they let him say, and not as complex dramatic screens or personae." Berryman had called Henry an "outlet," a "way of making my mind known." What Pinsky calls for is as simple (and difficult) as this:

—the right to make an interesting remark or to speak of profundities, with all of the liberty given to the newspaper editorial, a conversation, a philosopher, or any speaker whatever . . .

And this:

—talking, predicating, moving directly through a subject as systematically and unaffectedly as [one] would walk from one place to another.

If language in poetry as anywhere else, given its nature, must be abstract—and Pinsky lines up with the philosophical realists and against the philosophical nominalists—then this sounds a sensible enough program, and simple enough. But there are grave difficulties for someone who might need "to speak of profundities" rather than chat, or like a philosopher rather than a journalist, and maybe even be eloquent *in order* to make his mind known in a period, as Berryman says, "inimical to poetry, gregarious and impatient of dignity." The results in such a case might look at first to be affected, unsystematic, and very clumsy indeed in getting from one place to another. In such a situation, Pinsky observes in an earlier chapter on Berryman, "a contemporary poet has adopted an elaborate mannerism in order to speak simply." In what is surely the best thing on Berryman's style since Berryman's essay on Thomas Nashe, Pinsky writes:

> Perhaps the most important point to be made is that the colloquial words and the gag-words are not the words for which the extravagant style provides a kind of license or passport. Rather, the colloquial words help the syntax, the gags, and the personae in a general effort to admit another kind of phrase—like "a smothering southern sea"—just as in ordinary talk tough-slangy tag lines such as "all that jazz" often excuse and qualify a phrase the speaker fears may seem too elevated or pretentious.

Then he quotes the conclusion of 'Dream Song' 75 and goes on:

> It is precisely only the context that is ironic, the weird manner. The irony is only that of a man in pain assuming dialects and self-effacing tones in torments of embarrassment and diffidence, as to distract himself. That is, the phrases of celebration, and the poet's phallic pride in his book, are meant; the irony constitutes a sort of request for permission to use such phrases and to express such pride.

The main theme of Pinsky's near-polemic for discursive poetry, however, has to do with less complicated and ambiguous practitioners of it than Berryman sometimes is. The main theme, in fact, has to do with the implementation of what Pinsky calls the "prose virtues" in poetry, "a drab, unglamorous group, including Clarity, Flexibility, Efficiency, Cohesiveness . . . a puritanical assortment of shrews . . . [which] do not as a rule appear in blurbs." Having no sympathy for the "quasi-political terms by which practice in the art is spuriously divided," he praises poets as different from each other as J. V. Cunningham, Frank Bidart, and James McMichael. He is also enormously interested in poets like John Ashbery and A. R. Ammons and Frank O'Hara who, as it were, *negotiate* with the prose virtues and the discursive manner in their poems—and two of these three he clearly wants back from Harold Bloom, as examples for practicing poets, for *use*.

Among poets of the modernist tradition more or less committed to what he regards to be an unsound nominalist orthodoxy, he finds "overwhelming moments . . . when a poet breaks through into a kind of prose freedom and prose inclusiveness," transcends his anti-verbal prejudice in a "generosity of movement," and writes "with the freedom and scope of speech . . . inquiring, expanding." His examples include Eliot's passage on History in 'Gerontion,' the autobiographical and moralizing sections of Canto LXXXIII, and Williams' poems which are organized around "remarks." (It's a pity, in passing, that there is almost no discussion of contemporary British poetry in the book—Tomlinson gets a stanza quoted and Hughes gets a parenthesis—as there is much in Auden, Roy Fuller, Larkin, Davie, Tomlinson, Turnbull, Fisher, Prynne, Silkin, Tarn, and many others which would broaden and complicate the terms of his discussion. And what of MacDiarmid's later poems as some kind of test? Of patience and stamina, anyway. But Pinsky allows there is boredom even in Ammons.)

But I have been discussing the conclusion of *The Situation of Poetry*. The "situation," the problem of poetry in the modernist and postmodernist period is, according to Pinsky, chiefly to be seen in terms of a deluded nominalist orthodoxy among poets which, paradoxically, has continued to produce masterpieces for sixty years. Interested in "affinity" and "tradition" rather than "influence" (a concept which has recently taken on a Romantic meaning: "the irresistible force of one personality upon another"), Pinsky discusses "a climate of implicit expectation and tacit knowledge" which has changed and grown, and "technical means which may be shared." The cost to a contemporary of not sufficiently understanding his tradition will be conventionality and mannerism; the price of understanding it fully may be a compulsion to disown it, or silence.

Pinsky does not disown it. He does disown the conventionality and mannerism of certain of his knee-jerk contemporaries who have not struggled to understand the tradition in which they are writing. Tracing that tradition back to the Romantic period by way of a detailed reading of 'Ode to a Nightingale,' he concludes:

> . . . the Romantic poet regards the natural world nostalgically, across a gulf which apparently can be crossed only by dying, either actually or through some induced oblivion. The gulf is closely related to the gulf between words and things. Various philosophical descriptions might apply to the situation. The broadest of these . . . stems from the terms "nominalism" and "realism." Nominalism can be defined loosely as the doctrine that words and concepts are mere names, convenient counters of no inherent reality, though they may be useful means for dealing with the atomistic flux of reality. I understand philosophical realism as the opposite doctrine that universals—and therefore, concepts and words—embody reality. The Romantic poet tends to look for values to emerge from particular experiences—associated sense perceptions and states of mind at particular moments—and insofar as that is true, he is a nominalist. But insofar as he is a poet he must to some extent be a realist, for those reasons which may bear repeating: words are abstractions, sentences are forms disposing their parts in time, and rhythm is based upon the concept of recurrence or pattern.

Finding, therefore, "the ultimate goal of the nominalist poem . . . logically impossible"—and telling us in a footnote that, when Pound said "go in fear of abstractions," he was speaking rhetorically and not philosophically: he was calling for concrete referents—Pinsky concludes rather surprisingly: "But the pursuit of the goal, or the effort to make the gap *seem* [my italics] less than absolute, has produced some of the most remarkable and moving poetry in the language."

Seem. Pinsky is, in fact, passionately in love with poem after poem which his theories call profoundly into question. True, as I said earlier, nearly all of these poems are concerned with defining the dilemma itself, and he is not much amused by "vulgarisations" of the tradition where the dilemma becomes obscured ("A poem should be wordless / as a flight of birds"), or by various reductions (a poem appearing in *The Paris Review* which reads entire: "Bananas are an example"). Although it would be rash to say that Pinsky clearly prefers poems to principles (Winters: "We shall scarcely get anything better unless we change our principles"), the poems do absolutely come both first and last, providing both the source and a rigorous test of the principles. It is obviously safer (I don't say better) to proceed like Berryman, who is all scholarship and electric response, and to avoid being too concerned with theory.

What does Pinsky like coming out of this tradition? Those poems which demonstrate that the poet understands the bind he is in by making dear that he can't possibly write the poem he has written, or, better, those that demonstrate by their very existence that the poet can't possibly think what he seems to think, or, best of all, appreciates the terrible cost of thinking it, which sometimes leads to his abandoning the idea or hypothesis as a delusion: ". . . the fancy cannot cheat so well / As she is famed to do, deceiving elf."

> My proposition is that the difference between the dross and vulgarization on the one hand, and genuine work on the other, is a sense of cost, misgiving, difficulty . . . The peculiar, somewhat paradoxical project—to make an art's medium seem less what it is—produces brilliant techniques and new assumptions. Then, as generations pass, those techniques and assumptions come to seem the only way of writing. The original premises and difficulties of the style, and the original dilemma of mind, become obscured.

> The modern poems against which he tests the work of his contemporaries are Williams' 'The Term,' Frost's 'The Most of It,' and, supremely, Stevens' 'The Snowman.' Later on, there is much praise for A. R. Ammons' 'Motion.' Against these poems which he admires, Pinsky ranges work by poets both familiar and unfamiliar from the second-best all the way down the line to the absolutely awful, formulaic poems from what he calls the "surrealist-jackanapes" school and things like Lawrence Raab's 'The Word,' about which he says: "Without flying too far off the handle, I suggest that, in its oblique way, this is cant."

Yvor Winters begins a famous chapter by saying that "a poem is a statement in words about a human experience," and, in one of his poems which Pinsky has had occasion to quote elsewhere against the sort of work he doesn't like, writes of "Something one would never say / Moving in a certain way." But some of the finest poetry of the century has been written by people who believe that a poem is not a statement in words about a human experience at all, but, elusively yet triumphantly, an object made out of words that provides a human experience, and that poets are makers rather than sayers. Pinsky allows this, as I've said, investigates the assumptions and the work resulting from the assumptions, praises and censures, then sticks to his realist guns. It's very interesting that, in a passage on John Ashbery, he is willing to say this: "The language comes closer than one might have thought possible to being, itself, a nominalistic particular: pure, referring to nothing else, unique." The language is used, he says, like paint in a nonrepresentational painting. There is abstraction and then there is abstraction. This is the point at which another kind of book by another kind of poet might begin.

Pinsky is an eminently sane, enormously helpful and lucid critic of poetry. As the major poet of John Berryman's generation enters his sixties, one begins to look around hopefully for some younger talents who are able to take on the high responsibility of continuing the practice and criticism of the art in increasingly difficult times. Pinsky and a handful of other poets of his immediate generation—Hass, Peck, McMichael—promise and have indeed already accomplished a great deal. I would stress, precisely, the wholeness and tenacity and coherence of their work—which implies no sacrifice of energy, vision, or invention—after a period which has seen important poetry published which is sometimes seriously unhinged or severely misshapen or obsessively violent. As I must end this, however, I think I should do so with a quote from Pinsky which has to do with unusual clarities which can be achieved "out near the end of things," as Berryman has it. Taken broadly, what he says of sanity at work in poetry—even when emotion is nearly intolerable or "wonder interacts with a deranged or neurasthenic aspect of personality"—describes some of the highest achievements of Berryman's work as well as the strangely descriptive poems by Roethke, John Clare, and Sylvia Plath, which he discusses in the chapter this passage introduces, and which he admires:

> A "sane" work of art . . . is one which accomplishes its meaning
> consciously. Otherwise the meaning is the reader's creation, the
> art a symptom; sanity in writing is the tonal adjustment that
> changes confession into character-making. Authentic clarity is
> the style's proof that the fiction is true: not a patient's tortured,
> oblique version of a dream, but the authoritative dream itself,
> naked and magisterial.

Two Kinds of Autobiography

[The following consideration of prose by Michael Anania and Jiri Wyatt originally appeared in the title essay of my book called Reading Old Friends. *It was combined there with part of the piece printed earlier in this book about the critical prose of Robert Hass. Hass, I argue there, is also writing a kind of autobiography in his book called* Twentieth Century Pleasures.*

Literary memoirs are all too frequent now, and of course I have printed five of my own at the beginning of this book. If you happened to know John Ashbery or Robert Bly when you were sixteen, you do not hesitate these days to write it all up as a memoir, although you probably should. I have reminded myself of the attendant dangers of autobiographical writing when at work on these pieces, but the rewards seemed worth the risks. In the books discussed below, Anania and Wyatt have written the kind of autobiography now taught in American writing program workshops as "creative non-fiction." It's an ugly term, but there we are. The genre allows the autobiographer all the techniques of fiction, even certain falsehoods if they will make the story more interesting. I have allowed myself some cautious latitudes in my own memoirs. But the practice is fraught with dangers. Robert Lowell, who was always ready to do this kind of thing himself, was annoyed when his old friend Peter Taylor did it in his portrait of Lowell in the autobiographical short story Taylor called '1939.' But Taylor had anticipated both Lowell's annoyance and what I have just written in the story itself:

> I stand before the class as a kind of journeyman writer, a type of whom Trollope might have approved, but one who has known neither the financial success of the facile Harvard boy or the reputation of Carol Crawford. Yet this man behind the lectern is a man who seems happy in the knowledge that he knows—or thinks he knows—what he is about. And from behind his lectern he is saying that any story that is written in the form of a memoir should give offense to no one, because before a writer can make a person he has known fit into such a story—or any story, for that matter—he must do such violence to that person's character that the so-called original is forever lost to the story.

Of course Taylor went right ahead and committed what violence he needed on the "Harvard Boy," "Carol Crawford", and others in his story.

On the "creative non-fiction" continuum, Anania's The Red Menace *tends most toward fiction, Wyatt's* Against Capitulation *most toward recording the facts. But they are both ways of writing a memoir. I should also say that "Jiri Wyatt" is really Igor Webb. When* Against Capitulation *was published, an authorial pseudonym was still necessary to protect friends and family in the old Czechoslovakia. The Berlin Wall had not yet fallen, Václav Havel was still in prison, and the Czechs and Slovaks had not yet gone their separate ways as post-communist states.]*

§

I. *Against Capitulation*

Jiri Wyatt's *Against Capitulation* is difficult to classify generically; it is very much the prose work of a poet. Falling into two uneven parts—a twenty-five page essay published before the rest of the book was even conceived, and a sequence of twenty-three often oddly titled chapters ranging from childhood reminiscence through political analysis and travelogue to something like dream-vision and prose-poetry—the book deals with Wyatt's childhood in Fascist Slovakia; his later life in South America, the United States, Canada, and England; his trip back to Slovakia in 1978; and his attempts to clarify his thoughts about the Holocaust, revolution, socialism, Stalininsm, the 1960s, and his identity as a Jew, a son, a father, a Slovak, a New Yorker, a writer, and a radical. The sweep of the book is ambitious enough to require all of its unusual means. And it is good enough to take an honorable place beside the work of those more recently exiled Czechoslovak writers, Milan Kundera, Josef Škvorecky, and Jiri Gruša.

In Wyatt's book I find myself listening to a familiar voice—I have known the author for many years—telling both familiar and unfamiliar stories, advancing arguments I've heard in conversation many times and some that are entirely new. The name itself, however, is not familiar; it is a pseudonym made necessary for the same reason that other people's names and identities have been disguised in the book—to protect the men and women who, in the Holocaust of 1939–1945, saved the author's life. There is a certain irony in the fact that this is necessary. *Against Capitulation* begins with a scene set in a small bedroom with a single window looking over a bleak Manhattan landscape. Here the author's parents came "one surprising evening and announced matter-of-factly that they planned to change our family name." He was sixteen at the time. His parents said, "We're doing this for you. You don't know what it means to be Jewish." The book, then, has to do in part with "Jiri Wyatt" learning what it means to be "Jiri Weinwurm," learning, not perhaps until the visit to Slovakia in 1978, what it means to have been born "a Jew in the town of M——." But it also has to do with two forms of hubris—that of parents and that of children—and the literary means of discovering the nature of these while simultaneously engaged in attempting to regain the past without sacrificing the felt life of the present and learning, as Robert Hass says of Miłosz, "to dwell in contradiction."

In the spring of 1966 Wyatt occupied the office of J. Wallace Sterling, the president of Stanford University, with a group of war protestors. The first part of *Against Capitulation*—the essay that was published separately—concludes with a description of the occupation and an evocation of the period when "events invited a millennialist vision to which we felt egotistically equal." In the second part—the long account of the visit to Slovakia and its background—Wyatt writes of another millennialist vision, that of the Holocaust survivors who project onto their children a "raging, primal need to *see* themselves reproduced . . . The parents are possessed by a vision of their fulfillment so intense, so millennial, that they are wholly unaware that they are possessed. They, the parents, embody the message, and now the children will speak it." Because Wyatt finds "the experience of survival equivocal," he cannot accept Elie Wiesel's position that religious witness must be paid to those who "set eyes on 'an event that weighs on man's destiny.'" Wyatt's own experience of survival made Wiesel's notion that "persecution bestows upon the victims moral stature" less than self-evident.

> I lived what amounted to a life without moral example, embroiled in survival but lacking the dignity of an asserted self-respect or of a proud history. My parents retrieved from the Holocaust a determination that they would not be caught out again: out of the disorder forced upon them they would secure, less for them than for me, a permanent inviolable stability. This turned out to be an emphasis in their lives with

few affirmatives: the chief rules were don'ts, and the sum of these don'ts was a deadly practicality aimed against belief in any of its delusory and dangerous forms—against belief in anything but the worst.

Both Wyatt and his parents could not, he saw, have what they wanted—"They a vicarious triumph through me, and I my own life." Insisting on denying his parents their vicarious triumph by becoming himself, Wyatt attempted in high school to annihilate his past by taking hold of fate in a Sartrian manner and, free to choose his identity, trying to make "the authentic daily assertion of individual freedom." Insisting on belief—on belief in nothing but the best against his parents' fear of belief in anything but the worst—he became the politically committed radical sitting in the president's office at Stanford where "events invited a millennialist vision." But nightmares of his childhood in hiding mocked Sartre's *Being and Nothingness* with images of a past which he could no more escape than he could choose his dreams; and a sense emerged, after the fact, that there was something hubristic in "the pleasure of absolute certainty" sitting there in the Stanford president's office confident that the future would prove one absolutely right.

At about the time his daughter was born in 1970, Wyatt and his parents began to share "the suppressed history" of their lives between 1941 and 1945, and slowly his determination formed to visit Slovakia. Much of the long second part of *Against Capitulation* has to do with images—how they are manifested in dreams and nightmares, arise unexpectedly before the traveler, compose and recompose themselves and then dissolve, draw one to the past or lead one to the future or hold one in the present moment—images of justice, tyranny, life, death, pain, pleasure, and joy. The danger with images, as Robert Hass points out in his seminal essay on the topic in *Twentieth Century Pleasures*, is to cling to just a single one alone as if it embodied an entire truth. For example, the image of "a raving inarticulate parent, replete with impossible demands, posturing like an Old Testament prophet." Or of oneself as Stanford's Bob Dylan telling Wallace Sterling how he doesn't know what's happening, does he Mr. Jones. Images, says Hass, "either . . . dry up [and] are shed, or . . . are invisibly transformed . . . or we act on them in a way that exposes both them and us." "What do you want to go there for?" Wyatt's mother asked him when he told her that he planned to visit Slovakia. One reason was to trace to their source his primal memories that appeared to him "not as sequences of actions but as images accompanied by specific and powerful emotions. . . . My lost childhood, my forgotten sensuous past, this darkness rank with smell, taste, and terror—that was what I wanted." Another reason, he discovered, was to act on certain images which had begun to petrify in such a way as to expose, in Hass' terms, both himself and them—to form thereby another image, for example, of the figure making impossible demands and posturing like an Old Testament prophet. "One of my reasons for going," he says, "was to love my parents."

The journey itself begins in America with a visit to several surviving relations who might possibly give Wyatt information which will allow him better to connect those images which the word *past* conjures in his mind with the people and places he needs to see in order, at last, to ground them in a fully personal, historical, and geographical context. *Past* had conjured an almost contextless vision of interiors in sequence: "a ground-floor room . . . with windows at one end . . . my mother is ironing . . . outside the world is snow . . . soldiers on skis are working their way up the hill"; or another room, a mountain bunker with wooden boards to sleep on, a stool on which a child stands to suck his mother's breasts; or the house in M— where the child will not leave the window looking out into the darkness of the village as he waits impatiently for his parents to return.

But sometimes *past* had conjured other images—images which were not constricting or frightening, but which seemed to open into a world of peace accompanied by emotions "which approached euphoria." He remembered "being pulled by [his] father out of the mountains on a sledge . . . after the Russians had swept through [their] sector of the White Carpathians," and before that "crossing a brook or small stream under a stunning night sky" heading for a second bunker which his father had built higher in the mountains feeling "wonder and peace as we crossed that stream, exactly as if the forest and the overwhelming clear arc of the night sky and the stream were themselves a little in awe."

In Boston, Wyatt's uncle Pepo asks him "Who can you go visit . . . ? There's no one left." And in Atlanta his Aunt Sharon opens on her lap a box stuffed "with every scrap of paper—every railroad ticket, letter, note, telegram—from the years 1939–1945" which she has saved from a life of hiding, flight, and exile. She has kept all this to document their family's history and pass it on to their daughter, Wyatt's cousin Valery, who isn't interested. Valery's parents, like Wyatt's, had come to America "with the Holocaust raging behind them. They were, they knew, survivors; their lives had been threatened and spared, and they aimed to recoup what in truth they could not regain through the life they would give their children." Valery, in a style utterly different from the young Wyatt's, had abandoned her Jewish and Slovakian identity to survive the lives of her survivor parents. Wyatt tries to explain to his aunt. "Can you ask us to live for you? We didn't want to make your dreams come true, we just wanted to be ourselves." But his own situation in regard both to survival and identity is now more complicated than his cousin's, and he leaves for Bratislava with the names of "a few good people," an improved sense of geography, a year's tutoring in Czechoslovak under his belt, and a headful of images—including the box of papers open on his aunt's lap in Atlanta.

After being met in Bratislava by his cousin Miro, Wyatt almost immediately inquires after the quality of the cuisine in a restaurant in Hviezdoslav Square. He had come to Slovakia not only to look and see and listen and talk, but to touch and smell—and eat. He wanted "the food of memory"—chicken paprika, *gnochky*, and *palachinky*.

At the first opportunity, he goes to the restaurant on the square for lunch and sits at the table "with a virtually ritual anticipation, like a child," only to be profoundly disappointed when the food arrives and he finds that "he could have done a lot better had he cooked the meal himself." Or could he have? Perhaps the food of his childhood, the one "constant" of his childhood, was misremembered or "just wasn't to be had," lost, somehow, like so much else he was seeking.

This initial disappointment predicts the comically qualified sense of success at the end of the book when Slovakian cooking becomes the metaphor for Wyatt's ability to give his daughter the experience of his journey by writing and dedicating to her *Against Capitulation*. He struggles for several weeks after his return home to bake proper cheese *buchty* for dessert, experimenting again and again with the dough and a variety of cheeses. In the end, he serves it up. "The *buchty* looked good—just the right depth of brown, risen to a nice thickness . . . and they weren't bad—'yummy!' my daughter said. Not bad, but not quite right."

What Wyatt learns, of course, is that what was once available to him in Slovakia exists only as memory, as a past which can be given voice to and remembered more precisely as his early images and their attendant sensations are clarified and given back their defining contexts, but that past really does mean *past* if he should be asked (as he is by the Kafkaesque inquisitor he posits at the end of the book) to say who he is. He can no longer give "the perfectly simple answer: I am a Slovak Jew from the town of M—." He must journey among identities, understanding that the place of beginnings has been "a blank of darkness rank with sensuous power but entirely without definition" may be given definition in the course of the journey only to an extent which will be at best "Not bad, but not quite right." Although Wyatt does revisit the house in M—, it still lives chiefly in his mind's eye, in his memory. By being made more vivid the past becomes more vividly the past.

But the desire to embrace the past, or, rather, to embrace those images and icons of its absence which are present to him in Slovakia, is intense. After spending some time with his aunt and uncle, Monika and Joseph, in Bratislava, he travels by train to the town of M—where his cousin, Honza, shows him the house where he lived briefly after the war which, like other houses in the village, soon will disappear to make way for prefab high rises with hot running water. Calling himself for the first time "an autobiographer" or "at best the historian of an idea he cannot name," he wants nothing to change here, wants "the old streets to remain as a living model," though "he does not know of *what*." He begins to feel that he "had come on a foolish errand: to repossess what I could never have again . . . that house and gate across the road, so familiar, so alien."

Beyond the town of M— is the tiny village of Kamen, and beyond that the series of bunkers in the hills. Honza and Oliver, the Partisan who hid with Wyatt and his family in the bunkers, travel on with him to the home of Franzi Holub in Kamen with its "one street without any sidewalks" where the houses are "unpainted cement squares and triangles" and the look of the place recalls, Wyatt thinks, the set for the movie *Shane.* The Holubs' front room, where the Wyatts first had hidden, was the source of one of the primal, ungrounded images presented early in the book which, as it were, had brought him here. The image composes itself, decomposes, recomposes. His mother was ironing at the window and the German soldiers passed on skis. But what could his mother have been ironing? He had remembered bright, white linen—sheets. But they had brought nothing with them, not even clothing. And "what sort of iron would it have been?" Perhaps she was doing something else. And yet "I see her clearly at the ironing board at the back of the room, the steam swirling, whiteness the colour of snow fall."

Because it is too late in the year and the woods are wet and flooded, Wyatt never manages to get to the bunkers in the hills, the source of the other and more powerful images of pristine earliness, those which were accompanied by emotions "that approached a kind of euphoria." Later, when Franzi's slivovitz and sausages have run through his system, he goes into the field behind the house to defecate. "What I had come [to Slovakia] for," he says, "was lying in the mist of the hills behind me." The sources of his most powerful early memories and most vividly haunting mental images remain inaccessible, subject still to "longing"—a term that Wyatt earlier invokes perhaps because, as Hass says in his poem, 'A Meditation at Lagunitas,' desire must remain "full of endless distances."

In a later chapter, Wyatt considers another reason why the boy that he was could never fully come to life in him again, and why he could not repossess the house he lived in or even spontaneously and innocently grasp for the intense sensations, the "memories made palpable," which he sought. He no longer belonged in M—not only because "no amount of Slovak food could force from my identity the decades I had spent away . . . but also because grown up I had become an observer, a perennial third party, the one who writes."

When his cousins went to bed at night, he wrote in his notebook. Old images and their defining contexts were not only actively to be sought, but they were to be given a verbal shape and submitted, along with the perceptions of the seeker, to analysis. The same was true of new images and their defining contexts. "If I do not belong in M—," Wyatt wonders, "do I belong anywhere else?" The act of self-conscious observation and analysis itself alienates, deracinates such a "perennial third party." When the Kafkaesque inquisitor at the end of the book asks Wyatt, "Who, truly, are you," he desperately runs through a mental list of possibilities—"Fresser, Jew, Slovak, New Yorker, Radical, Writer (??), U.S. Citizen c. 1956, Socialist"—and jumps to his feet crying out "Jew." We understand that any of these answers would be wrong in Wyatt's journey among identities, but if I were forced to choose one for him from the list, it would be "Writer."

As a writer, then—but also as a Jew, a Slovak, a New Yorker, and a Radical—Wyatt seeks out or stumbles onto new images as well as old remembered ones, images and their defining contexts which establish a potent tension between the present and the past. It was inevitable, for example, that he should wish to visit Terezin Fortress and the medieval Jewish cemetery in Prague. One of the three epigraphs to *Against Capitulation* is a line from Geoffrey Hill's austere and shattering poem 'September Song,' with its note "born 19.6.32—deported 24.9.42." Hill's elegy for the child who died in one of the camps ends abruptly, as if he had intended to write much more and suddenly stops in disgust over having written anything at all, with the line Wyatt quotes: "This is plenty. This is more than enough." (One of Hill's constant preoccupations is the danger of committing what he calls "the tongue's atrocities." "Artistic men prod dead men from their stone," he writes in a poem on Auschwitz.)

Wyatt is not sickened by his own desire to meditate both on Terezin and in Terezin, consciously to collect images, or to write of what he sees and feels. He does not deny that "the unspeakable renders you blessedly speechless, since only silence is equal to your impossibly contradictory, besmirched emotion, and your awe," but he goes on to recognize that "silence is also incommunicable and opaque," which is why those writers on the Holocaust who "perceive its unique adequacy wind up composing sentences nevertheless."

Not sickened, therefore, by collecting and presenting images like the two white roses and the red one on a wooden table in the dormitory vaults "faded, pale, but brilliant and piercing the blankness and the utter silence of the cells" beside the faded note "in memory of R.F. who was a prisoner in this cell," he *is* sickened upon emerging from Terezin "to see people pursuing their innocently ordinary lives," and this involves him in some contradictions that he must learn to live with and write from. Upon leaving Terezin, Wyatt sees complicity written into the most common human activities—"the unexamined routine of the ordinary person appears vile. It appears to bear in its malleable commonsense the seed of all cruelty." The image at Terezin of human cruelty having become "stone, brick, and mortar," having become "that quintessential human creation: a building," makes him feel so "violated, soiled, and corrupted" that he cannot see a simple act in the present moment—"the ability to go shopping, say"—as not utterly tainted by corruption.

Images, as Hass points out, often say *this is.* But they also say, like Terezin, *this was,* or, like any *memento mori* (such as the brilliantly described stones in the medieval cemetery beside the Pinkas Synagogue) *this will be.* If the danger of clinging to the second or third kind of image is that one grows increasingly unable to live in the present, the danger of grasping at the first is that one grows increasingly unable to see the present responsibly as a product of the past with a future that depends on human will, or even other competing presents which cry out *these are* against *this is* because they're made invisible by the brilliance of an isolated moment. Wyatt, in fact, cultivates and presents such brilliant moments now and then, most notably in the image of a young woman on the Charles Bridge in Prague "tossing bits of bread to the gulls."

> The birds swirled round her. No sooner would she toss a piece of bread into the air than a gull would swoop to catch it. Each time this happened the woman's face opened into the purest delight, and she'd give out an enraptured little cheer. Over and over she threw her bread into the air and beamed with pleasure as the gull snapped it in his beak.

Wyatt calls this "a salvaged moment, beyond necessity and outside power." He has been walking the streets of Prague with a dissident and discussing Charter '77. Had the woman on the bridge heard of it? Was she here in 1968 when the Russian tanks rolled in? Would she have stood there throwing bread to gulls in 1943? Would she have known what went on in Terezin? Is she guilty of complicity in the repressions of the present regime, or gifted with the grace to live in the present moment, or both? Some of these questions are mine rather than Wyatt's, but they are all implicit in the little scene and its defining context. Looking over his shoulder for the police, he mentions his surprise that such things as feeding bread to gulls go on in the Prague of 1978, and his dissident friend says: "What do you expect, that life will stop?" Wyatt doesn't by any means. And although much of this book is obsessed with the past, the exhilaration of reading it, one realizes, comes from the vivid sense which it communicates of what it feels like to live the present moment to its fullest.

There is nothing for Wyatt to do but embrace the contradictions of his experience, and write as clearly and as honestly as he can out of his divided identity and multiple allegiances. It is a difficult balancing act—one achieved necessarily in the present, but with one eye on the future and one eye on the past.

There is a marvelous moment just before the three-part conclusion—the Kafkaesque self-interrogation, an analysis of broken covenants, and the *buchty* episode—when Wyatt is on the train from Mikulas to Bratislava. Although the train would not stop at M—, Honza and his family had insisted on waiting for it to pass under the large sign with the town's name written on it in order to wave and shout goodbye, and Wyatt wanted a last nostalgic look and to wave himself. As the train speeds past M— into the future, he frantically dives across the compartment to catch a final glimpse of his cousin and the sign with the word that more than any other stands for his past. "After a moment I became conscious that the wind was cold and that, the train careening at a fast clip, I was hanging dangerously halfway out of the window. In a fright I pulled myself back in. The thought flashed through my mind: I don't want to die. I love my life." Yes, and in a world where one *does* throw bread to gulls and say *this is* to the cacophonous *these are, this was,* and *this will be.*

Wyatt's account of his trip to Slovakia extends and in some ways responds to and interrogates the original short essay printed as the title chapter of *Against Capitulation.* That essay concludes with some firm judgments and what sounds like the making of a personal covenant, an affirmation "of the long Jewish resistance to oppression, or resistance to Fascism, and of the revolutionary Socialism which gave (and continues to give) that resistance shape and fire." By the end of the book, Wyatt writes about the breaking of covenants—between God and the Jewish nation, and between a purposeful History and mankind whose free and just millennium was to have been assured at the end of the dialectical spiral—in a world where old certainties, religious and political, no longer hold. The conclusion is full of questions and doubts rather than certainties and doctrines: "You set out on a journey to the place of origin with vague hopes, excitement, and more contradictory feelings than you can be aware of. You return enlivened and puzzled. Your puzzlement is your fate."

The questioning at the end even extends to the questioners, to the Czech dissidents and our own image of them in the West—the fact that, because these men and women have opted for clear consciences, we can deceive ourselves into believing "that the old certainties hold." Also, by the end of the book, Wyatt is thinking as much about his daughter as of his parents (a daughter whose birth I remember being announced on a card with a Vietcong guerrilla on one side and an inspirational poem by Chairman Mao on the other—whose message was *she* supposed to speak in 1970?), and wondering what it is he has to offer her. Instead of offering something like an affirmation of "the long Jewish resistance to oppression . . . and revolutionary Socialism," he offers her "what I have set down in these pages"—a sequence of images generating a narrative and ending in puzzlement.

The aim throughout this book is to understand (by puzzling over) the events experienced and the history recovered rather than to judge them. For this reason, images are truly sought, retrieved, shed, transformed, exposed, and discovered; the act of doctrinal judgment would simply have frozen some of them. I don't mean to imply an absence of political commitment at the end of the book; Wyatt is clearly still "against capitulation," and still a radical—even more so than before if a radical approach to our experience does mean getting at its roots. Ironically, he also, in the end, speaks the message which his parents and their generation embodied, bears them a kind of witness, and gives them, if not a vicarious victory, then perhaps a sort of vicarious strategic retreat or flanking action. Although it wasn't exactly what they had in mind, I wonder if they wouldn't have understood—and maybe even approved—had they been able to follow this journey to its end.

II. *The Red Menace*

Michael Anania's *The Red Menace*—"a fiction," he calls it; I call it an oral autobiography which he has dictated to himself—begins with the image of an atomic test on a television screen seen over the cereal bowls and milk bottles of countless American homes in the 1950s. I remember these tests well. The images certainly provided a bizarre focus for our scarcely conscious minds as, groggy and irritable, we stared uncomprehendingly at the black-and-white flickerings of those primitive TVs. For Anania, the images became a fundamental element in what he thinks of as "the snarl of things we call awareness." This is what we all were looking at and what it is that Anania's characters (his friends and/or antagonists) go off to school talking about.

> The screen was instantly blank, not bright, just blank; then slowly from its edges, as though seeping back, the gray of the sky circled in around a light at the center, which in turn began to grow outward against the recovered sky. The circle of light grew to the size of a baseball, darkening at the edges, rising on a column of smoke that ridged and fluted itself as it supported the ball, the ball itself grown smoky, flattening as it moved upward. The horizon was plain again, and to the right of the burgeoning cloud there were three thin streamers of smoke that rippled as they extended off the top of the screen. The wooden shed was gone. The screen belonged to the cloud, which stood still, or seemed still except for the constant enfolding of smoke shadows at the top and sides, and the constant pumping of smoke into the crown from the column below. The announcer droned on about height, times, size, and the picture changed.

"Jee-zus," one of the boys says, while the others rise "as though responding to a benediction." "Shee-it" "Fuckin' A" . . . "Damn Straight" the rest incant in their turn, reacting to various outrageous claims—"you know you could carry one of them things in a suitcase?"—made by one or another of them about the bomb. The jive, too, is part of the snarl of things which Anania says we call awareness and which, in his own case, we might just as well call memory. Anania is a great rememberer. My own method of dealing with the particular madness of the 1950s was simple—the cultivation of total amnesia. I hated and feared both the strange intensities and stultifying inertias of the decade, from its music, cars, movies, heroes, and politics to its style of sexual swagger or sexual innocence. As soon as it was possible to forget—at about the time, I suppose, of Kennedy's inauguration—I forgot. But Anania forces memory upon me. To some extent, his experiences were also mine—which was not the case, of course, with what Jiri Wyatt remembers from his childhood in Slovakia. But 1950s America is another country, too, and many of its characteristic or defining images are as simultaneously familiar and alien, once held up in their own authentically garish light, as a half-remembered room in an eastern European village is to a returning exile.

The snarl of things . . . awareness and the memory of awareness and the awareness of memory. Anania grew up in Omaha, Nebraska, and lived in a housing project named for Logan Fontenelle, the last chief of the Omahas. German on his mother's side, he got his "bits and pieces" of a Bremen pastoral mainly from his grandmother, who returned to Germany as an old woman after the war. His mother's immigrant experiences "foreclosed all but a few images of an earlier, green life in another world." Anania's father, whose southern Italian background made him something of a *don* both in his own mind and in the Calabrian community, died young after a life in which tuberculosis made steady work impossible. He shined shoes, sold papers, dealt cards, helped build a water wall for WPA, and ended up on welfare living "not so much by his wits as his sense of style."

Outside Omaha was the Macy reservation where some of Anania's friends, none of whom seems actually to live there, visit older relatives on weekends. Russell, the Omaha in Anania's high school who has a plan to steal the bomb, has the classic profile of the figure on a buffalo nickel and drives a Pontiac with its Indian hood ornament "jutting into the traffic." (Anania, importantly enough at the end of the book, drives a Plymouth with the *Mayflower* on its hood.) High school friends and acquaintances include a range of ghetto blacks, ethnic working-class whites, inaccessible upper-middle-class girls ("Cottonwood fluff"), and some truly violent delinquents for whom high school provided a kind of pastoral interlude "before the weight of lower-middle American life settled in" on them.

All the boys brooded on the bomb—made it their own "by right of attentive devotion"—while brooding with an analogous intensity on particular girls "attended to, watched carefully, offered the role of leading lady in the movies in our heads," and particular cars which were "nosed" and "decked" with "an almost Bauhaus purity" to the point that they resembled bombs or bullets. The music accompanying all of this was either black rhythm and blues (aggressively defiant and kept off the radio and out of downtown record stores) or early white rock 'n' roll. Movies in the mind were based on movies in the movie theaters, dangerously suggestive films like *Blackboard Jungle* on the one hand, and studies in the conflict between masculine honor and domesticity like *Shane, High Noon,* and *Rebel without a Cause* on the other. South of town was Offutt Air Force Base which, as headquarters of the Strategic Air Command, would make Omaha a certain target for a Soviet nuclear attack. Lewis and Clark stopped on their journey west to hunt on the river bluffs into which the SAC administrative building, a kind of inverted skyscraper, was sunk down to its lowest subterranean level where Curtis LeMay sat before the NORAD communications system dreaming of *grands prix* and his Ferrari, like a high school student before a blackboard dreaming of the dragstrip and his Olds or Merc.

Anania early on establishes a connection between the bomb and sex, and between both of these and the souped-up cars that looked like bombs in which sexual desire could be relieved in the backseat or, more often, compensated for by tearing down a country road at ninety miles an hour. The "Red Menace" of the title is simultaneously the threat of the bomb in enemy hands; a name given to Russell, the Omaha, by one of his classmates; the swollen phallus of the sexually famished but frightened teenage male; and any of several bright, fast, dangerous, and desirable cars. While Anania's book begins with an atomic test assuring us again of the actual possibility of the much imagined cataclysm of nuclear holocaust, it ends, after episodes in which the dilemma of sexual power, like that of political power, is seen to be powerlessness and defeat, with an emblem for the cataclysm in what he calls an "autoclysm"—an orgasmic crash, described in nearly pornographic detail, in which the car is "totalled" and everyone is killed.

If the autoclysm is the most memorable emblem in *The Red Menace,* it may be that 'The Real McCoy' is the most important. Readers of

Anania's poetry will remember the real McCoy, a revolver which Anania's father kept in a green steel box wrapped in a handkerchief, from an early poem in *The Color of Dust* called 'The Temper.' There as here, it represents something solid, authentic, and durable in the threatened and unstable atmosphere of Anania's world. This is the passage from 'The Temper':

> It is something to covet—
> what my father said of the real McCoy,
> the gesture and all of
> holding the revolver in his hand,
> tapping the butt on the table,
> saying, that is solid,
> more than this table, solid,
> tempered blue sheen thunk
> reflected on the table top,
> snubnosed, hammerless real McCoy.

In *The Red Menace,* the real McCoy surfaces in the third chapter, in which Anania's father successfully organizes a funeral for a woman who suddenly dies in the housing project, and then breaks up a neighborhood fight that develops in an afternoon of drinking when the group of pallbearers returns home. Anania's memories of his father constitute remarkable "islands of clarity," as he calls them, retrievable moments and images very like those presented in the early pages of *Against Capitulation.* Remembering his father's pleasure in breaking up the fight, Anania also remembers the day he sat him down at the kitchen table and showed him the gun which the young boy thought he might also have shown to the men in the fight in order to stop it. The gun "was a lesson in the weight and hardness of real things." Anania's father traces the crosshatch of the grip, turns it in the light to show off the bluing on the trigger guard and muzzle, and then, as in the poem, "holding it just above the table, he let the butt fall, thunk, and the whole kitchen seemed to shake."

Anania thinks his father was obsessed by "the spectacular reality presented by the surfaces of finely accomplished things—his gold watch, the case work on our Zenith radio, the leather box he kept loose tobacco in." He hankered, Anania thinks, "after a hard lustre in things, the deep burnish of the real in metal, the weight of leather, the flex in a hat brim of Italian felt." Well, the father's aesthetic, one feels certain, is also the son's, and the distance from the real McCoy to the cars customized with a Bauhaus purity to the textures of Anania's verse and prose is not very great. Anania admires energy, even deadly energy, held in elegant control, and the powerful sports car which he covets today is only the child of James Dean's customized 1949 Mercury in *Rebel without a Cause*.

Even when the energy is not held in control, elegantly or otherwise, Anania draws aesthetic implications and establishes implicit analogies. In the concluding 'Autoclysms' chapter, it is as if the real McCoy were no longer simply admired for its workmanship, but fired point-blank into somebody's face. Along with the final and appalling car crash in which four of his high school classmates are killed, Anania describes several others—including two close shaves of his own—and also the "corpse of a Studebaker Golden Hawk" that had been "front-ended," resting in a towing company garage. The Studebaker's windshield is fractured in such a way that the passenger's headprint is discernible and a cigarette, with a faint trace of lipstick on the filter tip, is embedded in the rubbery film of safety glass to which a few strands of blond hair are still attached. "The mangled front end, impacted bumper and grillwork, fenders closed like concertinas, all of it radiates from that collision in the glass, as though the whole wreckage were a crystal whose center was perfect and which grew amorphous only at its most extreme edges." He says that it verges on the sublime, and calls it "a geode . . . revealing in its deadly amethyst the impeccable record of the moment of impact." "Verges?" he asks. "It's hard to imagine anything more awesome, more eloquent in its obedience to natural law." And when he describes an accident in which he himself is involved as three cars and a boat being towed behind one of them "angled off into various ditches like billiard balls in a trick shot," he talks about "another kind of time" when "all the clocks changed," something that had to do "with the sudden perception of cause . . . as well as with increased adrenaline and focused attention, an instantaneous etiology that alters the perception of time." These are essentially aesthetic responses: that of the connoisseur (to the geode of the smashed Golden Hawk), and that of the artist himself tangled in the processes which he has unleashed but over which he loses control. Does aesthetic experience at its most intense require violence or danger? Must the real McCoy resonate with either suicidal or homicidal implications? Does the arsenal of nuclear weapons exist, as Armageddon may always have existed, "to intensify life?"

Another kind of violence entirely results in what one might call the book's alternate ending—violence done to Anania's system and perceptions by an experiment in sacred mushroom eating at the Macy reservation. After Whisky-Nose Louie—about whom more will be said in a moment—Russell, who is in fact the great-grandson of Logan Fontenelle, is my favorite among Anania's acquaintances in the book. Russell doesn't say very much, but he represents a great deal. And he is the one who is responsible for Anania's hallucinatory or visionary experience.

Russell is contrasted early on with a mixed Otto, Ponca, and Pawnee named John who wants to become a nuclear physicist and, as it were, acquire the bomb, which really means becoming a kind of Indian Oppenheimer who would build someone else's bomb and be someone else's scientist. Russell, who would steal the bomb rather than build it, "had never given up the essential secrets of himself as an Indian. Tough as he was, his real strength was in mystery. Remembering that early, his deep antagonisms to the society were crucial to that bomb-stealing vision of his." When Russell claimed that the Indians had taken the bomb off the testing tower in the desert and hidden it in a mountain cave at the end of an Apache trail that no one but an Apache could follow, what he understood . . .

> was what all the rhetoricians of apocalypse have always understood—that the signal points of our real fears are lying all about us and that turning them to any purpose is a poetic act of cultural alignments, a fine tuning, conducted through language, of what is already in scrambled view. Finally, the bomb is no more real than the stereotypical movie Apache, the painted desert no more tangible than the hulking Russian agent. There is no measured ontology to the stuff of this culture; there are only levels of energy. In one way or another everything in America is an icon.

When Russell and his cousin and uncle out at the Macy reservation share their hallucinatory mushroom with Anania so that they might "all dream together," Anania, thinking he's been poisoned, jumps in his Plymouth, and heads for home. On his way, he notices "a second highway brightly lit that veered to the right and upward, as though following the face of a steep hill that was not there." He tries to blink away the vision, but it persists; the car seems to be pulled by some kind of force toward this second road which "lifted and furled, banking as it turned westward, a finely worked contrail spiraling against the pure lapis of the summer sky." If this is the road not taken by the culture— and it clearly is—it's a road no longer takeable as well. Anania's car jolts to a halt in loose earth of the first road's shoulder, "weed crowns splitting across the bowsprit of the *Mayflower* at the point of the Plymouth's hood." After falling asleep in his car, he wakes to a final, fleeting vision: Russell and his cousin lifting the remains of the firebird which the cousin had earlier described to him, and placing it on its tail where "it looked more like a mushroom than a bird." In the form of a firebird, Russell and his cousin have the bomb. The visionary writing in these paragraphs of *The Red Menace* is exceptionally beautiful, and a good contrast to something like Hugh Brody's very plain account of the trail to heaven in *Maps and Dreams*. But the road Anania sees cannot be taken in his Plymouth. "We have come back to the Indian now for his secrets and his blessing," he says. "If he is smart, he will give us neither."

For the rest, there is a great deal of *talk* in this book—talk as when one says colloquially *"just* talk," the voluble bluster of verbal bravado—and much of it is hilariously funny. The best of the talkers is Whisky-Nose Louie, an alcoholic dishwasher at the grease joint where Anania works whose nonstop monologues make the jive of even the most advanced talkers at Tech High School sound amateurish by comparison. "He could go on . . . for eight hours, rasping out sexual advice, insult, salvation, and could curse longer without repeating himself than anyone I ever knew." One of his favorite subjects is the Communists and communism, and one set piece in a scene taking place in the grease joint is worth the price of the book. "You ever see the women that go around with Communists?" Louie asks. "Ugly and fat, every damned one of them, big fat arms, legs like pool tables. That's cause they hate good lookin' women, just hate 'em." "Louie," someone says, "that doesn't make any sense."

Course it doesn't. If they make any sense, they wouldn't be Communists. You meet a Communist, you ask 'em what he thinks about good-looking' women, then look out, cause you're gonna get a two-hour speech about capitalism and jewelry and widows with nine kids hitched up to plows and bankers and how a poor woman suffers for every jewel a fancy woman wears. All the while, he's got some quarter section a beef in a brown dress sittin' in the corner bitin' her fingernails. Never trust a man who's got a smart reason for havin' somethin' he don't want . . . I was in Portland one night, in a freightyard, not botherin' nobody, drinkin' Seattle wine with this here gandy-dancer. And up come this Communist. Spends half-a-minute talkin' 'bout the weather, then gets goin' on the capitalists and how they put us all outa work, and I says to him "Where's your fat girlfriend?" And he says he ain't got a fat girlfriend, and I tells him that the Communists fucked him straight cause he's entitled to a fat girlfriend. Then me and that gandy-dancer bust a gut laughin'. And he asks what's so funny, and I says, "They're s'posed to give you a fat girlfriend. It goes with bein' a Communist." And he says he ain't no Communist, he's a socialist worker. And I says, long as you're gonna be somethin' dumb, might as well be a Communist, cause a fat, ugly woman is better than no woman at all.

All this, needless to say, is *talk,* not conversation, and the book is electric with it in a variety of idioms. In the end, however, it is sad rather than funny. For *The Red Menace* ends with talk exactly like the talk that began it—the simultaneously aggressive and self-protective teenage jive which has an analogue in the gossip of adults. After the final autoclysm that kills Linda, Arnie, and Meatball and decapitates Darlene on a telephone pole guidewire, the talk echoes off into silence. "No shit, you could see 'em flying off in every direction. . . . Arms and legs out, towels, bathing suits, everything in the car." Anania has written a poem called '*Esthétique du Râle*' which is as intimately related to the conclusion of *The Red Menace* as 'The Temper' is to the episode at the housing project when his father takes out the real McCoy. It has to do in part with the degenerate history of modern art—from imagism and cubism to the work of minimalists and conceptualists and the "body art" of someone like Jack Broden—and with the deaths of modern artists, whether a James Dean, a Jackson Pollock, or an Albert Camus, in the autoclysms of the 1950s.

"Something is ending," Anania writes; and, "Perhaps it was too much / to ask them to resolve our difficulties." If artistic style, as Denis Donoghue maintains, is a compensation for the loss of conversation's true communion, then gossip, *talk*, a voyeuristic (and indeed a journalistic) focusing of attention on an artist's life and death, is certainly our compensation, and a very poor one too, for the loss of art. "We know / how the day went, the guest list / of the party down the road, the Cadillac's fish tail and impact" . . . Anania writes in his poem. And in the final lines of it a field of flowers as inauspicious as the jive about Darlene and Meatball waits, as talk, to receive the wreckage of one Red Menace among others:

> It is only in isolate flecks, swift
> and mutable, light finds its shape,
> all that the form fails to exclude,
>
> the almost unbearable clamor, every
> gesture ambled among traffic; this day
> or any other, talk settling in with the
> portioned words, meant, I think, to be
>
> a flower, a field of flowers, where
> the wreckage seems oddly comfortable,
> a seaside morning dew over bent metal
> and blue Quaker ladies, *le dernier cri.*

John Berryman

I: 1959–1969

Back when summer writers' workshops were still something of a novelty, I applied to one at the University of Utah at the suggestion of Peter Taylor, the short story writer and good friend of Robert Lowell's, with whom I had been doing some informal work at Ohio State University by virtue of being a high school senior at the "progressive" O.S.U. Lab School still operating on Deweyite principles on the Columbus, Ohio campus. Arriving in Salt Lake City straight from my high school graduation in June of 1959, I was seventeen years-old and totally unprepared to meet a man like John Berryman.

On the first day of the fiction workshop—the course he taught during the first week of the conference, taking over poetry from Stephen Spender in the second week—he passed out copies of three brief stories which I had submitted a few weeks before arriving. Having always been praised by my indulgent high school teachers for whatever writing I produced, I of course assumed that my genius was about to be proclaimed by this strange, intense man who placed the accents of words on unusual syllables and immediately struck an aggressive posture toward the small auditorium full of would-be writers by saying that, although he had just been told by Brewster Ghiselin, the conference administrator, to refer to us as "members" rather than as "students" he thought, nonetheless and on the whole, that "students" would do just fine. I can still remember my folly of leaning over to my right and proudly identifying myself to a fellow "member" as the author of the pages that were, alas, about to be annihilated.

The job done on the stories was as unremitting and detailed as it was devastating. I don't think a single sentence escaped his censure or ridicule. Though I was not so young as to be unable to weather this storm and profit from the beating that it gave me, a number of the more matronly "members" took it upon themselves to protest in various ways against what they took to be, I suppose, an inappropriately fierce critique of the naive scribblings of a high school senior. One of the ladies drew up a statement and tried to collect signatures; another left an anonymous letter under Berryman's door. The whole thing was terribly embarrassing. One of my defenders was a science fiction writer who was into Dianetics and Scientology. She encouraged me to come to her room and throw pillows at the wall while repeating some kind of Scientological incantation.

When Berryman finally left my poor stories behind and turned to something more substantial—a positive rather than a negative example of style—we were treated to another sort of incantation entirely, and one I've never forgotten. Berryman had asked us to read Stephen Crane's 'The Open Boat' and, when he began to discuss the story, asked us in his rhetorical manner what the different nuances seemed to be if we chose to place a primary stress on one word rather than the others of the opening sentence. For an entire morning he worked away on that sentence:

> "*None* of them knew the color of the sky." **or**
> "None of *them* knew the color of the sky." **or**
> "None of them *knew* the color of the sky." **or**
> "None of them knew the *color* of the sky." **or**
> "None of them knew the color of the *sky*."

Did it matter which word took the chief stress in this pentameter line of Crane's? Should one write pentameter lines in sentences of fiction, especially in first sentences? Did Crane do anything to curb our inclination to stress rhetorically a word on which a metrical stress might not fall? (This last was a question I found myself asking about Berryman's own work years and decades later.) Anyway, it was a marvelous display of pedagogical virtuosity and critical ingeniousness, and it was only a taste of what was coming. In spite of the shock of the opening day's workshop, I found myself warming to the man tremendously. On the whole, he let me off the hook after that first blast, although, from time to time, he would remark that the only person who had learned anything from him so far was "young Mr. Matt-i-as" (as he insisted on pronouncing my name both then and when we met again later on).

By the time I finally had a private meeting with Berryman in order to discuss my work, he had clearly become a little perplexed by the anonymous letters, petitions, and so forth on my behalf. I think he tried to apologize in a way by trying to find a few lines and images and sentences he could call "promising." I remember his urging me to read D.H. Lawrence's 'The Rocking Horse Winner' and Jon Silkin's 'The Death of a Son,' a poem he had also been pressing on Stephen Spender.

He said he would tell me at the conference picnic why he wanted me to read the Lawrence story and why he thought it was a masterpiece. In fact, he never returned to the subject, and I was too shy to bring it up again myself. At the conference, he also remarked that someone had told him that we looked alike. I can't think that we *did* look very much alike in 1959, but it's certainly true that we did later on—after my own features had begun to mature a bit and when we both were wearing beards. By the middle and late 1960s, this similarity in our appearance was something nearly everybody noticed and something that seemed to bother him. It was not just a matter of facial features, but also a question of characteristic gestures, mannerisms, personal tics. Much of it was in the hands—both their shape and length, and the way we used our hands when we talked. Years later a student of mine wrote and published a poem beginning:

> You, John, look like John. Matthias resembles a Berryman.
> Weary hair that sprawls like a hanging
> Garden of King Neb's dead grass.
> Vaulted forehead, wrinkles, fluting, the shrine
> Of a developed brain . . .
> Proud, dripping eyes . . . the schizoid clergyman
> Buried under one too many vows . . .

By the time of the conference picnic, all of the visiting writers—Berryman, Spender, and Herbert Gold—had begun to call Brewster Ghiselin "Mother Gooselin." Evidently, he took the personal welfare of his writers very seriously, felt that they should get to bed at a decent hour, and tried to keep them sober and respectable. I retain two images from the picnic: the tall and enormously ungainly Stephen Spender trying to play volleyball—always leaping in the air when he should have been firmly on the ground, and on the ground when he should have jumped—and Berryman, presumably pretty drunk, trying to run a straight line in the footrace he had organized, and running instead at a diagonal virtually tangent to the volleyballers and almost into a tree. Mother Gooselin was dismayed.

Berryman and I met again from time to time as we both grew older and as he became more and more famous. I saw him for the last time when he came to Notre Dame to read in May of 1969, just before my own first book was published. The students who sponsored his reading didn't tell me that he had checked into the Morris Inn on campus two days before the scheduled reading. For two days, they had left him alone in his hotel room without realizing what that might mean.

By the time I got to him he was in dreadful shape. His suitcase was full of cigarette cartons and bottles of Jack Daniel's, and he had been smoking and drinking alone for a long time. I managed to get some food into him and we took a walk around the Notre Dame lakes talking about Yvor Winters (under whom I had studied at Stanford) and Hugh MacDiarmid, whose *The Drunk Man Looks at the Thistle* Berryman admired and which seemed to me to be a possible source of influence on *The Dream Songs*. This he acknowledged. By the time of his reading, Berryman was in pretty good shape and read very well, dedicating the evening to my wife with whom he had flirted in his courtly way during dinner. Afterward, we had a small reception for him at our house. When everyone had left, I asked if I could read some poems to him to make up for the juvenilia he'd been obliged to endure in 1959. He listened attentively and made some acute observations. Then he signed two of my Berryman books. For my daughter, then less than a year old, he signed Dream Song 385, the beautiful conclusion to *His Dream, His Toy, His Rest*, that poem of thanksgiving which begins, "My daughter's heavier." For me, he signed the page facing his earlier signature in my old copy of *Homage to Mistress Bradstreet*. The first signature is dated "Salt Lake City, 19 June 1959" and the second, "Notre Dame, 5 May 1969." Just a few weeks less than an even decade.

II: *1976*

[The above was written as a letter to Paul Mariani in answer to a request for information pertaining to Berryman in the summer of 1959. Mariani was at work on the biography he published in 1990, Dream Song: The Life of John Berryman. *His was the second biography, John Haffenden having published his life of Berryman in 1982. In 1976, when I wrote the following review of Berryman's posthumous volume of prose,* The Freedom of the Poet, *I had of course read neither of these. Even by this date, I was still caught up in the self-dramatizations of my first poet-teacher. If Lowell's life was tragic, Berryman's life, on the evidence of Haffenden and*

Mariani, was often only squalid. As in the case of many other contemporary biographies, one learns things from both these lives that one might prefer not to know. Berryman at his most human and sympathetic appears in Saul Bellow's short memoir written as a preface to Berryman's unfinished novel, Recovery, *and Eileen Simpson's genuinely tender book about her first husband and his generation of writers,* Poets in Their Youth. *But when I reviewed* The Freedom of the Poet *for* The New Review *in 1976, I had not read Bellow or Simpson either.*]

John Berryman's *The Freedom of the Poet* is pretty much the brilliantly exuberant, but carefully discriminating, long, scholarly, sometimes dark and portentous, tough and often dead-accurate, evolving and passionate miscellany one had been expecting. In the wide range of its subject matter and learning—if not in its idiom—it recalls *The Dyer's Hand,* about the author of which book Berryman once said: "his opinions are important because they are his." One can say a good deal more about *The Freedom of the Poet* than that, but that to begin with: the opinions are important because they are his. Also, that it represents the concerns and commitments of Berryman's exceptional generation of American poets better than anything to come into print since the criticism of Randall Jarrell. It is a formidable performance and, immediately upon its publication, historical. The book will be read for a long time, in part because of its prose. In the end, the reader of this book grows to be more and more comfortable in the presence of a poet's increasingly familiar, persuasive, and compelling style.

The style is perhaps not as instantly apparent in Berryman's work as his editor and old friend, Robert Giroux, suggests in his Preface. In *Love and Fame,* Berryman writes of the earliest essay here collected, saying: "My girls suffered during this month or so, / so did my seminars & lectures & / my poetry even. To be *a critic,* ah, / how deeper & more scientific. // I wrote & printed an essay on Yeats's plays / re-deploying all of Blackmur's key terms / & even his sentence-structure wherever I could." This was a good many years before Berryman farted famously over "Rich Critical Prose" in Dream Song 107. But the style is there, in snatches anyway, in the prose as in the verse, from pretty early on. The prose is rich, critical, his. It also sidles up pretty close to the idiom of the mature poetry. By the time one gets into the middle and later essays, not to mention the several excellent short stories, there is some temptation to paste together a do-it-yourself Dream Song.

Friends, the hovering and plunging grief
Exceptionally sings. Wow! We put
Against it, then, a pretty
Round-faced wench, who, with Alfred Kazin
And his wife, edited
Her fiction—ah! I thought—

And missed the boat. God amuses himself;
Then man. Both these facts have been forgotten.
Windmills grind wheat
From which, Sir Bones, our bread is made. Irony
To the end. Fair enough!
You may wonder whether I dislike aestheticians.

A high and prolonged riskiness? The later
Men just drudged along: Lowell into spondees
And humped smash. Hardy's
Reputation has been furiously unstable.
Tell you a story. Until
A writer begins to bore us, O, it is .. .

. . . a matter of supreme importance that he handle characteristic materials characteristically." This from seven essays dated 1948, 1953, 1960, 1965, 1966, and 1967 (with a little help from a quote out of Nashe's *Unfortunate Traveler*). Along with the Boneses and the Os, you may include in your kit the following free-floating adjectives and adverbs: *delicious, adorable, spectacularly, American, ferocious, hallucinatory, intense, painful, marvelous, superior, sharply, foolish, irresistible, heavily, suicidal, little, ridiculous, ravishing, ominous, exquisite, brilliant, tumultuous, gigantic, radiant, Christian,* and *free*. It is mostly a vocabulary of praise, but a somewhat eccentric vocabulary. Add to that the somewhat eccentric syntax, which usually occurs when emotion is intense, along with the depth charges of emotion themselves, and you have the ingredients of the style.

"Most of us," Berryman writes, "never get to know many other human beings very well . . . We know people, perhaps, chiefly by their voices—their individual, indescribable, unmistakable voices." We can sympathize with Saul Bellow, who knew Berryman's voice as well as anybody, when his friend Dennis Silk asks him, while he's off in Israel writing *To Jerusalem and Back,* to "read some of [Berryman's poems] in Berryman's own manner." Says Bellow: Well, he can try.

The manner, the voice, was disconcerting and was meant to be; difficult to reproduce or imitate, it was unforgettable once actually heard. It *is* unforgettable. Thinking about the occasionally eccentric syntax of the prose, I realize that, in part, I'm remembering certain exaggerations of pause, pitch, and pace—of rhythm and punctuation— which Berryman was inclined to impose on any text at all, whether it was the first paragraph of Stephen Crane's 'The Open Boat' (which is the first thing I ever heard him read), or one of his own poems, or somebody else's poem, or an essay. There are strange hesitations; periodic sentences are drawn out oddly or else rushed along; unstressed syllables sometimes get stressed. In the Library of Congress recording you can hear two statements became quasi-questions in Berryman's reading of Dream Song 4, as well as the audience's response—a confused response? It is nervous laughter—following his reading of the last stanza of the terrifying (and funny?) Dream Song 29. I'd have given a lot to hear Bellow's reading of that one. Berryman worries over the poem in his essay about his own stylistic development.

Some reviewers have found the Elizabethan essays which constitute the first eighty-seven pages of *The Freedom of the Poet* somehow unimportant, the work of a scholar who is not necessarily a poet. They are certainly wrong. These essays seem to me absolutely central both in terms of their scholarly and critical merit as excellent and useful studies of writers who matter intensely to Berryman—Marlowe, Nashe, and Shakespeare—and, even more importantly, as angles on certain characteristics of Berryman's poetry which begin to show themselves as early as the 'Nervous Songs' and the sonnets.

Before any of these essays was written, Berryman had come in 1936 to Clare College, Cambridge, "a burning, trivial disciple of the great Irish poet William Butler Yeats," as he called himself at the time. At Cambridge, along with the *Fitzwilliam Virginal Book,* he stumbled on to Brian Boydell who, as he says in *Love and Fame,* "introduced me to the music of Peter Warlock // who had just knocked himself off, fearing the return / of his other personality, Philip Heseltine. / Brian used to play *The Curlew* with the lights out, voice of a lost soul moving." What Warlock, the arch-Elizabethan among modern English composers, once Heseltine, alias Rab Noolas, alias Huanebango Z. Palimpsest, set from the poems of W. B. Yeats for the ears of his burning, trivial disciple was, among other lines, these:

> No boughs have withered because of the wintry wind;
> The boughs have withered because I have told them my dreams.

You can hear that last line—first sung, but afterward whispered—on the EMI recording by Ian Partridge. It will break your heart, as doubtless it did Berryman's. In an excellent essay in *Cambridge Review* for May 1974, Kevin Barry, commenting that "a more apt description of Berryman's achievement in *The Dream Songs* would be hard to find," quotes Wilfred Mellers writing on Warlock in *Scrutiny* for March 1937.

> The songs have passed beyond any mere self-expression. There is, therefore, nothing fantastic in the fact that Heseltine should have been able, as no one else has been able, to reinterpret the Elizabethan art song and the English folk song on which that art form depended, in purely modern terms . . . Whereas the technique of the "Elizabethan" or folky song is comparatively straightforward and diatonic, here the melodic lines are twisted and contorted.

By the time he writes *The Dream Songs,* Berryman is as much a contemporary Elizabethan among poets as Warlock was among composers. (It is odd, in passing, that no composers—have they?—have gone to work on *The Dream Songs.*) The distance between Warlock, Boydell, and the Cambridge of 1936 and the essay introducing Thomas Nashe's *Unfortunate Traveller* of 1960 is not very great. In that essay Berryman distinguishes between two kinds of style.

> The notion "style" points in two contrary directions: toward individuality, the characteristic, and toward inconspicuous expression of its material. The latter is the more recent direction (George Orwell a superb practitioner); we may range it with T. S. Eliot's intolerable and perverse theory of the impersonality

of the artist; it may have something wrong with it. Nashe is an extreme instance, perhaps the extreme instance, of the feasibility of the first theory.

Berryman likes the first theory, likes extravagance, likes the abundant energy—held just in check by convention or contrivance or will—of the impetuous stylists from Dekker and Nashe all the way up the line to Pound and Dylan Thomas. (I will qualify this in a moment.) Quoting a passage from *The Unfortunate Traveller* which Berryman regards, in fact, as relatively tame, "a suggestive but median passage, though exalted in the close," he appreciates: (1) "Inversion or rearrangement for rhythm, emphasis and simulation of an (improved) colloquial"; (2) physicality and active verbs; (3) a self-consciousness which is "alert" rather than "laboured"; (4) an "anti-pedantic" (apparent) spontaneity which is, however, "showmanlike"; (5) a "queerly schizophrenic" division between the Marlowe side of image patterns, representing "Learning," and the Shakespeare side, representing "Daily Life"; (6) a "complicated simultaneous double movement" worked out in terms of a tension between democratic and hierarchical values; and (7) "a peroration at once highly rhetorical and rather casual, pathetic, and joyous." An enthusiasm for such a style as he here describes brings him at least half-way to his own, in verse as in prose, if not the whole way. Now the qualifications. He can also admire and practice himself, restraint, austerity, delicacy, and inconspicuous expression of material. In a "period as licentious as our own," he can admire a Waller or a Henry Reed, though he is "far from wishing to produce" either of them. He can even admire some of Dreiser, "who wrote like a hippopotamus," observing that "no style may on occasion be preferable to some aspects of Melville's lengthy and deplorable affair with Shakespeare."

Still, his own affair is with Shakespeare—and Marlowe and Nashe and Cervantes and Monk Lewis and Whitman and Yeats and Pound and Lowell—with writers who have produced at some point in their careers—early, middle, or late—sustained displays of prodigious energy. *The boughs have withered because I have told them my dreams.* It all depends on what you dream, and on what you tell about what you dream, and with how much power. "To be free of unruly and discreditable desire," he writes of *The Tempest,* "is the heart of the play's desire, and even in this does Prospero participate, released from the intoxications of hatred and might." But Marlowe dreams otherwise: Marlowe who "wrote simply to gratify himself . . . whose mind had no popular cast . . . who flaunted himself . . ." Marlowe, says Berryman, "twice at the summits of his art" damns himself for his two favorite and finally fused obsessive vices for either of which, indeed, he could have been burned. "The impression is unavoidable that he *enjoyed* writing these scenes, *and* was excoriated. His sinister art ran exactly with his life."

W. H. Auden, whose last great poem, *The Sea and the Mirror,* is about *Tempest,* came to believe that it is the business of art to disintoxicate and disenchant rather than the reverse. But the artist is extremely likely to be self-intoxicated and enchanted by his own work. So Auden wrote the 'Horae Canonicae,' brought down the curtain on magic, wrote bad poems on purpose, wrote libretti, wrote light verse. Berryman, tossed back and forth between the Marlowe and Prospero sides of himself, also wrote a 'Horae Canonicae' (which fails, certainly, to sustain a comparison with Auden's), taught *Job* to his seminar, taught *Luke,* taught Freud's *Civilisation and its Discontents* and Herman Feifel on the meaning of death. Although he is moved beyond words by Prospero's "retirement" (in the 1962 essay and later, always), he did not, on the evidence, exorcise the Marlowe from his make-up, or disenchant and disintoxicate himself. In many of the tortured later poems, he tried to. (And in 'Eleven Addresses to the Lord,' he nearly wrote his Canto CXVI, a poem fit to retire on, ripe, serene, transcendent.)

There is a retrospectively sad paragraph from the 1962 essay in which Berryman wonders how it is "that Stephan and Trinculo have or can have no part in this general redemption" at the end of *The Tempest,* and remarks: "Possibly it is because they are drunk. Irrational, self-set outside reason, they stand beyond the reach of the ruler's redemptive design. *They* think they are 'free,' of course." In a very late interview which might have been a part of this book, Berryman says (not *intentionally* parodying Alvarez parodying Berryman): "The artist is extremely lucky who is presented with the worst possible ordeal which will not actually kill him . . . And I think that what happens in my poetic work in the future will probably largely depend . . . on being knocked in the face, and thrown flat, and given cancer, and all kinds of other things short of senile dementia . . . I hope to be nearly crucified."

This sort of intoxication would not seem to be a condition of freedom either.

But was it? Can it be? Given a certain theology, a teleology, a necessity requiring recognition perhaps different from that impinging on, though ignored by, most men? And given the habitual practice from an early age of what Berryman calls "a terminal activity, taking place out near the end of things, where the poet's soul addresses one other soul only, never mind when"? And if this activity aims, as he says, "—never mind *either* expression or communication—at the reformation of the poet, as prayer does"? In the face of such a conception of poetry one had better, until all the evidence is in, if it ever is, reserve the matter.

There are less than ultimate reasons for writing poetry, too, and, mostly, *The Freedom of the Poet* has to do with those. "Love of the stuff and of rhythm, the need to invent, a passion for getting things right, the wish to leave one's language in better shape than one found it, a jealousy for the national honor, love for a person or for God, attachment to human possibility, pity, outletting agony or disappointment, exasperation, malice, hatred." It is a fine list.

As Berryman moves from one of these reasons to another, as each of them in turn becomes his subject, there is much talk along the way about pronouns. Berryman regarded himself, rightly, as a master of the pronoun, which "may seem a small matter, but she matters, he matters, it matters, they matter." His discussion of his own ambiguous pronouns in the concluding essay of part 4 of his book, following the loving consideration of Whitman's 'Song of Myself,' Pound's masks and personae, 'J. Alfred Prufrock,' and Lowell's 'Skunk Hour,' illuminates what is for him far more than a useful convention or powerful tradition, what is indeed "a necessity in a period inimical to poetry, gregarious and impatient of dignity." That is beautifully put, and he's certainly right about the period. The gregarious and impatient citizen is also right to feel that Berryman, like most modern poets, wants it both ways: (1) "That's good-old, charming-old me talking there, sweetheart"; and (2) "I didn't say that, officer! *Persona* said it. Let me alone." (I've noticed while looking into Warlock/Heseltine/Noolas/Huanebango's setting of Yeats in *The Curlew* that this exemplary heteronymic composer pressed D.H. Lawrence for libel, or, at least, forced a change in the travesty of himself—himselves?—which we get in *Women in Love*. Sometimes these things are at least legally more simple than meets the critical eye.) Introducing 'Skunk Hour,' Berryman says: "One thing critics not themselves writers of poetry occasionally forget is that poetry is composed by actual human beings, and tracts of it are very closely about them. When Shakespeare wrote 'Two loves I have,' reader, he was *not kidding."* Four pages later, he says: "The necessity for the artist of selection opens inevitably an abyss between his person and his persona . . . The persona looks across at the person and then sets about his own work." So Lowell; so "I." He doesn't tell us if the fairy decorator or the summer millionaire or the hermit heiress have any rights; nor whether Shakespeare's two loves had or have. It is an interesting problem.

For the rest—and there is *so much* in this nervous, jagged, and problematic book—I should point at least to these things: the excellent discussions of Isaac Babel and Stephen Crane; the treatment of "enslavement" in the lives and work of Fitzgerald, Dreiser, and Ring Lardner—an enslavement which Berryman finds to be the result of typical vague yearnings on the part of an outsider for whatever object, love or fame or money, in a culture disastrously split between the intellectual and the popular; the powerful justification—I was almost going to say the redemption—of "new critical" methodology in his often stunning, detailed, and moving readings of poems, stories, passages, novels, lines; the excellent fiction, suggesting that if Berryman had not become Berryman he might have become, say, Peter Taylor instead; and his omnivore's ability to call up all opinion and scholarship on a subject, sort it out, compare everything with everything else—was there any book he hadn't read?—eliminate what didn't matter to him, make the unusual or unforeseen point, and, in a word, teach.

In 1959, at the University of Utah in the early days of what Donald Hall calls *poebusiness,* Berryman found it hilarious when the administrator of one of those summer "writers' conferences" told him he must call all of us "members" rather than "students." If *we* were members, *he* certainly wasn't; but he, if anyone, knew what it meant to belong to the unregistered guild from which all but the truly gifted are barred. We can profit from being his students. Out in Salt Lake City, he quoted Ralph Hodgson, who figures in the last Dream Song, as he quotes Ralph Hodgson in *The Freedom of the Poet:* "I don't try to reconcile anything; this is a damned strange world." And then he went on and tried.

III: *2010*

It took me a long time to realize that Berryman's reputation had been slipping on the literary stock market. As a teacher, I made his work central to my syllabus and continued on my enthusiastic way only half-aware that Elizabeth Bishop had overtaken not only Berryman but even Lowell. Was Berryman's eccentric style too odd to last? Was it in fact so odd that it was difficult to tell homage from parody? Berryman had been a hero for me and I, like him, "had from my beginning to adore heroes / & I elected that they witness to, / show forth, transfigure: life-suffering and pure heart," as he writes in a poem from *Love and Fame*. In workshops, I would always require an imitation Dream Song, and I was inclined to teach the first seventy-seven songs as a kind of anti-sonnet sequence to outflank my postmodern students' contempt for the sonnet while actually managing at the same time to convey the possibilities of sequence in a lengthy group of poems in more or less fixed form.

Part of what came to bother me was that the student imitations or parodies (and there is plenty of self-parody in Berryman himself, both intentional and unintentional) were too good; it wasn't difficult to master the machinery and even make it sing. And these they wrote while also making clear to me that they didn't really *like* what they could easily do or the model that let them do it.

Other former students and deep readers of Berryman had a similar experience. David Wojahn, for example, in *Mystery Train*, the title sequence of which book is his Berryman-influenced cycle of sonnets about rock and roll, writes on the fifteenth anniversary of Berryman's death:

> My students
> find your poems "cranky and obscure." A dull-witted Brit
>   has written your
> unreadable life. I suppose you won't age gracefully, and some
>   of your books, *Love & Fame*
> and your gibberish sonnets plainly are no good.

In her book *Unmentionables*, my own former student, Beth Ann Fennelly, writes in a cycle of fifteen imitation Dream Songs that "my students love you not at all," and Kevin Young, attempting to introduce Berryman to a new generation of readers in the American Poets Project *Selected Poems*, feels obliged to begin like this:

> Who would rather take a week teaching Berryman's *Dream Songs* than an hour with the self-contained 'For the Union Dead' by Robert Lowell or Elizabeth Bishop's 'The Fish'? Far harder to explain Berryman's slapstick. When I dare to teach the poems, I find that for every *I don't get it* there are four more *I can't stand its.*

But Kevin Young goes on: "Inevitably [there is] one kid who gets a gleam in her eye, or a smirk on his face, and says nothing—until conferences, when I hear them confess how much they like Berryman."

Such "kids" are rare, but they tend to be people like Beth Ann Fennelly—not so much "students" as "readers" who would probably have found Berryman on their own, and who are independent enough of literary fashion to hear an original voice when it's speaking to them. Jarrell was right when he said "The gods have taken away our readers and given us students," but among the students a reader now and then emerges—someone hunched over a book they love rather than one they study out of obligation, a couple of Dream Songs in a class having sent them to the first 77, and then *His Dream, His Toy, His Rest*, and then back to *Bradstreet*, and maybe even the biography of Stephen Crane and the great short story 'The Imaginary Jew.' As the students settle down to the canonized Elizabeth Bishop, the reader reads: "I'm scared a lonely. Never see my son." Reads: "Men psalm. Man palms his ears and moans." Reads: "My mother has your shotgun." Reads: "Henry likes Fall. / He would be prepared to live in a world of Fall / For ever, impenitent Henry. / But the snows and summers grieve & dream."

These Berryman readers tend to recognize each other's smirks and gleaming eyes. But they also tend to keep quiet about their discovery. They read him, as it were, in secret, in the dark. There are no Berryman conferences to attend. The workshop they are taking quickly moves on to more fashionable poets.

Perhaps the best account of this experience of reading Berryman in the dark as a secret passion comes from Wojahn, his former student at the University of Minnesota. In his anniversary poem from which I have already quoted, he anticipates by several years his acquaintanceship with Berryman, and by several decades the experience of readers from Fennelly's generation:

> Eighteen, and dazed on Pakistani hash, I'm reading
> > in a commune bedroom
> *The Dream Songs* for the first of endless times that year.
> > No Henry pyrotechnics here,
> no elegy: I won't describe the moment,
> > the staring, rapt
> from that February bedroom, the almost-but-not-quite-weeping,
> > steaming pipe and coffee,
> Muddy Waters growling from the stereo. Sunset, the neighbor below
> > can't start his car,
>
> and soon I'll dress and ride the bus to work,
> > my watchman's job,
> pace thirty-seven hallways until dawn, *Dream Songs* and
> > a flashlight in my hand,
> pages wreathed in yellow light . . .

Although the commune, the hash, the Muddy Waters and the watchman's job are all optional, the intense focus is required to get from the greatest Dream Songs what they promise and, eventually, deliver: news of the "long / wonder the world can bear & be."

A year ago I read an essay submitted to *Notre Dame Review* that tells a similar story. Eventually published in the journal as 'Speaking Over Graves,' the piece surprised me by recounting James McKenzie's experience of Berryman's 1969 reading about which I had written to Paul Mariani many years earlier. I had not forgotten McKenzie, though I hadn't seen or heard from him in forty years. The main reason why I remembered him was that during that same year I had been called from a room in which I was part of a committee conducting his Ph.D oral examination to answer a phone call informing me that my father had just died. A moment before we had been talking about Roethke's 'My Papa's Waltz,' and Berryman's elegy for Roethke, Dream Song 18, among the first of a very long sequence of elegies in the *Songs*. So my memory of my father's death is all tangled with Roethke, Berryman, and a student whose literary competence I had been asked, in the strange way of university English departments, to interrogate.

McKenzie's essay has to do with poetry, fathers, graves, elegies, reading. As it happened, the author had never attended a poetry reading before he heard Berryman in 1969. He describes Berryman as "frail, wobbly, uncertain, trembling, hiding, it seemed, behind his horn-rims, his tangly beard, the podium, the pages of his text itself," and then remembers hearing "his powerful voice keening and filling the auditorium." McKenzie was an army veteran of twenty-eight, a little older and with more experience of the world than most graduate students, but he had been sold the proposition that he was now a professional student of literature—a student, not just a reader. But he left the reading with the elementary sense that he had heard poetry become a "human, living thing," and that from that point on he demanded more from literature, although he might have to keep that "more" entirely to himself and outside the dialogue with any professors or the discourse in any professional paper. The world could bear and be: that was the news from that "ongoing American musical tradition, now global, rooted in African-American music and history, field hollers, gospel, minstrel even, Leadbelly, Robert Johnson, [and] carried [in Berryman] all the way back to the court of King David. Dance and sing one's blackest sorrows, no matter what they may be; keep on keepin' on."

The essay ends with a visit to Berryman's grave at Resurrection Cemetery outside Saint Paul where McKenzie pours a libation and utters some quiet words. Had the kid with a gleam in her eye or a smirk on his face passed by, they might not have seen themselves as the grieving man who had been reading Berryman all his life, but they would have sensed "Our wounds to time, from all the other times, / sea times slow, the times of galaxies." This in a place where "the snows and summers grieve & dream."

There is an essay in Stephen Burt's recent book, *Close Calls with Nonsense,* called 'My Name Is Henri: Contemporary Poets Discover John Berryman.' The title itself makes one wince, and so do the quotes that Burt culls from a book he admires—Mark Levine's *Debt.* This is what happens when one latches onto the surface of Berryman's style without having any particular reason to use it or a psychological compulsion that produces all the jive and angst the equal of Berryman's own.

> My name is Henri. Listen. It's morning.
> I pull my head from my scissors, I pull
> The light bulb from my mouth – Boss comes at me
> While I'm still blinking . . .
> I am Henri, mouth full of soda crackers.

Burt considers a range of poets who "channel" Berryman in their different ways: Liz Waldner, Jeremy Glazier, Joanna Fuhrman, Lucie Brock-Broido, Susan Wheeler, Kevin Young, and Mary Jo Bang. For the most part, the same thing is wrong with their Berryman-influenced work that is wrong with Levine's. Burt gives plenty of reasons why Berryman might be a good influence on the poets in this group, but on the evidence one must conclude that he has often been a bad influence. Regretfully, I would also have to say that as much as I admire most of Beth Ann Fennelly's poems, her sequence 'So You Waved: A Dream Song Cycle' is probably her least successful extended work. The famous wave, the bridge, and the suicide are particularly dangerous territory for someone "channeling" Berryman. Burt writes of poets using suicide as "an attention-getting device." Only when he comes to Frank Bidart, a poet who never imitates the stylistic surface of Berryman's work, does Burt have a strong case for an efficacious influence as Bidart "appears to adopt some of Berryman's obsessions into a style of his own . . . portraying [in] his oeuvre theatrical performances of extended mourning by a fractured and guilty self" where an entire poetics derives fundamentally from the elegiac impulse. It is also worth looking for a deeper Berryman influence in books by two other poets not mentioned by Stephen Burt—Geoffrey Hill's *Speech! Speech!* and Kenneth Fields' *Classic Rough News*. But from my own perspective, the best homage to Berryman is simple enough: Not imitation, but reading and re-reading—if necessary by flashlight up and down some thirty-seven hallways on a watchman's job, like the young David Wojahn.

So what should one re-read? After fifty years of reading Berryman, I think his most successful and ambitious poem is *Homage to Mistress Bradstreet*. The childbirth scene in *Bradstreet* has sometimes been celebrated, and even independently anthologized, but the whole poem

is unique in post-World War II literature and something no one at all
has tried to imitate, or could if he did try. The poem takes great risks
both with elements of its narrative and in what appears to be a prosody
derived from Hopkins (as much as Berryman himself denied this). I
have read this poem dozens of times from the summer I first opened it,
uncomprehendingly, in 1959. (FSG should reprint the gorgeous first
edition, two stanzas to a page, with the original Ben Shahn illustrations;
it is the most beautifully produced book of poems I have ever held in
my hands.) Next, one should read *77 Dream Songs* straight through.
Aside from a dozen or so in the long *His Dream, His Toy, His Rest*,
the first seventy-seven are the best seventy-seven. They are of course
not equally fine, but it is necessary to read enough of them so that
not only a thematic pattern emerges but also the outline of a plot.
The narrative difficulties of *The Dream Songs* are more like those in
Pound's 'Hugh Selwyn Mauberley' or Auden's 1930 *Poems* than 'The
Waste Land.' There is a kind of story, and one must try to follow it.
Many people have noticed that individual Dream Songs do not make
good anthology pieces, as moving as many of them are in their context.
Berryman thought of his *Dream Songs* as a long poem, and he believed
that a long poem created a world for its individual parts to breathe in.
It is necessary to inhabit the world in order to breathe with the best of
the songs. And that is really enough. There are a few good poems in
the early *The Dispossessed*, but most of them lean too heavily on Yeats
or Auden. The sonnets, published too late and perhaps better lost, are
mostly weak, while the poems in the last two books, with three or four
exceptions, are a prosy record of the poet's personal collapse and the loss
of his brilliant talent. I think the best selections of Berryman's work are
the old Faber and Faber *Selected Poems 1938–1968* and Kevin Young's
American Poets Project volume. Both include too many sonnets,
though the date of the Faber volume allows it to escape the obligation
of culling through the wreck of *Love and Fame* and *Delusions, Etc*. Best
of all would be a book combining *Bradstreet* with the first seventy-seven
songs. Any poet deserves to have his reputation depend only on his very
best work.

And not to depend at all on his biography. "How wrong and petty
any life is," writes David Wojahn. Three years after Wojahn walked
through those hallways reading *The Dream Songs* by flashlight, he
became Berryman's student,

an acned college kid, and in the class I took from you
    all three hundred of us,
your teaching assistants not least, feared you and your wrath,
    feared the days when,

at the desk you lectured from, you'd sleep the class's
    first half hour, waking
with a start to mumble gossip on the Medicis. Two months
    and you'd be dead,
a story we all know, waving from the guardrail to passersby . . .

Sometimes I'd see you
    eating breakfast alone,
Gray's Drug lunch counter, shaky and—I don't know—drunk
        already,
    a hand that trembled
around the egg-yolked fork. The bridge was utterly
    nondescript, the one

I aimlessly walked that day, and every day for six
    uneventful years.

When I first read Beth Ann Fennelly's 'Say You Waved: A Dream Song Cycle,' I was brought up with a start at number 10, which staggered me by imagining, at its conclusion, my own death. Addressing Berryman, Fennelly generously remembers that her Notre Dame prof "called your birth scene / in *Bradstreet* the best he knew. Huffed I, / feministically, eighteen. / Now I, twice bairned, admit he's right." In Berryman's work, death lurks behind or beside every birth. And so she concludes, "When . . . Matthias crosses over, help him / from the boat." Actually, I would rather spend eternity with just about anyone other than John Berryman. But, disembarking, it would be an honor to take the hand of the poet.

Some Notes on the English Poetry
of Göran Printz-Påhlson

[This concluding essay-memoir reprints without revision a piece written for the Swedish journal Tärningskastet *in 1981. By that date Göran Printz-Påhlson's reputation in Sweden was beginning to wane, due in part to his long residence in Britain. Also, though much of his poetry written during the long period of our collaboration on translating Swedish poetry was in English, his work in this language was mainly known by his friends and colleagues. Only one book was published in English, a collector's edition of* The Green-Ey'd Monster. *In Sweden, Göran was chiefly remembered for his seminal critical book of 1958,* Solin I spegeln *('The Sun in the Mirror'). It was through the* Tärningskastet *special issue on Göran's work that I became acquainted with Lars-Håkan Svensson and Jesper Svenbro, his two most important Swedish advocates. Eventually, Svensson and I ended up co-translating the selected poems of Svenbro, while both Svensson and Printz-Påhlson translated books of my own. After Göran's death, Svensson, Svenbro, Richard Berengarten and other friends and family members began going through files of correspondence looking for more English poems. It turns out there are a lot more than anyone imagined, and a new essay on Göran's work would need to take account of these. For my own purposes, however, I want to leave this collaboration and friendship as it stood in 1981 when Göran's work in English seemed about to find some readers. In the end that really didn't happen, but at this writing one is hopeful that it still might. Robert Archambeau has edited a book of Göran's English prose and verse which is comprehensive and which will, with any luck, soon be published. This essay, like others in my book, is a memorial to a friendship—as well as the memory of a time when poets still sent poems and letters through the mail and across the sea. Göran's letters—and we exchanged hundreds—always included something unexpected, like the inscrutable poem (if it is a poem) that fell out of an envelope when I gathered up some letters for the Printz-Påhlson archive at the University of Lund. I have no idea what it is all about, but that was often the case with Göran's learned conversation and discourse, and I'm happy to sign off with the interlinear italic questions that I might have asked him.]*

§

Shortly after I first met Goran Printz-Påhlson in 1973, he and I and the British poet Richard Burns gave a reading together at Clare Hall, Cambridge, where Printz-Påhlson was a Fellow. We all read from our translations that evening, as well as from our own poems, and Printz-Påhlson amused the audience enormously by reading a poem from *Gradiva* three times—twice in English and once in Swedish. 'When Beaumont and Tocqueville First Visited Sing-Sing' was, in fact, originally written in English. It appears in *Gradiva* translated by Printz-Påhlson himself into Swedish. Discovered there by an American reader of Swedish poetry, it was translated back into English and published in a literary journal. The new English version, obviously enough, was quite different from the first. Printz-Påhlson's reading of the three poems that night formed a comic triptych with an elusive moral. But the adventures of the Beaumont and Tocqueville poem do not end there. A year ago, I picked up Lars Gustafsson's *Forays into Swedish Poetry* and discovered that the one poem chosen from Printz-Påhlson's work to represent him among his Swedish forbears and contemporaries was the ubiquitous 'Nar Beaumont och Tocqueville forst besokte Sing-Sing'—translated back into English for the American edition of the book, this time presumably by Gustafsson. Such are the hazards risked by extraterritorial types who are determined to write memorable work in more than one language. The fate of this poem is almost worthy of an extended treatment by Nabokov—or of a short one by Borges.

The Beaumont and Tocqueville poem is not the only curiosity to be found in *Gradiva*, for it is surely not typical—or so I must assume—for a volume of Swedish poetry to conclude with a 'Summary' which, in fact, consists of three poems in English on the subject of American comic strip characters. In a note on the 'Summary,' Printz-Påhlson says that he has so named the section "in order to show that you don't have to be less serious when you write about Superman . . . than you do when you write about the Rosenbergs." Like several of the Swedish poems in *Gradiva*, the three concluding poems in English are written in rigorously metrical rhyming quatrains, and it is in the making of these quatrains that much of the "seriousness" to which Printz-Påhlson refers in his note resides. But there is another kind of seriousness involved here as well which goes beyond the seriousness of good craftsmanship—a reorientation of imaginative energies which was perhaps stimulated when Printz-Påhlson began translating English and American poets and took up residence in English-speaking countries, initially in America (1961–64) and afterward in England. In a very interesting poem addressed to the American mathematician Newcomb Greenleaf, Printz-Påhlson writes:

> . . . When I met you & Connie
> I was ambitious, crisp, refractory, European. You & America
> taught me to flatten my desire onto the untoward topology
> of the ingenuous . . .

The English poems in *Gradiva* may well represent an early meeting of sorts between the ingenious mind of the poet and the ingenuous American phenomena he has come to love—a "flattening," as it were, of an ambitious theme to occupy the two dimensions of the quintessentially unambitious comic strip. At any rate, the poems about 'Superman,' 'Bringing up Father,' and 'The Katzenjammer Kids' make use of a highly idiomatic American English with great energy and authority when they are at their most knockabout and boisterous—slapping together rhymes like "mad pursuit" and "doesn't care a hoot," "something cute" and "He is a fruit," and so on—and then suddenly sound rather British when they grow reflective. These concluding quatrains of 'Bringing up Father,' for example, remind me of the early work of Donald Davie (which Printz-Påhlson has translated) in such representative poems as 'Remembering the Thirties' and 'The Garden Party.'

> We can forgive our ancestors the mere
> Deception of their ruthless living lie
> But hardly the brutality to leave us here
> And rot away and stink and simply die.

> This goes to show that feeling is without pretence,
> Construing the unbearable (as our pun gets slyer)
> In bringing up our fathers in the awful sense
> Of exhumation of a dreaded sire.

Ambitious, that. Perhaps even crisp, refractory, European. It is good for the poems that they can accommodate both the sophisticated thought and craftsmanship of the poet as well as his exuberant response to what is actually a kind of folk art.

It is folk art, in fact, which has recently come to occupy Printz-Påhlson a good deal whether he is on his British or his American turf. Between the publication of *Gradiva* in 1966 and (in English) *The Green Ey'd Monster* in 1980, Printz-Påhlson has written considerably more than I suppose most Swedish readers are aware of. And yet there was indeed a dry period, a time when perhaps the question of whether to write in Swedish or English became sufficiently problematic that the flow of poems in both languages all but ceased. I can imagine Printz-Påhlson during this fallow period waiting for the tardy arrival of his muse while the music of Scott Skinner or Dock Boggs wailed on that scratchy old machine in Stapleford. While I've been treated to many recordings both in Stapleford and Cambridge, I have trouble remembering who's who among Printz-Påhlson's elect of hillbillies and highlanders. I do, however, have a letter in my files telling me that "the fiddler James 'Scott' Skinner is the inventor of a very influential cross-bowing plonking, drawing-room style of fiddling." I think it is safe to assume that Skinner's fiddling, like Printz-Påhlson's wonderful poem in homage to his style, *takes off*. The piece is short enough to quote in its entirety.

> The kelp is not enough. Two hundred
> thousand wet sea-birds every
> minute serve the mind with writs of constraint
> in *pizzicato* dancehalls all over
> the moody crags. A lonely kipper
> is seen to flounder in the volatile traffic
> leaving his ladder, embarking
> for France, land of cotillons and plenty,
> prognathous and proud in the strathspey
> prattle of little Jacobite girls in terror.
> Far, far away, o dominie, from
> glamour-grammar grit and the sweet
> mountain smell of mossy socks in Allenvale!

If Skinner's invented technique stands, say, in a relationship to traditional fiddling somewhat analogous to Eliot's "individual talent" and *that* tradition, it is probably more important to note that any Scots fiddling, however sophisticated or exportable, will be "connected with the unchanging flow of life, accepted values, rustic stability, indigenous belonging and such"—a point Printz-Påhlson makes about the pre-Eliotic received sense of the word *traditional* in a recent essay on Tranströmer. But if all kinds of traditional or folk or ethnic music are in one sense deeply conservative, they are in another sense radical and subversive in an age of centralized economies, political control from distant capitals, pressure of all kinds for social uniformity, and an international style in painting, literature, and music (whether of the symphony orchestra, the jazz band, or the rock group).

If that lovely kipper—taking off like Skinner's fiddling—must sojourn in France for a while, prognathous and proud as any Stuart Pretender, he may well return strengthened by his flight to the valley of the Spey to work with all those other trouts and herrings for Scottish devolution (while, doubtless, dancing the Birks of Invermay or the Braes of Tullimet with many a pretty Jacobite). Skinner's style, like the Scots poetry of Hugh MacDiarmid, has a political as well as a strictly aesthetic meaning. It is interesting in this context to remember that Printz-Påhlson and Jan Östergren have, for several years, discussed the possibility of translating MacDiarmid into the Scanian dialect, and that Printz-Påhlson's long poem in Swedish, '*Gläd Dig, Du Shåning*,' can be seen, as he has written in a recent letter, as "a kind of Scanian version of *A Drunk Man Looks at the Thistle*"—MacDiarmid's most successful and sustained poem in his unique synthetic reinvention of the Scots vernacular.

Though the nitty-gritty of the mountain moss in Allenvale may be "far, far away, o domine," from the hills of Dock Boggs, the poem in homage to Boggs' music makes a point not unrelated to the Scott Skinner piece. The tone, too, is similar in many respects to that of 'Scott Skinner,' as is the character of the humor. It is the idiom, of course, characterized by those "sourmash blandishments" and "gridiron reverberations," that bluegrass "bushwhacking" of God's melodies, and the "clodhopper shovel / smack in the kisser," that measures the distance between the two.

There are gridiron reverberations
in the hills, sourmash
blandishments bleating
from the sheriff's office.

Ah, the *gavroche* innocence of a barnyard rape!

He offers a smile, mild
as pick-axe handles a
mile wide which kindles
the hide of rutabagas:
their red necks swabbed
by cool, pale blue grass
in the abstracted stare of poverty.

Bushwhacking the melodies of God
for the breakdown of brushfires,
he nurtures illustrious health
with the grating pap
of pink indigence,
plucking the lure of life
from the audible *mouchoir* moment
when distant authority suppurates
the blueridge landscapes of childhood.

Raw death: a clodhopper shovel
smack in the kisser.

While the region festers in the "benign neglect" of a centralized political system, Boggs' music is efficacious. For the staring poor, he nurtures health with the pap of indigence itself—his singing. Even raw death, like raw music, has something to be said for it, the contrast being (to use Robert Lowell's distinction between two kinds of poetry) the "cooked" death of the modern urban hospital with all life-support systems buzzing and blipping until the last mechanically assisted breath and artificially stimulated heartbeat. This is another good poem, by the way, as confident in its (highly idiomatic!) dealings with America as the Scott Skinner poem is in its dealings with Scotland. It is itself, however, "cooked" rather than "raw." Nothing could be more carefully contrived (in a totally non-pejorative sense) than that marvellous imagery of the rutabagas having their red necks swabbed in the pale blue grass. Printz-Påhlson, though often drawn to the down-home subject, is always, as a poet, crafty and sophisticated and urban. He loves Dock Boggs—not, however, close-up in the local sheriff's office, but from the relatively safe distance of a speaker system in Cambridge, London, or Lund. Nor is this in any sense hypocritical. The politics of the poem are deeply felt in part as a result of the distance.

When the politics gets closer to home, however, the distance disappears. 'Odradek,' a frightening and brilliant poem based in part on Kafka's little parable, 'The Cares of a Family Man,' is dedicated to Printz-Påhlson's old friend and publisher, Bo Cavefors, who was, at the time, the target of civil and criminal proceedings by the Swedish authorities which were interpreted by many in Sweden as a kind of legal harassment aiming at censorship. In a letter to me dated 28 April 1980, Printz-Påhlson breaks off at the bottom of one page only to begin again in great consternation at the top of another. "Next morning at 7. Awakened by an express letter. It contained clippings from Swedish newspapers telling us that Cavefors was convicted in the proceedings for 'obstruction of fiscal control and suppression of documents.' As Bo had been detained on suspicion of much more serious crimes, the judge very generously considered it quits. But nobody offered to give him restitution for the unfounded slur on his reputation that any conviction in a criminal court entails." 'Odradek' arrived in the mail a few days later.

In Kafka's parable, Odradek is the name of the strange mechanical creature representing all sorts of obscure and seemingly benign forces of denial that lurk in the house of the narrator—in the garret, the stairway, the lobby, the entrance hall. Initially, it appears to be "a flat star-shaped spool for thread." But it is "not only a spool, for a small wooden crossbar sticks out of the middle of the star, and another small rod is joined at a right angle. By means of this latter rod on one side and one of the points of the star on the other, the whole thing can stand upright as if on two legs." The thing is "extraordinarily nimble and can never be laid hold of." Also, it can talk. In Printz-Påhlson's poem the "cases"—locative, instrumental, and accusative—are intended to have both a linguistic and legal meaning, as well as the more general sense of sets of circumstances or affairs and the informal one referring to peculiarities or eccentricities. Here is the poem:

> *Odradek*
>
> *Es klingt etwa so wie das Rascheln*
> *in gefallenen Blättern*

Their cases are locative or instrumental.
Here, in this place, I see the leaves falling
on the fabulously stayed crosses and inscriptions,
as they fell on the Homeric simile of generations.
You have heard them, the little dissuaders,
whispering in the attics, or from behind the creaking stairs,
with their busy spools and laughter, seemingly
from no human lungs. You proceed to ask:
What's your name? Answers: Odradek.
Where do you live? *Unbestimmter Wohnsitz.*
They cannot die but cease to exist
when you do not listen. In another place,
in Paris, a car is stopped: a little dog
in the lap of a young girl exploding
like a ripe autumnal fruit in her hands. Her
lover is already carved in half by bullets.
There are cleaner cases, more winsome
uses for the accusative. Do not heed them anymore.
Here we all die, in bits and pieces.

For Bo Cavefors

Although in these brief remarks I have felt I should limit my commentary to those of Printz-Påhlson's poems which are short enough to be quoted in full, it would be entirely misleading to leave the impression that all of his work in English is in the mode of 'Scott Skinner' and 'Dock Boggs' or in the mode of 'Odradek.' Along with 'Acrobats on the Radio,' the letter-poem to Newcomb Greenleaf from which I quoted a few lines earlier, there are three other middle-length poems of an epistolary and/or discursive kind: 'To John at the Summer Solstice' (the companion piece for the Greenleaf poem), 'My Interview with I. A. Richards,' and 'Comedians' (dedicated to Kenneth Koch).

All of these are, to some extent, poems about poetry (or at least about language), and therefore all of them lead very naturally to Printz-Påhlson's most ambitious poem in English, *The Green Ey'd Monster*, a poem that Richard Burns has accurately called "a playful, witty, profound, sad, funny, serious poem, which combines all the Swedish, American, and English influences on his earlier work in a brilliant synthesis." It is, he says, "one of the finest long poems written in English (and what is more, in England) which I have read in the last ten years." Poems about poetry . . . Well . . .

> Before it had become fashionable to write poetry
> about writing poetry, it was considered
> so exceedingly difficult that it was next
> to impossible,

. . . begins the poem to Kenneth Koch. By the end, however, through the agency of a little girl who learns in the course of the poem to swim without water-wings and then "without air, / without rhythm, without metaphors" . . . and who says "'Wait a minute, / I am being used as a metaphor now,'" 'Comedians' concludes:

> But there she is wrong. The poem, if it is any good at all,
> is never about writing poetry: but rather about
> making jokes, or love; or deceit; once again she (in
> spite of her perky independence of mind) and the reader
> have together been lead up that proverbial old
> garden path. But, in that case, consider a boy
> on the first day of spring when the rain has just stopped,
> playing marbles up that old garden path,
> water-logged still by the rains . . .

. . . and we must return again to the beginning. The conclusion of *The Green Ey'd Monster* is similar.

> My song is
> soon to end, but don't mistake
> my placid tone for equanimi
> ty. Most of all it is itself
> a metaphor, in which the

vehicle is missing but the
tenor, in wonderful belcanto warblings
goes on and on and on.

And then, *Encore, da capo*, the voice sings.

There is no way for me to give any brief sense of the complexity of *The Green Ey'd Monster*. Formally, it may be even more ambitious than the title poem of *Gradiva*. In a letter of 14 January 1980, Printz-Påhlson wrote: "I do hope that you can see what I am trying for in the new poem: in the intersection between the farcical and the pathetic for instance, in the constant worrying about synchronicity (in a strictly non-Jungian and non-superstitious sense) and diachronicity—alternative worlds, but more in the strictly logical meaning of the phrase. I tried to clarify it in my poem 'Comedians' (which should be the writer-reader relation) and I am using it on a grand scale in *The Green Ey'd Monster*." This will indicate at least some of the poem's essential preoccupations—although, of course, it gives little account of its shape or movement.

The first section of the *Monster*, 'The Mezzotint,' is, in fact, my favorite. We are asked again and again to "imagine a picture." Again and again, the picture dissolves. "But this is not the picture," we are told. It is not the "manor-house in Salop. or Derbyshire"; it is not the "Italian villa on the bleak Dalmatian shore"; it is not the "mandala / of Oriental opulence and splendour / straddling the world"; it is not even the work of the "mimeobionic, infraquarcine, microplane android artist" whose crime is re-creation of the Past, the "palinpoietic activities" which are, "as every callow space cadet will know, punishable / by Eternal Life." But . . .

> imagine two lovers who have long since ceased
>   to talk
> to one another, or who will go on talking to them-
>   selves, whispering *quarrel, gauntlet, equinox, soon,*
>   *same, graves.*

> This is the same picture, the same
> treasure-filled *Spelunca,*
>   darkness scratched from the dry copper plate.

Every conversation is inbetween these two,
    not between the maiden and her ravisher, nor the child
    and God, nor the artist and his shrunken world.

It strikes me that what Lars Gustafsson wrote in conclusion about the much-travelled Beaumont and Tocqueville poem also applies to the world of *The Green Ey'd Monster* opened up by 'The Mezzotint.' I want to conclude these notes by quoting it. Gustafsson argues that the Beaumont and Tocqueville poem sees the entire modern world as a prison:

> The poem is part of a sequence entitled *Carceri Suite*. This name alludes to a series of engravings by the eighteenth-century Italian artist, Piranesi, a remarkable suite of gigantic, labyrinthine prisons, an indoor universe of deep arches and endless cavities of hewn stone. Printz-Påhlson's work has the same melancholy authority, the same desolate, windy dream quality—*dream* and yet, *reality*.

There are other qualities, as Richard Burns suggests, which are also characteristic of *The Green Ey'd Monster*, but in the end I feel it is the "melancholy authority" and "desolate, windy dream quality" that Gustafsson finds both in Piranesi and the *Carceri Suite* that continues to dominate.

Interlinear Dialogue with a Poem found with Letters from Göran Printz-Påhlson

So, at last, there is one thing we have in common
The habit of assuaging the country mist:
But reading here about it I'm not sure at all if I'm to
Find the mist in country outside of Malmö, or Cambridge,
Or for that matter in the country just beyond South Bend,
An Indiana town you rather inexplicably
Enjoyed. Nor can I be sure, squinting at an old-fashioned
Carbon copy on an old-fashioned onion skin,
If this "assuaging" should occur
Because there is one thing we must not allow,
In particular in the autumn when the
Pastures are trivial, leaves playful,
Or, if we did allow this thing, just what the consequences
Might become. This is how I figure: a description
Of any kind of narrative (as I a daughter
Asleep from drinking, left alone), *a narrative that must,*
We suppose, have something to do with "trivial" pastures
And "playful" leaves, as well as with the afore-
Mentioned "assuaging" of the country mist. But "as I a daughter"?
It certainly wakes one up, even from a narrative
Not properly described. And does one, GPP, "describe"
A narrative, even "(as I a daughter,
Asleep from drinking, left alone)"? Or just get on with telling?
I sometimes used to leave
You alone, asleep from drinking, in the Clare Hall
Common room after lunch. That would have been in 1976–7,
Year of our collaboration, a memory
That makes me wonder, too, if
This is not a self-translation from the Swedish,
Something that you often did, as in the case, for instance,
Of the famous 'When Beaumont and Tocqueville First Visited
Sing-Sing,' a poem which still, I understand,
Causes problems for your editors: Put it in
The 'Poems in Swedish' section, or later on, page 85 ff,
The 'Poems in English' part?—since
This is the time I don't come from

357

But rather the opposite, like St. Augustine,
Another installment in my debt to you
My darling Janet. *I do, I think, remember Janet, or*
Maybe I confuse that name with Annette, who woke us both
From time to time when we were feeling "rather the
Opposite," like St. Augustine, therefore both incurring
An installment in our debt. Negation NEGATION
Sounds apocalyptic when at least you can speak and say
At least I can speak now and not
At that omen (I was a poet once and
Then) miraculously (read an old
Acquaintance. *Who was that? And why does this*
Parenthesis not close? I'm glad to speak now too, but
Why not "at that omen"? (To the omen, through the omen,
For the omen, five the omen, six?)
Are you a poet here, or only once (upon a time)
And then. When—Oh Miracle!—an old acquaintance
Came up riding with a text in writing saying
"Read an old acquaintance for your sins!" And isn't this the IS
That is first-order logic when
Consensually agreed on, or words to that effect?
That is why this poem is called 'The
Decline of the Supernatural,' although its
Title is 'On What Was As Near To
Happiness,' *or 'Interlinear Dialogue with a Poem*
Found with Letters From Printz-Påhlson'
But dedicated to Henry Mayhew
And the memory of Clive Jenkins.
School children will require a gloss or so, a moss
Or so beneath a tree out somewhere in the country where
They might lie down and dream, assuaging mist.
The open parenthesis runs on. A gap of space, a hiss:
I do only countenance arithmetical order
Which is the stark nonsequitur of most
Vengeful fathers. *Line break and page break: then*
Forgive me, as vulgar as a poem mentioning Chomsky
(*Where, exactly?*) incognito there,
Or whales,   or wage demands   *may be*

Notes to the Essays

Notes to 'Kedging in "Kedging in Time"', pp.39–56

[1] I have done this kind of thing once before, in 'Places and Poems: A Self-Reading and a Reading of the Self in the Romantic Context from Wordsworth to Parkman' which appears in my book *Reading Old Friends: Essays, Reviews, and Poems on Poetics, 1975–1990*. (SUNY, 1992). I repeat here a few things that are also said in that essay.

[2] Two poems from my *New Selected Poems* appearing in this book, 'Some Letters' and 'Geneva Pension,' deal with some of the same backgrounds. Many of the earlier poems in sections II and III of the *New Selected* have to do with the Adams house in Suffolk. 'An East Anglian Diptych' is a full-scale celebration of the region, and is discussed in the 'Places and Poems' essay.

[3] Emily Young's work is featured in *Notre Dame Review*, #20, Summer 2005, and can be seen on her web site, www.emilyyoung.com

[4] "*Petrarch* and *Sorato* followed, turrets slowly turning, firing at embrasures . . . the returning Admiral" is from *Savrola* and not, like most other borrowings, signalled by italics. The text merges here with the author's thinking about the implications of his work as he "puts aside his pen to pour himself another gin."

[5] This is a complicated history. See Andrew Boyle, *The Riddle of Erskine Childers* (Hutchinson, 1977); Thomas J. Cox, *Damned Englishman* (Exposition Press, 1975); Jim Ring, *Erskine Childers* (John Murray, 1996); Burke Wilkinson, *The Zeal of the Convert* (Second Chance Press, 1985).

[6]   Kedging

        's all you're good for
        someone said. Is what? Your good

        and for it. Not to fear: O all your
        goods so far. Your good 4.

        Your goods 5 and 6. With a little tug
        At warp. So by a hawser winde

        Your head about. Thirty nine
        Among the sands your steps or

        Riddle there. Who may have
        Sailed the Alde is old now, olde

        And addled, angling still for some
        Good luck. So labor, lad: *when other*

Moiety of men, tugging hard at kedge
And hawser, drew us from

The sand? Brisk and lively in the
Dialect East Anglian. Ain't so well

As I was yesterday, for I was then
Quite kedge. Even though I pull and

Pole and persevere I'm blown to
Windward. Winding still. Warping so

As not to weep, cadging as I can.

[7] In *Downhill all the Way*, Leonard Woolf prints extensive records of the Hogarth Press sales of Virginia Woolf's books. In its first year, *Jacob's Room* sold 1,182 copies. By contrast, *The Thirty-Nine Steps* sold 25,000 copies during its first year and *Greenmantle* 30,000 copies in its first year, 50,000 in its second. Nor has *Jacob's Room* (so far) outlasted Buchan's books. Neither *The Thirty-Nine Steps* nor *Greenmantle* has ever been out of print. Sales figures, through many different editions, of Childers' *The Riddle of the Sands* are even more impressive.

[8] There's a bit of smoke and mirrors at this point in the poem. It may look as if Tsar Nicholas himself led the attack. Of course he could not have done so, though it was "his" cavalry insofar as he was Tsar. The attack was led by Grand Duke Nicholas.

[9] This was Thomas Dilworth, critic and biographer of David Jones. Any reader of *The Anathemata* will know that the tin-trade sailors of 'Middle Sea and Lear-Sea' have their own difficulties, like Childers' gun-runners, with the weather around Land's End when "Albion's brume begins to thin away."

Notes to 'Poetry and Murder', pp.74–98

[1] Richard Elman (1934–1997) was the author of twenty-five books, including *The Reckoning, Lilo's Diary, The 28th Day of Elul, Ill-At-Ease in Compton, The Poorhouse State, A Coat for the Tzar, Tar Beach, Disco Frito,* and *Namedropping*. He taught at many American universities, including Columbia, the State University of New York, Stony Brook, and Notre Dame. For several years he was a regular commentator on National Public Radio.

[2] Janet Holmes, *The Green Tuxedo* (South Bend: University of Notre Dame Press, 1999), p.56.

[3] Ibid.

4 'The Lamson Case,' *Time* Magazine Archive Article, Sept. 11, 1933. http://www.time.com/time/magazine/article/0,9171,746015,00.html [Accessed December 6, 2009].

5 Email letter from Kenneth Fields, Winters' last student assistant and collaborator on the anthology *Quest for Reality*, 14 December 2005. "If you read the brief (the brief's about 600 pages long) you can see Winters' style on every page."

6 The pamphlet lists Frances Theresa Russell as co-author, but she did very little of the actual writing. Winters was at that time only an instructor at Stanford and he wanted the pamphlet to carry the weight of a senior professor at the university. Looking perhaps for another credential to establish his own authority, he is also identified on the title page as "regional editor for the west of *Hound and Horn*." (Even Thom Gunn, in his notes to the Library of America edition of Winters' *Selected Poems*, gets the academic rank wrong, calling Winters a "professor." For a long time Winters' status at Stanford was insecure, and he was perfectly well aware of the personal risks he was taking in publicly defending a person widely perceived as a campus wife-murderer.)

7 R.L. Barth (ed.), *The Selected Letters of Yvor Winters* (Athens: Ohio University Press, 2000), p.228.

8 Thom Gunn (ed.), *Yvor Winters: Selected Poems* (New York: The Library of America, 2003), p.101. There is a very fine essay on the Lamson poems by David Reid: 'Rationality in the Poetry of Yvor Winters,' *Cambridge Quarterly*, Vol. 34, No. 1 (2005), 1–21.

9 Kenneth Rexroth, *The Collected Shorter Poems* (New York: New Directions, 1966), p.198. Rexroth and Winters appear to have been close friends for a while.

10 Ibid.

11 Gunn (ed.), *Yvor Winters: Selected Poems*, p.102.

12 R.L. Barth (ed.), *Selected Letters*, p.229.

13 Frances Theresa Russell and Yvor Winters, *The Case of David Lamson* (San Francisco: Lamson Defense Committee, 1934), p.86.

14 Kenneth Fields in conversation.

15 Tom Zaniello, 'Yvor Winters,' *Dictionary of Literary Biography* 48, edited by Peter Quartermain (Detroit: Broccoli-Clark, 1986), p.449.

16 Frances Theresa Russell and Yvor Winters, *The Case of David Lamson*, p.83.

17 Gunn (ed.), *Yvor Winters: Selected Poems*, p.104.

18 R.L. Barth (ed.), *Selected Letters*, p.233.

19 Ibid.

20 Richard Elman, *Namedropping: Mostly Literary Memoirs* (Albany, SUNY Press, 1999), p.19.

21 Thom Gunn, 'On a Drying Hill,' *The Southern Review* (Autumn 1981), p.692.

[22] Ibid., p.693.

[23] Richard Elman, *Namedropping*, p.15.

[24] An extremely impressive short story, available in Gunn's *Yvor Winters: Selected Poems* and the Swallow Press *Collected Poems*.

[25] Richard Elman, *Namedropping*, p.22.

[26] Dennis J. White, 'Winters Chill,' Letters to the Editor, *Stanford Magazine*, January/February, 2001. British readers probably need to be told that Bobby Knight was a particularly irascible basketball coach at the University of Indiana, famous for things like throwing chairs at referees and players during games.

[27] Ibid., Helen Pinkerton Trimpi, 'Winters Chill.'

[28] Richard Elman, *Namedropping*, p.43

[29] Ibid., pp.39–45.

[30] Ibid.

[31] Richard Elman, *An Education in Blood* (New York: Scribners, 1971), p.26.

[32] R.L. Barth (ed.), *Selected Letters*, p.410.

[33] Ibid., p.412.

[34] Ibid.

[35] Richard Elman, *Namedropping*, p.44.

[36] Yvor Winters, 'The Significance of 'The Bridge' by Hart Crane, Or What Are We to Think of Professor X,' in *In Defense of Reason* (Denver: Alan Swallow, 1943), pp.577–603.

[37] R.L. Barth (ed.), *Selected Letters*, p.399.

[38] Richard Elman, *An Education in Blood*, p.27.

[39] Ibid., p.28.

[40] Richard Elman, *An Education in Blood*, p.61.

[41] R.L Barth (ed.), *Selected Letters*, p.410.

[42] Richard Elman, *An Education in Blood*, p.62.

[43] Readers unacquainted with the Yvor Winters canon of great poems should look up the fascinating anthology edited by Winters and Kenneth Fields, *Quest For Reality* (Chicago: Swallow Press, 1969). The poems range from Thomas Wyatt's 'Remembrance' to Thom Gunn's 'In Santa Maria Del Popolo.'

[44] Richard Elman, *An Education in Blood*, p.454.

[45] Simon Schama, *Dead Certainties* (New York: Knopf, 1991), p.263ff.

[46] Frances Theresa Russell and Yvor Winters, *The Case of David Lamson*, p.21.

[47] Simon Schama, *Dead Certainties*, p.265.

[48] Gunn, (ed.), p.91.

[49] David Lamson, *We Who Are about to Die: Prison as Seen by a Condemned Man* (New York: Scribners, 1936), p.xi.

[50] Simon Schama, *Dead Certainties*, p.269.

[51] J.V. Cunningham, *The Collected Poems and Epigrams* (Chicago: Swallow Press, 1971), p.118.

[52] Ibid., p.83: "So love by love we come at last, / As through the exclusions of a rhyme, / Or the exactions of a past, / To the simplicity of time [...]"

Notes to 'Grand Old Dirty Old Men', pp.120–152

[1] Along with the poems of W.B. Yeats and Octavio Paz, works discussed in this essay include: Yasunari Kawabata, *House of the Sleeping Beauties and Other Stories*, trans. Edward Seidensticker (Kodansha International 1980) and *Beauty and Sadness*, trans. Howard S. Hibbett (Vintage 1996); J.M. Coetzee, *Giving Offense: Essays on Censorship* (Chicago 1996) and *Diary of a Bad Year* (Viking 2007); Guy Davenport, *Tatlin* (Johns Hopkins 1982), *Da Vinci's Bicycle* (John's Hopkins 1979), *Eclogues* (North Point 1981), *Apples and Pears* (North Point 1984), *The Jules Verne Steam Balloon* (North Point 1987), *The Drummer of the Eleventh North Devonshire Fusiliers* (North Point 1990), *The Death of Picasso* (Shoemaker & Hoard, 2003), *A Balance of Quinces: The Paintings and Drawings of Guy Davenport*, ed. Erik Andrson Reece (New Directions 1996), *Wo es war, soll ich werden* (Finial Press 2004); Octavio Paz, *The Double Flame: Love and Eroticism*, trans. Helen Lane (Harcourt Brace 1995); *An Erotic Beyond: Sade*, trans. Eliot Weinberger (Harcourt Brace 1998); Georges Bataille, *The Story of the Eye*, trans. Joachim Neugroschel with essays by Susan Sontag and Roland Barthes (Penguin 1982); Edward W. Said, *On Late Style: Music and Literature Against the Grain* (Pantheon 2006).

[2] Quoting the same texts in 'How to be an Old Poet: The Examples of Hardy and Yeats' (*Sewanee Review*, Spring 1997), Samuel Hynes is concerned with Seventh Age poets, not six-and-a-halfers. Citing the last four lines of Jacques' speech, he says: "You must recognize, as I do, that those lines don't accurately describe old Hardy, or old Yeats, or any other Old Poet. And yet ... I am caught by Shakespeare's sense of age as diminishment and loss—*sans, sans, sans*, what Hardy called time's "talking's away"—and of oblivion. And so, even though it isn't quite fair, I think of this poetry as Seventh Age poetry: poetry that is about the reality of loss-in-time, and how to live with it, and make poetry out of it."

[3] Sister Kate Benedict's web site is very funny, and worth looking up: http://www.katebenedict.com/dreck/contents.html. Although I think she misses with Yeats, she scores well identifying clunkers in another dozen, mostly modern, poets. Shades of D.B. Wyndham Lewis' *The Stuffed Owl: An Anthology of Bad Verse*, recently re-issued by New York Review Editions.

[4] All biographical information about Yeats comes from R.F. Foster's *W.B. Yeats: A Life. Volume II. The Arch-Poet* (Oxford 2003).

[5] *Speaking the Unspeakable* (SUNY 1993) is Peter Michelson's revision of

his 1971 book *The Aesthetics of Pornography*. Though *Speaking the Unspeakable* is expanded to include cinematic works and pornogrtaphy written by and for women, I have a particular fondness for the original book and the associations it has for me with the zeitgeist of the 1960s and my friendship with the author when we both were young. Both versions of the book are highly recommended

6 Edward W. Said, *On Late Style: Music and Literature Against the Grain* (Pantheon 2006). Quoted frequently in this essay, Said's book is important in many ways. Though it avoids discussing the erotic in "late style," surely a major omission in his argument, the book is deeply moving as well as intellectually cogent. Like his own piano performances, these considerations take him beyond the political. The book to read beside *On Late Style* is Octavio Paz's *The Double Flame*. Two other unlikely companion volumes—their size and design are almost identical—are Paz's meditations on Sade in *An Erotic Beyond* (Harcourt Brace 1998) and Guy Davenport's *The Logia of Yeshua* (Counterpoint 1996), his beautiful co-translation, with Benjamin Urrutia, of the sayings of Jesus.

7 For this essay I have been reading Sontag's 'The Pornographic Imagination' in an afterword to Georges Bataille's *The Story of the Eye* (Penguin 1982), where it appears together with Roland Barhes' 'The Metaphor of the Eye.'

8 Wyatt Mason, 'There Must I Begin to Be: Guy Davenport's Heretical Fictions,' *Harper's Magazine* (April 2004), p.87. In *Secreted Desires: The Major Uranians*, Michael Matthew Kaylor comments, p.408ff., that "Mason's article [is] the only serious, critical engagement of Davenport that approaches him on his own terms, especially in regard to the erotic elements within his fiction, elements usually considered anathema and attacked as representative of Davenport's 'polymathic pederasty.' The difficulty that scholarship has in approaching Davenport's fiction is observable in the following 'disclaimer' by Samuel R. Delany: "I start by saying I have no notion what Davenport's sexual persuasion might be. [...] My disclaimer is sincere. I don't know. [...] Whatever his sexual fixes, [Davenport] nevertheless produces work saturated with pederastic resonances." The scholarly impasse described by Kaylor has recently been bridged by André Furlani's excellent *Guy Davenport: Postmodern and After* (Northwestern 2007).

Notes to 'The Poetry of Roy Fisher', pp.192–217

1 Roy Fisher, *19 Poems and an Interview* (Pensnett, Staffs.: Grosseteste Press, 1975), 15, 17, 18. The interview was conducted on 19 November 1973 by Jed Rasula and Mike Erwin, and it is the best source available for getting a

sense of Fisher's intentions in his work up through at least the 'Handsworth Liberties,' nine parts of which appear among the 19 poems. Subsequently referred to in notes as *Grosseteste Interview*, and in text as *GI*.

2 The "Large Glass," of course, refers to Marcel Duchamp's 'The Bride Stripped Bare by Her Bachelors, Even.' In 'Then Hallucinations,' the prose sequel to the 1962 Migrant Press edition of *City*, the following sentence appeared: "This city is like the Bride of Marcel Duchamp; and when she is stripped the Glass needs to be broken and carted away."

3 Ernst Von Glaserfield, 'An Introduction to Radical Constructivism,' in *The Invented Reality* (London and New York,: W.W. Norton & Company, 1984), 24. Had I not been such a realist on my drive through Studebaker Corridor, Fisher's language might have stimulated a sequence of perceptions which seemed to "fit" rather than to "match" or "correspond to" what we passed. Von Glaserfield writes: "The metaphysical realist looks for knowledge that matches reality . . . In the epistemologist's case it is . . . some kind of 'homomorphism' [that concerns him], which is to say, an equivalence of relations, a sequence, or a characteristic structure—something, in other words, that he can consider the same, because only then could he say that his knowledge is of the world . . . If, on the other hand, we say that something fits, we have in mind a different relation. A key fits if it opens the lock. The fit describes a capacity of the key, not of the lock" (21–22). Fisher sought a key for a topography presenting itself as "an indecipherable script." Such a key might fit in several locks—in Birmingham or elsewhere.

4 Donald Davie, *Thomas Hardy and British Poetry* (London: Routledge & Kegan Paul, 1973), 11.

5 Ibid., 188.

6 Ibid., 152–172.

7 J.D. Needham, 'Some Aspects of the Poetry of Roy Fisher,' *Poetry Nation* 5 (Winter 1975), 74–87.

8 Davie, *Thomas Hardy*, 166–167.

9 Along with Davie's argument see Peter Barry, 'Language and the City in Roy Fisher's Poetry,' *English Studies*, 67:3 (June 1986), 234–249. Barry summarizes Shklovsky's famous doctrine by saying that "what literature does is to make us see reality as if for the first time by subverting our habitual modes of perception and 'making strange' things to which we have become so accustomed that we no longer really perceive them at all." This is certainly one of the things that Fisher is sometimes up to in his poems, and it is frequently discussed by his critics. But I am primarily interested in something rather different.

10 *Grosseteste Interview*, 34. All further references in text.

11 The following, for example, is from *The Ship's Orchestra*, not *City*: "Swung from the arms of the gaslamp that was the only light in the street; a street

greenish black, among factories. The long linen sack was twisted round and round and was unknotting itself in slow revolutions, with all the weight at the bottom. As it turned, the moisture caught the light, coming through the fabric from top to bottom, but not dripping." And this is from *City*: ... The creature began to divide and multiply . . . I could see people made of straws, rags, cartons, the stuffing of burst cushions, kitchen refuse . . . a long-boned carrot-haired girl with glasses, loping along, and with strips of bright colour, rich, silky green and blue, in her soft clothes. For a person made of such scraps she was beautiful."

[12] Quoted in William C. Seitz, *The Art of Assemblage* (New York: Doubleday and Company, 1961), 73.

[13] John Ash insists in 'A Classic Postmodernist' (*Atlantic Review* [New Series] no 2, p.46) that Fisher's Birmingham is also Baudelaire's Paris and "the hallucinatory Petersburg of Andrei Bely and Aleksandr Blok (which is also Mandelstam's 'Petropolis'). Against all odds, Birmingham has become an aspect of Fisher's ideal, 'Pan-European city of art.' This is a triumph of art, but the triumph is accompanied by a sense of loss: the real city, the whole, escapes."

[14] *The Dictionary of Modern Thought*, ed. Alan Bullock and Oliver Stallybrass (New York: Harper and Row, 1977), p.39.

[15] In the Sheppard interview, *Turning the Prism: An Interview with Roy Fisher* (London: Toads Damp Press, 1986) he said, "I wasn't aware that [Davie had] exactly written about my work in that book," and to Ash (op cit, p.44), he wrote that he was no part of a tradition ending with "a full house for Philip Larkin."

[16] Ash, 'A Classic Postmodernist,' 46.

[17] Davie, *Thomas Hardy*, 171.

[18] Barry, 'Language and the City,' 246.

[19] See Michael Hamburger, *The Truth of Poetry* (New York: Harcourt Brace, 1969), chapters 2–4. Hamburger identifies this self as "the everyday person, the citizen and employee, the family man" and even the "*poète maudit* who might well have no servant to do his living for him." p.58.

[20] Peter Barry, 'Language and the City,' 248.

[21] This is true in spite of the "Tedium of talking again, / or at last, about composition and art" because "there's no other topic to be had" ('Lesson in Composition'). The poem "has always / already started" even though the speaker may dislike "mentioning works of art" ('If I Didn't').

[22] *Roy Fisher*, an autobiography appearing in *Contemporary Authors: Autobiography Series Vol. 10* (Detroit: Gale Research Inc., 1989), ed. Mark Zadronzny.

[23] Gerald L. Bruns, *Heidegger's Estrangements* (New Haven and London: Yale University Press, 1981), 164.

[24] Fisher has said that *The Ship's Orchestra*, "along with a lot of things I do," was rigorously composed in an additive form. That is, each section was written

in an attempt to refer only to what I had already written in that work, and without any drive forward at all" (*GI*, 14). An improvisational work must obviously involve a "drive forward," however sharp its turns and "changes of direction."

[25] What "has always / already started" in 'If I Didn't' is also a process which ultimately locates lost time in memory: "under whatever progression / takes things forward / there's always / the looking down / between the moving frames / into those other movements / made long ago or in some / irrecoverable scale / but in the same alignment and close to recall." The double spiral of this process—the movement forward which loops one back again—also prefigures the form of *A Furnace*.

[26] Roy Fisher, 'Handsworth Compulsions,' *Numbers*, 2:1 (Spring 1987), 24–28.

[27] Ibid., 25.

[28] Ibid., 27.

[29] Jacket note to *Matrix* (London: Fulcrum Press, 1971).

[30] Cf. the beginning of 'Calling' in *A Furnace*, where the stained glass window of a church, broken by a pick-handle or a boot, has been "cobbled / into a small / new window beside the Dee."

[31] Marjorie Perloff, *The Futurist Moment* (Chicago: University of Chicago Press, 1986), 150.

[32] Paul Klee, 'Creative Credo,' *Theories of Modern Art*, ed. Herschel B. Chipp (Berkeley: University of California Press, 1970), 182.

[33] Francisco J. Varela, 'The Creative Circle: Sketches on the Natural History of Circularity,' *The Invented Reality*, 320.

[34] It is also a genetic calling, in which the double vortex functions as the DNA molecule: "The ghosts' grown children / mill all day in the Public Search Office / burrowing out names for their own bodies . . . Genetic behaviour, / scrabbling, feeling back across the spade-cut / for something; the back-flow of the genes' / forward compulsion . . ."

[35] This essay, 'Signs of Identity,' was originally intended for a Donald Davie *Festschrift*. Crozier's anthology, *A Various Art* (Carcanet Press, 1987) in a sense picks up where *23 Modern British Poets* ended, anthologizing Fisher's work with poetry by, among others, Anthony Barnett, David Chaloner, Veronica Forest-Thomson, John James, Tim Longville, Douglas Oliver, J. H. Prynne, John Riley, Iain Sinclair, and Crozier himself. The passage is quoted with the author's permission.

[36] It is also, like parts of 'Calling,' about a return to Nature and the countryside.

Notes to 'Modernisms: Five Poems', pp.269–279

On April 12, 1963, Ekelöf wrote the following to Leif Sjöberg about the icon which was in his possession: "Basically she is an old Xoanon made of olive wood, an olive plank, dead, which is the icon painted on her. She is standing here on my chest of drawers by the way, and she always has flowers near her. She is constructed in such a way as to make it possible to undress her—the child (on a stool, standing, in a Byzantine emperor's garments), the veil, the cloak, the seven arrows of pain in her left breast, yes, the breasts and the stomach and the arms and everything until you get to the holy tree, which you could not fell in Attica with impunity."

Xoanon: ancient wooden image in Greek temples; icon
Panayía: Greek—Our Lady
Basmá: a repoussé metal (usually silver) covering over some icons, allowing only the face and hands to be seen
Maphorion: a veil-like headdress covering head and shoulders of all female saints and The Virgin Mary.
Hodigítria: The Guide; Mother of God icon
Philoúsa: Loving Virgin; Mother of God icon

CPSIA information can be obtained at www.ICGtesting.com
Printed in the USA
242710LV00001B/3/P

9 781848 611689